SMITHEREENS
STRANGE ORCHESTRA
BEFORE THE PARTY
THE OLD LADIES

T0347884

Rodney Ackland

Rodney Ackland

PLAYS TWO

SMITHEREENS
STRANGE ORCHESTRA
BEFORE THE PARTY
THE OLD LADIES

Introduction by
Michael Hastings

OBERON BOOKS
LONDON

First published in this collection in 2001 by Oberon Books Ltd
521 Caledonian Road, London N7 9RH
Tel: +44 (0) 20 7607 3637 / Fax: +44 (0) 20 7607 3629
e-mail: info@oberonbooks.com
www.oberonbooks.com

Strange Orchestra first published in 1932, *The Old Ladies* in 1935 and *Before The Party* in 1950, all by Samuel French Ltd.

A catalogue record for this book is available from the British Library.

PB ISBN: 9781840020885
E ISBN: 9781783192182

Two photographs and one painting supplied courtesy of Terry Todd.

Every effort has been made to contact the copyright holders.

Cover illustration: Andrzej Klimowski

Cover typography: Jeff Willis

Printed and bound by Marston Book Services, Didcot, UK.

Visit www.oberonbooks.com to read more about all our books and to buy them. You will also find features, author interviews and news of any author events, and you can sign up for e-newsletters so that you're always first to hear about our new releases.

Contents

Mabby Poole

INTRODUCTION

Michael Hastings

I was Literary Manager for the English Stage Company at the Royal Court Theatre in 1987. An exacting and fraught job, which has been honourably held by a number of playwrights.

Since George Devine founded the ESC in 1956, the brief is to bring on new work with a kind of rigorous appraisal, keep faith with a quirky brand of leftish republicanism always there in the tiny rooms and narrow corridors, and somehow attract the best actors and directors available.

George did have that one rule in 1956 – *the right to fail.* There was another side to him though. He had a strong sense of parallel histories in our culture. In 1956, I was employed as a trainee actor/writer at the Royal Court (implausible actor/ virtually illiterate writer at the time). Devine had just staged a ponderous verse drama, *Don Juan,* by Ronald Duncan. With sets by Johnny Minton, George had persuaded the excellent Rosalie Crutchley and Stephen Dartnell on board. The language of *Don Juan* was a portentous mix of John Drinkwater and Ezra Pound. The development of character and ideas was so stylised, it took at least two interminable speeches for any of the desperately overworked actors to get on or off the stage. I have a pale memory of Don Juan himself taking almost twenty minutes to cross stage left to right there were so many lines to speak. Clad in toga and sandals, the actor was reduced to a version of that slow prat dream walk immortalised by Little Titch. I asked George why he was stepping back into a world of literary pastiche? He said – 'This is the type of play no one else will do. What is more – it has a verbal beauty'. Yes, but – I intervened. 'So don't have a go at me about my intentions. I have a theory that the novel and the poem has had its revolution this century. For some reason the theatre has not. I have to experiment with all kind of plays'.

He looked at me, fairly confident nothing he had said would change my mind about that verse play, 'And besides – the author is a friend of mine and he's on the Committee'. That did it. I boiled up. It took me many years to give a coherent reply to that kind of quixotic artiness.

By 1987, the Royal Court had a weekly system of going through play scripts. Eight or ten or so – apprentice directors, casting directors, actors, writers, gather on Friday mornings. Each one of us brought back a couple of plays having read them over the week. Comments on each play were carefully recorded. Plays were entered onto a system somewhat frighteningly known as 'the grid'. Jim Cartwright piles into the room late. Pulls out a very large manuscript he'd read on the train. It has the look and temerity of an ancient Norse saga in rhyming couplets. What have you got there, Jim? 'This one's a fat rascal!' Jim sighs.

One Friday in 1987, I put on the weekly grid two plays by Rodney Ackland – *The Dark River* and *The Pink Room* (later *Absolute Hell*). I read out a few small notes I'd made. The former was set in 1937, but not performed until 1943. And the latter was a rewrite of a much censored 1949 version. I pointed out that Ackland was perhaps one of the most important unsung playwrights in the country. He was almost a theatrical contemporary of George Devine. And, to its undying shame, this theatre has never attempted an Ackland play. Nervous silence. Never heard of him. Is he still alive? What are the plays about?

Perhaps I was a little bit too cavalier. I suggested that all the very English middle-class characters in *The Dark River* were touched in one way or another by the Spanish Civil War. And in *Absolute Hell*, the hopelessly drunk Christine, the owner of a West End drinking club, surrounds herself with a savage array of characters who, for the most part, are doing their utmost to drink World War Two under the table. A gun is fired at a ceiling. A theatre critic is rudely excoriated, loses her wig and passes away. And two young men who are lovers have a bitter quarrel over a woman. The original production, in 1949, even toned down with more heterosexual proclivities, was described as an 'insult to the British nation', and a critic on the *Sunday Times* reported he was a witness 'If not at the death of a talent, at least of its very serious illness'. (A familiar tack certain gormless critics revert to, a poisonous meme, and the kind of notices both John Osborne and Simon Gray have cheerfully collected). Yes, I believed Rodney Ackland was still alive. Last heard of in Richmond, cruelly rumoured to have been found begging on the High Street outside Sainsburys.

It didn't take the Royal Court long to decide against the Ackland plays. They were vaguely interesting as historical items, but the business here is to mount new writing. Somehow there wasn't enough confidence in the curious dialogue, half insulting half gleeful, as if the author hadn't quite found the target.

The following year, Sam Walters produced a stunning production of *Absolute Hell* with Polly Hemingway at the Orange Tree Theatre, Richmond. Sheridan Morley described the play as one of the greatest theatrical experiences of the year. And Francis King acutely diagnosed that the entire play was a portrait of inmates of their own self-inflicted Concentration camp.

Clearly, something had begun to stir in theatre memory. There has been a small but ever-growing army of supporters who have never ceased putting forward a case for Ackland's plays. This has been led by the indefatigable Frith Banbury, with Sam Walters, Polly Hemingway, Simon Curtis, Hilary Spurling, Anthony Page, Judi Dench, James Hogan, Eric Glass, Tom Conti, Nicholas Dromgoole and Terry Todd.

Rodney Ackland was born Norman Acland Bernstein in 1908. His mother was a musical comedy star and a dancer. (She performed under the name of Ada Rodney. Although she was born Emily Diana Lock on her birth certificate). His father, Nathan Bernstein, became a successful businessman, and the family prospered for many years with a large house, servants and cars in Southend. Sudden irreversible bankruptcy brought the Bernsteins to the verge of ruin. And Rodney got his first acting role at the age of fifteen. He played 'Medvedeff', an elderly police inspector, in a production of *Lower Depths* by Gorki, at the Gate Theatre, Floral Street, 1924. He wrote two early and somewhat immature full-length Plays, *Improper People*, 1929, and *Dance with No Music*, 1931, and was soon plunged into the modern theatre world of Owen Nares, Theodore Komisarjevksy, Mrs Patrick Campbell and Ian Hay. In all, Ackland wrote some sixteen plays and adaptations and a number of film scripts. His scripts for films include two classic movies – Emeric Pressburger's *Forty Ninth Parallel,* and Thorold Dickinson's *The Queen of Spades,* with Edith Evans. In 1950, Ackland met Mabby Poole, the daughter of the playwright Frederick Lonsdale, and they were wed a couple of years on. There is also a memoir by Ackland and Elspeth Grant, *The Celluloid Mistress,* published 1954. Mabby died in 1972 after a long and very happy if erratic life with her husband. Ackland constantly found himself in regular demand by the Inland Revenue, and as a consequence of this he changed his address sometimes as frequently as he changed his shirt. Rodney Ackland died aged 83, in 1991, in the kind care and custody of Terry Todd and his family, to whom Rodney owed a unique and considerable debt of loyalty and friendship.

In retrospect, it is difficult to understand how George Devine at the onset of the English Stage Company, or, later, Peter Hall at the National Theatre, or Trevor Nunn at the RSC, could have overlooked Rodney Ackland. The powerful theatre group HM Tennent Ltd firmly closed their door in his face. Of the critics, TC Worsley, JC Trewin and Kenneth Tynan still held some respect for his plays. The Rank Film Studios, Ealing and Elstree were no-go for Ackland, even though he had written Edith Evans' greatest film role.

There was an occasional outlet for the plays on BBC Radio. But publishers Samuel French maintained at least two plays in print. What caused this situation? Was it a matter of his bile and contempt for the complacencies and narrow-mindedness of middle English society albeit disguised in sensible three act corsets? Well, that other playwright from the 30s, Keith Winter, expressed just as much hatred for the cosy piano and footstool drawing-room play. In fact, in Winter's 1934 masterpiece *The Shining Hour,* not only does the good upright wife burn herself to death, he allows her death to become a sacrifice for the two shits who decide they are made for each other and must run off together from the wrecked household. Then, there was the forecast of war in *The Dark River*:

ALAN: I've been in Spain recently. I've seen the results
    of air raids there. Thousands of people massacred
    because they had no deep shelters. And that's what'll
    happen in this country before long unless we do
    something about it...

Are we to imagine this was more than the West End could
take in those years of Beaverbrook and appeasement? Surely,
Giles Romilly and Christopher Caudwell had already brought
the news back of the atrocities at Ronda. If anything, Ackland
possessed a braying supercilious despair. And perhaps this
marked him down as a Cassandra to avoid. There seems to
have been a quality inside Ackland which would not quite
play the cultural game. Glimpses of his Buddhism...the
fatalistic glee with which he avoided income tax officials...a
comedy of occasional bisexual encounters...incidents when
the penniless playwright offered astonished cab drivers a hasty
exchange of body fluids in lieu of the fare...the unashamed
borrowing and relentless dependence on fathomless loyalty
from a few old friends, never once stopping to thank the person
or be obligated in any way for the smallest kindness...his
instinctive wish never to speak again to someone he little knew
but who had forked out for a sudden Ackland emergency...

It is possible he has always looked upon us with a cold
taciturn eye. And is that what has kept the rest of the English
theatre at bay? His curmudgeonly tone behind the writing.
And the pain so barely concealed in his sense of horror,
significantly in the character of Elizabeth in *Absolute Hell*, for
she knows she has lost her best friend in Ravensbruck, but it
seems so much more important to go out, hail a cab, and burn
dark until dawn in yet another nightclub:

ELIZABETH: If only Sam *were* having an affair with
    Douglas Eden – at least that would be something
    I could understand – but to give up everything to go
    flouncing off to India in search of what? – in the hope
    of finding what? Some revolting old 'fakir' squatting
    on a tin-tack glowering at his navel? Who's going to
    reveal to Sam 'the Meaning of Life', 'the truth' about

why we're here and what we're for and the – in my
opinion undoubtedly sadistic and hideously imbecilic
purpose of it all.

Was it really necessary to condemn this play for its
unpatriotic flavour at the close of World War Two? Do we
detect that old canard from the ranks of the narrow-minded
English culture? It seems that Ackland did something quite
unforgivable in his writing. And there was no Cyril Connolly
or Herbert Read to speak up for him. And yet this bitter voice,
the sound of forensic disgust, was far from unique in the wider
contemporary world. The central character of *Journey to the
End of Night* by Louis-Ferdinand Celine inadvertently finds
himself in a French nightclub studying the *café-crème* with
similar self-lacerating auscultation:

> CELINE: Only their eyes were sad. Eyes are not enough.
> They were singing the defeat of life and they didn't see
> it. They would find out later, maybe, where the end all
> that was, when they were rosy no longer, when the
> pitiless grime of their own foul country had enveloped
> them all again, their great horsy thighs, their little
> bobbing breasts, the sordidness already had them by
> the neck, they wouldn't escape.
> It was within. No costume, no painted scene, no
> lights, no smile to deceive. To impress this thing of
> misery; it knows its own; wherever they may hide, it
> roots them out; it merely takes its pleasures, allowing
> them to sing till their turn comes, allowing them all
> the absurdities of hope. Unhappiness is whetted,
> soothed, excited in that way.
> Our real misery, the ultimate misery, entertains us
> thus.

I don't know if one should quite go that far on seeing your
first squad of hoofers in a dance club, but Ackland and Celine
definitely shared Sartre's hatred of viscosity, that quality of
non-authentic knowledge of the real world, which reduces one
to a living fear of existence. If we do not confront our darkest
despair with an honesty, measure it and reinterpret it against
our codes of behaviour, then we risk spending our lives blind.

For so many, hope and decency died after Auschwitz and Truman's US atomic bombs on Japan. Hitherto optimistic phenomenological psychiatrists committed suicide in their deserted clients' waiting rooms. Teams of Nazi scientists threw away their swastikas and flew west toward the Eisenhower years. Many exhausted liberal academics in Eastern Europe unrestrainedly embraced Stalin's plans for the rebuilding of a common state at the cost of some twenty million lives. In England the unploughed fields and the wrecked factories slowly returned to life, women were laid off work and returned reluctantly to the kitchens, and under the Bretton Woods agreement we borrowed untold millions which had to be repaid dollar for dollar. Our own empire had quietly exhausted itself, from Suez to Pitcairn Island, and the pink on the world's map was in retreat before the might of the Republic of chewing gum.

Meanwhile, in London, everything was left to that robust intellectual Binkie Beaumont, at HM Tennents' Ltd, with his delightful menage and his many theatres, to keep the middle England spirit of genteel hope and class achievement merrily burbling along. And he did it so well, with his hollies and his ivies and his waters of the moon. The fox furs were out again in the stalls of England, and one could begin to hear again that tongues' bray of clownish arrogance in the rush for the gin-slings at the interval. More useful perhaps to check up on the world's theatre concurrent with *Absolute Hell* around the late forties. O'Neill's *The Iceman Cometh* had just opened in New York. Sartre's *Huis Clos* in Paris. Eliot's *The Cocktail Party* in Edinburgh.

Christine Foskett, the central character in *Absolute Hell*, doesn't know if her licence to sell alcohol will be revoked, she is humiliated by an American GI she loves, haunted by a crazed spiritualist out of her window, at least four of her club members entirely depend on her for moral sustenance, and ultimately she is deserted by the two friends she has helped through thick and thin – Elizabeth, the classy whore who would prefer to fuck for pleasure; Hugh, the gay civil servant who so desperately wants to know what the difference is when his lover Nigel runs off with a woman: it is Christine who accepts these betrayals and failings, and, ultimately closes down the club in the name of despair. They may all meet again, her, her clients and lovers, all of them her children in the softly glowing drinking night, but never again on her terms in her nightclub, *'La Vie en Rose'*. But Ackland does not allow her anything more than a stoic's end. She weaves her way remorselessly blithe, unblinkered, unbowed, crying out in the dark of 26th July, 1945. Going to her fate eyes wide open and in full knowledge, and angry to hell at the stars for casting such dice. But she has not lost a certain capacity to love, and is burdened by a tolerance only one drunk can share with another. For have no doubt Christine Foskett (perhaps based on the real life Olwen Vaughan of the French Club) is killing herself with booze. It is her living. It is also her dying. And that remains the blind corner in her eye she can never see out from. Perhaps it is this very unblinkeredness in Ackland, this open heart surgery of the soul which has caused such offence.

O'Neill's Hickey in *Iceman* has returned to the saloon bar to tell them all he is so cured, he never need come, he has found the good woman of his life. As the drinks go down, Hickey slowly confesses he has killed this woman. The weight and depth of empathy on stage is produced by the extraordinary realisation of this in all the other saloon bar regulars. Their knowledge of Hickey's truth becomes a choral hymn of bathetic understanding. Something hapless but unbowed, not unlike Christine Foskett's last cry of rage, empowers these bedraggled slaves to alcohol. Perhaps we should stop calling this drug alcohol, better to call it a natural crutch for human strength in the face of cold wretchedness. But ultimately, disease from alcohol, provides no sentimental or softening antidote for the victim. There comes a point in the disease when the body no longer demands intake in quantity. The failing kidneys only require a brief rehearsal of intake. The body now rejects overload. And the mind works lucidly beside these very cruel chemical desiderations of the body. Possibly, both Christine and Hickey, have now forgotten what it is like to be without the sentiment of moderate drinking. They have reached an unblinking plain of clarity where their bodies can never again achieve the early kind of boozing innocence. Faced with his or her despair, no matter a disease which is killing them both, Christine and Hickey ultimately possess an azure eye.

This is not the case for plays like *Huis Clos* or *The Cocktail Party*. Here the playwrights address the agenda of despair in highly conceptualised schemes. Sartre chooses to unravel the idea of tedium in immortality. Eliot chooses an obscene and tortured death on an ant-hill for the mistress in order to achieve expiation. (Perhaps not so surprising; most of Eliot's scripts are packed with dour guilt about throwing 'useless' wives to their death). What all four plays have in common, and in resolute affinity with the world at the time, is a wish to tackle the failure of the human nerve.

Those who have anathematised Ackland at home for not quite playing the game or fitting the bill, may not have noticed the sombre reflectiveness, or wanted to attend to the harsher honesty in his eye. I suggest Rodney Ackland's achievement as a playwright belongs in a much broader frame of reference. It was the critic Hilary Spurling who remarked that Ackland remains the only serious playwright whose work will bear comparison, in point of imaginative strength and emotional delicacy, with the novelists and poets this country produced between the wars – Powell, Waugh, Greene, Spender, and Auden.

In this second collection of plays by Ackland, here are four plays which do much to entrench his own particular brand of caustic nerve on a more domestic scale.

Smithereens began life as an immature piece in 1934, *Birthday*; but was extensively reworked and carefully revived in 1985, with Katherine Parr and Lucy Fleming. *Strange Orchestra* was directed by John Gielgud in 1932, and immediately transferred to the West End. The third play *Before the Party* was written in 1948, and had a successful West End run with Constance Cummings. Our fourth play – *The Old Ladies* by Rodney Ackland is an adaptation from the novella by Hugh Walpole. A three-hander, it is very much a performance piece for character studies. And it was first performed in 1935, when the three old women were played by Edith Evans, Mary Jerrold and Jean Cadell; and directed by John Gielgud.

In *Smithereens*, the time is still set in the thirties, in a very stuffy and traditional upper-middle English household at 25, Adelaide Gardens, South Kensington. Among the Moorhouse-Rees family is an unmarried daughter, the 29-year-old Rosamund. When you dissect the play, it is Rosamund's journey which most counts. The principal non-Equity performer on the stage is a large late Victorian china vase, which is very difficult to avoid as a symbolic device. Mary and Sylvie are sisters, and they share the house with their brother Alfred who is reduced to a wheelchair. They have a cook and a chauffeur. Mary still in her fifties is a deeply insular person, prone to narrow-mindedness. And it is understandable how her husband Howard Rees simply walked out on her and the two daughters – Lallah and Rosamund. Mary appears to hold the family purse-strings, and for a woman born somewhere in the 1880s, in order to keep control of the family she has adopted this priggish role. Lallah is 32, and is married to a young solicitor and they still live in the large house at Adelaide Gardens. Lallah wants kids, she wants a home of their own, but she is not prepared to rock the household boat. In many ways, the older generation of Sylvie and Alfred seem far removed from Lallah and Rosamund. They have both experienced rough days. Alfred's much adored wife Jessie died. And his sister Sylvie gave up a suitable beau called Bertie in India to return to England to look after her crippled brother. And the great hideous vase in the room was the much prized possession of the late lamented Aunt Jessie. Alfred and Sylvie bear the brunt of Mary's constant harping. They were born Edwardians, and somehow what seems best is to keep the family together behind the tired curtains.

A certain Mrs Ormerod gives a very large and noisy bohemian-type party over the road. There is a hint of frenzy and decadence about the riotous noise, and Rosamund knows the young man she loves, Marcus, is most probably being more decadent than anyone else at the party. Then, comes a moment, when Marcus hurls himself into the genteel rooms of the Moorhouse family and promptly destroys the precious giant vase of Aunt Jessie's.

Marcus is a wild drunken spirit, filled with DH Lawrence and James Joyce, he has acquired a small reputation as a novelist. Not quite an Evelyn Waugh, nevertheless there is something mischievous and over-confident about his own natural gifts reminiscent of the young David Garnett. Mary is shaken up enough by the presence of Marcus, but is shocked beyond all civilised grief when she finds out that Marcus has lent Rosamund a copy of *The Well of Loneliness*.

Marcus now only wants Rosamund to run away with him to Paris. Start afresh. Live on French pennies in the artists' quarter. He is filled with hatred for those who condemned Roger Casement to be shot. His implacable war against philistines and the rage in his soul for having served in a great war devoid of motive keeps bright love beating in Rosamund's frozen heart:

MARCUS: Well, that was it. After all the mud, blood, filth and idiocy I couldn't wait to get my candle well and truly lit. What I hadn't realised – was that the enemy at home had used the war as an excuse to pass so many footling little repressive, strangulating laws that when at last the heroes returned to the land made fit for them, our right little, tight little sceptred isle had been turned into nothing so much as a right little, tight little reformatory for retarded children.

Of course, Marcus is referring to everything that Mary stands for. Of course, Rosamund is head over heels in love with him. But the situation becomes soured. There is another young woman called Jo from Mrs Ormerod's party over the road. She bears the same surname as Marcus. She is always seen in his company. When Rosamund confronts Marcus over this, he swears he is not married to this woman. A couple of years ago they announced to friends they were wed, the truth is – it was only a silly prank.

Whilst the large ugly vase is being repaired, Rosamund and Marcus make plans to run off. Marcus begins to call Rosamund his 'Molly Bloom' and it is by no means clear if Rosamund actually grasps the meaning of her new name. Mary gets even tougher with her sister and her brother. A row emerges. Alfred and Sylvie could be thrown out on a whim. Now Alfred threatens to take his wheelchair and walk the streets like a beggar. Now Sylvie insists she will sail back to India and see if that Bertie chappie will have her back. And Rosamund hears about a small studio apartment in an artistic corner of London which is shortly to let.

It is this unknown quantity – the young woman Jo, who confronts the unworldly Rosamund. Jo has had wonderful free and open sex with Marcus ever since they first met. In fact, according to Jo, she is a sexaholic. And to get that you don't need a wedding ring. Rosamund is still prepared to run off with Marcus, until Jo lets slip how often she has cheated on him. And how many men she needs to keep her bed filled. We learn that Jo and Marcus have also sworn to go to Paris on the midnight train. And Jo breaks down in front of Rosamund. Jo has cheated on Marcus again and again because that is the only way she can keep him. They are made for each other in their curiously frenzied lives of sex and betrayal. And on these terms, Jo knows she is the only woman for him. On the appointed hour of escape, Rosamund doesn't take the taxi to the station for the famed 'Golden Arrow' Night Express to Paris. She makes a discreet phone call, and inquires if that studio apartment is still available. It is. She packs her suitcase.

It is difficult to grasp the sexual implications of this play until mother and daughter share the stage. The silent anger waged between Mary and Rosamund has as much to do with frigidness as it has with the new class of youth. There is something in Rosamund's response to the woman Jo which is made out of forlorn revulsion. Whatever it was that separated her mother from her father Howard, something of that distaste for life has transmitted itself to Rosamund. Rosamund knows she cannot compete with the wild and woolly largesse of Jo's rampant love. Jo and Marcus may fuck each other to death in Paris, they may cheat and holler and lie to each other for the rest of their days, but it is a bed they are prepared to lie on. Quietly, and discreetly, but not entirely defeated by all this, (bemused, certainly), Rosamund prepares to take a room of her own, and perhaps write.

In the early thirties the fragile fabric of the traditional drawing-room comedy came under certain criticism. Various young playwrights emerged – Lionel Britton, Merton Hodge, Anthony Kimmins, Edward Knoblock, Ronald Mackenzie and Dodie Smith. With the exception of Mackenzie, it soon became apparent the West End was only interested in new voices as long as they sang the old songs of genteel status quo. This horror of touching politics or any other serious matter was peculiar to the English theatre. When shows from Budapest to Chicago vigorously explored modern issues, the London public was entertained with slight comedies about the fat-headed activities of a tiny minority of the population. Our theatre, instead of becoming a mirror for the broad range of society, turned itself into a box of chocolates. But among a few writers there was an inclination to bite back albeit in the disguise of a traditional offering. Both Ackland and Ronald Mackenzie entered 1932 with new plays which possessed a kind of subversive inner language.

In Ackland's *Strange Orchestra* rootless young ninnies assemble in Vera's Chelsea apartment. Vera ekes out a modest income renting rooms. Mackenzie's play *Musical Chairs* was, on the surface, a virtual make-over of *The Cherry Orchard*. A family in eastern Europe selling up all its possessions. Retreating to Paris. An affair with a maid who is eventually left behind in the great house. Plus the mind-numbing *tabula rasa* of the required grand piano and French windows. But if one looked more closely, you could glimpse through the French windows a blood red thunderstorm gathering over Europe behind the matinee idol John Gielgud at the piano making a fist of the ivories. Stitched into the fabric of a drawing-room play was the foreboding sound of the jackboot and moral despair of a pugnacious capitalist family on the run.

One gets a glimpse of the theatrical temperature of the time with these two plays. Ronald Mackenzie's original title for his play was *The Discontents*. Gielgud immediately sensed death at the chocolate box office with a marquee banner like that, and demanded a new title. Initially, Mrs Patrick Campbell opted to emerge from retirement and chose to play the central role in *Strange Orchestra*. But after a few days of rehearsal, she announced she could not go on. And the actress Laura Cowie stepped in to fill the role of Vera. Mrs Campbell was discovered in full retreat from playing the part of a broken down baggage of a woman of uncertain moral standards and no visible means of support who readily admitted to being a single unmarried mum. Is it possible she hadn't actually read the play before rehearsals began? One garrulous thought emerges – perchance she just counted her lines and tossed the script aside on the sofa.

Raffish must have been the word for it. Vera the Bohemian landlady has a wildly indiscreet affection for the young Val who is supposed to be in love with Vera's daughter. A couple – Jimmie and Laura – are so infatuated with each other they slip up and down the bannisters like entwined seals. Vera's younger daughter Jenny is the most vulnerable. Jenny is the victim of a progressive disease of the eye, and will soon go completely blind. She is an innocent, but inside she cannot believe anything will last. She is sure there has to be an end in sight to the most rapturous of situations. She has fallen hopelessly in love with a penniless artist. Peter the artist duly arrives with a very convincing patter, and a suitcase full of unsold small canvasses. He has God-like looks, and at least one other tenant, Freda, is smitten to the floor. Jenny accepts the fact that Peter may only be hers for a short while. He is too good to be for ever. Her mother insists the new arrival has a decent room, and as landlady and all-seeing-eye of the hectic house Vera announces she will sleep on the couch in the front hall. Soon, Peter is extracting funds out of Jenny, and that suitcase is filled with stolen paintings. Peter is not that kind of artist. He is skilled in wrecking women's lives.

Vera is not the ideal mother to have in moments like this. She's seen Peter flirt with the other tenant, the vivacious Freda. She knows Peter will do his worst to her own daughter, Jenny. Even with Jenny's impending blindness, Vera is unable to offer her much help:

> VERA: I love my children. I want them to be happy,
> and they can't have happiness until they've come
> right up against evil and faced it and got over it for
> themselves.

PETER: You think I've been good for Jenny, then?
That's a relief because I've been more fond of her
than any girl I've done this on before. Do you know,
I nearly didn't go tonight. I've enjoyed this affair so
much, and Jenny was so charming, I thought, why not
prolong it a bit more. But as she herself suggested it
should end in a fortnight, I carried on with my
original plan. You see, she's not very different from
any of these other girls really.

Jenny becomes blind in the third act. Peter is wanted by
the police as a serial thief and seducer and is now on the run.
And even young Val's romance with the other sister Esther
hits the rocks. Val is almost on the verge of taking himself and
his unfinished novel to a remote and closed monastery. Vera
presides over this mayhem from her bed in the front hall.
Nothing seems to surprise her. All her tenants have revealed
themselves as fools when in love. It is here where Ackland
produced his surprise. We are invited to sympathise with
hard-headed Vera, it is at least a way of surviving she suggests.
Then, from a room upstairs by the bannister rail comes the
smell of gas. The inseparable lovers Jimmie and Laura, those
writhing seals of the upper corridor who are never out of bed,
have tried to commit suicide. Why? Why? asks Vera. Because
they know their love for each other can never get better.
Everything else to come in life will be a miserable shadow.
Better to end it now, at least their intense love will stay like
this for ever. It will remain constant between them like memory
sealed in formaldehyde.

Ackland confronted Vera with something quite novel to
her. Here was Vera who hardly demurred when her man left
her – 'I didn't say life was at an end. I said, I've got myself.
Nothing anyone can do to me really matters. And soon afterwards
I got the idea of painting the furniture'. But Vera would never
understand what drove the young lovers to such limits. When
Vera is confronted with their all-consuming and agonising
rapture, no longer can she sustain the act of the shallow bohemian
gypsy surrounded by young things. She's revealed to us in all
her limitations as a self-serving phlegmatic Roman, who dimly
blinks in the irrational light of unutterable happiness.

As for blind Jenny – she has one last confrontation with the cad Peter. He is on the run from the police and needs a few quid to see him through. She will help him once more. And he'll make a run for it for the last time.

> JENNY: No, I wasn't in love with you. It wasn't you at all.
> PETER: Who was it then?
> JENNY: Not you. It was someone I imagined.

Afterwards, in the front room, her sister Esther gives Jenny a bouquet of flowers. Jenny can smell them. Jonquils. They are lovely. They each have little surprised faces. Jenny wears a beatific expression. It's a play of manners, in which the writer suddenly asked his audience to strip down the trivial emotions, and find in love a form of inspired wisdom. More hard work perhaps than the West End punter of the day had in mind.

After World War Two, the late forties was a very productive time for Rodney Ackland. He lived in London with a successful designer, Arthur Boys, and together they worked on a number of film scripts, in particular *The Queen of Spades*. Arthur Boys had an undoubted influence on Ackland, and it is no great leap of the imagination to detect this in the intense and doomed love affair between Hugh and Nigel in *Absolute Hell*. Working with Tyrone Guthrie and Edith Evans, Ackland adapted Dostoevsky's *Crime and Punishment*, and Ostrovsky's *The Diary of a Scoundrel (Too Clever by Half)*.

Between 1948 and 1950, Ackland became a Buddhist, *Crime and Punishment* went to New York, it seems the relationship with Arthur Boys faltered, and the playwright fell in love with Mabby Poole, who worked in film production at the time.

Ackland embarked on an adaptation of a short story by Somerset Maugham – *Before The Party*. The play ran for a hundred performances in the West End with Constance Cummings, and was televised in Britain and America. The success of the play helped the foundation of his new life with Mabby, and for a time they lived together in bucolic circumstances in Cornwall.

Of all his plays, *Before the Party* is the most carefully constructed. It unwinds like the workings of a fine clock. Although set very deliberately in the Surrey belt of lawn tennis courts and Charles Voysey cottages, one could be misled for taking that at face value in an Ackland play. We are in the home of the very upright Aubrey Skinner who soon expects to stand as a Tory MP. His daughter Laura is a widow at 28. David Marshall, a travelling salesman with a deft eye for black market petrol, is in love with Laura. This doesn't go down at all well with the clear-blue-water-between-us customs of the Skinner tribe. Laura is a tragic widow whose husband recently died in West Africa. And David has an unexpected background in World War Two when he was fighting for Tito in Yugoslavia. Twists and turns successfully unfold in this comedy of manners before a happy outcome is found. Yes, we have the clipped voices over the Surrey hedgerows, and the cries to the cook for toad-in-the-hole and bread-and-butter-pudding, but on closer inspection at least one servant is still virtually a card-carrying Nazi and Laura's sister has a pathological hatred for Jews. Rodney Ackland is something of a cony-catcher with his West End audience. Although the mirror he holds up does look jolly disarming, underneath there is a cold and dispassionate nerve in the work. But the play is really about two hardened young people – Laura and David, who have both murdered people and for various official reasons got away with it. One is tempted to ask – Just who is the audience applauding at the close of this play?

I jump a few years. In 1989, Simon Curtis left the Royal Court as an Associate Director. He'd been garlanded with praise for one of the best productions of a new play in the decade – Jim Cartwright's *Road*. BBC2 TV offered Simon a unique slot to produce modern and classic plays on television under the banner of 'Performance'. Simon's first instinct was to seek out Rodney Ackland and mount a major production of *Absolute Hell* with Judi Dench and Bill Nighe and Francesca Annis in the first season. The director was Anthony Page, and I was asked to pull in the structure of the play from almost three hours to a 120 minute length.

At the time, Rodney was living with Terry Todd and his family on the upper floor of a high rise council block in Richmond. Rodney had a room of his own with a vista window.

There were piles of clean clothes and neat boxes filled with manuscripts. The central heating roared even in the summer. And a hint of Dettol and Daz pervaded the nostrils. Rodney was 82, and very weak. He had returned from a second visit to the hospital. He was suffering from the effects of pleurisy and was certainly in no fit state to write. I found a way of pruning the text, without losing any of the characters. My one regret was having forfeited the dance of the drunken GIs and their animal masks which ended up in an orgy over Christine's boozed and helpless body. Rodney came to rehearsals in his wheelchair. He appeared even more frail. On one occasion he cried a little. Silently. Terry Todd wiped Rodney's face. Don't worry about a few tears, Terry said to me, he's as tough as old iron and he don't want no sympathy from any of you. And don't think Rod's on the grateful train. He knows how good this play is.

While shooting the play in the studio, I don't think I've ever seen a director work so hard as Anthony Page. There were tremendous time constraints. Anthony orchestrated the flow of short scenes with wonderful skill. The play uses the whole breadth of a stage to reflect one group upon another. The very nature of this type of writing makes it impossible for the actors to have substantial runs at a scene. Anthony's cameras scrambled to get return shots to cover the narrative. Bill Nighe had an unusual way of building up steam. Between takes, he asked me to march at furious pace with him down corridors and along studio catwalks. Now and again testing his lines with a staccato breath. On the last night in Studio One we had run out of production time. The clock was well past midnight. The crew reassembled and assured Anthony they'd get to the end with him. Sod the clock. Bill and Francesca wrapped up their scenes with great style and acumen. Judi Dench took time to carefully deliver the last exhausted moment when Christine Foskett can only cry out at the dark. It looked to be there. Judi said she'd go once more. And she did. At the last, the entire crew and remaining cast burst into applause.

Rodney Ackland saw a tape of the production shortly before he died. He wasn't going to give anything away, but I knew he was pleased. Anthony Page and Simon Curtis visited him again.

There were phone calls and offers to produce some of the other plays. Rodney spent more time in bed. He looked at me as if to say – something has been restored. The wheelchair became irrelevant. Terry and Debbie Todd did everything they could for him. Then he died.

I got a phone call from Terry. Would I come round? Rodney's birth certificate had gone AWOL. The doctor was on his way. There were all these piles of manuscripts in cardboard boxes. The kids had to be collected from school. There was a man on the blower from the Inland Revenue. (What did *he* want?) Rod's agent was on his way. And a German impresario needs a quick answer like. He'll translate and mount a touring production of *Absolute Hell*, take it from city to city as an epic about the British nation at the end of the war. Why does he want to do that then? Well, said Tel, he thinks a German production of this play will be a raving success. Why is that, then? Because he says that's how the Germans like to see us at the end of the war – on our knees, out of our skins, completely doolally, shooting flies off of the ceiling, and having unproductive rows between two gay men over a woman who we never meet.

When I arrived, there was Terry on the phone pretty much at the end of his tether doing his best to answer the questions of a virtually incompetent obituarist from a tabloid paper – yes, that's right, he's dead. Rodney's dead. He's definitely dead... (pause) Why? You want to come round and see him?

Picked my way through the cardboard boxes in Rodney's room. It was too hot in there. Had to open a window. Rodney won't mind. Rodney's head lay on a double cushion. Gave him just enough leverage to oversee everything in the room. There was some form of cotton padding up his nose, his chin stuck out firmly and those Inland Revenue panic lines on his forehead were melted away. Down the hall the phone wouldn't stop ringing and the kids' TV volume was on full whack. The children had come back from school.

One of Terry's daughters, a mite with Alice hair and a wonky blue bow, edged her way into Rodney's room. She stood by the bed and studied Rodney. Then she leaned across and pinched his cheek. After she let go with her fingers, the firming up epidermis failed to return. The pale skin retained the contour of the pinch. The little girl looked at me – 'Grandad Rodney's not smiling, you know'.

He certainly wasn't.

Michael Hastings
London 2000

Rodney Ackland and Mabby Poole

SMITHEREENS

Characters

HENRIETTA DUCIE

ROSAMUND MOORHOUSE-REES

LALLAH BROOKES

JOHN BROOKES

MARY MOORHOUSE-REES

ALFRED MOORHOUSE

SYLVIE MOORHOUSE

MARCUS EVERSLEY

JO

VINCE

DONNA

EDDIE

Smithereens was first performed at the Theatre Royal, Windsor, on 1 September 1985, with the following cast:

MISS DUCIE, Katherine Parr

ROSAMUND, Lucy Fleming

LALLAH, Angela Down

JOHN, Peter Gale

MARY, Phyllis Calvert

ALFRED, Andrew Cruickshank

SYLVIE, Sheila Burrell

MARCUS, Gregory Floy

JO, Kate Coleridge

VINCE, James Hall

DONNA, Joanna Dickens

EDDIE, Neale Goodrum

Director, Frith Banbury

A house in South Kensington some time
in the early thirties

Act I: March

Act II: Three weeks later

Act III: The following evening

ACT ONE

Towards the end of March some time in the early thirties.

The first floor drawing-room of an upper-middle-class terraced house in that area of London where Kensington merges into Chelsea.

The room is in darkness except for the faint light from a street lamp which, shining obliquely past the ornamental ironwork of a shallow balcony, past half-open French windows, makes visible in the embrasure the bulging shape of a late Victorian china vase, top-heavy on its too slim rosewood stand. After a second or two a light is switched on, apparently from a corresponding room across the road, and a long, clearly defined patch of light is thrown half on the wall and half on the drawing room carpet. A burst of hilarious, raucous laughter is heard, a gramophone starts to play, and shadows move and frenziedly dance in the patch of light.

Suddenly a voice is heard talking to itself in the drawing-room. It comes from the direction of a wing-chair, lost in shadow, back to the door, its occupant, MISS HENRIETTA DUCIE, aged seventy-two, so effaced by the obscurity that, were it not for the quick-flicking movement of knitting needles and the light-catching whiteness of the wool that is being knitted, there would be little evidence that there is anyone in the room.

MISS DUCIE: Dretful creatures! Perfectly dretful!... Not a gentleman among them... Look at the girls too. *My word!* If only poor Papa were still alive... (*She is about to continue in this vein but hears someone approaching the room and shuts up.*)
(*ROSAMUND comes in. The unexpected noise and movement from across the road brings her up short.*)
ROSAMUND: Oh.
(*For a moment she remains transfixed, then hurries to the window and, transfixed again, stands staring out at the antics of the people across the road. Crossing the room, she hasn't noticed MISS DUCIE in the wing-chair and is still unaware of her.*)

LALLAH also, who now appears in the doorway, has her attention immediately riveted and doesn't glance in MISS DUCIE's direction. Both girls wear dinner dresses: LALLAH's pretty, almost fussy, ROSAMUND's unobtrusive, almost dowdy. LALLAH is in her early thirties, ROSAMUND thirty-three.)

LALLAH: Oh! Those people have arrived then... How exciting!

(Crossing to join her sister, she brushes past a new ebony stand, better and larger than the one supporting the vase, its legs protected by brown paper, straw, etc., which has apparently been dumped in the middle of the room and left. But LALLAH is too intent on the new neighbours to spare it more than a glance.)

And having a party already...

ROSAMUND: Lall, stand back a bit – too *shaming* if they caught us staring in at them.

LALLAH: Oh Ros, look, do look at that man dancing all by himself – I wonder if it's – no, it can't be, he's too...or *is* it?

ROSAMUND: It's that *woman* I'm fascinated by – see the one I mean?

LALLAH: Goodness, yes!... What *has* she got on her head?

ROSAMUND: A tea cosy.

LALLAH: *(Peering.)* Oh help! It's that Queen Anne cosy Mother gave Mrs Ormerod for Christmas!

ROSAMUND: *And* repaired by Goosey's own fair hands.

LALLAH: *(After a slight pause.)* You know, poor old thing, Goosey really is becoming a pest, an absolute pest, poor old thing. *(A hand behind her back, she fiddles with a fastening at her waist.)* Ros, see to my dress at the back, will you?

ROSAMUND: *(Kneeling down behind her.)* Keep still a minute.

LALLAH: You know, I am really getting sick to death of having to tear perfectly good clothes apart simply to ensure that Goosey has enough mending to do.

ROSAMUND: Poor old thing.

LALLAH: Oh, thank you, darling – yes, that's much better – and…

(*Her voice dies away. The ball of white wool from which MISS DUCIE has been knitting has fallen from her lap with a soft, tiny thud, drawing LALLAH's attention to the shadowed part of the room; ROSAMUND, following the direction of her sister's gaze, draws in her breath and both girls remain frozen. The ball of wool rolls towards them across the carpet. LALLAH is the first to break the appalled silence.*)

Goosey! What are you doing sitting in the dark? (*She switches on a nearby table lamp.*) Oh look, you've dropped your wool…here it is, Goosey dear. Oh – uh – Mrs Ormerod's nephew seems to have arrived… Oh, and Goosey, how do you like the new pedestal for Uncle Alfred's vase? It's from Rosamund and me as a surprise. We –

ROSAMUND: (*Kneeling beside it, she has started removing the packaging from the new pedestal.*) Lallah, do come and help or they'll have finished dinner.

LALLAH: Oh, sorry, terribly sorry, Ros. (*She kneels and gets to work untying string.*)

ROSAMUND: What are you knitting, Goosey? Something for Mother?

MISS DUCIE: Needlewoman! Sempstress! Miss Henrietta Ducie, daughter of the Late Lieutenant Colonel. Her services as a needlewoman were all she had to offer, trudging wearily from door to door.

ROSAMUND: Well, thank heavens your weary footsteps finished up at *our* door, Goosey.

MISS DUCIE: A queen! Your angel mother: angel ever bright and fair. She made a promise to herself then, she made a vow that for your dear Mamma she'd work her fingers to the bone.

ROSAMUND: Yes but surely you could take things a little more easily now that – uh – now that you're –

MISS DUCIE: So old.

ROSAMUND: I wasn't going to say that.

MISS DUCIE: Oh, yes you were. But she is not a hundred-and-ninety yet, she is not even eighty. No, and she is not deaf.

(*ROSAMUND and LALLAH are abashed.*)

LALLAH: (*After a moment; uncertainly.*) Er...Goosey?

(*But ROSAMUND signals her to keep quiet and she does so. MISS DUCIE goes on knitting with redoubled fury. ROSAMUND removes the last piece of wrapping paper from the new pedestal.*)

ROSAMUND: Well, there it is. What do you think? (*A pause while she looks at it.*) *I* think we must have been a bit potty, suddenly buying it like that.

LALLAH: *I* don't. You wait and see how thrilled they'll be.

ROSAMUND: (*Starts collecting up brown paper and pieces of string from the floor.*) Come on, Lall, help me clear this mess up.

LALLAH: Oh sorry, darling. (*She picks up a single piece of wrapping paper and stands with it.*)

ROSAMUND: Goosey, what *are* you doing?

(*MISS DUCIE, her knitting abandoned with her sewing bag on a chair is painfully bent over, making snatches at the litter on the carpet.*)

Do leave it.

LALLAH: Goosey, do stop! It's not for you to do.

MISS DUCIE: It *is* for me to do. (*Dropping back onto the carpet the scraps of litter she has collected, she stalks out.*)

LALLAH: (*Gazing after her, reflectively.*) It must be so ghastly being as old as Goosey. (*Pause.*) ...Do you know, (*Pause.*) the only time John and I are ever alone together is in bed at night, and then, I'm always so tired I go right off to sleep, and then, when I awake in the morning...

ROSAMUND: Do you mean that...er...Lall, do you mean that er...you and John can never – you know –

LALLAH: Rosamund! Don't be so *foul!*

ROSAMUND: Sorry, I only –

LALLAH: Ros, *please!*

ROSAMUND: Anyway, I was going to say why don't you and John go away for a weekend together sometimes?

(*LALLAH's answer is an exaggerated sigh.*)

Yes, I know…Mummy…

LALLAH: (*Picking up some of the rubbish.*) Ros, did you send
those first chapters of your book to the publishers?

ROSAMUND: (*Coming out of an abstraction.*) Sorry, Lallah –
did I what?

LALLAH: You said you were going to take the plunge and
send as far as you'd got to some publishers in the hope
that they'd…

ROSAMUND: Commission me to go on with it. Which
couldn't be less likely.

LALLAH: But have you sent it yet? Have you actually –
(*She is interrupted by a burst of laughter and shouts from
across the road, then a crash as though someone has chucked a
bottle out of the window.*)
What on earth are they up to now? (*She rushes across to a
vantage point for peering.*) Ros, do come and look –

ROSAMUND: (*Rather too quickly.*) No, I don't want to.
I can't be bothered. (*She glances towards the windows then
goes out of the room.*)

LALLAH: (*Thinking she is still there.*) Oh help! Now a sort of
tramp's just come in…he's got an accordian…

ROSAMUND: (*Returning with a carpet-sweeper.*) Lallah,
please don't let them catch you staring at them! (*Then she
sets about tidying up the litter.*) Come on, do help.
(*With an effort LALLAH withdraws her attention from the
party and joins her sister.*)

LALLAH: You never told me if it *was* him or not…
Was it?… Oh, do tell.

ROSAMUND: What d'you mean, 'do tell'? *I* don't know
any more than you do.

LALLAH: I say, I just thought – that book of his that you
were so mad about – what was it called? – it had a photo
of him on the back – do go and get it and then we can –

ROSAMUND: Oh, Lallah, I haven't seen it for ages.
I expect I lent it to someone.

LALLAH: How maddening. (*Crossing to an armchair she is
about to sit down but stops short.*) Oh, help! Jelly is *naughty!*

Look at this! A 'hugeous' great bone! (*Holding it up for
ROSAMUND to see, she lets the wrapping-paper etc. in her
other hand fall to the floor.*)
(*MISS DUCIE comes back.*)

MISS DUCIE: (*As ROSAMUND gets to work with the carpet-
sweeper.*) That's enough. (*Advancing on her.*) That's enough
of that, young woman. (*Grabbing the sweeper.*) This is
Miss Ducie's work from now on. *C'est le premier pas qui
coûte.* (*She gives a vicious jab with the sweeper, and its
contents: dust, fluff, carpet-pile, etc., fall out.*)

ROSAMUND: Goosey, dear, stop being so silly.
(*Taking up a coal-scuttle from beside the fireplace, she drops
a handful of rubbish into it and then, going on her hands
and knees, starts to shovel the mess from the carpet-sweeper
into it as well.*)
Do something for me, will you? Be a lamb and tippy-toe
down to the dining-room and see what they're up to.
(*MISS DUCIE jumps up from the wing-chair where she
has perched herself with an obstinate expression, grabs her
sewing-bag and knitting, crosses with staccato steps to where
ROSAMUND kneels beside the carpet-sweeper, bundles the
whole lot into the coal-scuttle and exits briskly.*)

LALLAH: (*After a moment in which she and ROSAMUND gaze
at each other open-mouthed.*) She was quite three feet away
from me, but – stale sherry…phew! (*Intending a humorous,
schoolgirl gesture of waving a hand in front of her nose, she
realises the hand has a bone in it.*) Oh, gosh, it's got meat
on it still!… Well, I'd better 'replace it where I found it',
or Jelly will start 'creating.' (*With great care she replaces the
bone and, turning round starts lowering herself into the chair.*)

ROSAMUND: Don't sit on it!

LALLAH: (*As she jumps up.*) No, don't!
(*They both burst into laughter. LALLAH brushes the seat of
her dress with the back of her hand.
JOHN BROOKES looks into the room as though uncertain
who is going to be in it. His expression relaxes when he sees
the two girls.*)

ROSAMUND: You're back late, John.

LALLAH: Johnny, what happened?

JOHN: Sorry, love. I got held up.

(*LALLAH runs and throws her arms round him.*)

LALLAH: (*Drawing back to look at him after they've embraced and kissed.*) You look so white and tired, Johnny. Doesn't he look white and tired, Ros?

JOHN: Yes, all right, all right – don't fuss me, Lallie. I'm tired and I'm white.

LALLAH: Of course you are, poor little thing. Now, if I were you I should have a nice quiet bath and a nice quiet dinner. I'll see Cook about it.

JOHN: (*He kisses her affectionately.*) Have the others finished yet?

LALLAH: Oh, they must have by now.

JOHN: Thank God for that.

LALLAH: Don't be so beastly.

ROSAMUND: (*Returning the coal-scuttle to its place.*) Lallah, do let him say what he feels for once.

LALLAH: Well, even if he does find our family irritating and stupid he might at least try to disguise the fact.

JOHN: I'm continually disguising the fact.

LALLAH: You mean you *do* find them –

ROSAMUND: Lallah, did you *hear* yourself then? You sounded exactly like 'a nagging wife.'

LALLAH: Oh, I *know.*

(*A particularly violent outbreak of party noises across the road.*)

JOHN: Good-God-our-help-in-ages-past! (*He crosses to the windows.*) La Vie de Bohème, eh? And how long are we supposed to put up with this?

ROSAMUND: Lallah, how long did Mother say Mrs Ormerod had let the house for?

LALLAH: Till they get back from Nice; it's while he's having his own house redecorated.

ROSAMUND: Oh...it'll be a few weeks then.

LALLAH: Ros, do look, he's going to play the accordion – (*She pulls the windows open wide. Accordion music swells out.*) What fun. (*Dancing up to JOHN, jigging her shoulders exaggeratedly.*) Darling, come on – *on y danse, on y danse...*

JOHN: Not now, Lallie! I'm too tired and too white.

LALLAH: Oh, please!

JOHN: Lallah! I don't *want* to.

LALLAH: (*She looks at him for a moment then droops
despondently and moves away.*) Oh...all right... I'm sorry.
(*ROSAMUND goes hurriedly to the windows and closes them.
The accordion music and the sounds from the party are reduced
to mere background noises. MISS DUCIE comes back.*)

MISS DUCIE: Your Aunt Sylvie is still fiddling with her
grapes and complaining, your Uncle Alfred's drinking
port and well away with some off-colour anecdote and
your dear mamma is *pas-devant-les-domestiques*-ing and
fingering a peach. Such is the state of affairs on the
dining-room front. (*She takes a long shuddering whistling
breath through rounded lips, marches, bridling, to the wing-
chair, collects her sewing-bag and knitting, dumps them back
into the coal-scuttle and makes for the door.*)

ROSAMUND: Goosey, do stop this ridiculous attitude...
Goosey!
(*MISS DUCIE pays no attention; reaching the landing, she
goes up the stairs and out of sight.*)
...John, be a lamb and help me get this vase up.
And (*Indicating the old pedestal.*) we'd better get this
wood-wormy old thing out of sight somewhere.
(*He goes to her assistance.*)

JOHN: Chut! I think they're coming up.

ROSAMUND: Oh, quick then, John!
(*They have lifted the vase onto the floor and now lay down
the discarded pedestal behind the sofa.
LALLAH's mother comes in; a handsome woman in her middle
years, MARY MOORHOUSE-REES.*)

MARY: (*With forced, artificial brightness.*) Well, children,
I thought I'd have my own little Private View of the
famous pedestal before the others come up.

ROSAMUND: (*Together.*) Here it is then – *voilà!*

LALLAH: (*Together.*) Lo and behold!

MARY: Oh, yes, your Uncle should be very pleased.
(*She stops short, freezes; a crescendo of party sounds from
across the way makes her aware for the first time of what is
going on in the house opposite.*)

I was right then! (*Crossing to the windows to have a good look – after a moment, turning back to the room.*) Well, one thing you can be certain of: I am *not going to put up with it.* Lallie, stand up straight, dearest, you're getting quite round-shouldered. Look at Baby, Baby doesn't stand like that.

LALLAH: Mummy, John was kept late, he's only just got home, he's had no dinner, nothing to eat, I thought I'd go and tell Cook –

MARY: I wish he'd arrange to dine at the same time as everybody else. Alfred and Sylvie will begin to think that our conversation isn't lively enough to entertain a tired business man.

JOHN: But I often get a great deal of entertainment from your conversation.

LALLAH: Mother, a solicitor is not 'a businessman' and you know that perfectly well.

MARY: What is that bone doing in the armchair?

ROSAMUND: You know what a scene Jelly makes if she's deposited a bone somewhere and comes back and finds it gone.

MARY: Yes, but somebody should see to all that.

LALLAH: (*With an air of defiance.*) John, I'm going down to see Cook. Would you like –

JOHN: Lallie, I don't want a meal – I had something sent in at five o'clock – all I want is a bath.

A SHRILL VOICE: (*From downstairs.*) Madam!

MARY: (*Springing up.*) Oh! Alfred's been telling Hopkins one of his stories. Come along Lallah, I cannot cope with them any more on my own.

(*She goes out, LALLAH following.*)

LALLAH: (*Turning at the door, she addresses JOHN in a stage-whisper.*) Just have a *wash* for the time being! And I'm going to order you some delicious sandwiches!

MARY: (*As she starts down the stairs.*) Yes, what is it, Hopkins? (*LALLAH joins her. JOHN and ROSAMUND are alone.*)

ROSAMUND: (*Breaking the silence between them.*) Were you late home on purpose? To avoid having dinner with the family?

JOHN: Yes, of course.

ROSAMUND: But John, I'm there too, it's just as –

JOHN: Yes, but you belong to the tribe.

ROSAMUND: That makes it worse, I suppose.

> (*There is a pause filled with rueful thoughts. Suddenly JOHN snaps out of it.*)

JOHN: Oh, I got that book you wanted (*Getting it from his pocket.*) in Charing Cross Road at lunchtime.

ROSAMUND: 'Work in progress'? Oh, thank you. You are a lamb.

> (*He gives it to her.*)

I've been longing to get hold of this.

JOHN: I... I couldn't resist a quick glance at it on my way home...

> (*He waits for a reaction but ROSAMUND is intent on the book's opening passage and doesn't hear him.*)

and...surely it's a confidence trick?... The man's a charlatan.

ROSAMUND: (*Looking up at last.*) Oh, sorry... What? What did you say?

JOHN: I said the man's a charlatan.

ROSAMUND: What man? James Joyce?

JOHN: I mean it's not even English. May I have it for a moment? (*Taking the book from her he reads out.*) 'Anna Livia plurabelle' – what's that supposes to mean?... 'Sing me songs of stem and stone. Of Shem and Shaun'... 'Hither and thithering waters of. Night.' Now if you can tell me that that's –

ROSAMUND: May I have it please?

> (*She holds out her hand for it; he gives it to her.*)

JOHN: Ros...have I upset you?

ROSAMUND: Thanks.

> (*She crosses to an escritoire, opens a drawer puts the book inside and closes the drawer on it. There is a crash of broken glass from across the road.*)
>
> (*Alarmed.*) What's that?
>
> (*JOHN runs to the window. ROSAMUND joins him, peering over his shoulder.*)

They're mad... Oh, do stand back, they'll see us.

JOHN: What's that woman got on her head?

(*MARY enters in a rage.*)

MARY: (*Crossing to the window and glaring out.*) It's iniquitous!
No consideration for other people. None whatsoever! As
I said to Mrs Flitch at the bridge club, 'Any man who
could write such vile books is bound to be a bounder.'

ROSAMUND: 'Bound to be a bounder'?

MARY: Baby, don't always try to turn anything serious into
a joke.

ROSAMUND: But how can you say somebody's books are
vile when you've never read a word of them?

(*LALLAH has come back into the room and joined her mother.
MARY clutches her arm.*)

MARY: Oh, look, Lallah, my Queen Anne cosy, that I got
Miss Ducie to do all that intricate work on, stuck on
some horrible woman's head!

LALLAH: Oh, dear! But Mummy, it won't do the cosy any
harm.

MARY: Of course it will do harm. Horrible women like that
never wash their hair.

(*JOHN starts for the door but MISS DUCIE, carrying a
tray, comes in and, peering round short-sightedly, makes for
him.*)

MISS DUCIE: Ah! Here he is, alone and palely loitering.
(*Proffering the tray.*) Gentleman's Relish.

JOHN: That's very thoughtful of you, but…um…

MISS DUCIE: You see? They left out of account the
fighting spirit of the daughter of my dear papa, the late
Miss Ducie.

JOHN: You can't call yourself 'the late'. You couldn't be
more alive.

MISS DUCIE: Better late than never. (*She places the tray on a
nearby table and starts to go.*)

LALLAH: (*Through stifled laughter.*) But Goosey, what
happened? I asked *Cook* to make sandwiches.

MISS DUCIE: They wouldn't do. I told her *I* would do them.

LALLAH: Oh help! And she *let* you? – but what did she say?

MISS DUCIE: What one would expect. Irish curses!
Obscenities from the bog.

MARY: You must not interfere with staff, Miss Ducie.

MISS DUCIE: If only my papa were here he'd take a horsewhip to them!

ROSAMUND: But Goosey, do you mean to say that your father used to stalk into the kitchen and horsewhip the cook?

MISS DUCIE: Most certainly he did! In his Indian days, when he was serving his country in India.

ROSAMUND: Well, I'm sorry, but I think it's utterly revolting. It makes one ashamed of being English.

MISS DUCIE: (*In a hoarse whisper; leaning towards her.*) My dear Princessy, don't you think it's time you acquainted yourself with the fundamental rudiments of how to behave? (*She straightens up and bridles out of the room, adding:*) If you wish to pass as a lady, that is.

ROSAMUND: She really is getting beyond any kind of joke!... Mummy, honestly, what made you take her on in the first place?

MARY: You know about that, darling. I've told you.

LALLAH: (*Under her breath.*) Five thousand times at least.

ROSAMUND: I mean she was a complete stranger, wasn't she?

MARY: (*She ponders for a moment.*) Well...she broke down and cried in front of me.

(*Seated outside MARY's line of sight, LALLAH now starts to mouth MARY's words as her mother speaks them, accompanying the childish mockery with exaggerated mime.*)

I could see right from the start – as soon as she was shown in here – that she was well–bred and came from a decent background and that it couldn't be *her* fault that she was destitute. And of course my instinct was right! She'd had a very reasonable amount left her by her father, but she'd invested it with an American Trust Company and then The Crash came and of course she lost every penny. She'd been trudging about all day, she'd had nothing to eat but a pot of tea, a Bath bun and a single solitary sausage – Lallah, are you behaving like a stupid schoolgirl?

LALLAH: No, I don't think so.

MARY: Well, stop being so ill-bred. I'm sorry, Baby, where had I got to?

ROSAMUND: You were going to say 'and one could be certain the sausage had no proper meat in it.'

MARY: (*Turning to ROSAMUND.*) No, and that's when she broke down and cried like a child and I thought, 'Good heavens, poor woman, I can't have her crying like this.' So I rang for some tea for her and engaged her to do the sewing and mending for us. You would have done the same, Baby. Anybody with a vestige of ordinary decent feeling would.

LALLAH: But Mummy –

MARY: Just a minute, Lallah... Yes, they're coming up by themselves. Run along and see if they need any help. (*LALLAH runs out.*)

MARY: Oh dear! And the vase has been left on the floor. (*ROSAMUND goes to put the vase on the new pedestal.*)

JOHN: Well, if you'll excuse me, I think I'll... (*He is making for the door, but MARY stops him.*)

MARY: John, be a good boy and help Rosamund up with it.

ALFRED: (*Off, on the stairs.*) I can manage, my dear. Plenty of time. The drawing-room won't run away.

LALLAH: (*Rushing back into the room.*) Perfectly all right, they're puffing up the stairs under their own steam.

JOHN: Two antique puff-puffs from the early days of rail. (*Nobody laughs.*)

ROSAMUND: Oh, do come on – as we've organised a 'surprise' we might as well do it properly. (*JOHN goes to help ROSAMUND with the vase.*)

MARY: That's right. Get it quite in the centre. Disgusting people! (*She has involuntarily glanced out of the window.*) (*ALFRED and SYLVIE appear at the door, but, before she has time to stop herself, LALLAH has run and shut it in their faces.*)

LALLAH: Oh dear! I didn't mean to do that!

MARY: You're forgetting yourself, Lallah. Open the door at once.

LALLAH: We don't want to spoil the surprise.

ROSAMUND: Well, it's ready now.

LALLAH: (*Shouting.*) You can come in. (*She flings the door open.*)

(*ALFRED and SYLVIE enter. ALFRED has on a baggy dinner suit with a soft shirt; he limps and assists himself with a stick. SYLVIE is wearing a stiff semi-evening dress. Her hair is nondescript grey, very thin and cropped ludicrously short. She is rather deaf, so people shout when addressing her. ALFRED's habitual expression is a smile, SYLVIE's a frown.*)

ALFRED: *There's* a nice trick to play on your old uncle.

SYLVIE: What's the matter with you, Lallah?

MARY: I'm afraid she was rather excited, dear. She forgot herself.

SYLVIE: What? Forgot what?

MARY: She forgot herself.

SYLVIE: What have you forgotten, Lallah?

LALLAH: Nothing, Aunt Sylvie.

ALFRED: Herself.

SYLVIE: Forgotten herself. Never heard such gibberish.

(*ROSAMUND can no longer suppress her laughter. It bursts forth, followed by JOHN's, LALLAH's and ALFRED's. Even MARY laughs deprecatingly. Then they stop, there is another wave of laughter from across the road. The effect is momentarily frightening. They all look at each other.*)

(*To whom it has been inaudible.*) Why are you all looking so silly? Like stuck pigs. Nothing but a lot of stuck pigs, I call you.

ROSAMUND: Oh, never mind. Uncle Alfred, we've got something to show you, *and* Aunt Sylvie.

ALFRED: All right, my pretty. Now, what is all this going on across the road?

(*He hobbles to the window, followed by SYLVIE.*)

SYLVIE: Alfred! Alfred! Take hold of my arm, or you'll fall and hurt yourself.

ALFRED: Thank you, my dear. That's right. I don't know what I should do without you.

(*They are now near enough to the window to see across.*)

ROSAMUND: (*Hoping to draw their attention to the present.*) Be careful of that awful old pedestal, Uncle. It's got very wobbly lately.

ALFRED: (*Intent on other things.*) So am I, my dear. What with my old Boer War leg, I'm getting wobbly too. Wobbly on the pins. (*He suddenly shouts to SYLVIE.*) Funny lot of devils they seem to be.

SYLVIE: Horrors. Nothing but horrors, I call them.

JOHN: Well, er... I'm just going up to make myself respectable.

ALFRED: Now, my boy, don't you go running away directly I come in.

JOHN: Well... I'm rather grubby...

SYLVIE: Now come along and sit down, Alfred.

ROSAMUND: No! No, don't go away from the window yet.

ALFRED: I knew you girls were up to something. Come on, now, out with it.

LALLAH: Oh, go on, Ros, tell them.

ROSAMUND: Don't you notice anything different about the room, Uncle?

SYLVIE: What is it, dear? Speak up.

ROSAMUND/LALLAH: Don't you notice anything different about the room?

(*The old people look at each other in puzzlement and then gaze around them.*)

LALLAH: Give them a clue, Ros.

(*A pause.*)

ALFRED: God bless my soul! What is it? A new pedestal? Magnificent! Well, I never, what a beauty, eh?

(*ROSAMUND is glowing with delight.*)

SYLVIE: Well, there! What grandeur. How delighted Jessie would be to see it.

LALLAH: (*Together.*) Rosamund spent all the money she was saving up.

ROSAMUND: (*Together.*) Lallah spent all the money she was saving up.

ALFRED: The silly girls. Come and give your uncle a kiss, my pretties.

(*ROSAMUND and LALLAH do so in turn.*)

SYLVIE: And isn't your old aunt to get one?

ROSAMUND: (*Together.*) Yes, of course.

LALLAH: (*Together.*) Of course, Auntie.

ALFRED: A typically Moorhouse thing to do. Always ready to give up everything for another Moorhouse.

MARY: Come and sit down, both of you, or you'll be tired out with so much excitement.

ALFRED: (*Hobbling to an armchair, assisted by SYLVIE and his stick.*) God bless me! What's this – a bone? Well, here's a how-d'ye-do – a man can't sit in his own chair because Madam Jelly doesn't like her bones moved. Jelly?... Jelly? Come and get your bone – Bad girl! Messing up the drawing room. Jelly? You're a dirty bitch!

MARY: Alfred!

ALFRED: Well, I'm not going to call her a dirty *dog*.

JOHN: I'll go and get her.

LALLAH: No, call her, she'll come if we call.

ROSAMUND: She's got three suitors now.

SYLVIE: What? Disgusting, I call it. We must keep her in. We can have a box of earth for her.

ROSAMUND: She's in love with the dachshund I believe.

SYLVIE: Rubbish, Rosamund.

MARY: Do call her, Ros, poor Alfred's waiting to sit down.

ROSAMUND/LALLAH: Jellyjellyjellyjellyjellyjelly.

(*They are at the door now and JELLY waddles in, her tail wagging. She is obviously overfed.*)

LALLAH: (*Dropping on her knees before her.*) Darling little darling. Mummy's pet. Mummy's pretty. Little fat woggums.

ALFRED: What you want is a baby, Lallah.

LALLAH: Uncle, don't.

MARY: Don't say such things, Alfred.

(*A pause.*)

SYLVIE: (*In a wheedling tone.*) Where's Auntie's pet, then? Come and get her nice boneys.

ALFRED: Here you are, my pretty.

ROSAMUND: Here's the bone, Jelly. Look. It's not been moved.

(*She points to it. When JELLY has seen and approved,
ROSAMUND puts it in her mouth and lifts her up, bone
and all.*)
I'll take her downstairs. Here, John, you take her down.
(*She hands JELLY to him.*)

JOHN: (*With meaning.*) Thank you, Ros.
(*They exchange quick collusive smiles. He carries JELLY to
the door.*)

SYLVIE: And tell them down there whatever happens she's
not to be let out!
(*JOHN shuts the door behind him. ALFRED sits down.*)
(*Fussing the cushions.*) Are you quite comfortable, Alfred?

ALFRED: Yes, thank you, my dear.

MARY: Now, where will you sit, Sylvie?

SYLVIE: Over here, dear (*She sits down.*)

MARY: (*Fussing the cushions.*) That's better. Alfred's a bit too
much for you sometimes.

SYLVIE: Thank you, my dear. I don't know what I should
do without you.

LALLAH: Mother, do come and sit down, you've been
whizzing about all day.

MARY: Thank you, dearest. (*Seating herself.*) I shall take a
cachet faivre when I go to bed.

SYLVIE: John? Where's John? Lallah's husband. Why does
he run away directly we come in?

MARY: Is your hand cool, Lallah?

LALLAH: (*Touching her own cheek.*) No, it's rather hot. I'll put
it on the window and cool it. (*She crosses the room.*)

MARY: No! Don't. You don't want to go over there.

LALLAH: (*Who obviously does.*) I'll make the blood run away.
(*She holds up her hands in the air and wriggles them.
Lowering her hands.*) Oh! Oh! How awful! How terrible!
How absolutely *shaming*!
(*LALLAH, hiding her flaming cheeks in her hands, runs as
far from the window as she can and collides with her husband,
who is just entering the room. He clasps her to him.*)

JOHN: (*Together.*) Steady on, Lall. What *are* you doing?

MARY: (*Together. Rising.*) What is the matter? You shouldn't
frighten us like that.

ALFRED: (*Together.*) God bless my soul!

ROSAMUND: (*Together.*) Lallah!

SYLVIE: (*Together.*) What is it – a mouse?

LALLAH: (*Tearfully.*) Somebody opposite thought I was *waving* to them, and they waved back.

JOHN: A nice friendly gesture.

SYLVIE: What's the matter with the girl? Hysterical I call it.

LALLAH: (*As she and JOHN sit together on the music-stool.*) I felt such an idiot.

JOHN: *They* were the buffoons, Lallie, not you.

(*He puts his hand over hers and presses it. LALLAH looks at him affectionately.*)

MARY: (*Looking round at them.*) My head's bad, Lallah.

LALLAH: Sorry, I forgot.

(*She starts towards MARY but ROSAMUND gets there first and taking up a position behind her mother's chair, places a hand on MARY's forehead. MARY is disconcerted and rather annoyed but she can only say:*)

MARY: Thank you, dear.

LALLAH: Thank you, Ros.

(*She sits down next to JOHN again. There is silence for a moment.*)

ALFRED: (*Returning to his contemplation of the vase.*) I remember as if it were yesterday. We saw it in the shop, Jessie and I. We stood there gazing at it and we both thought... It was that same afternoon that I broke it to her about going to sea. Your poor Aunt Jessie, she did cry. 'What's the good...?' On the Stock Exchange or on the sea, that's what I had to choose. I chose the one that would make your aunt happy. The next evening when I got home, I opened the front door and what a surprise! There was the vase!

SYLVIE: Yes. She got the vase for him.

(*A pause.*)

MARY: Why don't you play us something, Ros?

LALLAH: (*Together.*) Yes, do, Ros. (*Rises.*)

SYLVIE: (*Together.*) What's that? Play the piano?

MARY: What do you say to something from *The Mikado*, dear?

LALLAH: (*Springing up and going to ROSAMUND.*) Oh, Ros, do you remember the time we all went to *The Mikado* together? I must have been about eight.

SYLVIE: Come near *me* and talk. Don't leave your old aunt out.

(*They move over to her so that they make a little group: ALFRED, SYLVIE, MARY, LALLAH and ROSAMUND. JOHN is left sitting at the other end of the room.*)

ROSAMUND: We were remembering when we all went to *The Mikado* together.

LALLAH: Do you remember, Aunt Sylvie?

SYLVIE: I should say so!

(*They laugh. JOHN laughs just afterwards.*)

LALLAH: And wasn't it funny! I thought the theatre must be one of those strange, not-very-nice places called for some unknown reason 'A Public House'.

MARY: But, my dear, you shouldn't have known such places existed.

ALFRED: There you are Mary! Found out at last! Used to leave you outside, Lallah, while she went in to booze a pint of porter.

(*He chuckles uproariously, and the others laugh too.*)

MARY: Well, come along, Ros, I thought you were going to play to us.

(*The others, with the exception of JOHN, chorus 'Yes, do play something,' 'Do play!' etc. etc.*)

LALLAH: Here you are, *The Yeoman of the Guard.*

ROSAMUND: (*Looking through music.*) Yes, let's have *The Yeoman of the Guard.* (*She sits at the piano, arranging the music in front of her.*)

ALFRED: (*Singing.*) I have a song to sing-o.

LALLAH: (*Singing.*) Sing me your song-o.

SYLVIE: Bertie took me to see *The Yeoman of the Guard* the night before he went back to his regiment in India. Ah, dear me, poor Bertie.

JOHN: Come and sit here, Lall.

LALLAH: Oh, hullo, Johnny. Wait a minute.

(*ROSAMUND starts to play.*)

ROSAMUND: ...'Were I thy bride...' Come on, Aunt
Sylvie.
(*She goes on playing for a minute or two, then looking round
at her aunt sees that the old lady's eyes have filled with tears.*)
Oh dear... (*She stops playing.*) Auntie, what's the matter?

SYLVIE: 'I'm not thy bride', she says at the end. That's what
I said to Bertie. Ah, well, poor old Alfred, Jessie gone
and his Boer War leg, you couldn't expect me to go and
leave him.

MARY: You were wonderful, Sylvie, wonderful.

ALFRED: Yes, wonderful woman your sister, Mary. Don't
know what I should have done without her.

SYLVIE: Nor I without Mary, Alfred. You don't think I'd
have put up with you all these years if I hadn't had Mary
here as a companion. Not likely! But I never got on with
her husband.

ALFRED: Nice chap. I liked Howard Rees. Sorry when he
went to live by himself. Tch. Tch. Great pity.

MARY: (*Shutting her eyes as though in pain.*) That'll do, Alfred.

LALLAH: Play something else, Ros. Something jolly.

ROSAMUND: All right, wait a minute. I'll find something.

LALLAH: (*Looking through a music-album.*) Here's one
I rather adore. It always makes me think of when
Mummy took us up to Hampstead and we saw the
roundabouts.

ROSAMUND: And she wouldn't let us go on them.

MARY: I should think not. You don't know what you might
have caught.
(*ROSAMUND starts to play.*
*LALLAH's choice has fallen on 'Over the Waves', an antique
waltz, ubiquitous at this period as background music for
fairgrounds, variety halls, circuses, and in the repertory of
street barrel-organs. The Moorhouses and their Moorhouse-
Rees sister now resign themselves contentedly to the habitual
conclusion of their day: a creeping paralysis of after-dinner
torpor while the comfortable sounds of familiar music and
the comfortable sight of Aunt Jessie's vase help in lulling
them towards bedtime and the oblivion of sleep.*

Uncle ALFRED has just reached the point where it is evident that his next breath will merge into a snore when, with peace-shattering abruptness, the doors of the drawing-room are flung open and a flushed and out-of-breath MISS DUCIE bursts into agitated view.)

MISS DUCIE: *Prenez-garde!* Everyone *prenez-garde!* Those dretful creatures – she's let one in! (*A glance over her shoulder.)* And he's coming up the stairs!

(Glaring scorn and indignation at the intruder, she draws herself up, bridling, as MARCUS EVERSLEY, an extraordinarily attractive, dark young man of thirty-two, in a high old state of drunken euphoria and almost dream-like recklessness, brushes past her into the room.)

MARCUS: Don't run away – don't get up – don't sit down – don't wet your cami-knicks – (*His eye on the vase he weaves towards it.)* I'm so drunk I'm invisible – Gotcha!

(With a sudden pounce he grabs the vase, raises it above his head so that the people gathered in the window opposite can see, and lets out a prolonged cry of triumph of the Ancient Greeks:)

Elelelelu!

(Shrieks, cheers, whistles and laughter from his friends. But before he can carry out his intention of dashing the vase to the floor, ROSAMUND has rushed into the balcony and is struggling to get it away from him.)

ROSAMUND: Let go! – let go of it! – let go!

(He lets go and ROSAMUND, finding the vase unexpectedly in her hands, immediately drops it. It smashes to pieces.)

MARCUS: Butterfingers!

(Turning to face the open-mouthed bated-breathed family, he makes a sweeping gesture which nearly topples him.)

Massacre of the Philistines! Collapse of stout parties!

(Applause from across the road. Acknowledging it, he swings round, steps to the balcony rail, and, clasping his hands together, shakes them in the traditional self-congratulatory gesture of a boxer who has won.)

ROSAMUND: (*Meanwhile.)* I don't know *how* that happened... I'd got it *away* from him, I... Oh, God! I am sorry...

(*MARY and SYLVIE have risen to their feet, LALLAH, at the smashing of the vase, has uttered a staccato, uncompleted scream, and ALFRED bursts into tears.*)

SYLVIE: (*Hurrying to comfort him.*) Alfred, don't!... Oh, my poor boy! Oh, Alfred!... (*She too bursts into tears.*)

ALFRED: All those years...all my life that...and then for a drunken scoundrel...

(*MARY hurries to comfort her sister.*)

MARY: Sylvie! You mustn't. You'll make yourself ill. Sylvie! Alfred!... Oh, it's so *unfair!*

(*MARY bursts into tears. LALLAH runs to her.*)

LALLAH: Mummy, darling, it can be mended – it *can* be, I'm sure it can – oh God, Johnny! (*Now it is her turn to burst into tears.*)

(*JOHN goes to her.*)

JOHN: Lallah, don't...it's all right, sweetheart.

LALLAH: Beast! The horrible beast to do a thing like that! (*JOHN looks round at the balcony where MARCUS is signalling to his guests across the road. The room is now in complete uproar. Freeing himself from LALLAH's embrace, JOHN crosses with quick, light steps to the French windows, pushes them shut and locks them.*)

MARY: That's right, John! Now he's trapped.

LALLAH: Oh, I'm sorry... I'm so sorry, Johnny, I can't stop crying.

JOHN: (*His arm round her again.*) Come on, Lall – for God's sake!

(*MISS DUCIE, who, immediately after the smashing of the vase, has vanished from the doorway now reappears with the carpet-sweeper and shoves her way, purse-lipped and stony-eyed, through the emotion-stricken family. LALLAH's sobs are gradually merging into something different, which now resolves itself into shrieks of laughter.*)

LALLAH: Oh, my goodness, now I'm having hysterics!... I'm having *hysterics!*

MARY: Take Lallah up to bed, John and give her some aspros. Then I want you to find Collins and tell him to go straight out and fetch a policeman.

JOHN: (*As he leads LALLAH, still laughing and sobbing, out of the room.*) Be much simpler to phone the police station.

MARY: Very well, *leave* it to me, *I'll* do it.

MISS DUCIE: (*Having swept, with her hand, the bits of broken china onto the floor from the arm of an armchair where ROSAMUND has dropped them, she is now pushing ineffectually at them with the sweeper.*) Useless contrivance. Hercules sweeping up the horsedung.

MARY: Now what happened, Miss Ducie? Who let that person in?

MISS DUCIE: One foot inside the door and the female village idiot simpering and giggling...
(*Her attention is caught by movements on the balcony. Through the glass MARCUS can be seen pulling crazy faces and making crazy gestures into the room.*)

MISS DUCIE: My...*word!* What a rotter!

MARY: Then it was Hopkins who let him in?

MISS DUCIE: (*On her way out, still clutching the carpet-sweeper.*) Dolt of a girl!... Prize idiot!... Put against a wall and shot.
(*ALFRED suddenly notices MARCUS making a devilish grimace through the window glass, his index fingers either side of his temples pointing upwards in imitation of a devil's horn.*)

ALFRED: Look at him there! (*He gets to his feet, waving his stick with impotent fury.*) Young blackguard!

SYLVIE: Alfred! Alfred! Come upstairs, dear... Mary is going to telephone for the police.

MARY: Yes, go along, both of you. There's nothing you can do, try and get some sleep...
(*She glances apprehensively at the balcony where MARCUS, having retired to the balustrade, is more or less out of sight, and starts manoeuvring the two old people, muttering and mumbling, out of the room and up the stairs.*)
Baby, you'd better stand guard.

ROSAMUND: It was all my fault. I shouldn't have interfered – I –

MARY: Don't talk *nonsense*, Baby. He was going to smash it anyway. Now keep an eye on him. I'll be down in a minute.

ROSAMUND: Yes, all right.

MARY: Take care, won't you. I shan't be long.

(*ROSAMUND waits until they are out of sight then turns to face the balcony. MARCUS is smirking at her with a questioning expression, his state of reckless, drunken euphoria apparently unchanged. She starts towards him but goes first to close the double doors before hurrying across the room and pulling open the French windows.*)

ROSAMUND: How could you have *done* such a thing?

MARCUS: Gorgeous angry girl – Rosamund. Rosamund! Rose of the world! My visible worm will seek out your bed of crimson joy if you're not careful – why are you hissing at me?

ROSAMUND: Just go, will you? Come on, quickly – please! (*She has started to lead the way but, unable to contain herself, stops short and turns on him.*) How *could* you? It was so cruel, so horrible.

MARCUS: But I did it for you, love, you know that, don't you – I adore your tits.

ROSAMUND: Oh, stop this ridiculous drunken rubbish.

MARCUS: But you asked me to do it, you begged me to.

ROSAMUND: I *begged* you to? How can you *say* such a thing?

MARCUS: Now listen, love-dove, you cast your mind back, as they say in the law courts – God, I could gobble you right up top to bottom – to the moment when you got off with me in the post office this morning –

ROSAMUND: I did not 'get off' with you. Why do you try to drag everything down to a level of commonness?

MARCUS: There speaks your mother's girl.

ROSAMUND: But it's a completely wrong choice of words to describe what happened.

MARCUS: What words would *you* use then?

ROSAMUND: Look, when I was standing at the counter, sticking on the stamps for Chatto and Windus, and I turned round and saw you smiling at me, what made me smile back was that you'd become so much a part of my life. Your novel, your book reviews – I followed them religiously every week –

MARCUS: Religiously?

ROSAMUND: Yes, religiously – All the marvellous books you introduced me to. They've opened up areas of my mind that had been completely closed – Sh!... Oh, my goodness. It *is* Mummy! Hide! Hide somewhere!
(*As MARY is heard approaching ROSAMUND runs to the double doors and, opening one of them, stands holding it so that to get into the room, MARY would have to push past her.*)
Oh, Mummy, it's too dreadful! I'm terribly sorry –

MARY: My poor Baby, what is it? What's happened?

ROSAMUND: I glanced away for a moment and when I looked back I couldn't see him. He was gone.

MARY: But –

ROSAMUND: He must have climbed over and dropped to the ground.

MARY: Oh, well... I didn't really welcome the idea of policemen tramping all over the house tonight. Of course if you hadn't got the vase away from him he could have been charged with damage to property.

ROSAMUND: Oh, I know! I couldn't be more sorry. I could kick myself!

MARY: And what was John doing standing there?

ROSAMUND: Well, I'm sure it could be patched up with rivets or something.

MARY: Well, you'd better go to bed, I'm sure you could do with a good night's sleep as well as any of us.

ROSAMUND: Yes, I really could.

MARY: (*Kissing her.*) Goodnight then, pet. I'll leave you to turn the lights out. (*Sighing deeply she trails up the stairs.*) I simply could not have coped with policemen on top of everything else tonight...

ROSAMUND: Goodnight, Mummy.

MARY: I think I'll take *two cachets faivres* when I get to bed. (*ROSAMUND comes back into the room, closes the doors quickly and carefully and turns to MARCUS.*)

ROSAMUND: So what was I saying? What was I saying when Mummy –

MARCUS: That I'd opened up something of yours which had hitherto been closed.

ROSAMUND: Yes, I mean everything opened up for me –

MARCUS: Which had hitherto been closed?

ROSAMUND: I'm trying to say that I returned your smile in the post office exactly as I would have with an old friend I'd known for years. And *how* that could be interpreted as 'wanting to get off.'

MARCUS: All too evident. You thought, 'I know what I'll do! Never mind old Chatto and Windus. I'll give Marcus Whatsisname 'the eye', get off with him and get him to take this stuff home and read it and then give me his *absolutely honest* opinion – '

ROSAMUND: How could you know what my thoughts were? How could you *possibly?*

MARCUS: By your subsequent actions. Look what happened. You *did* plead with me to take your stuff home and read it. And I did exactly that.

ROSAMUND: ...How do you mean? Did exactly what?

MARCUS: I took it home. And I read it.

ROSAMUND: Oh, you didn't!

MARCUS: And I formed an 'absolutely honest' opinion about it.

ROSAMUND: ...Oh *dear!*... Oh well, I might as well know... So what did you think? Am I a writer? You did really read it?

MARCUS: I not only read it, I re-wrote it.

ROSAMUND: *Re-wrote* it?

MARCUS: Quite a lot of it.

ROSAMUND: Oh Lord!... You don't think I'm really a writer?

MARCUS: My dear girl, shut-up. Do you imagine for a moment that I'd spend one fraction of a fractured second of my irreplaceable time re-writing anyone who wasn't a writer?

ROSAMUND: No, I don't, when I come to think of it... But... I'm longing to ask you – do you think the subject I've chosen for this novel –

MARCUS: Never mind about that – settle the other question first. Do you remember, after we left the post office together, what your reply was when I told you that we'd been seriously considering buying catapults and taking pot shots at the objectionable vase in your first floor window? You said, 'What a spiffing idea! I've always longed for some kind friend to stump into the drawing-room and smash the bloody thing!'

ROSAMUND: I did not say that and you know I didn't! What I said – I remember exactly – I said 'You know that scene in *The Idiot* where Prince Myushkin goes to this reception and the moment he sees this priceless vase knows he's going to finish up by accidentally smashing it – and, of course, does? Well,' I said to you, 'I keep looking at our vase lately, and ever since I read the book, I can't help thinking, 'If only Mummy would give a big reception and ask someone like Prince Myushkin to it.'

MARCUS: There you are. Exactly what I said you said.

ROSAMUND: Oh, there's no point in going on with this conversation. I can only think that deep down you're thoroughly ashamed of –

MARCUS: *Ashamed?* You think I'd be *ashamed* of *any*thing I'd done to strike a blow against The Enemy?

ROSAMUND: The enemy?

MARCUS: Yes! The Enemy!

ROSAMUND: A formidable enemy I must say!

MARCUS: Now listen, Rosamund, you listen to me. I spent two filthy squalid years of my life being a brave boy and murdering Germans – because I'd been told that they were the enemy. But it wasn't the Germans who were the enemy. It was nauseating, lying toads who *told* me that they were: the fine old upright, implacable British Philistines who'd connived with the armaments manufacturers to organise their profit–making holocaust –

ROSAMUND: This isn't *true*, is it?

MARCUS: So wait a minute, let me finish – so when it was over – when the Armistice was signed – I was nineteen, and – d'you remember the title of my novel – nearest I've got to writing a best-seller?

ROSAMUND: *A Lovely Light?*

MARCUS: Yes, and remember where I got it from. Edna St.
    Vincent Millay? 'My candle burns at both its ends, It will
    not last the night, But ah! my foes, and oh! my friends, It
    gives a lovely light.' Well, that was it. After all the mud,
    blood, filth and idiocy I couldn't *wait* to get my candle
    well and truly lit. What I hadn't realised – was that the
    Enemy at home had used the War as an excuse to pass so
    many footling little repressive, strangulating laws that
    when at last the heroes returned to the land made fit for
    them, our right little, tight little sceptred isle had been
    turned into nothing so much as a right little, tight little
    reformatory for retarded children. It didn't take me long
    to find out. To start off my candle-burning I thought it
    would be extremely fitting to go to the nearest pub.
    Sorry. Can't serve you. Past closing time. I book into a
    hotel. Invite a woman into my room. Banging on the
    door. A detective appears. No wedding ring? Out. Not
    allowed. I go for a stroll in Hyde Park. Down by the
    Serpentine I see a bunch of little boys being chased by
    a policeman because they're not wearing bathing
    trunks. I get to work writing. It's Sunday, I run out of
    paper. Off to get some. Stationers cum sweet shop.
    They can't sell me any paper to write on. Not allowed.
    It's Sunday and that's the law. Well can't they at least
    slip me a notebook – just a little one to jot my ideas
    down before they evaporate and are lost for ever? Not
    likely! They'd been caught before like that. Can you
    imagine it? *Agents provocateurs* to stop a writer writing.
    The Enemy triumphant. I made a vow to fight them
    tooth and nail and from then on never let a day go by
    without committing some outrageous act against them.

ROSAMUND: Look, I understand completely what you
    feel but why work it off on my family? *They* didn't pass
    these idiotic laws.

MARCUS: They voted into power the idiots who did pass
    them. And look at the atrocities! Never mind the atrocities
    of the so–called Huns – what of the atrocities of the

English philistines? I needn't remind you of what they did
to poor old Wilde because he found men more attractive
than women, or bother you with how they treated Dilke
because he found two women at once more attractive than
one, but they burned Hardy's *Jude the Obscure*, they seized
the paintings of D H Lawrence; they banned Joyce's
Ulysses and are almost certainly responsible for him going
blind –

ROSAMUND: Sh! Do keep your voice down. Listen!
(*Tiptoeing to the double doors, taking the greatest care, she
opens one of them a few inches and looks through the crack.*)

MARCUS: (*Has followed her and continues his harangue
without a break and with no attempt at lowering his voice.*)
They shot Roger Casement not because he was a traitor
– which he wasn't – but because he was a sexual heretic;
they hanged Edith Thompson not because she was a
murderess but because she copulated with her lover in a
railway carriage; they announced that they'd rather give
glasses of prussic acid to their daughters than copies
of that innocent little lesbian love-story *The Well of
Loneliness* –

ROSAMUND: Anyway I can never quite think what a
woman and another woman are supposed to do together.

MARCUS: (*With a shout of laughter.*) 'Oh, Rosamunda!
Rosamunda, oh!'

ROSAMUND: Chut!... Sh! for goodness sake!
(*She makes for the doors. MARCUS's laughter increases in
volume. This so alarms ROSAMUND that she turns and
rushing back across the room and claps a hand to MARCUS's
mouth.*)
Do stop it! Do *stop!* Everyone in the house will hear.
(*He pulls her hand from his mouth but still keeps hold of it.*)

MARCUS: (*Through his laughter.*) 'What do two women do?'
I don't believe you know what a *man* and a woman do...
do you?

ROSAMUND: (*With a half-hearted attempt to pull her hand
away.*) Oh, don't be so silly!

MARCUS: Would you like to find out?

(*She doesn't answer; they stand without moving, holding each other's eyes.*)

Would you like me to teach you?

(*A pause.*)

Of course you would. That's what you want, isn't it? Come on, Ros, that's what you want. Why not? (*And then, throwing back his head as though yelling at the top of his voice, though the words come out as a sort of whispered shout.*) 'Do what thou wilt shall be the whole of the law!'

ROSAMUND: (*Breaking the spell and getting her hand away.*) Stop talking drunken rubbish.

MARCUS: Look, why don't you snap out of it, say shucks to your Christian upbringing and be yourself? Do what thou wilt!

ROSAMUND: Yes but what *I* wilt is a very different thing from what *you* wilt – it's my own personal feelings – nothing to *do* with any Christian upbringing.

MARCUS: It's *everything* to do with it: your inhibitions, your Kensington way of life, everything! 'Thou hast conquered, O pale Galilean, and the world has grown grey with thy breath!'

(*A pause.*)

That shocks you, doesn't it?

ROSAMUND: Nothing Swinburne wrote could shock me. I love everything he wrote. Including that poem – and those particular lines. Which I always find magical.

MARCUS: 'Thou hast conquered, O pale – '

ROSAMUND: Oh, goodness, yes! They're such lovely words, and –

MARCUS: Well, I'll be damned! Does that mean that you agree with old Spindleshanks that, thanks to the pale Galilean –

ROSAMUND: Oh, I wasn't talking about the meaning, I meant the sounds of the words, the music they make in juxtaposition with each other. And the *feel* of them, the texture... 'Thou hast conquered, O pale Galilean, and the world – '

MARCUS: (*Who has been listening to her, open-mouthed.*) Jesus
God! She's a wordswoman! A gloriously scrumptious
female girl – and she's a wordswoman! And darling –
forgive all my nonsense, I'm serious. So tell me – Do you
get drunk on words? I mean do you get magnificently lit
up spinning and delirious?

ROSAMUND: ...Yes, I think I do. (*Pause for thought.*) Yes,
I do, of course I do! Frequently.

MARCUS: This is terrific! We share a secret vice, we're
both word-addicts. Word addled! Word addled word-
addicts! We'll go on binges together. Delirious!

ROSAMUND: Now that's a heavenly word. 'Delirious' –
'Delirious'... 'Illyria' 'Delirious in Illyria!'
(*They both burst into delighted laughter.*)
I meant – I meant 'delirili' – Oh, I can't say it now!

MARCUS: You're word-drunk already. You're absolutely
pissed on words. Listen, what are your favourite set
pieces to get you started off on a word binge?

ROSAMUND: Er...what are yours?

MARCUS: Anything gets me going... Estate agents on a
to-let sign, solicitors on a brass plate: Numbleby and
Dimble; Slatterpass and Prosper –

ROSAMUND: (*Laughing.*) Oh, yes! Mine's much more
ordinary, rather obvious in fact. I say obvious because –

MARCUS: Never mind about that. What is it? Come on,
come on, what?

ROSAMUND: Softly walk over the Western wave, Spirit
of Night...
(*MARCUS joins in; they speak in unison.*)

ROSAMUND/MARCUS: Out of the misty Eastern cave
Where all the long –

MARCUS: No, no, skip the opening, let's start with
'Wrap thy form in – '
(*He crosses and stands facing her, very close. Their eyes lock.
She joins him in the second line and they speak in unison.*)

ROSAMUND/MARCUS: 'Wrap thy form in a mantle grey
star–enwrought

Bind thy hair the eye of day
Kiss her till she be weared out,

Then wander o'er city and sea and land
Touching all with thy opiate wand
Come...long sought.'
(*MARCUS has been bringing his face closer and closer till now their lips are almost touching; he is just about to take advantage of this when:*)

JO: (*Voice from the street.*) Marco! Marco!

MARCUS: Oh, buggeration!

ROSAMUND: For God's sake go and stop them – Mother or somebody will hear.

MARCUS: (*He has dashed onto the balcony and is now leaning over the rail.*) Yes? What is it?

JO: I say, duckie, I shouldn't stay there much longer. Haven't they got the law on you yet?

MARCUS: I'm talking to a gorgeous Kensington lovely – and she's a wordswoman! Terrific!
(*He comes briskly back into the room.*)
Drizzledick and Wackerbater's!

ROSAMUND: Gascoigne, Pease and Frisco!

MARCUS: Meaney, O'Beaney and –

VOICES: Marco! Marco!

ROSAMUND: Oh lor'! Oh, do stop them.

MARCUS: I'm off.
(*He makes for the balcony.*)

ROSAMUND: Where are you going? You can't –

MARCUS: I have already. You told your mother about it. See you over there? (*He runs to the railing and climbs over.*)

ROSAMUND: Oh, do be careful.
(*He drops out of sight. She goes to the balcony and looks over.*)
Are you all right?
(*He doesn't answer at once. She follows him with her eyes as he gets up and crosses towards the house opposite, then stops and calls to her.*)

MARCUS: (*Off.*) Pratfanger and Bosticock!

ROSAMUND: Chatto and Windus!

MARCUS: (*Off.*) Boosey and Hawkes!
(*She bursts into laughter, watching him for a moment, then comes back into the drawing-room and stands thinking with a sort of tucked-in smile. Her lips move as she turns over*)

another 'name of a firm' that has occurred to her; then voices
it but so low the words are only audible to herself; delighted
with the sound of this latest inspiration, she runs on to the
balcony and leaning over the rail, calls as loudly as she dare!)

ROSAMUND: Rumbellow, Crumbold, Finchingfield and
Tinch!

(*She waits for a response but none comes. She shrugs and still*
with her tucked-in smile, hurries back into the drawing room,
gives herself a hasty glance in the looking-glass over the
chimneypiece, grabs up a shawl which is draped over a chair,
turns out the lights and rushes from the room.
There is a yell of laughter from over the way. The music is
quite loud now, and the shadows of the people at MARCUS'
party are thrown on the floor and the wall. The fragments of
the broken vase glisten. ALFRED, in a night-shirt and dressing
gown, hobbles into the room.)

ALFRED: (*Mumbling.*) Must have a bit of Jessie's vase...just
a piece to keep...

(*He stoops down to pick one up, but in doing so the window*
of the house opposite is brought into his line of vision. He
jumps as if he has been shot.)

Good God Almighty! Mary! Mary! Mary!

(*After a second MARY rushes in, in her pyjamas, her hair*
half-down. She switches on the lights.)

MARY: (*At the doorway.*) For heaven's sake, what's the matter?

ALFRED: It's Rosamund! She's there! With them! Over
there! Sylvie! Sylvie!

MARY: (*Rushing to the window.*) What do you mean? What's
the matter with you? Oh! Oh! It's Rosamund!
Rosamund! She wants to kill us all.

(*SYLVIE rushes in, in her night-clothes.*)

SYLVIE: (*At the doorway.*) Who's calling out? What is it?
Heavens above, what are you doing?

ALFRED: It's Rosamund! There! Over there. Look! She's
gone mad!

SYLVIE: (*Rushing to the window.*) With the horrors? Ros?
Dancing with the horrors? Monstrous I call it! Monstrous!

MARY: Oh! Fetch her back, someone! Fetch her back!

(*JOHN and LALLAH appear in their pyjamas, and join the group at the window.*)

JOHN: What on earth's the matter?

LALLAH: Oh! It's Rosamund! It's Ros! Ros! (*She goes into shriek upon shriek of hysterical laughter.*)

MARY: What is happening to us? This is the end of everything. What will happen to us now?
(*JELLY waddles in, wrapped in a blanket and joins the group in the window.*)

End of Act One.

ACT TWO

Three weeks later. Sunday. Early afternoon.

The family, more or less stupefied by their midday meal, have just finished coffee. Only ROSAMUND is absent. ALFRED, SYLVIE and JELLY are asleep. MARY, looking desperately worried, is moving about restlessly, occasionally glancing through the window. JOHN, sitting a little distance from his wife, is gazing abstractedly at nothing and singing to himself in an undertone.

JOHN: 'Oh God our help in ages past,
    Our – '
MARY: John, please! (*She points a forefinger angrily to her lips, then points to the sleepers.*)
JOHN: (*With a start.*) Sorry. (*There is silence again, then he whispers to LALLAH.*) Do you know where the *Sunday Times* is?
LALLAH: The *Sunday Times*?
JOHN: I haven't had a chance to look at it yet.
    (*They both wander about looking under cushions and chairs. MARY still moves nervously to and from the window.*)
LALLAH: You haven't seen the *Sunday Times*, have you, Mother?
MARY: Sh!
LALLAH: Wait a minute! Perhaps Aunt Sylvie's sitting on it.
    (*Running to her sleeping aunt, she bends down and peers beneath her.*)
MARY: Lallah, what *are* you doing?
LALLAH: (*Straightening up guiltily.*) It's not there anyway.
JOHN: Look, isn't that it, under Uncle Alfred?
    (*LALLAH hurries to see.*)
LALLAH: I won't wake him. (*She is already pulling at the paper on which UNCLE ALFRED is sitting but only succeeds in tearing a piece off.*) Oh!
MARY: Now don't litter the room.
LALLAH: I...I'll put it back. (*She pushes it under ALFRED.*)

JOHN: Wait a minute, let *me*. (*He takes hold of the paper and starts pulling at it gently.*)

MARY: Have you *no* consideration?

ALFRED: What? What? What's that?

(*ALFRED wakes up.*)

JOHN: Oh dammit! Yesterday's *Morning Post!*

ALFRED: Just having forty winks.

JOHN: Uncle Alfred, for mercy's sake go to sleep again.

LALLAH: Have you seen the *Sunday Times*, Uncle?

ALFRED: *Sunday Times?* Yes, Jelly's torn it up and eaten it.

MARY: Eaten the *Sunday Times?*

LALLAH: She is *naughty*. (*She picks up JELLY, gives her a tap and puts her outside the door.*)

SYLVIE: (*Opening her eyes.*) Well, what did he want to see in the *Sunday Times?*

JOHN: Nothing, Aunt Sylvie. Only the score.

SYLVIE: Score?

LALLAH: The cricket score.

MARY: When I'm nearly out of my mind with worry I think it extremely inconsiderate that people should be thinking about 'scores'.

JOHN: But, after all, she's only gone out to lunch or something –

MARY: I don't know *where* she is – or with whom – or *what* sort of places she takes herself off to till all hours. Lunch!

LALLAH: Anyway, perhaps on Sundays they have dinner instead of lunch like we do and then supper in the – Mother?... Has something *happened* this morning? – I mean something that's upset you – because you've –

MARY: I don't wish to discuss the matter. Not now or with anybody. Ever.

ALFRED: (*Together.*) Lowest of the low. Out of their minds, the whole lot of them.

SYLVIE: (*Together.*) Disgusting I call it.

(*MISS DUCIE, her face flushed, comes in with a pile of sewing. She crosses, none too steadily, to her usual chair, plumps down into it and makes a pretence of applying herself to her work. Except for ALFRED, who continues with his observations, everyone looks slightly uncomfortable.)*

ALFRED: Young blackguard. Ought to be shot. Let him show his face here. I'd shoot him. Like a dog.

MISS DUCIE: Well...she'll be for the high jump next week, that young woman. When the verdict of guilty is brought in.

LALLAH: Goosey, what *are* you talking about?

MISS DUCIE: A lesson to us all. Letting down the side. Though, of course, the family is not 'quite'.

SYLVIE: (*Together.*) What does she say? What's she saying?

LALLAH: (*Together.*) But what family, Goosey? What family are you – ?

MISS DUCIE: A signor Mussolini is what we need in this country. *My word!* He knows how to deal with them. A good dose of castor oil. Then she'd have no need to shoot him.

LALLAH: To shoot *Mussolini?*

MISS DUCIE: Dretful creature. Drunk in a mews at three in the morning. There she was, a revolver in her hand. Ah, well...(*She makes off again, unaware of the trail of sewing she is dropping on the carpet.*) And now she will be hanged by the neck until she is dead. Although her parents are not 'quite'. *My word!* Not by a long chalk... or even with a barge-pole.

(*As soon as she is out of earshot LALLAH and JOHN explode with the laughter they have been holding in check.*)

ALFRED: What's the matter with the woman?

JOHN: (*As, breathless with laughter, he picks up the pieces of MISS DUCIE's sewing.*) Inferior sherry, if you ask me. Gone straight to her frosty pow.

SYLVIE: What? What's that? Frosty what?

LALLAH: Pow, Aunt Sylvie.

SYLVIE: Pow?... Pow? What's the matter with the girl? 'Pow.'

MARY: (*In a low but compelling voice.*) You, all of you, read the papers – you at least, John, must be only too aware what Miss Ducie was referring to –

JOHN: The Barney case.

MARY: (*With increasing intensity.*) – and why she chose to make these terrible observations about it –

JOHN: Yes, but I think we should take account that she –

MARY: I don't care how much sherry she may have had and whether or not her pow has been affected by it – Lallah, stop it! This is a serious situation.

LALLAH: Mummy, I *knew* something had happened this morning.

MARY: And God alone knows what horrors we may be called upon to face... Because she's on the same road as this appalling Mrs Barney. They all end there, those sort of creatures – they all end there, every one of them.

JOHN: It's three o'clock, Lallah.

LALLAH: Oh yes, yes. We're going for our Sunday walkies, Mother. Won't be long.

(*JOHN is already at the door.*)

SYLVIE: What's all this?

LALLAH: We're only going to Kensington Gardens. Back at teatime. (*She hurries after her husband.*)

MARY: Lallah, wait a minute, please.

(*LALLAH stops short.*)

LALLAH: (*After a pause; turning to MARY.*) Yes?

MARY: Aren't you being a little selfish, dear?

LALLAH: Well, after all, Mother, John and I don't get much time to ourselves.

SYLVIE: That's not the way to speak to your mother. I don't know what you were saying but your face looked most rude.

LALLAH: Oh dear, I didn't mean it to be.

MARY: Lallah, dearest. Who's to look after your uncle and aunt when they go for their afternoon walk?

(*A pause.*)

LALLAH: But Mother, what about *our* afternoon walk – John's and mine? Can't Collins take Uncle for a drive somewhere?

MARY: You know your Uncle dislikes the car. Besides, he and Collins *encourage* each other.

LALLAH: Encourage…?

MARY: You know quite well what I mean, Lallah. With their jokes.

LALLAH: Yes, but Mummy –

MARY: Oh please spare me all those 'yes-but-Mummies' –

ALFRED: Pipe down, Mary, can't you? Go on then, my precious. Off you go for your walk. I'll do without mine. Don't you worry about me.

LALLAH: No! No, Uncle, of course not. I wouldn't dream of it.

SYLVIE: There's a good girl. I'd offer to push the bath-chair myself if I could.

(*JOHN comes in buttoning up his coat.*)

JOHN: Ready, Lall? (*He stops short, seeing what has happened.*) Oh… Is it…all off then?

MARY: Don't blame us, John. If Rosamund had been here, but…

JOHN: Lallah's going to do it. *I* see.

(*LALLAH has begun to weep, she pulls out a handkerchief.*)

LALLAH: Oh don't. John, don't. Oh Mother I'm sorry…

MARY: Never mind, Lallah, it's all right. You shall have your walk. I'll do without my afternoon's rest. *I'll* wheel the bath-chair.

LALLAH: No, Mother, no!

MARY: Now go on, dear, we all have to make little sacrifices.

ALFRED: Be quiet, all of you. Lallah and John can go for their little outing and Mary can lie down and sleep off her lunch. I'll go without my walk.

SYLVIE: Go without your walk, Alfred? Not if I know it. I'll wheel you myself if I drop dead on the pavement.

MARY: Sylvie, I said *I* would wheel the chair.

LALLAH: No Mummy, I'll do it. John, dear, why don't you go for a nice walkies by yourself, darling?

JOHN: Oh, for mercy's sake, Lallah! Do what you like, go and enjoy yourself. I'll wheel the chair.

LALLAH: If you wheel the chair I shall come too.

MARY: Alfred and Sylvie, get ready. I'll be down in a minute.

LALLAH: Oh Mother dear, wait a minute. It's all so awful, it's too bad of Rosamund. Of course I'll come – the least I can do when you're giving up your afternoon's rest.

MARY: That's my Lallah.

ALFRED: There we are, then! A nice little family promenade.

SYLVIE: What? Are we *all* going?

JOHN: Yes, Aunt Sylvie, every one of us.

(*ROSAMUND has come back and is trying to sneak upstairs without being seen, but ALFRED spots her.*)

ALFRED: Hey, young lady! Where are you off to?

ROSAMUND: (*In a bright voice which, nevertheless, contains a tremor.*) Hullo... Have you had a nice nap, Uncle?

SYLVIE: As if it matters to her who's had a nap and who hasn't.

MARY: (*With a quick glance round at ROSAMUND, and then deliberately looking away from her.*) Cook has kept something hot for you but I imagine you have already eaten.

ROSAMUND: (*She comes down.*) Mother, I told you I should be out at lunchtime.

MARY: Oh yes, of course, I forgot you have all your meals out now.

ROSAMUND: You know that isn't true, Mother. Why exaggerate? It's so humourless. I'm sorry Mother, but it is.

JOHN: Well, come on, Lall, what about getting your things on?

SYLVIE: You'll be able to have your rest after all, Mary, as your daughter deigned to come back in time to take us out.

ROSAMUND: Yes, but I'm sorry but I can't.

(*JOHN and LALLAH stop short in the doorway. They all – except MARY – stare at her.*)

MARY: You can't *what*, Rosamund? If I may ask.

ROSAMUND: I'm afraid I can't take them... I... I have to go out again.

(*ALFRED suddenly bangs his stick on the floor and hurries out of the room. She makes a little imploring gesture towards him.*)

ROSAMUND: Uncle...

(But apparently he doesn't hear. SYLVIE hurries away after him.)

SYLVIE: Alfred! Now don't go upsetting yourself. *(As she passes ROSAMUND she says bitingly.)* Selfishness personified!

ROSAMUND: Oh, Aunt Sylvie –

(But SYLVIE hurries out.)

LALLAH: Ros, do go with them. It would save such a lot of unpleasantness.

ROSAMUND: I'm sorry, Lall.

LALLAH: Oh, darling, *please!*

ROSAMUND: I *told* you.

LALLAH: Oh, Rosamund, really! All our Sunday ruined. *(She flounces past her sister.)*

ROSAMUND: Lallah...

(But LALLAH doesn't answer. When JOHN passes her ROSAMUND takes hold of his arm to stop him.)

John... *You're* not furious?

JOHN: *(After a pause.)* Not with you. *(He follows LALLAH.)*

(ROSAMUND and MARY are alone together. MARY glances round to see if ROSAMUND is still there but immediately looks away again. ROSAMUND hesitates, is about to speak but, daunted by the implacability of the back of her mother's head, turns to go.)

MARY: *(Suddenly.)* Just a moment, Rosamund. Close the door please.

(ROSAMUND does so then waits in anxious expectancy. But MARY remains silent.)

ROSAMUND: *(At last: bursting out.)* Oh Mother, *do* stop being like this. Can't you possibly be *real* with me just for a moment? Do try. Or how can we say *anything* to each other? *(She waits for a response but receives none.)* ...Mother please... Look, all that's happened is that I've made a new set of friends.

(She pauses, but MARY gives no indication of having heard.)

Oh, I know you made up your mind from the start that they were irresponsible, immoral and unprincipled. But Mother, they're the most principled people I've ever met.

It's *because* of their principles that they refuse to let their lives be tied down by... Oh, *do* stop looking at me like that. Mother, what on earth's the matter?

MARY: Now listen to me, Rosamund. There's something we have to discuss of a very serious nature. Very serious indeed.

ROSAMUND: Well I could hardly be *more* serious.

MARY: Something that might very well land us – all of us – in the police-courts.

ROSAMUND: In the p – ?

MARY: Yes, in the police-courts. Now I'm going to ask you a very serious question. And I hope I can rely on you for a truthful answer. Do you understand me? However horrible or shameful, I want the truth.

ROSAMUND: For heaven's sake, what *is* it, Mother?

MARY: Very well then. Will you please tell me...how came that *filth* – that indescribable *filth* – in the drawer of your bedside table?

ROSAMUND: (*After a minute; in despondent self-reproach.*) Oh *dear* – Oh Lor'... (*Then furious at her own stupidity.*) I *knew* I should have put it somewhere else... You mean *Lady Chatterley's Lover*.

MARY: I mean *Lady Chatterley's Lover*.

ROSAMUND: (*In sudden alarm.*) Mother, you didn't *read* it, did you?

MARY: Quite enough to make me ashamed to look any decent person in the face.
(*LALLAH, dressed for the Sunday walk, comes in. She looks from one to the other.*)

LALLAH: Oh! (*She goes out.*)

MARY: You haven't answered my question. How came you by that disgusting book?

ROSAMUND: I didn't *come by* it.

MARY: Don't lose your temper and shout at me, Rosamund.

ROSAMUND: I wasn't. I was simply saying that I didn't 'come by' the book, it was given to me.

MARY: May I ask by whom?

ROSAMUND: Oh, what does it matter? It was given to me, that's all.

MARY: Yes, I can imagine by what sort of person.

ROSAMUND: No, you can't! You can't even *begin* to imagine (*She concludes in an undertone.*) what sort of person he is.

MARY: I certainly find it difficult. The sort of creature who could bring himself to give disgusting filth to a decently brought-up young girl to read –

ROSAMUND: Bernard Shaw said *all* decently brought-up girls should be given it to read.

MARY: That doesn't surprise me.

ROSAMUND: And Mummy, have you forgotten – on my next birthday I shall be thirty-four.

MARY: That has nothing to do with it. And I don't wish you to call me Mummy any more.

ROSAMUND: Not call you – ?!

MARY: I find it quite insupportable to be called Mummy by anyone who has read a book like that. All I ask is that you take that filth out of the house and return it to the unspeakable cad who gave it to you.

(*Icy with rage, ROSAMUND stares at her mother, and makes for the door.*)

I suppose you'll even deny that he was disgustingly drunk.

ROSAMUND: Oh, good heavens, Mother, everybody gets drunk sometimes. And – and you've no right whatsoever to criticise and – and vilify someone who went through all that mud and horror fighting *your* war –

MARY: So I'm responsible for the Great War now.

ROSAMUND: Oh, you know what I mean, I mean people of your age, Mother – of your generation. You needn't have *accepted* the war propaganda, you needn't have believed the lies. But you wanted the War, didn't you?

MARY: That's enough, Rosamund. I need scarcely ask where you've picked up all this Bolshevistic balderdash. It's a betrayal of everything our poor boys, our gallant lads, laid down their lives for.

ROSAMUND: (*In a suppressed voice.*) Marcus was one of our brave boys and gallant lads.

73

MARY: Oh, don't twist everything I say!

ROSAMUND: (*Almost inaudible.*) *And* he was decorated. (*A pause.*) If only you could have met him – just once – and talked to him, I'm sure you'd get –

MARY: I have met him.

ROSAMUND: (*After a pause.*) Yes, but –

MARY: Sick on the floor in front of everyone. A drunken lout.

ROSAMUND: *What?*

MARY: I said he was a drunken lout.

ROSAMUND: Very well then. (*Rapidly becoming beside herself.*) That really is the end between us, Mother – that's the end of our friendship. (*She makes for the door, but turns.*) If you *knew* how ludicrous it was to use a word like that about someone as – as beautiful – and as elegant – about someone who's a distinguished and acclaimed novelist –

MARY: I wouldn't call it very elegant and distinguished to break into people's homes and deliberately destroy their most treasured possession.

ROSAMUND: He didn't destroy it, I did.

MARY: You know as well as I do you were trying to stop him.

ROSAMUND: Oh, I know that's what I *thought* I was doing. But all the time – don't you understand? I *wanted* to see it smashed to pieces. In my subconscious mind I'd wanted to for years.

MARY: There is no such thing as the subconscious mind.

ROSAMUND: What?...

MARY: It's simply a term invented by German Jewish brain specialists to make more money out of the people.

ROSAMUND: (*After staring at her mother for a moment.*) Is that what you genuinely believe? I suppose you really do, you genuinely believe it.

MARY: Don't look at me like that, Rosamund! How dare you look at me like that?

ROSAMUND: I wasn't looking at you like anything. I was simply trying to work out how to explain Freud to you.

MARY: (*She starts to weep.*) I can't stand much more, I really can't...

ROSAMUND: (*Going to her, kneeling down, embracing her.*)
Oh Mummy, don't...don't...please darling, I can't bear
to see you so unhappy...

MARY: Stop making me unhappy then.

ROSAMUND: Poor Mummy, do you think I want to? Why
should I make you miserable? If I'm wrong let me work
it out for myself.

MARY: Oh, Baby...if he were a decent sort of man, a man
you could marry in the ordinary way – but this low,
drunken rotter...

(*ROSAMUND freezes: she starts to get to her feet but MARY
restrains her.*)

MARY: You *must* listen to me! You *must* listen. For my sake,
darling – for all our sakes – give it all up – come back
to your family, Ros. Don't break our hearts.

ROSAMUND: Mother, I cannot go back to a life I don't
believe in any more.

MARY: Don't believe in what? What is it you don't believe
in?

ROSAMUND: Everything our lives are based on in this
house. Mother, it's no good. It simply is no good!

MARY: Well, it's been good enough for me and for Alfred
and Sylvie for the last twenty years!

ROSAMUND: But it wasn't good enough for Father!

(*MARY makes a sudden panic–stricken movement of her
hands.*)

ALFRED: (*Coming in.*) It's not a bit of use you two silly
women sitting and arguing, you're obstinate as mules
both of you. Come along, Mary, we're waiting.

SYLVIE: (*Coming in behind him.*) Where's Jelly's lead? She's
not going without her lead, poor lamb.

(*LALLAH enters with JELLY on a lead. JOHN follows
behind.*)

Oh, she's on the lead, is she? Now, don't let her go on
any account, Lallah.

LALLAH: No, Aunt Sylvie.

SYLVIE: (*Defensively.*) Not that she wants to, mind.

ALFRED: Nonsense, Sylvie, of course she wants to.

SYLVIE: Be quiet, Alfred. Nothing of the sort.

ALFRED: Well, she's a damned unnatural animal then.

SYLVIE: You disgust me. Are you coming or not, Mary?

MARY: No, go for goodness sake! I'll meet you coming back.

(*As she says this JOHN slips outside the door with LALLAH holding his arm. SYLVIE is after them like a shot.*)

SYLVIE: Lallah! Lallah! Is she on the lead properly? (*Off.*) Alfred! Alfred!

ALFRED: Yap! Yap! Shut up yapping! (*He hobbles out.*)

(*MARY wilts, pulls out a handkerchief and starts crying again.*)

ROSAMUND: (*After watching her in helpless silence for a moment.*) Mother, if only you wouldn't take everything so *personally*. It's not against *you*, it's not against the family; it's my generation against yours. It can't be helped, it – it's a matter of historical necessity.

MARY: (*Wearily, tearfully; closing her eyes.*) ...'historical necessity'...

ROSAMUND: (*Suddenly.*) Look, it's just occurred to me, the whole thing is most perfectly expressed in a book I'm reading. Wait a minute, I've got it upstairs – (*She makes for the staircase.*)

MARY: (*Going onto the landing and calling after her.*) Rosamund! If you dare to come down and start reading me passages from –

ROSAMUND: Oh *Mother!* It's by Chekhov. Short Stories by Anton Chekhov.

MARY: Anton who?

ROSAMUND: Chekhov.

MARY: (*Her voice still choked by tears.*) Well, if that's that Russian whose plays they put on at Barnes or somewhere, Mrs Brent at the Bridge Club went and it's utter rubbish; a man says to a woman, 'Good afternoon, how are you?' and she replies 'My little dog eats nuts.'

(*ROSAMUND is already out of sight up the stairs. MARY returns to the drawing room. She heaves a bitter, exasperated sigh. Voices from an open window across the road draw her attention. She stares in their direction for a moment, comes suddenly to a decision, crosses back to the double doors and, after a quick glance up the stairs, closes them and goes resolutely to the telephone. A brief hesitation while she recollects the number she is about to ask for and lifts the receiver.)*

Sloane five-o-six-two please... Hullo... Is that...uh Mrs Ormerod's house?... Is Mr...uh...Mr Eversley there?... Well, would you tell him Mrs Moorhouse-Rees would like to speak to him... I see...how long do you think he'll...? Yes, if he'd telephone me as soon as he comes in. Thank you...what?... I beg your pardon? Who is that?... To whom am I speaking?... *Who?*

(She continues listening for an aghast moment, then hearing ROSAMUND returning down the stairs, she hangs up. Crossing back to the sofa, she sits down stiffly and remains so, looking stunned. ROSAMUND hurries in with a book.)

ROSAMUND: *(Closing the doors.)* Now Mother, you must listen – just a minute... Um...*(Coming into the room and searching for her place.)* Oh yes...*(She looks up.)* You see, the young man has broken up with his upper-middle-class father and got himself a job as a labourer –

MARY: Rosamund, I think I'd better tell you –

ROSAMUND: Just a minute, Mummy – in a minute.
' "Well?" my father sighed, "I must ask you to remember how, in this very room, I reminded you of your obligations to your family and your class. But you mocked at every word I said and you introduced your sister to your deplorable ideas which have now brought about her downfall and her shame." '

MARY: Stop! Stop! Rosamund, are you trying to break it to me gently that Lallah –

ROSAMUND: Oh Mother!...of *course* not! *(Resuming reading.)* ' "Isn't it about time," I demanded, "that you started to ask yourself what is the purpose of living as we do, without art, without culture, immersed in triviality, and with a set of values utterly outworn which still you cling to." '

(*The telephone rings. MARY gives a start and goes to answer it. ROSAMUND, arrested in full flight, stands, book in hand, feeling foolish.*)

MARY: Yes?... Yes, well, I'm anxious to meet you and speak to you and I suggest you come over for half an hour... Yes, she is here... By all means...within five minutes. But I must ask you not to be later. Very well, then. I shall expect you. (*She hangs up and turns to face a ROSAMUND open-mouthed with astonishment and dismay. After a pause.*) You've kept on saying that if only I could meet him.

ROSAMUND: Yes, I know – I know...

MARY: What's the matter then?

ROSAMUND: It's all so...so totally unexpected.

(*A pause.*)

MARY: Will you tell me something please?... Is his – is his mother with him?

ROSAMUND: Marcus' mother? No, why should she be?

MARY: No, I didn't think she was.

ROSAMUND: But –

MARY: Rosamund... (*A heavy, pregnant pause, then:*) Did you know that Marcus Eversley is a married man?

(*ROSAMUND draws her breath in to reply, but before she can do so MARY continues.*)

And that his wife is over there now?

ROSAMUND: Oh, they must have just got back then.

MARY: You...you mean you *know* her?

ROSAMUND: Well, of course. Naturally I do... She's rather futile as a matter of fact.

MARY: You mean...you mean you and she *speak* to each other?

ROSAMUND: Oh, *Mother*... Look, he'll be here, he'll be on the doorstep – what are you going to say to him? (*A ring at the front door.*) Oh Lor'!... Mother, quickly, you must tell me, *what* are you going to *say?* (*On her way to the staircase leading to the ground floor MISS DUCIE pauses at the drawing-room doors.*)

MISS DUCIE: Pull up the drawbridge! Women to the ramparts with cauldrons of boiling oil!

MARY: That's quite enough, Miss Ducie. Hopkins will open the door.

MISS DUCIE: (*Continuing to the staircase which she starts to descend.*) Hopkins is lying down with what she calls a 'my-grain'. Planning to give her notice by the looks of it. Dretful creature!

MARY: *What?* (*Hurrying on to the landing, she leans over the banisters.*) Miss Ducie! Have you been having a scene with Hopkins and she's threatening to leave?

MISS DUCIE: (*Off, she sings untunefully, from 'The Mikado'.*) 'She will never be missed... She will never be missed...'

MARY: Oh, good heavens! (*She moves distractedly to the next flight of stairs.*) Rosamund, try to cope with her, will you? (*Hurrying up the stairs.*) I simply cannot be expected to cope with *everything* –

(*As MARY goes out of sight upstairs the front doorbell rings.*)

ROSAMUND: (*Calling down in a frantic stage whisper.*) Goosey!

MISS DUCIE: (*Off...her footsteps are heard crossing the hall.*) My...word!

ROSAMUND: *Goosey!*

(*Sounds of the front door being opened.*)

MISS DUCIE: (*Off.*) Young man, I have a bone to pick with you.

MARCUS: (*Off.*) Dear and famous Miss Ducie, I am expected –

MISS DUCIE: (*Off.*) Play *up!* Play *up!* And play the game!

MARCUS: (*Off.*) – by the lady of the house.

ROSAMUND: (*Leaning over the stair rail; in the same frantic stage whisper.*) Marco! Marco!

MISS DUCIE: (*Off.*) You know the poem that comes from, young man?

MARCUS: (*Off.*) Are you alone? (*He can be heard coming upstairs two at a time.*)

ROSAMUND: Quickly – in the drawing-room.

MISS DUCIE: (*Off; laboriously mounting, behind MARCUS.*) 'There's a deathly hush in the close tonight'...

(*MARCUS comes purposefully past ROSAMUND into the room and turns, waiting for her, brimming over with elation and eagerness and the effect of lunchtime drinks.*)

ROSAMUND: (*Still in the doorway; as MISS DUCIE comes into sight.*) Goosey, do go and lie down or something. (*She comes quickly into the room, closing the doors.*) Marc!... Coney – quickly – before Mother comes down, I *must* put you *au fait* with –

MARCUS: (*Briskly.*) How is your passport?

ROSAMUND: My passport?

MARCUS: Is your passport in order? Not expired or –

ROSAMUND: I've only used it once, the year we went to Dinard, so –

MARCUS: Good. Splendid. Come here.

ROSAMUND: Don't order me about like –

MARCUS: (*Together, in mocking unison with her.*) some horrible caveman.

ROSAMUND: (*Together.*) some horrible caveman. (*Laughing.*) Well, *don't* anyway. (*He shuts her up with a mouth to mouth kiss.*)

MARCUS: (*When the kissing is finished; quickly, before she can speak.*) Listen, Pozz, unbemuse yourself, uncross those beautiful eyes and pay attention. At any moment, during the next two or three days I want you to be poised for flight – Elizabeth Barrett Browning, packed, ready and in your running shorts. As soon as I give you the signal you'll nip down and join me outside, I'll have a car waiting and vroosh! We're off! *D'accord?*

ROSAMUND: But of course, darling – absolutely...the only thing is –

MARCUS: Yes?... What *is* the only thing?

ROSAMUND: Oh, nothing really, I just wondered why the sudden mad rush.

MARCUS: Because I've got to get out! I've got to get back to work. Do you know how long it is since my last book? Two years. *Two years*, Pozzy. I've got to start writing again.

ROSAMUND: But –

MARCUS: And don't bring up those 'literary' pieces I churn out for the *Week-End Review*. I'm talking about *writing*. I don't say I haven't had blocks in creativity before. But never for so long.

ROSAMUND: Coney, tell me later. At any moment
Mother –

MARCUS: Let me finish. Ages ago, soon after I started,
I worked out a quick cure, a sure-fire method, if the
creative juices looked like drying up, of getting them
flowing again.

(*While MARCUS continues ROSAMUND goes nervously to
the door, opens it slightly and looks anxiously up the stairs.*)
First of all I have to induce in myself feelings of
contempt and superiority. So I go to the Lower Ground
Floor of Lyon's Corner House, where there's a Ladies'
Orchestra playing the ballet music from *Faust* – and sit
myself at a table. In this Mecca of the lower-middle
classes I let my gaze wander over the tea-laid tables at
which, in all their smug pretentiousness, their invincible
Philistinism, they sit. And, God, do I despise them! Do
I feel superior! (*He pauses.*)

ROSAMUND: (*Shutting the door, but staying by it.*) Yes? Go
on, go on. I'm listening.

MARCUS: Then I start to particularise, to observe –
groups, couples and individuals. To watch, to eavesdrop
and to infer. And a change is taking place already.
Interest! And now we're under way. Interest gives way to
understanding. Understanding develops into sympathy,
sympathy slips into empathy, and in no time at all I'm
identifying with them. These people are no longer apart
from me. *I* am *them.* A miracle! I feel like Walt Whitman
proclaiming that he is all men and women, and that
every sort and kind of human being is contained within
himself. But where, for instance, Walt tells us, 'I am the
hounded slave, I wince at the bite of the dogs,' for me it's
'I am the woman in *pince-nez* with a poached egg on
toast, who winces at the commonness of the fat little man
sitting opposite her!' And I *am* the fat little man and I
am saying: 'I'm sorry… I'm sorry… Well, I've said I'm
sorry. What d'you expect me to do, kiss your arse?'
(*ROSAMUND gives a quickly suppressed laugh and returns
to him, still keeping an eye on the door.*)

And so on and so forth with everybody in sight. And suddenly all ideas of identifying myself with others are swept away – in a wild uprush of delight at the strangeness, the ridiculousness, the sheer impossibility of it all, and at the same time I'm overwhelmed by an acute awareness of my *vocation*... When I'm not writing I'm only half alive. For two bloody years now the cure has only lasted as far as the front doorstep. The moment I've passed it – distraction! distraction! That's why I've got to get out! How can I *expect* to write? – how is it possible to string even two words together creatively, when I'm whirling on a non-stop roundabout –

ROSAMUND: (*Suddenly stiffening.*) Sh! Listen!...
(*She pulls away from him, crosses towards the doors and, halfway there, checks herself and stands tensely. MARCUS follows and, just as the tenseness of her attitude relaxes and she turns to him, he clasps her again.*)

MARCUS: And another thing – a proposition! Do you *know*, Pozzy, that we could do the-beast-with-two-backs fifty times a day or eighty times a night whenever or wherever we happened to feel like it? Down in the coal cellar, under the bed, on top of the wardrobe – *and we could get a licence for it!* Imagine! A Performing Licence! And from then on, whenever we were performing – no matter how outrageously – it'd be in the hilarious knowledge that our performance was being smiled on, approved of and connived at by the Enemy! By Stanley Baldwin and Mrs Baldwin, by Baden Powell and the Lord Chamberlain and Kipling and Beaverbrook and the whole poxy crew of them right up to George and Mary in Buck House!... So what about it! Pozzy, what about it?

ROSAMUND: What?... Sorry, Marc, I was only listening with half an ear. I'm so petrified of –

MARCUS: You didn't hear a word.

ROSAMUND: I heard something about the top of a wardrobe. Marc, what *were* you saying?

MARCUS: I was saying, 'A pox on everybody, why don't we get married?'

ROSAMUND: (*After a pause.*) Oh, stop clowning!

MARCUS: If you think I'm not serious, here you are, here's the ring... Don't you like it?

ROSAMUND: It's not a ring...it's a sort of bracelet.

MARCUS: No, it isn't, it's a ring.

ROSAMUND: How *can* it be a ring?

MARCUS: It *is* a ring, I promise you it is. (*Then suddenly, with a shout of laughter.*) It's a *nose* ring.

ROSAMUND: Oh, you are a brute! (*Flinging it across the room so that it falls behind the sofa.*)

MARCUS: So what about the proposition?

ROSAMUND: What proposition?

MARCUS: The 'proposal' then. I've made an offer for your 'hand.'

ROSAMUND: As you *are* married, I don't see the –

MARCUS: Who told you that?

ROSAMUND: Told me what?

MARCUS: That I'm married.

ROSAMUND: But you *are.*

MARCUS: What? To Jo? We're not married. You've been listening to gossip.

ROSAMUND: But...if you and Jo aren't married why is she Mrs Eversley?

MARCUS: Because that's what she's known as. (*A blank pause.*) Look, two or three years ago we were hard-up and Jo and I felt we could do with some presents, so we sent cards out saying we were getting married on a specified date and would they come to drinks afterwards.

ROSAMUND: ...Well, *really!*... And did they bring the presents?

MARCUS: Yes.

ROSAMUND: And you hadn't been married at all?

MARCUS: No.

ROSAMUND: ...You're not pulling my leg?

MARCUS: I'm pulling your arm. (*He has grasped her hand and is pulling her towards him; holding her close, he speaks into her ear, kissing it.*) So what about it?... What about it, eh? Yes?... Yes? Come, on, Molly Bloom – *Yes!*

(*At that moment MARY comes in. MARCUS and ROSAMUND move hastily apart.*)

MARY: You must excuse me, Mr Eversley; trouble with the staff, which I'm trying to smooth over. I'll be with you in a few moments.

(*She glances sharply from one to the other and goes out, closing the doors. Before MARCUS can say anything, ROSAMUND motions him to silence, runs to the doors and listens till she hears MARY starting up the stairs, then swings round to face him.*)

ROSAMUND: (*In a fierce whisper.*) Marco. What happened – *She found Lady Chatterley!*

MARCUS: *What!*...and *read* it?

ROSAMUND: Enough to make her 'ashamed to look any decent person in the face.'

MARCUS: Oh my sacred aunt! (*In convulsions of laughter he collapses on the sofa.*) Jesus, Mary and Jezebel!

ROSAMUND: Marco, stop!... Do stop, she'll hear.
(*He attempts to speak but is so convulsed that he can't manage a coherent word and rolls about, hugging his diaphragm.*)
Coney, please!

MARCUS: Do you think she – do you think she – oh my God! – do you think she got to where – to where Connie runs out into the rain, starkers, in her galoshes and goes flump! on all fours in the mud, and – and old Mellors is pounding up behind her, tearing his flies open? Can you *imagine* your –

ROSAMUND: I'm sorry, I can't laugh, I can't bear making fun of Mummy.

MARCUS: (*Flatly.*) Oh. (*And then again in the same way.*) Oh. (*A pause.*) – Is this the beginning of the rot?

ROSAMUND: What do you mean?

MARCUS: The first warning of a steady but rapidly accelerating erosion of resolve?

ROSAMUND: ...All I said was I didn't like making fun of Mother. I know it's stupid of me –
(*MARCUS joins in.*)

MARCUS/ROSAMUND: – but I can't help feeling sorry for her.

ROSAMUND: (*She laughs weakly.*) ...But I do – most desperately sorry.

MARCUS: Look here, you could stop the rot now. (*A chopping movement with his hand.*) Like that.

ROSAMUND: Yes, I know, I know. But do try and see, however much I *want* to, I can't just...

MARCUS: So you're going to let me down.

ROSAMUND: You're being horribly unfair. – It'll mean a complete break with my family and that's something I've kept putting off and putting off. Well, now it's come to it. I –

MARCUS: All right, all right, now it's come to it your mother and your family are going to be very upset.

ROSAMUND: It isn't a case of being 'very upset,' Mother will be heartbroken! They all will.

MARCUS: Then you'll have to choose, won't you?

ROSAMUND: (*After a pause.*) Marco, all I'm asking is for time to get my breath and think clearly about what I'm doing.

MARCUS: How long will that take you?

ROSAMUND: I've made up my mind already, I'm sure I have, just give me an hour, two hours, half an hour, anything...

MARCUS: (*With a shrug, looking at his watch.*) What about... seven o'clock then? Tonight. Will that give you long enough?

ROSAMUND: Oh, golly, yes! Of course, of course it will.

MARCUS: So, by seven tonight, having reached your foregone conclusion, you'll let me know whether you're coming or not.

ROSAMUND: Stop sounding like a waspish schoolmaster... Coney?...darling, I do love you... Whatever happens, don't ever forget that I love you very much.

MARCUS: I don't care a damn how much you love me! What's it amount to if you're going to back out and let us both down?

(*ROSAMUND says nothing. They hold each other's eyes. MARCUS crosses to a wing-chair and, throwing a leg over*

the arm, pulls a mouth-organ from his pocket and abstractedly
plays a piece of 'Bal Musette' dance music.)
(*Singing.*) '*Amusons-nous...de dou-dou-dou...*' We'll be
dancing to this in the Rue de Lappe unless you insist on
buggering everything up...
(*Tears spring to ROSAMUND's eye but she says nothing.*
When she does speak after a moment or two it is in flat, dry
tones devoid of affection or emotion.)

ROSAMUND: When it comes to seven o'clock...how
will I – ?

MARCUS: Use the piano. Thump out a message.

ROSAMUND: (*After a pause.*) What will I play then?

MARCUS: Whatever you like. What was that kitchy waltz
you were strumming when I... (*Singing.*) Dah dudderdah
dee... You could jazz it up a bit. (*He gets to his feet and*
crosses to the piano.)

ROSAMUND: Don't start playing *now*...do have some
sense.
(*But his fingers are already descending on the keys.*)

MARCUS: ...Syncopate it... (*Playing.*) ...and it'll mean
(*Singing.*) *Ma*rcus, I'm *co*ming with *you*
I've got *no*thing to *lose* but my *chains*...
(*He jumps up abruptly and, swinging round, grips her by the*
arms.) For God's sake, Pozzy, it's your life... And my life.
And my work too. *And* yours. Get tough.
(*With a tinkle and rattle of tea things the doors are pushed*
open and MISS DUCIE appears behind an overloaded
tea-tray. She is in difficulties.)
Hey, look out! – (*He hurries to help her.*) All right... I've
got it.

MISS DUCIE: Thank you.

ROSAMUND: (*Indicating a table.*) Marcus, here... (*Then, as*
he puts the tray down.) Oh...um er, this – is Miss Ducie,
Marcus. Miss Ducie –

MISS DUCIE/MARCUS: We have met.

ROSAMUND: Goosey, did Mother ask you to –

MISS DUCIE: Young man, why are you letting down the
side?

MARCUS: Because, Miss Ducie, I have joined the other side.

MISS DUCIE: (*She starts reciting.*) There's a deadly hush in the close tonight –

MARY: (*Entering.*) What on earth – ? What are you doing, Miss Ducie? What is this tea doing?

MISS DUCIE: It is *my* doing. (*Making her way out.*) I took it upon myself. (*She goes out, closing the doors.*)

MARY: (*Breaking an uncomfortable, uncertain silence.*) Well...as tea seems to be here... (*Moving towards the tea-tray and seating herself behind it.*) – Won't you sit down, Mr uh?... Do you take tea in the afternoon?

MARCUS: Oh, indeed, yes, the cup that cheers but not inebriates. And so much more refreshing than whisky.

MARY: (*After a moment.*) Milk?...or do you like lemon?

MARCUS: Whichever you prefer.

MARY: Do you take *milk* in your tea, Mr uh? Or do you take *lemon*?

MARCUS: Um...er – *you* choose for me.

ROSAMUND: (*In a sharp undertone.*) Marcus! (*Then in her normal voice.*) Mother, he takes milk and two lumps.

MARY: (*As she pours the tea.*) And how have you liked living in this district, Mr uh? Rather too quiet perhaps? Though convenient for the West End – which we seldom visit nowadays. Except to see *Cavalcade* of course. (*Passing MARCUS his cup.*)

MISS DUCIE: (*Pushing open the doors for JELLY, who waddles in and makes for ROSAMUND.*) In you go – go on in – that's right! *My word!* Making a nuisance of yourself. (*She retires, closing the doors.*)

MARY: Sit down, Rosamund. (*Handing her a cup.*) I thought Jelly went with the others.

ROSAMUND: No. Aunt Sylvie wouldn't let her because –

MARY: (*Quickly.*) Oh, I see...uh – pass Mr Uh the sandwiches, Rosamund.

ROSAMUND: *Eversley* – Mr *Eversley*, Mother.
(*She passes the sandwiches and he takes one.*)

MARCUS: Thanks.
(*A long pause.*)
(*To JELLY.*) Come on, boy. There's a dirty old doggie. What's his name, Mrs Moorhouse?

ROSAMUND: (*An impatient sotto voce.*) *Rees* – Moorhouse-
Rees!

MARY: What *is* the *matter* Rosamund?... Her name is Jelly.

ROSAMUND: (*After a pause.*) Mother – !

MARY: – And – uh – are you writing any more books, Mr
– uh – Eversley?

MARCUS: Books? Oh, yes! Scribble, scribble, scribble.
Morning, noon and night.

MARY: Really? I wouldn't have thought you could find
time for all this work.

MARCUS: (*Offering his sandwich to JELLY.*) Here you are,
old fat-gut... Does he eat cucumber?

MARY: Jelly eats anything.

MARCUS: Including nuts? Your little dog eats nuts?

MARY: I beg your pardon?

MARCUS: Your little dog eats nuts?

MARY: I can't think where this idea of dogs eating nuts
comes from. It would simply choke them. I hope you
never offer them any.

MARCUS: You hear that, Jellybelly? No nuts.

MARY: Rosamund, put Jelly outside, will you?
(*ROSAMUND does so.*)
And how much longer, Mr – uh – Eversley, are you
planning to stay at –

MARCUS: Pulling stumps at any moment, Mrs Rees.

MARY: You will have to be very busy, I imagine, restoring
the house to the state in which you found it. Mrs Ormerod
is, I believe, nothing if not particular and meticulous.

MARCUS: Mrs Rees, that's a solo for the xylophone.
Particular and meticulous, particular and meticulous,
sometimes real pernickety and other times ridiculous.

ROSAMUND: Mother, I don't know what made you ask
Marcus over but (*With a glance at her watch.*) time's
getting on and I'm terrified that –

MARY: Yes, all right, all right, Rosamund. Mr Eversley, as a
writer, not, I gather, without repute, I would like to ask
you to give me your professional opinion as to whether
Rosamund has any aptitude for writing, for becoming a
writer –

ROSAMUND: Please stop it, Mother! It's too bad of you!

MARY: Would you say she has it in her – by hard work and application – eventually to write a best-seller?

ROSAMUND: No, she has not! Mother, for heaven's sake!

MARY: Will you please not shout at me?

ROSAMUND: It's absolutely shaming! If you don't stop I'm going out of the room.

MARY: Would you say, Mr Eversley – (*But before MARCUS can say anything a voice yells to him from out in the street.*)

JO: (*Off.*) Marco?... Mah-ark! Have you got your keys? I've locked myself out.

MARCUS: (*In exasperation.*) Oh *God*... (*Jumping up and hurrying onto the balcony.*) Maddening woman – they're probably at the bottom of her handbag.

JO: (*Off; meanwhile.*) Mah-ark?... Marcovitch! Can you hear me? (*Then as he moves forward.*) Ducky, throw your keys down, will you?

DRUNKEN MAN: (*Voice off, half yelling, half singing.*) Wotcher me old brown son, how *are* you? Wotcher me old brown son –

MARCUS: I haven't got them, I think I've left them in the – hold on a minute, I'll come down. (*Feeling in his pockets, he steps back into the room.*) The most infuriating woman. She only has to step outside the front door and it's 'Oh, I've left my keys on the gramophone!'

MARY: Are you speaking of your wife, Mr – uh – ?

MISS DUCIE: (*Off, from the entrance hall.*) Straight up. You'll find him in the drawing-room.

JO: (*Off; her voice approaching and then ascending the staircase.*) Ducky, I'm sure I saw you pick them up and 'pocket' them –

VINCE: (*The owner of the drunken voice, singing as he mounts the stairs behind her.*) Ours is a nice 'ouse, ours is, what a nice little 'ouse ours is...

MARY: (*Simultaneously.*) What is Miss Ducie thinking of? (*She springs up and, crossing the room, pulls open the doors just as JO reaches the landing.*)

JO: (*Addressing her.*) Oh darling, isn't it hell leaving one's keys inside, one feels there's some dreadful symbolism in it, 'Love Locked Out', but it's oneself who's done it. (*She is in the room by now.*) Ducky, haven't you found them? (*MARCUS grabs her handbag.*)

MARCUS: Here, give me that.

(*He looks inside and then emptying its numerous contents onto a nearby chair starts to go through them. Close on JO's heels and still singing 'Ours is a nice –'ouse', VINCE passes MARY on his way into the room, then suddenly stops and, swinging round, stares at her.*)

VINCE: Good God, Ivy Compton Burnett!... Madam, I salute you! (*He brings his heels together in a steel-spring military salute. ROSAMUND, distracted, hurries to intervene.*)

ROSAMUND: Oh Mother – this is Alastair Vincey –

VINCE: Allow me, Madam, to pay homage.

(*He drops to his knees.*)

ROSAMUND: Vince, stop it – please. You're drunk.

MARY: Disgusting!

VINCE: What's up with *her?* Think I was going to bite her ankles?

ROSAMUND: ...Darling, don't worry, I'll get rid of them somehow.

(*DONNA looks in and peers round. In her early fifties, she wears a flowing black cloak and wide-brimmed, flat-crowned hat tied under the chin.*)

DONNA: Is that the abominable Vincey on the floor? Eversley, abominable Vince is disintegrating into the carpet.

MARCUS: Come on, Vince. You're not together. Pull yourself...

VINCE: Blotting paper! Blotting Paper! Show me the way to go home, Donna. It's time that you took me home to bed...

DONNA: Haven't you taken in the fact yet, Vincey, that my home is no longer yours? I don't want you there any more – or any other male.

JO: Aren't you being a little harsh on poor old Vincey? – Where can he go?

MARCUS: Donna will put him up when it comes to it.

DONNA: She won't.

MARCUS: (*To DONNA.*) The trouble with you is that you have become an enthusiast.

DONNA: I am an enthusiast. I agree with Virginia Woolf. It angers me that the human race should be designated Mankind. 'Man!' – Women are the Race, the Human Race. Man is – an afterthought, an excrescence, merely a piece of fancywork.

VINCE: Hey, I ever tell you the latest 'Bobby an' Annabelle'?... They'd been having one o' their twice-nightly free-for-alls – an' they both pass out an'... Hey, you know what' cucumbers smell of?... Ghosts... Cucumbers smell of... (*Collapses.*)

MARCUS: Watch yourself!

DONNA: I've realised with shame that all the years I've owned my studios I have accepted the convention that a painter was a man. Well, just as women can now look forward to having 'rooms of their own' to write in, I think they should have studios to paint in.

MARCUS: (*Trying to get bottle.*) No, Vince, no. Come on, let's have it.

JO: Look what Vince has got!

DONNA: And here I was provided with the means to bring out the unsuspected talent of women who might otherwise go from womb to tomb without ever putting brush to canvas. (*Indicating MARY.*) Take that woman, for instance, God knows what masterpieces she may have locked up inside her... If only she were given the chance.

JO: Well, why don't you give it to her.

DONNA: That's exactly what I am going to do.

JO: Let go of the Gordon's, Vincey. All our little pink tongues are hanging out.

DONNA: (*Sitting next to MARY.*) Dear Lady, when the time comes to find out *who* you really *are*, come to me. (*ROSAMUND returns.*)

JO: Foxy drinks! Foxy drinks! Who's for Foxy drinks?

ROSAMUND: I told Goosey if they got back before these people have gone, to keep Alfred and Sylvie downstairs.

JO: (*To MARY.*) Darling, are you having some? Go on, it'll do you good.

ROSAMUND: (*To MARY.*) Tea in the morning room.

JO: (*Handing MARCUS a cup.*) Oh, Marcus. You do look sweet. Don't you think he looks sweet? Donna?

DONNA: No, he looks rather surly to me.

MARCUS: I consider myself badly treated and I am behaving like a spoiled brat.

DONNA: Behave like a spoiled brat and you'll be a man my son.

VINCE: What...eh...

ROSAMUND: Oh gosh! Vince is coming to. (*She rushes to him.*) Now is the moment surely to. (*She shakes him.*) Vince!

VINCE: What! Eh! So next thing she sits up and in comes old Bobby with his loaded tray, coffee, milk, toast, butter –

ROSAMUND: Yes, yes, yes! And he brings the whole lot crashing down on her head – and that's supposed to be hilarious. If you *want* to give the impression that you're heartless, callous and without any kind of human feeling you certainly succeed.

VINCE: Bollocks!

(*Enter MISS DUCIE and a cab driver.*)

MISS DUCIE: Who hasn't paid the cabbie? Pay up! Pay up! Or he'll have every excuse for turning ugly.

JO: Ugly! With that gorgeous slim figure.

DONNA: Oh, Driver, I'm sorry you had to wait. How much do I owe you?

JO: Nothing at all or whatsoever, ducky-ducky. This is my treat. (*Going up to the CABBY.*) Darling, where did you come from?

CABBY: What? Before I picked up 'er in the 'at? Tufnell Park.

JO: Look, how much to book you in advance? For the rest of the day?

CABBY: Cost you a lot of money, Miss.

JO: Here you are, here's a fiver to go on with.

CABBY: Ow!... Ow, thanks very much, Miss, ta.

JO: Is your name Eddie?

CABBY: Eddie? Nah, Ernie.

JO: Oh no, dear, all my young men are called Eddie. So Eddie, I suppose you've got a wee wifie?

EDDIE: Got a what?

JO: Waiting up for you every night? A wee wifie?

EDDIE: Nah, I got a bloody great big one.

JO: *What?* What did you say?

EDDIE: I said I got a bloody great big one.

JO: (*With a shriek.*) Eddie, *je t'adore.* Darling, I knew it! I knew it!

(*Loud Laughter. MISS DUCIE becomes beside herself.*)

MISS DUCIE: You call yourselves ladies? Call yourselves gentlemen? Savages! Kaffirs! (*And off she squiffily takes herself, yelling.*) Fuzzy Wuzzies! Fuzzy Wuzzies!

JO: (*Through another burst of laughter, herself helpless with it.*) It's not *true!*... It's not *true!*... Oh my God... *Fuzzy Wuzzies!*

(*The laughter stops abruptly at the sound of MARY's voice. They had almost forgotten she was there.*)

MARY: Would you please leave my house, all of you. I'm not feeling very well. Please go home. Ros, ring for Hopkins. No, don't. Show them out yourself.

ROSAMUND: (*Going to her, protectively.*) Mummy!

MARCUS: (*Still not quite in control of his laughter.*) Ros, I'm sorry about all this. But it just *happened,* didn't it – whole thing was a mistake.

ROSAMUND: I think, perhaps, everything's been a mistake.

MARCUS: Oh, you think that, eh? (*Then, after a split moment in which they hold each other's eyes.*) Come on, (*To his friends.*) I'm clearing out – better all push off, Rosamund's mother's not well.

(*MARY suddenly stands up, her hands trembling.*)

MARY: Oh yes, I am. I'm trying to keep my feelings under control, that's all. But I can't do it, I cannot! I shall speak out! And it's my duty to speak out. You come here with your foul manners and your monkey-house morals, with your filthy language and your strident voices, and turn what had been a nice, quiet residential street into something like an alley in the slums on Mafeking Night! Well, with foul-mannered people I can be foul-mannered too. Just because you may have written some pretentious novel, or painted some 'advanced picture', with four eyes and two noses where their chins ought to be, you think you can flout every code and convention of civilised behaviour that ordinary decent people live by. You think it's 'modern' and 'intellectual' to disregard other people, live your own lives, as you say – but you're Chicago gangsters. What is the difference? Will someone please explain to me what is the difference between people like you and Chicago gangsters? You're just as wicked. Don't think I don't know you're trying to ruin my daughter's life! Don't think I don't know it! But you imagine for a moment that I'll let you? You think that I'd permit it? I *won't* – I will not *permit* it, I'll fight you tooth and nail. I've written to Mrs Ormerod complaining of Mr Eversley, and if she doesn't do anything I shall sit down and write the whole sordid story to the Kensington Borough Council. (*ALFRED comes in, followed by SYLVIE.*)

ALFRED: Hullo! Hullo! What's all this set-up?

SYLVIE: Good gracious! What is it?

ROSAMUND: (*Intercepting her uncle.*) No, no, Uncle, it's nothing, please go away.

ALFRED: Who are all these young people, then?

MARY: *Miss Ducie!* Did Miss Ducie suggest you should come up here?

SYLVIE: She said there was a party. Whose party?

DONNA: (*On her way out she stops and turns to MARY.*) I'm in complete agreement with what you said about Picasso. In my opinion he'd have done much better to have stuck to his Blue Period.

ALFRED: Who is this lady?

JO: Eddie, you coming?

ALFRED: Now, my dear, don't you go running off because of me.

SYLVIE: Alfred! Who's that? Look! Look! Over there, that man –

ALFRED: What? What? What is it you say?

SYLVIE: That young man over there –

ALFRED: (*Recognising MARCUS.*) God almighty! Daring to show his face here!... Get out! Get out! D'you hear me?

MARY: Alfred!

LALLAH: (*As with JOHN and MISS DUCIE she appears in the doorway.*) What are they doing?

ALFRED: (*Advancing on MARCUS, his stick raised.*) I'll show you.

ROSAMUND: (*Together.*) Uncle, don't!

JO: (*Together.*) Eddie, stop him!

EDDIE: Steady on, sir, watch out.

(*He removes the stick from ALFRED's hand just in time to save MARCUS from being whacked across the face with it.*) You can be *done* for that, you know.

ALFRED: (*Breathing heavily, he supports himself on a chair.*) ...Give me that stick.

EDDIE: Only if you're good. We don't wanna see nice old elderly gentlemen in the Scrubs, do we?

(*ALFRED stretches out a trembling hand and EDDIE, seeing that there's no fight left in him, relinquishes the stick.*)

ALFRED: (*Getting his breath; to MARCUS.*) Go on, go on, young man...while I'm still in control of myself.

(*MARCUS' attention is deflected to VINCE who, saluting MARY again and falling on his knees before her, is now about to kiss the hem of her skirt.*)

MARCUS: (*Rushing forward, he yanks VINCE to his feet.*) For Christ's sake, Vince!

VINCE: (*As MARCUS propels him out of the room.*) ...a bloody genius...you read *Brothers and Sisters?* Respectable matron, married for years, finds out her husband's her brother. Everything in her life is based on incest. So know what she does? Buggerall!

(*By this time he and MARCUS are out of the room.*)

...there's the genius, all she does is buggerall.

(*They go out of sight but VINCE's voice can still be heard receding down the stairs.*)

...finds out her husband's her brother an all she does is buggerall...

DONNA: (*To MARY.*) Well, don't forget – if it comes to it – The Studios, Ellanby Gardens, Fulham Palace Road. Jo, may I borrow your Eddie to run me home?

JO: (*She and EDDIE are on their way out.*) He'll have to let me in first, Eddie, I've lost my keys – have you ever been a cat-burglar?
(*With DONNA bringing up the rear, EDDIE follows JO across the landing to the staircase.*)

EDDIE: What, me? Nah, Miss, not in my line.

JO: (*Off, as all three go down the stairs.*) Don't tell me you can't shin up a drain-pipe with the greatest of ease...
(*A moment later the front door is heard closing. LALLAH has started to weep and in the comparative stillness her sobbing becomes audible.*)

SYLVIE: You must have taken leave of your senses, Mary, sitting here, taking tea with them.

ALFRED: You should have kicked them out.

MARY: Will you please not all turn on me. My nerves are stretched to the limit.

JOHN: You are an ass, Ros, asking them here.

ALFRED: (*Together.*) It's about time you knew better, my girl.

ROSAMUND: (*Together.*) I *didn't* ask them!

MARY: If you must know the truth, I am responsible for their being here.

ALFRED: (*Together.*) You?

LALLAH: (*Together.*) Mother!

SYLVIE: (*Together.*) What?

JOHN: (*Together.*) Good Lord!

MARY: You're all so concerned about what's happening to Rosamund but I'm the only one who does anything to help her. And when I do you all turn on me.

ALFRED: You silly, meddling woman.

ROSAMUND: Look, please everybody, the whole thing is entirely my fault.

SYLVIE: That's as may be but Alfred has no right to insult his sister.

MARY: I'm inured to insults.

ALFRED: (*To SYLVIE.*) What are you putting your spoke in for?

SYLVIE: Be quiet, Alfred, my spoke's as good as yours.

MARY: You call me meddling but it seems to me the meddling was done by you. What reason was there for

your bursting into the drawing-room? Miss Ducie, it is
your fault. And I must ask you to go. At the end of the
week, I've had enough.

MISS DUCIE: Very well. There are always the Homes for
Decayed Gentlewomen. At least I should be amongst
Nice People.

ALFRED: Now see what you've done.

MARY: You may not think it but I mean Miss Ducie to go.

SYLVIE: And what right have you to tell Miss Ducie to go?
I'm her employer just as much as you are.

JOHN: Oh, for mercy's sake, what is the point of all this
bickering?

ROSAMUND: Aunt Sylvie! What's happened to us all?

SYLVIE: You to ask what's happened when the root of the
trouble lies at your door!

ROSAMUND: Yes, it does, it does, I know it does, I've
admitted it, so why can't you –

MARY: So you're Miss Ducie's employer, are you, Sylvie?

ROSAMUND: (*In desperation.*) Oh *Mother!*

MARY: It's you who engages staff, is it?
(*As MARY goes relentlessly on, ROSAMUND turns away with
a groan.*)
So it's you who takes on all the wearisome business of
engaging them and sacking them? How is it then – and
isn't it extraordinary? That I should have worked my
fingers to the bone to run the house for you for the last
thirty years.

SYLVIE: Rubbish. You run it for yourself. Mrs Moorhouse-
Rees this, Mrs Moorhouse-Rees that! What have I been
made to feel like? A poor old dependent.

MARY: So that's the thanks I get, bringing my family here to
make a home for you and Alfred. Who drove my husband
away? Who drove Howard from me with her mean,
nagging, selfish ways? You did, Sylvie, you know you did.
I sacrificed my life for you, Sylvie, and that's all the
thanks I get. (*She collapses on the sofa and bursts into tears.*)

LALLAH: (*Running to her.*) Mother! Darling Mummy!

ALFRED: Nothing but a lot of squawking women!

JOHN: Come on, Lallah.

MARY: Oh. So my daughter's not allowed to comfort me now.

JOHN: What good will it do – everybody sitting around weeping?

LALLAH: John, how *can* you?

MARY: Every minute he's been in this house he's tried to make me look foolish. And now he's trying to make Lallah hate me!

JOHN: Does it look as if Lallah hates you? Well, you may not have succeeded in your object of making her hate me, but if you're not very careful, I shall end up hating her!

LALLAH: No, John, no! (*Wailing, she gets to her feet and goes to him.*) You don't mean it? Johnny, say you don't mean it... I'd kill myself. I would, I'd kill myself! Why did we ever *come* here, John? We've never had a moment's happiness together since we came.

MARY: What happiness have I ever had?

LALLAH: (*She lets go of JOHN and turns to her mother.*) Oh! I realise now! Why you've never wanted me to have a child.

MARY: Lallah! I've never said any such thing.

LALLAH: Yes, you have!

ROSAMUND: No, you must have misunderstood –

LALLAH: But she did! Hundreds of times! She said she didn't think I ought to. She frightened me out of it.

MARY: I never had any such intention. As God's my witness.

JOHN: Why have you told Lallah she oughtn't to have a child then?

MARY: (*Weakly.*) I don't know.

SYLVIE: *Did* you? Did you say that? Oh, I'd believe anything of you now. A wicked woman I call you. A wicked woman.

ALFRED: Shut up! Why must you always chip in and make things worse?

SYLVIE: And you shut up yourself, Alfred. I've had enough from you. More than I can stomach. After all these years of looking after you as if you were a child. I ruined my life for you. My life was out in India with Bertie, as Bertie's wife. But no! I threw all that up. Break Bertie's heart and mine, too, so that I can come here and help you, with Jessie gone, and your leg. And what have I had for it? Rudeness from you and treated as nothing by Mary and the children. Year in, year out. Uncle Alfred this, Uncle Alfred that! Aunt Sylvie sometimes remembered as an afterthought. But who gets the best presents on their birthday? Who gets favourite dishes? Who's king? The king and the slave I call it.

ALFRED: And a fine life mine's been, hasn't it? Fine sort of king. When Jessie died my life stopped. What's it been since? With Mary putting me in my place for doing what's natural and you at me all the time, yap, yap, yap. Well, you may not know it, but you'll be pleased to hear I had thoughts of marrying again, not so long after poor Jessie died either; but I didn't do anything. No, I let it go. Made the greatest mistake of my life so that we could live happily together, so that I could make a home for you all. And this is the result – eking out what's left of my blasted life with a lot of *damn silly women!*

LALLAH: (*Together.*) We're not silly, Uncle! We're not silly.

MARY: (*Together.*) You've no right to speak like that!

JOHN: (*Together.*) Oh, come on, Uncle Alfred!

SYLVIE: (*Together.*) Wicked old man. Wicked! Wicked!

MARY: (*As they all go on shouting.*) Sylvie! Lallah! John!

(*There is a sudden silence.*)

I think we've all forgotten ourselves.

(*The silence is broken again by a torrent of sound. ROSAMUND has run to the windows and opened them and is sitting at the piano thumping out 'Over the Waves' as loudly as she can. The others stare at her. She continues playing.*)

End of Act Two.

ACT THREE

Some twenty-four hours later. It is not quite dark yet. There is no illumination from the house across the road. ROSAMUND is standing with the telephone receiver to her ear; she has an air of having been waiting almost hopelessly for her call to be answered. With an occasional glance towards the windows, she continues listening, then recalls the operator.

ROSAMUND: Hullo?... There's still no reply from that number... Yes, leave it, I'll try again later.

(She sighs and, crossing the room, pulls the windows open and looks out but there is no sign of life in the house opposite. Anxious and on edge, she turns back into the room and is starting to pull off the short, outdoor coat she is wearing when lights come on on the first floor of Mrs Ormerod's. ROSAMUND flings the coat towards an armchair and turns to the window again. She watches for a moment, then with an expression of relief and half-apprehensive hopefulness, returns to the telephone and picks up the receiver.)

...Sloane seven-six –

(She doesn't complete the number: someone is coming and, with a movement of guilty haste, she hangs up. SYLVIE enters, switches some lights on and potters over to an escritoire.)

Are you looking for anything?

SYLVIE: *(Snapping at her.)* I can find it quite well, thank you. *(She ferrets about without success.)* Ridiculous, I call it, no ink in the house!

ROSAMUND: Here, let *me*... No, there doesn't seem to be any.

SYLVIE: What's that new bracelet you're wearing?

ROSAMUND: What, this? It's a nose-ring.

SYLVIE: Rubbish. What d'you mean, a nose-ring?

ROSAMUND: A ring to wear in the nose.

SYLVIE: Disgusting I call it.

(LALLAH puts her head round the door.)

LALLAH: Have you seen Jelly anywhere?

ROSAMUND: No, I haven't. (*She goes to the windows again and tries to make out what is happening across the road.*)

LALLAH: Oh dear!

(*After a moment ROSAMUND turns to her, LALLAH's manner becomes conspiratorial. She whispers.*)

What's Mother doing? Still lying down?

ROSAMUND: I don't know. Aunt Sylvie, I've got (*Looking in her bag.*) a perfectly good fountain-pen here.

SYLVIE: Can't stand the things. (*On her way out.*) Hiding the ink. Most peculiar I call it.

LALLAH: Oh, I'm sorry, Uncle.

(*She makes way for ALFRED as he comes into the room. He and SYLVIE stop short at the sight of each other.*)

SYLVIE: (*With exaggerated politeness.*) Excuse me.

(*ALFRED grunts and hobbles farther in.*)

I've got a letter to write. (*Muttering, she goes out.*)

ROSAMUND: Do you want anything, Uncle?

ALFRED: What? Want anything? I don't know what I want. Collins! I want Collins to take me somewhere.

ROSAMUND: Do you want me to find him?

ALFRED: (*His manner becomes conspiratorial.*) Where's your mother? Lying down still.

LALLAH: (*In the doorway.*) Oh, I'm sorry.

(*She makes way for MARY, who is very pale and almost incredibly frigid and dignified. During the ensuing scene her tone remains icy.*)

MARY: Is no one having tea?

(*She indicates a table on which is set a laden tea-tray. ALFRED grunts and hobbles out. MARY heaves a tragic sigh. She asks.*)

Have you any idea where the aspros are, Rosamund?

ROSAMUND: There are some in the bathroom I think.

MARY: Thank you. (*In a lower tone.*) What's your aunt doing?

ROSAMUND: Looking for some ink.

(*MARY turns to go. LALLAH hurriedly moves out of her way.*)

LALLAH: Oh, I'm sorry.

MARY: Thank you. (*She goes.*)

(*LALLAH buries her face in her hands. She sobs helplessly once or twice.*)

LALLAH: Everything's so ghastly... Oh, dear! (*She runs out. Left alone, ROSAMUND goes to the window again then returns to the telephone.*)

ROSAMUND: Hullo... Hello?...um... Sloane three-o – (*But again she hears someone coming and puts down the receiver without completing the number. Someone kicks at the doors and she runs and opens them. MISS DUCIE is revealed staggering under the burden of something resembling a very large hat-box.*)

Goosey! (*Backing into the room she helps her lower the box onto the floor.*) Why didn't you get Collins to bring it up?

MISS DUCIE: ...dumped it in the hall: there it was.

ROSAMUND: Goosey, sit down, you don't look at all well.

MISS DUCIE: (*She sits on the nearest chair, recovering herself, then announces.*) I've been poisoned.

ROSAMUND: (*Her attention on the window opposite.*) Poisoned?

MISS DUCIE: By the Irish peasant woman. The whole of yesterday I was suffering from the effects.

ROSAMUND: (*Who has crossed back to the telephone.*) ...Goosey, be a lamb and keep cave for me; tell me if you hear Mother coming.

MISS DUCIE: All I can recall now is some kind of quarrel with your poor mamma and that she gave me my marching orders.

ROSAMUND: Sloane three-o-six-two, please... Yes... there's been no reply all day and now it's engaged all the time... Yes, if you would, please... (*Then, after glancing up at the sound of MISS DUCIE leaving the room.*) Hullo?... Yes, I see, thank you... No, no, don't do that, I'll try again later.

(*She puts back the receiver, sighs and, first making sure that no one is coming, drags the box to the back of the room and hides it behind a screen, straightening herself as MARY appears.*)

MARY: (*She seats herself behind the tea-tray.*) Are you not having tea?

ROSAMUND: No tha... Oh, yes – thank you, I will have just a cup.

MARY: Every mouthful will choke me. (*She pours a cup for ROSAMUND and hands it to her.*)

ROSAMUND: (*After a pause.*) Has anything been seen of Jelly yet?

MARY: I really couldn't tell you.

ROSAMUND: She seems to have disappeared since last night. (*A pause.*) Is it your head?

MARY: (*Showing a bottle.*) I am taking these to steady my nerves.

(*MISS DUCIE comes in again; she is holding a letter.*)

MISS DUCIE: ...Telephone directory – the Home for Indigent Dependants of Commissioned Officers. I've written to them for admission (*Holding up the letter.*) but was uncertain of the address.

ROSAMUND: (*As MISS DUCIE collects the directory from the top of the escritoire and starts to go up.*) Wouldn't you like some tea, Goosey?

MISS DUCIE: (*On an indrawn breath.*) No-o-o-o thank you.

MARY: One would think some*body* would come down to tea when I went to all the trouble of ringing for it.

MISS DUCIE: If it is of use I will take it upon myself to sound the gong. (*She goes.*)

ROSAMUND: Poor old Goosey! Don't you think she should be stopped from sending in the application?

MARY: I really couldn't tell you.

ROSAMUND: It sounds so dismally depressing.

MARY: Oh, but it will be seventh heaven for her after living here. A home for deaf and dumb paupers with the plague would be a happier place to live in than this house with me. I thought that was something every one agreed on.

(*The gong sounds. LALLAH appears nervously in the doorway.*)

Are you having tea, Lallah?

LALLAH: I don't know – I – no, thank you. (*She turns to go.*)

MARY: You'd better have something.

LALLAH: Just...some tea then.

(*She comes into the room and sits down, MARY hands her a cup.*)

MARY: It's no good doing without food.

(*ALFRED, his overcoat on, looks in, but seeing MARY, hastily retires.*)

Aren't you going to have any tea, Alfred?

(*He comes back.*)

ALFRED: Tea? I'm going out. Collins is taking me out somewhere.

MARY: The car won't be ready for five minutes. You'd better have some tea.

ALFRED: (*Hobbling to a chair and sitting.*) Tea? What's the good of tea?

MARY: Here's your uncle's cup, Rosamund.

(*As she takes it to him, SYLVIE comes in holding a bottle of ink and a pen.*)

SYLVIE: Nice place to keep the ink. In the medicine cupboard! (*To ALFRED.*) Would you mind moving, please? I want to write a letter.

ALFRED: (*Moving his chair for her.*) Sorry. Beg your pardon.

MARY: Will you have some tea, Sylvie?

(*SYLVIE sits at the escritoire and prepares to start a letter.*)

ROSAMUND: Mother said you would like some tea, Aunt Sylvie?

SYLVIE: Who said so?

ROSAMUND: Mother. Would you like some tea?

SYLVIE: Tea? If I want tea I shall go to a restaurant the same as I did for lunch. I don't want people working their fingers to the bone for me.

(*MARY weeps quietly but recovers with an effort and bravely drinks her tea.*)

Going to write a letter. Letter!

MARY: (*To LALLAH.*) Will nobody eat a muffin? Lallah?

LALLAH: No, thank you.

MARY: You'd better have one.

LALLAH: No, really.

MARY: (*Holding them out.*) Here you are. Take one.

LALLAH: I couldn't eat it.

MARY: Will you please have a muffin?

LALLAH: I...couldn't...eat it.

MARY: (*Dramatically.*) Very well! (*She replaces the muffins on the tray.*)

LALLAH: Oh Mother, I didn't mean it like that. I will have one. Yes, please give me a muffin.

MARY: No...no...don't have one. Don't eat anything at all. (*LALLAH ostentatiously takes two.*)

LALLAH: Will *you* have one, Mother?

MARY: (*Taking one.*) Thank you.

LALLAH: Ros?

ROSAMUND: (*Taking one.*) Thank you.

LALLAH: Please, Uncle Alfred. Have one too. Look, there's only one left.

ALFRED: I don't want a muffin.

(*But he leans forward and takes one. They all sit nibbling helplessly. They go on eating. Tears drop from LALLAH's eyes onto her muffin. ROSAMUND goes behind MARY and, over her sister's shoulder, hands LALLAH a handkerchief.*)

SYLVIE: Rosamund, how much is the fare to India?

ROSAMUND: I'm afraid I've no idea, Aunt Sylvie. (*SYLVIE looks at MARY and ALFRED to see what effect her question has had. Apparently it has had none. ROSAMUND returns to the window to watch.*)

SYLVIE: (*To ROSAMUND, but with her eye on the other two.*) If I told you what to do, do you think you could arrange about selling some shares for me... No, doesn't matter, I'll do it myself. (*She turns back to her writing.*)

MARY: Will you have some more tea, Alfred?

ALFRED: Got to get off to the club. Arrange about a room there.

MARY: I beg your pardon?

ALFRED: Arrange about a room at the club.

MARY: Collins will let you know when the car's ready. (*She pours herself out some more tea. JOHN looks in. He is in a state of barely concealed excitement.*)

LALLAH: Johnny, you're back early tonight.

JOHN: Come upstairs directly you've finished.

ALFRED: Well, either go or stay, my boy, we're all in a draught.

MARY: Perhaps you'd like some tea.

JOHN: No thanks!

LALLAH: (*Grimacing and nodding at him.*) Do have some tea, John.

JOHN: Oh!... Yes, all right. Thanks. I will just have a cup. (*A pause.*)

SYLVIE: How do you spell cantonment?

JOHN: Cantonment?

LALLAH: What on earth's that?

SYLVIE: It's the place where they live – where the people live in India.

JOHN: C.A.N. –

SYLVIE: All right. I can spell it. (*She returns to addressing her envelope.*)

MARY: Sylvie, forgive my asking, but are you thinking of going to India?
(*There is no reply.*)
Would you mind asking your aunt, one of you, whether she is going to India?

ROSAMUND: Aunt, Sylvie, Mother wants to know whether you think of going to India?

SYLVIE: Who wants to know?

ROSAMUND: Mother.

SYLVIE: I've every intention of going to India.

MARY: Thank you. And how about you, Alfred? You're taking a room at the club, I gather?

ALFRED: (*Getting to his feet he hobbles to the door.*) Best to fix things up as soon as possible.
(*ALFRED grunts and goes out.*)

MARY: Do you mind not hovering round the window like that, Rosamund?

ROSAMUND: Sorry, Mother.

MARY: And you, of course, will be going away.
(*ROSAMUND says nothing.*)
Could you tell me about what date? I don't want to be curious, but, you see, I'd like to know because of the arrangements.

ROSAMUND: (*In a low voice; not looking at her mother.*) I can't tell you at the moment.

MARY: Anyway, you'll let me know as soon as it's decided.
And how about you, Lallah? When will *you* be leaving?

LALLAH: Oh Mother! Oh dear! Oh, isn't it awful!

MARY: Perhaps, John, you could be a little more explicit.

JOHN: Well, as a matter of fact, I took the afternoon off
to go flat-hunting and I have come across quite an
agreeable little place not far from here. I thought of
taking Lallah along to have a look at it.

MARY: (*After a pause.*) I shall sell up the house of course.

LALLAH: Mummy, you can't do that! Where could you go?

MARY: Don't worry about me, dear. I shall go to one of
those private hotels – boarding houses.

LALLAH: Mother darling, no! (*She springs to her feet, but in
doing so, upsets her cup.*)

MARY: Do be careful.

(*JOHN mops up the tea with his handkerchief. MISS DUCIE
appears.*)

MISS DUCIE: Here she comes. The fatted prodigal daughter.
(*JELLY waddles in, very dishevelled and covered in mud.*)
Yes, and so eager to get up to her wickedness, she
wouldn't even spare the time to take her lead off. Aren't
you ashamed of yourself? Letting the side down in the
gardens all night my *word!*
(*MISS DUCIE withdraws.*)

ROSAMUND: Oh, *Jelly!* Where have you been, you
naughty old dog? What have you been up to, eh?
(*JELLY wags her tail and looks silly.*)

LALLAH: (*Kneeling and embracing her.*) Poor little lovums.
What hasms been up to? Dirty little naughty.

MARY: For goodness sake, take her out of the drawing
room, Lallah.

LALLAH: Come along then. Mummy's little queen.
(*Putting her outside.*).

MARY: Who let her in the garden? The door into the gardens
is always locked. Somebody must have deliberately
opened it for her.

LALLAH: But who would do a thing like that when she's –
you know – not very well…

JOHN: Somebody in the kitchen perhaps.

ROSAMUND: It wouldn't be Cook.

MARY: It's Miss Ducie! That's who it is. Miss Ducie, out of pure perversity.

LALLAH: What about Hopkins? Mightn't she have done it?

SYLVIE: (*Getting up from the escritoire she starts to make her way out.*) Cook, Hopkins, Miss Ducie. It wasn't any of them. *I* let Jelly loose myself.

(*The doors close behind her. A pause.*)

JOHN: Oh, Ros, that's the most pathetic thing I've ever heard.

MARY: *Pathetic?* It would be funny if it weren't disgusting.

ROSAMUND: It isn't disgusting or funny, Mother, it's just horribly pathetic.

(*MARY stands up abruptly.*)

MARY: Of course I know I'm an imbecile. But never mind, I'll soon be amongst my own kind, faded, unwanted women in boarding houses. The only sort of people fit to associate with me.

(*She goes. ROSAMUND, JOHN and LALLAH exchange meaning glances. All three open their mouths to speak. The telephone rings.*)

ROSAMUND: (*With a start; nervously.*) I'll answer it. (*She goes to the phone.*) Hullo?... Yes, *do*, please. Thank you... Marco! Oh, thank heavens! Coney, listen, I sent the message to you – but you weren't there. I looked across and everything was dark...Of *course* I meant it. And... (*Suddenly her face falls.*) Hullo?... Hullo?... (*She takes the receiver from her ear, looks at it with a puzzled expression and, hanging up, turns to the others in dismay.*) He's rung off.

LALLAH: (*Uncertainly.*) Ros?...were you planning to elope with him?

ROSAMUND: We planned to go away together... If you want to know the truth, I'm in love with him, I love him. So if you're going to start criticising, I don't want to hear.

LALLAH: (*Reproachful tears starting.*) I wasn't *going* to criticise you. I'd no *intention* of criticising you.

JOHN: Now don't you two start.

ROSAMUND: Lallie, I'm sorry, but if you *knew* what it's been like for me. The whole of today I've been trying to get him on the phone. And then when I do he puts the receiver down on me.

JOHN: He's probably haring across the road to see you. At this very moment.

ROSAMUND: Do you think so? Oh, but Goosey would poke her nose in and Mummy would come down! – for heaven's sake run down into the street and stop him! (*Intent on their conversation, no one has noticed MARCUS clambering onto the balcony and, in two steps, reaching the French windows which are ajar. He pushes them open.*)

MARCUS: Pozzy!

LALLAH: Oh!...you did make me jump.

ROSAMUND: Marco!... (*Then, weakly.*) Oh, Coney...
(*JOHN makes a gesture to her meaning, 'You see? I was right.' Taking from his pocket a key with a label attached he holds it up for LALLAH to see and, with a jerk of his head towards the door, leads the way out. Rather reluctantly, and with one or two backward glances, LALLAH follows. ROSAMUND and MARCUS wait for them to go before turning to each other.*)
Coney, what happened? I've been nearly demented – not knowing –

MARCUS: Come here... Come on, come here.

ROSAMUND: ...Why?... (*But she is already moving towards him. As soon as she is within reach MARCUS grasps her and pulls her close.*)

MARCUS: (*Hugging her.*) Because I can't wait to get in touch with reality again!

ROSAMUND: (*After a moment; half jokingly but in a tear constricted voice.*) Is that your other name for me, then 'Reality?'

MARCUS: Ros, I can't *tell* you, I thought we were all washed up, I thought that's it, then. That's that. And then I start losing myself, we were in the Fitzroy and, in the thick of all the boozing and shouting, I thought – or somebody thought, well the thought came – 'Who *is* this? What's he doing here? Who is it he thinks he is? Who does *who* think *who* is?' I felt myself falling apart. It was terrifying, a true night-black panic! And then another thought came, 'Rosamund! Get that girl back, grab her! Grasp her! Grasp her! Wrap yourself around her! Get *with* her! And you'll stop falling to pieces, stop feeling scattered and whirled around like a fistful of confetti in a high wind.'

ROSAMUND: But has it worked? Has it *worked*, Coney? Are you all right again?

MARCUS: Am I all right? I rushed out into Charlotte Street and got a cab and I was already halfway back to being the one who got off with a girl in the post office and who thought he'd lost her by behaving like an eighteen-year-old buffoon. I didn't get your message yesterday but I've got it now. Do you still mean it? Pozzy, do you still mean it?

ROSAMUND: (*Pulling his head down she presses her lips to his ear.*) Yes! The answer is Yes! Yes! Yes! Yes! Yes!

MARCUS: No last minute compunction about the family? (*She shakes her head.*)

You're sure about that?

ROSAMUND: Look, (*Displaying the bracelet.*) this shows how *unretreatingly* I've made up my mind.

MARCUS: Good God! The nose ring!

ROSAMUND: Oh Coney, it was all my fault, I shouldn't have snapped at you like that, I can't tell you how miserable I've been about it… Oh, let's hold each other.

MARCUS: (*To music which has been heard from across the road since he came in and left the windows open, MARCUS starts tearing ROSAMUND round in a mad, capering dance, singing.*) And the farther off from England, the nearer is to France… The nearer, nearer, nearer, nearer is to France!

ROSAMUND: Stop! Stop! Marco, stop! Mother will come in and –

MARCUS: So Mother will come in and she'll see us dancing.

ROSAMUND: No! No! That's the last thing I want. (*Abruptly he stops dancing and goes quickly to the double doors.*) What are you *doing*?

(*He locks them.*)

ROSAMUND: What's the good of *that?* She'll only start banging on the door and –

MARCUS: I shall take a flying leap out of the window. (*He resumes his mad dancing, seizing her by the hand pulling her round with him.*)

ROSAMUND: Marco, listen...stop being so mad, and listen... Marco –

(*Suddenly he lets go of her and stops dancing. They stand looking at each other, getting their breath.*)

MARCUS: What?

ROSAMUND: I'm packed, ready, and in my running shorts. All I have to do is fling a few things into a travelling bag. Marco, I want to go *tonight.*

MARCUS: But naturally. What are you fussing about?

ROSAMUND: Do you mean it? You really agree?

MARCUS: Tonight! Tonight! Of course tonight!

(*The record across the road comes to an end.*)

Now listen. Tonight. What we'll do, Victoria. Midnight. Couchettes. We snuggle down, a spell of shut-eye, then 'You can look now! Paris!' By God, Pozzy, you'll have to put up with Paris being presented to you by the man who *owns* it, who in fact created the whole works –

I shall be shaming! Come on, what are we waiting for?

(*Pulling her towards him, kissing her.*) Rozpoz, beautiful, you get that bag packed.

ROSAMUND: I'll have to choose the right moment: when everybody's dressing for dinner. After the first gong. How long will you – ?

MARCUS: I'll have a cab waiting. I'll signal you from the street. (*He disengages himself and starts for the balcony.*)

ROSAMUND: Do be careful.

(*She is about to follow him but sounds from the first floor landing pull her up short and she stands listening; then seeing that MARCUS has also stopped she begs him in an urgent whisper.*)

ROSAMUND: Go *on* – do go! I believe that's Mother.

MARCUS: (*Swinging round and coming back to her.*) And I'll tell you what we'll do: a few weeks in Paris and then off

111

to Berlin. And I promise you, Pozzy – no, no, stop
agitating, nobody there, false alarm – I promise you that
life in Berlin –

(*They both freeze at the sound of a door–handle being turned.*)

MARY: (*Off.*) Rosamund?

(*The door-handle is turned again and the door shakes.*)

Rosamund, have you locked the door?

ROSAMUND: (*Mouthing the words as she urges him towards
the balcony.*) Go on...go on!

MARY: (*Off.*) Will you please open the door. Rosamund, do
you hear me? What is going on in there?

(*ROSAMUND looks trapped. MARCUS gives her a reassuring
look, accompanied by a gesture, 'Leave it to me,' and crossing
swiftly to the double doors, unlocks and pulls them open,
taking MARY completely by surprise.*)

MARCUS: Hullo, Mrs Moorhouse-Rees, how are you? (*He
crosses to the staircase.*) The rain doesn't seem to be
keeping off. Oh, *not* to be in England now that April's
there.

(*A moment later the front door is heard closing. Both MARY
and ROSAMUND, confronting each other, seem about to say
something emotional, dramatic and urgent and both open their
mouths to do so. But nothing comes of it and the awkward
silence starts stretching until ROSAMUND breaks it by
muttering something almost inaudible as she slips past MARY
and goes upstairs.*)

ROSAMUND: Sorry Mummy...get something from my
room...

(*In a state of extreme agitation MARY crosses to the fireplace,
hides on the chimneypiece a key she has been concealing in
her hand, and stands breathing heavily.*)

MARY: (*She paces up and down distractedly, then stops and,
going to the door, calls in a subdued voice.*) Miss Ducie!...
Miss Ducie!...

(*A wave of noise from over the road causes her to hurry across
the room to the windows.*)

Hooligans.

(*MISS DUCIE comes in.*)

Oh, Miss Ducie...

MISS DUCIE: You wish her services?

MARY: Oh, Miss Ducie, I hope you didn't take too seriously what I said yesterday. I wasn't at all well.

MISS DUCIE: Well, there's no harm done, I haven't posted the letter yet.

MARY: Miss Ducie, Rosamund's running away, she's going abroad with that wicked, *wicked* man from Mrs Ormerod's.

MISS DUCIE: We'll have to stop her, won't we.

MARY: But I can't think what to do. I've taken the key of her room and hidden it –

MISS DUCIE: Better try delaying tactics. For instance... we could put all the clocks back.

MARY: Put the clocks back.

MISS DUCIE: Make her late...miss trains. (*She starts for the door.*) I'll put the hall clock back half-an-hour and –

MARY: (*Making for the drawing-room clock.*) And I'll do the same for this one. (*She stops short.*) But this is perfectly futile. She could look at her wristwatch.

ROSAMUND: (*Bursting into the room.*) Mother, you haven't locked my door and taken the key, have you?

MARY: I should have thought that sort of thing is more your department.

ROSAMUND: (*With a shrug.*) Perhaps the lock's got stuck or something. (*But she turns back to MARY in spite of herself.*) Oh, Mother! (*She runs across to her and, kneeling down, puts her arms round her.*) Poor, dear, tired Mummy...
(*MISS DUCIE tactfully leaves the room as ROSAMUND continues.*)
Darling, please believe, in spite of everything, I do love you.

MARY: (*Melting over her.*) Oh, my baby...don't leave me.

ROSAMUND: (*In a harsh voice.*) Mother!
(*Jumping up, she runs from the room. MARY rises, trembling, but with queenly dignity.*)

MARY: Well, Miss Ducie, I know what I must do. There's only one way that I can stop Rosamund going tonight. (*She opens her bag, takes from it a small pill-box, shakes a few white tablets into her hand, turns to address MISS DUCIE and finds her gone. Then she calls.*) Miss Ducie! Miss Ducie!

(*She rises and is making for the door when MISS DUCIE returns.*) Oh, Miss Ducie, I have the most fearful headache. Have you some aspirins?

MISS DUCIE: But...aren't those aspirins in your hand?

MARY: Five, that's all, they're the only aspirins in the house. Surely you must have some.

MISS DUCIE: Not me! I don't believe in drugs. If *I* have a headache I simply –

(*LALLAH comes in, followed by JOHN. She is glowing with high spirits.*)

LALLAH: John's found a flat! Quite near here, just across from South Kensington Station: it's one of those mews flats and it's heavenly!

JOHN: I should hardly call it heavenly.

LALLAH: Of course, the rooms *are* rather tiny –

JOHN: Dwarfish.

LALLAH: The bedroom's a sort of duck-egg blue – and the bed's too big for the room, really, but we bounced about on it for a bit and it's absolutely scrumptious... Mother! What's the matter?

MARY: Nothing. Nothing at all.

(*She returns the pills to her bag and starts to go, MISS DUCIE having preceded her.*)

...I'm glad to know you and John will have a cosy little home...

LALLAH: (*Quickly.*) I don't see why we shouldn't have a few people in for dinner sometimes. You know, sort of intimate little dinner parties.

JOHN: They'd have to be. The dining-room only measures about nine feet by six.

LALLAH: Oh help!

JOHN: Never mind, we'll have to cultivate some nice midgets.

(*ROSAMUND comes in hurriedly. She has a small suitcase in one hand and some night-clothes etc., in the other.*)

ROSAMUND: Quick! Shut the door, John.

LALLAH: What on earth are you doing?

ROSAMUND: Marcus and I are going abroad. I'm getting out while I can.

JOHN: (*Together.*) Good for you, Ros. D'you want any help?

LALLAH: (*Together.*) Oh Ros. Where – whereabouts are you going then?

ROSAMUND: Paris and then Berlin. Yes, you could do something for me, John. Have you some spare cash to cash me a cheque? (*She opens the suitcase and starts jamming her things into it.*)

JOHN: (*Starting for the door.*) I'll see what I've got. Will twenty-five pounds do you?

ROSAMUND: Oh, plenty, you are a lamb.

(*JOHN hurries out.*)

LALLAH: I'll keep cave.

(*She takes up a position from which she can see onto the landing. ROSAMUND goes on packing.*)

ROSAMUND: Mother locked the door of my room so I couldn't get in; she'd forgotten the airing cupboard!

LALLAH: That was lucky – Ros, I must tell you, John's found a flat for us!

ROSAMUND: I *am* glad, darling.

LALLAH: I do wish you had time to see it. It's above what used to be stables and has its own little staircase leading up to the front door – I know we're going to be happy there. Look out, here's Uncle. (*They bundle the suitcase and ROSAMUND's night-clothes out of sight as ALFRED comes in.*) Oh, hullo, Uncle, d'you want anything?

ALFRED: What? Want anything? I don't know what I want.

LALLAH: Did you go to the club?

ALFRED: Club? No. No, I didn't go to the club. Thought I'd go tomorrow. (*He grunts and goes out.*)

LALLAH: (*Taking up her stand by the door again.*) Oh yes! So do you know what it reminded me of? Grace Moore in *One Night of Love.* Everybody leaning out of their windows and bursting into song.

(*JOHN comes back with a wad of bank-notes.*)

JOHN: (*As he hands the notes to ROSAMUND.*) Twenty-five.

ROSAMUND: Thanks, John, you're a lamb.

(*Puts the money in her handbag, tears the cheque out, gives it to him and applies herself to re-packing.*)

115

JOHN: (*Taking it.*) Thanks, Ros...anything else I can do?

ROSAMUND: Oh blast! I haven't packed any toothpaste – doesn't matter, doesn't matter! Don't go for it!

JOHN: I'll just nip up to the bathroom.

ROSAMUND: It's not worth it – I'll get some –
(*But he has gone.*)
(*Starting to pull her coat on.*) Nobody's lurking, are they, Lallah?

LALLAH: It's all right, coast's clear.

ROSAMUND: (*With anxious uncertainty.*) He's supposed to signal me from the street when he's got a cab, but...
I've half a mind to go straight across.
(*She goes onto the balcony and looks down into the street.*)

LALLAH: (*Deserting her post.*) You will write? Let me know where you are.

ROSAMUND: No cab there yet.
(*MARY makes a sudden dramatic entrance. Pale and staring-eyed she stands, half collapsing against the wall.*)

LALLAH: Oh!
(*For a second or two she hovers between her mother and the suitcase which she tries to conceal. The suitcase falls to the floor, spilling its contents. MARY comes slowly into the room. LALLAH becomes aware of her mother's expression.*)
Mother! Mother, whatever's the matter?

MARY: Oh, I feel so peculiar... I've never felt so peculiar.
(*Her eyelids droop and close and she drops on to a chair. ROSAMUND comes in from the balcony.*)

LALLAH: Ros, quickly!... Oh, Mummy darling...
(*Unloosening MARY's dress.*) Water!... Ros, get some water, hurry. And smelling salts.

ROSAMUND: (*As she hurries out.*) Oh Lord!

LALLAH: John! John! – oh, he's getting the toothpaste...
Mummy!
(*Pause.*)
It's Lallah, Mother.

MARY: (*Opening her eyes.*) Don't tell Ros. You won't will you? *Whatever happens.* But I've just taken eleven aspirins.

LALLAH: What!

MARY: I put you on your honour not to tell.

LALLAH: But Mother... (*She looks, and finds bottle.*) That was in the medicine cupboard, wasn't it? – there were only four or five left, so, Mummy you couldn't have taken eleven.

MARY: Oh! Four or five! Eleven! What difference does it make? You're only supposed to take two.

ROSAMUND: (*Coming back with a glass of water.*) What happened? Did she faint or something?
(*LALLAH makes way for her and she kneels down, holding the water to MARY's lips.*)

MARY: (*Feebly.*) Is that Rosamund? Thank you...something's going round and round in my head, and my ears are singing.

ROSAMUND: Poor Mummy...do you think an aspirin would do any good?

MARY: Come closer to me, baby... Don't leave me darling – you won't, will you, when I'm so ill –

ROSAMUND: Mother, don't *say* things like that to me! It's, it's so *unfair.*

MARY: If you only knew how ill I am.

JOHN: (*He has come downstairs and is watching from the doorway.*) Hadn't you better get going, Rosamund. (*He holds up a tube of toothpaste for her to see and drops it into the open suitcase.*) Lallah and I can look after your mother.

MARY: Ros dear, I'm much too ill to be left.

JOHN: I can't stand this. (*He turns angrily and goes upstairs.*)

ROSAMUND: (*With sudden resolution, controlling herself.*) I'm going to phone the doctor.

MARY: No, no! Wait a minute. Rosamund, come here. Come here, I want to tell you something.
(*She stretches a hand out, inviting ROSAMUND to take it. The invitation accepted, she turns a piteous, imploring gaze on her daughter.*)
You might as well know, darling, I overheard everything that went on between you and that man just now. I heard him using every kind of cheap trick and subterfuge to get you to run away with him. Can you wonder that I feel so ill? Not that I blame you, darling, but I see now

that you're besotted with this man. All I ask is that you postpone it. Think of your mother. Think of what she went through – what she underwent –

(*She clings to ROSAMUND. ALFRED hobbles in.*)

ALFRED: What's going on? Screeching and shouting.

MARY: Alfred! Rosamund's going off with that scoundrel. Can't you say something?

ALFRED: Madness, that's what it is.

MARY: Ros, you're not going? Say you're not going!

ROSAMUND: I *can't*, Mother. How *can* I say it?

MARY: Lallah! Lallah darling, you ask her.

LALLAH: Oh, I don't know... I – Ros, perhaps it is the wrong time now to –

ALFRED: Why don't you listen to what your mother says instead of running off like a lunatic?

ROSAMUND: Oh, Uncle, surely you understand! What made you want to go and live at the club?

ALFRED: Club?... Club?... Mere suggestion, that's all. No intention of living at the club.

MARY: There you are, you see, Rosamund. Your uncle's not going. Stay with your mother until she's a little better. Dearest, think of the lovely times we could have together – like, we used to, darling, when you were children and we all went to *The Mikado.*

ROSAMUND: 'When we were children' – we *were* children, it was a thousand years ago.

(*SYLVIE comes in and with a quick summing-up glance at the rest of them makes for her favourite chair.*)

SYLVIE: Tch! Nothing but scenes lately, morning, noon and night. What is it now?

ALFRED: She's taken it into her head to go running off with that young scoundrel.

SYLVIE: Out of her mind. Ought to be locked up.

ROSAMUND: (*Suddenly hard.*) Well, I'm going to finish packing. (*She makes a movement towards the suitcase.*)

MARY: Ros!... Oh, *you* say something, Sylvie.

SYLVIE: Oh, now, come. What about you poor old aunt? What's her life going to be without you to cheer us all up?

ROSAMUND: But you said you were selling some shares and going out to India.

SYLVIE: India! Out of the question. Couldn't address Bertie's letter.

ROSAMUND: Aunt Sylvie, don't you see? You and Uncle and Mother and even Goosey, it's too late for you to alter your lives now. It's too late. But I won't go on with this same old life here until it's too late for me as well!

MARY: Now listen, Rosamund. Have you ever known me to tell you a lie?

ROSAMUND: Oh Mother! I don't know, I can't remember.

MARY: (*With an air of having been triumphantly vindicated she turns to ALFRED and SYLVIE.*) You see? You can all bear witness that never have I been know to tell my children a lie. Until today, that is. Until this evening. I'm afraid I have to tell you, Rosamund, that in a last desperate effort to save you, I've taken eighteen aspirins.

ROSAMUND: (*Going to her.*) Mother! You silly ass!

ALFRED: Make yourself ill!

SYLVIE: Eighty aspirins? She'll kill herself.

ROSAMUND: Mummy! I think I'd better phone the doctor after all.

MARY: No! Don't do that!

ROSAMUND: You haven't really taken eighteen, have you?

MARY: Oh, I don't know. You couldn't expect me to count them. If you'll promise to stay with me, that's the only sort of doctor I want.

(*ROSAMUND's face hardens into an expression of exasperation and despair.*)

SYLVIE: Pros or prins were they? Pros or prins?

MARY: I beg your pardon.

SYLVIE: Were they *aspros* or *aspirins?*

MARY: Aspros I think.

SYLVIE: Nothing to worry about then... Don't affect the heart, it says so.

MARY: (*Indignantly.*) My ears are ringing and something's going round and round in my head.

LALLAH: (*Sotto voice to ROSAMUND.*) She'd only got five. Five! (*She runs out.*)

ALFRED: Be all right when she's had some dinner.

SYLVIE: That's right.

MARY: Yes, stay and have dinner with your family, Ros, and we'll talk it over quietly.

(*The gong sounds.*)

SYLVIE: There, it's time to dress.

MARY: Now you see, we'll go and dress and come down to dinner in our customary way. Go along, Sylive. Go along, Alfred.

ALFRED: Be able to talk sensibly with a bit of dinner in our bellies. (*He hobbles out.*)

SYLVIE: (*Following him.*) She'll run away while we're dressing.

MARY: She will do nothing of the sort.

SYLVIE: How do you know she won't?

MARY: (*Turning at the door she says deliberately and with barely concealed triumph.*) I put you on your honour not to go. (*And she follows her sister.*)

(*From across the road a piano is heard being played. ROSAMUND sits down weakly on the sofa and is shaken for a moment by something which is neither laughing nor crying but a mixture of both. After a moment or two she comes to a decision. Bundling her spilled clothes into the suitcase, she takes up her case, gives the drawing-room a last look of farewell, and all eagerness for the new life she is about to embark on, moves to the door. But she doesn't go out. Instead she retreats backwards as the door is pushed open and JO comes in.*)

ROSAMUND: What are you doing here?

JO: (*She is terribly agitated.*) That dotty old woman – what's she called? Goosey – let me in.

ROSAMUND: What do you want?

JO: (*A moment's silence then she bursts out.*) Rosamund, you can't *do* this to me! You simply can't do this.

ROSAMUND: Oh. (*A pause.*) I'm sorry, but I don't see that it's any concern of yours.

JO: You know, don't you, that I'm Marco's wife.

ROSAMUND: No, I don't know. You and Marcus aren't married and you never were, I know *that.*

JO: (*After a slight pause.*) But does it matter? Do *you* think it matters? Everybody accepts me as his wife, so what's the difference? Tell me, *what is the difference?*

ROSAMUND: Not so loud, Jo, please. You may like to think of yourself as Marco's wife, but you don't care for him. And you never have.

JO: Not care. Me? Me?... God, this is insane! It's ludicrous! I dote on him, I love that man as much as anybody *could* be loved!

ROSAMUND: How could you love him when you scarcely let a night go by without taking some man or other into bed with you?

JO: What's that got to do with caring and loving? One doesn't 'care' for a gorgeous dinner and feel 'love' for it. One eats it. And never wants to see it again.
(*A pause.*)

ROSAMUND: Well, I must go. Do you mind letting me by, please.

JO: (*With a despairing gesture; brushing her hair from her eyes.*) Oh God...listen to me, just for a moment. If only you could understand what you were doing to me then perhaps you wouldn't go.

ROSAMUND: Then I don't want to understand.

JO: (*After a pause.*) You don't know what happened to me, Rosamund – when I was a bloody tiny tot – I was a terrified small child of nine years old and I was raped. By my own father.

ROSAMUND: Oh good God!... Good God! Jo...

JO: Oh! I know everybody says I'm just a raving sex-mad nympho – but I never gave way until after Marco decided he wanted a change of diet every now and then. And now – I've become addicted. I'm an addict. But, Rosamund, listen – I could give it up, without a moment's thought, if Marco and I could be together again. God... (*Brushing past ROSAMUND, she sinks into a chair.*) A drink, a short drink of some kind?

ROSAMUND: You do look rather white – only it would mean –

JO: No, no, it doesn't matter... (*She breaks down and starts to weep.*) I'm sorry, but I'm in such an emotional state.
I mean when I finally got it out of Marco that you were going away together... Marcus is my home – you see, I haven't any home but Marcus!

ROSAMUND: But...but what about your parents? Your family?

JO: I tell you I've had nobody to turn to, nobody at all. Until I met Marco.
(*She waits for a response but ROSAMUND remains mute.*)
Oh Ros, what's going to *happen* to me? What's going to become of me if you take Marco away? Listen! You know these old girls you see huddled up in the exit doorways of the London Pavilion – dressed in filthy old rags and with newspapers to keep out the cold...that's *me*. I absolutely know it! That's how I shall finish up if you take Marco away – I will, I know I will...huddled in rags and newspapers, and...and... (*Her voice becomes choked with sobs.*) all purple-faced and hideous, from m-m-methylated spirits...

ROSAMUND: I don't see why you should be so certain that –

JO: Well, what *else* could happen to me? I haven't got well-off parents and relations. I haven't a talent for anything. But darling, listen to me, Ros, listen – if you were to back out now, and I were to go to him – Oh, I know it's a devastating thing I'm asking –

ROSAMUND: Don't make me give him up. Please, please don't make me!

JO: What do you mean, *make you?* How can I *make* you do anything? I'm asking this of you because you're understanding and compassionate.

ROSAMUND: I wouldn't give him up for my mother, my family, why must I give him up for you?

JO: *Why? Why?* What can I say? I could say 'because I love him.' But what would be the point? You love him tóo. All right, don't deny you love him – but my love for Marc, it's...oh dear sweet Rosamund, can't you understand this?... My love for Marc is the one sane, decent thing I've got... And I'm his sort of person. (*She collapses, seems to go completely to pieces, hiding her face in her hands, shaken with sobs. ROSAMUND looks down at her with increasing perturbation.*)

ROSAMUND: Come on, Jo...come on now...

JO: (*The sobs gradually diminishing as, with hiccups and catching of breath, she gasps out.*) I thought if you could send him across a note – you could say your mother was taking it so badly – that you simply couldn't bring yourself to go, he'll be in such a state of turmoil – you know what Marco is – all teed-up for the Golden Arrow tonight and wanting more than ever now to get out of this bloody country, he won't care much whether I come with him or not. And that will give me my chance! Rosamund? (*ROSAMUND says nothing.*) Oh, ducky... Will you write the note now?

ROSAMUND: (*As though from a distance.*) What?... Yes, write the note. (*But she makes no move to do so.*)

JO: There isn't much time, is there... I mean, if...

ROSAMUND: I'm *going* to do it, I'm *going* to do it!

JO: You really will?

ROSAMUND: I'm going to do it, I told you.

JO: (*She gives a noisy sigh of relief and sinks onto a nearby chair.*) Thank God! (*After a moment, seeing that ROSAMUND is standing turned away from her and still as a statue, JO suddenly produces a flask of whisky and treats herself to a long, furtive swig. Wiping her mouth with her hand, she is only just in time to whisk the flask out of sight as ROSAMUND, emerging from her trance-like immobility turns in her direction.*) I don't know what made me say 'Thank God' when what I meant was 'Thank Ros.'

ROSAMUND: (*Flatly.*) Yes... (*She takes a fountain-pen from her handbag and, crossing to the escritoire, sits at it, her back to JO. After a while she stirs herself to pull a sheet of writing paper towards her. But merely sits staring down at it. Unobserved behind her, JO,*)

with quick cautious glances, produces a lipstick and 'flapjack'
with which she starts making up her face.)

ROSAMUND: (*Suddenly erupting though without raising her
voice.*) I can't do it! I'm sorry, I cannot write this lying
rubbish!

JO: (*Who has hastily stowed away the make-up.*) ...You're not
going through with it then?
(*Pause.*)

ROSAMUND: (*Turning to her impulsively.*) I'm sorry, I'm
sorry, Jo. Don't take any notice of that. (*She turns back to
the desk.*) Jo, my family are almost certain to look in on
their way down after the second gong goes.

JO: Oh, I don't want to run into *them*. (*She starts to go, but
turns at the door and says hesitantly.*) Ros?... I feel I must...

ROSAMUND: Please...don't.

JO: No... (*Then with a lasting glance at ROSAMUND she
murmurs almost inaudibly.*) Try not to be too un – (*She
stops short.*)

ROSAMUND: (*Still staring down at the writing paper.*) What?

JO: Nothing.

(*She goes quickly, closing the drawing-room door.
ROSAMUND waits, listening, till sounds from ground floor
tell her that JO is out of the house. A constraint seems to be
lifted and she gets to her feet and paces the room, her emotions
made audible by occasional low-toned, furious utterance of
disjointed words and sentences on a single theme. She sits at
the desk again. With a great lung-emptying sigh of anger and
despair and she takes up her pen and starts writing: quickly,
so as not to give herself time to think. She is folding the note
when the sound of MARCUS's mouth organ – his favourite
'Bal Musette' music – floats up from the street. ROSAMUND
gets to her feet, moves towards the balcony, stops, hesitates
and, all at once, breaking down, abandons herself to grief.
After a few minutes MARCUS stops playing. ROSAMUND
manages to control herself, and pulling the nose-ring off her
wrist and wrapping the note round it, she goes onto the balcony.
MARCUS, who has started to play again, stops abruptly and
whistles two cheerful notes of greeting. But with a gesture of*

*negation ROSAMUND throws the note and the ring down
to him and running back into the room closes the French
windows and stands for a moment holding them as though
they might burst open and let MARCUS back into her life.
Then, as if to make this doubly impossible she draws the
heavy curtains. After that she dries her eyes and, crossing to
the mirror, makes some attempt to hide the, traces of her
tears. Having done this she goes to the door and looks out onto
the landing.)*

ROSAMUND: Oh, Goosey? If... Mr Eversley knocks at the door will you...not open it?

MISS DUCIE: (*Off.*) That's the spirit.

ROSAMUND: And make sure nobody else does.

MISS DUCIE: (*Off.*) Play up. Play up! And play the game!

*(ROSAMUND comes back into the room and almost immediately
MARY comes in, her dinner dress not yet fastened at the back.)*

MARY: Oh, Ros...

ROSAMUND: You heard what I said to Goosey?

MARY: Yes, dear. What...have you...?

ROSAMUND: He's going abroad.

MARY: You mean...for good.

ROSAMUND: I don't know.

MARY: You don't know. Then... (*Pause.*) Then you've finished with him.

(ROSAMUND nods.)

Oh, thank God!

*(She hurries back to the landing. A knock at the front door.
ROSAMUND draws herself up.)*

(Calling up the stairs.) Alfred! Sylvie!

(She returns to the drawing-room.)

Oh, my dearest, everything's going to be all right! We'll forget these last few weeks as though they were nothing but a horrid nightmare.

*(She kisses her daughter tenderly. ROSAMUND, controlling
her trembling with difficulty, waits tensely for the next knock.)*

There, baby, you see your mother's not such an old fool after all. (*Sniffing, she dabs her nose with a handkerchief.*) Do me up at the back, will you dear?

(*ROSAMUND obeys her mechanically. ALFRED comes in wearing his dress trousers and stiff shirt and holding a collar.*)

ALFRED: What's all this? Has Ros come to her senses, Mary?

MARY: Didn't I say she would?

(*A knock at the front door, louder this time.*)

ALFRED: There's a good girl, Ros. Nothing to look so glum about. Cheer up for Chatham and Dover. Give your old uncle a kiss, my dear.

(*ROSAMUND touches her lips to his cheek.*)

Come on, this won't do. Tears? You're a big girl now.

MARY: (*Blowing her nose.*) Let me do your collar for you, Alfred.

ALFRED: Thank you, my dear. I don't know what I should do without you.

(*SYLVIE comes in in her dressing-gown.*)

SYLVIE: Were you calling out, Mary? What is it? Has she given him up?

(*A knock at the front door, louder than ever, followed by a succession of knocks. ROSAMUND suddenly rushes across the room and closes the drawing room door which has been left open.*)

MARY: It's all right, Sylvie. Everything's going to be all right.

SYLVIE: I'm very pleased to hear it. Give your old aunt a kiss, my dear.

(*She holds out her arms. ROSAMUND without any emotion crosses to her and, as with ALFRED, merely touches her lips to the ancient cheek.*)

Sorry if I said unkind things to you. All forgotten now.

LALLAH: (*Bursting into the room in her cami-knickers over which she has thrown a peignoir.*) What's happening? What's happened?

MARY: Go and get dressed, Lallah! – like that in front of your uncle.

(*A rapid machine gun fire of knocking is heard from downstairs.*)

ROSAMUND: For God's sake close the door after you.

(*She runs and bangs it to herself.*)

LALLAH: Sorry – sorry darling. Aren't you going then? Aren't you going after all?

ROSAMUND: No, I'm not. Silly, isn't it. After all those preparations.

MARY: Lallah, dearest, we're all going to be happy again. Our life will be just like it was before. Don't you be the only one to spoil it.

LALLAH: Why should I spoil it, Mother?

SYLVIE: What's this box here by the screen?

ROSAMUND: It's the vase. It's mended.

ALFRED: (*Together.*) Jessie's vase! Jessie's vase mended!

SYLVIE: (*Together.*) The vase? Put together! Where is it?

MARY: (*Together.*) Oh, but my dear, how wonderful!

LALLAH: (*Together.*) Quickly, the vase. Where is it? Do let me see it again!

(*Everyone but ROSAMUND converges on the screen and in a second LALLAH comes from behind it, triumphantly carrying the vase.*)

ALFRED: Stupendous, I call it!

SYLVIE: Very good of you, Rosamund.

ROSAMUND: (*Without expression.*) Mr Eversley paid.

LALLAH: Let's put it back in it's old place of honour.

MARY: Yes, do, my dear. The pedestal has looked rather empty.

LALLAH: Someone pull the curtains back.

ALFRED: Here, let me, my dear.

ROSAMUND: No!

(*He doesn't hear her and continues to pull them back. LALLAH and MARY lift the vase onto its pedestal.*)

ALFRED: Well, I never thought to see Jessie's vase in its old place again.

SYLVIE: Rivets! Nothing but rivets!

MARCUS: (*Voice off, from the street.*) Rosamund?... Rosamund?

(*ROSAMUND looks trapped; she gives a frantic glance around the room then goes quickly to the escritoire and sits at it, her hands pressed to her ears.*)

(*Voice off. A last appeal.*) Pozzy, for God's sake!... For God's sake, Pozzy!

(*JOHN appears in the doorway. Except that his tie is not yet tied he is dressed for dinner.*)

JOHN: (*In a low, shocked voice.*) Lallah!

LALLAH: Oh John, Ros isn't going after all, nobody's going, the vase is mended and we're all so happy and everything's going to be like it was before...

JOHN: (*After a pause.*) Will you say that again, please?

LALLAH: Wha...wha...what do you mean?

JOHN: I'm asking you to repeat what you said to me then.

LALLAH: Oh dear...what *did* I say?

(*ROSAMUND takes her hands down from her ears and looks at her sister as LALLAH continues.*)

I said... I think I said, 'Ros, isn't going and we're all so happy, and – everything's going to...to be... (*Her voice trailing away.*) like...it...was before...

(*JOHN, glaring at LALLAH, gives vent to a monstrous and almost indescribable sound: a cry, a shout, a growl, a snarl; suddenly up comes his clenched fist. LALLAH flinches, but instead of hitting her he smashes it with painful force into the wall.*)

Johnny!

(*He stares at her for a moment with a piercing concentration of anger that leaves her trembling and stalks out of the room. Tears spring to her eyes, LALLAH stands rooted, fingers pressed against her tightly-closed lips, and making faint whimpering sounds.*)

MARY: (*Brightly.*) Here? What are we all doing, walking about half dressed and half undressed? I never heard of such a thing! Come along Alfred, come on, Sylvie. There's some lovely mulligatawny soup to start with and, for a special treat, jugged hare. All such silly-billies at lunch not eating anything. Go on, be off with you. We'll have the second gong going.

(*By this time she has shooed them all outside. Except ROSAMUND.*)

Aren't you dressing tonight, Ros?

ROSAMUND: I haven't the time.

MARY: Well, cheer up. Cook's making one of her Cabinet Puddings. I know you can never have enough Cabinet

Pudding, can you, darling? And (*Confidentially.*)
I thought we'd go off on our own tomorrow afternoon,
shall we? Go to a matinee.
(*ROSAMUND says nothing.*)
We'll keep it as our own little secret then... You see, your
mother isn't such an old fool after all, is she, Ros?
ROSAMUND: No Mummy, I agreed you weren't.
MARY: Thank you, dearest. (*She turns to go but turns back.*)
You know, the time will come when you'll look back on
all this and you'll thank your lucky stars that, in the end,
your good sense and your love for your family prevailed
and you listened to my advice. (*A pause; then, almost
hesitantly.*) Ros?
ROSAMUND: Yes Mother?
MARY: Try not to be too unhappy. (*She gives her daughter a
little pat and takes herself off, pausing at the foot of the stairs
to call cheerfully.*) Don't be late down.
(*ROSAMUND waits until her mother is out of earshot then
springs into action. First she goes and attends to her suitcase.
Then she hurries to the telephone. She lifts the receiver and
waits, nervously impatient.*)
ROSAMUND: Hello? Sloane five-eight-nine-five please –
Hello, is that the taxi rank? Will you come to twenty-five
Adelaide Gardens please. Now. Immediately. Yes, that's
right, just round the corner... Oh, and...hello...are you
still there?... Look. I shall come down and be waiting for
you...yes, so there's no need to knock or ring... Thank
you. (*She hangs up. Waits for a moment, then lifts the receiver
again.*) Hello?
(*Apparently no one answers. The sound of voices in the street
causes her to wince and pucker her brows as though with a
headache. The voices belong to MARCUS and JO and to others
who are calling desultory goodbyes. Turning her back on the
balcony, trying not to hear, ROSAMUND gives all her
attention to the telephone.*)
Hello?...are you there? Freemantle nine-three-four-six
please... Hello! Is that Donna? (*She lowers her voice even
further but the tone is more urgent.*) Rosamund. Donna,

listen, is that studio of Vince's still free?... Oh *good*...
The thing is, do I qualify? I'm not a painter, but I am
a writer who's a member of the human race and
I desperately need somewhere of my own where I can
be myself and write. So... Oh, thank goodness. Well,
from tonight, if I could... Indefinitely... Yes, now...
Donna, I can't thank you enough. In about a quarter of
an hour then.

(*She drops back the receiver and goes for her suitcase. As she
takes hold of it the loud honking of a taxi horn brings her up
short. Exasperated, she dashes, case in hand, onto the balcony
and leaning over the balustrade, calls out.*)

Coming. I'm just coming down. Don't hoot any more!
Won't be a minute.

(*She swings round, and in her haste to escape from the drawing
room, knocks into the pedestal. The repaired vase is sent flying
and shatters to smithereens. ROSAMUND pauses only for a
quick intake of breath before she is out of the room, across the
landing, down the stairs and into the street. As the front door
closes the second gong sounds. Someone is beating it with a
fury of excessive energy and the booming, great, clangour –
echoing hollow sound grows, expands, swells and reverberates
through the house. Doors are heard to open. Then the sound of
voices as MARY, ALFRED and SYLVIE emerge from their
rooms and make their way down the stairs to dinner.*)

The End.

STRANGE ORCHESTRA

Characters

VERA LYNDON

GEORGE

VAL

ESTHER
Vera's daughter

FREDA

LAURA

JIMMIE

JENNY
Vera's daughter

GORDON
Vera's son

PETER

SYLVIA

Strange Orchestra was first performed at the Embassy Theatre, Swiss Cottage, and later at the St Martin's Theatre, London on 27 September 1932, with the following cast:

VERA LYNDON, Laurie Cowrie

GEORGE, David Hutcheson

VAL, Robert Harris

ESTHER, Mary Casson

FREDA, Nadine March

LAURA, Carol Rees

JIMMIE, Leslie French

JENNY, Jean Forbes-Robertson

GORDON, Clifford Bartlett

PETER, Hugh Williams

SYLVIA, Elizabeth Astor

Producer, John Gielgud

The scene throughout is the hall of
Vera Lyndon's flat near Chelsea

Act I: Evening

Act II: Evening. Three weeks later

Act III: Morning. Some weeks later

ACT ONE

*The hall of VERA LYNDON's flat near Chelsea. Evening. It is
extremely untidy and littered with hand-painted furniture. The front
door is at the back of the stage to the right. Two doors in the right
wall lead to bedrooms. Another door down left also leads to a bedroom.
Through an archway up left are two short corridors. One going off
left parallel to the footlights, leads to the kitchen: the other, which
goes towards the back of the stage to the bathroom and more bedrooms.
A staircase left leads up to yet another bedroom.*

*The most conspicuous object of the room is a large divan. On the edge
of this is seated VERA, who is about forty, and inclined to be stout.
Before her is a moveable oil-stove. She has no shoes on, and is balancing
a tray on her lap and eating a hard-boiled egg and buttered toast.
From a room on the right comes the sound of a ukelele and a voice
singing 'Make Yourself a Happiness Pie'. Presently the singer comes
from his room. He is a hearty young man named GEORGE, and is
wearing a dressing-gown. Leaning against the door, he continues
playing.*

VERA: Ooh, go away, you awful boy.

GEORGE: (*Down below the door.*) I say, Mrs Lyndon, don't
you think this is rather decent? (*He strums.*)

VERA: Oh, how awful! Do go away. I don't like you. I don't
know why I ever let you come here. Besides, you owe
me some rent.

GEORGE: I... I know. I'm fearfully sorry, but it's only for
one week...

VERA: Well, the only reason I've let you live here is
because you've paid *regularly*, so if you don't you'll have
to *go*, because you're much too awful and masculine to
have about the place.

GEORGE: I'll pay you both weeks at once on Saturday. (*He
turns on the gramophone.*)
(*VAL, a wild and unhappy-looking man, bursts out of his
room down left.*)

VAL: Do please stop making that horrible row! It's dreadful!
I can't write a word, let alone think.

GEORGE: All right. All right. You haven't bought the place. I've a perfect right to play.

VAL: Not here, this is Vera's room, and I'm trying to write in mine.

VERA: Oooh, do go away, you awful boys.

(*GEORGE takes the gramophone off.*)

VAL: Go away when she tells you.

VERA: (*Rubbing her chest.*) Oooh, that egg's given me indigestion.

GEORGE: Rotten, what!

VERA: No, quite new laid.

VAL: Ha, ha!

(*He goes back to his room and slams the door.*)

GEORGE: What did he say? (*He sits right of table and puts his feet up on a chair, bringing it down slightly.*)

VERA: I don't know. (*She drinks some tea.*)

GEORGE: (*Strumming quietly as he speaks.*) It was about five in the morning before I got back from that party last night. It was great. You know – finished up with all the lights out. There was a girl named Sylvia there. She was marvellous. (*He sticks out his lower jaw and strums viciously.*)

VERA: (*Shuddering.*) Oooh, how awful!

GEORGE: (*Stops strumming.*) What did you say, Mrs Lyndon?

VERA: (*Standing up, her mouth full.*) Stop calling me Mrs Lyndon, and go away. (*Crossing to him.*) My vibrations are quite out of tune with yours this evening.

GEORGE: Look here, do you really want me to go? (*He gets up.*)

VERA: Yes, I do.

(*GEORGE strums.*)

And don't play any more.

GEORGE: Oh, all right, rather. I'll put the old uke away. Cheerio!

VERA: Oooh!

GEORGE: What's the matter? (*Looking rather bewildered, he goes into his room down right.*)

(*VERA takes the tray and goes towards the kitchen, but changes her mind, and going towards VAL's doors, says:*)

VERA: Val, you dear little thing, are you working?

VAL: (*Off.*) I'm sort of trying to, but I can't. Shall I come and be cheered up?

VERA: Yes, do, darling. It's nice and warm in here.
(*As she speaks she walks back to the divan and sits on it, placing the tray beside her. VAL comes from his room down left.*)
Poor ickle Val, you look so sad and miserable.

VAL: Oh well, I am. Foully – *horribly* miserable. There you are, self-pity. Vera darling, may I put my head on your bosom and cry?

VERA: If you want to, dear.
(*VAL goes to her and puts his head on her bosom. He makes one or two meaningless sounds and then sits up straight.*)

VAL: It's no good, I can't.

VERA: (*Putting her hand through his hair.*) You dear little thing!

VAL: Don't call me that, darling.

VERA: I can't help it, you're my own favourite little lodger! (*With a heavy sigh.*) I wish I was a beautiful young cutie and then I'd make you fall in love with me and we'd be so happy. Now come on, let me cook you something nice in the kitchen.

VAL: I owe you six weeks' rent. I can't sort of go on accepting things from you and never giving you a penny. It's wrong.

VERA: Never mind! I'll add ten shillings to Freda's rent – a big room like that's worth it, and she's got plenty of money.

VAL: (*Laughing.*) You are sweet, Vera dear. Some things are right and some are wrong. Don't be silly.

VERA: Your vibrations are wrong, dear, that's the whole trouble.

VAL: (*Getting up and walking across to the table.*) Is that why I haven't had a word accepted for weeks, and why my novel's turning out pure bilge?

VERA: It's all vibrations, dear.

VAL: (*Turning to her.*) Well, it *isn't* bilge, it's grand.

VERA: I wish you'd have some food. Come along. (*She rises.*)
(*GEORGE starts to strum loudly off down right. VAL runs across and bangs on his door. The music stops. VAL sits down above table. There is a pause which he breaks by saying:*)

That horrible George is in early. I suppose the rest of the rabble will arrive soon. (*Crossing to VAL.*) I don't care what you say about the lodgers, Jenny and Esther are all right. None of my three children are rabble. But I never quite know what Gordon means: sometimes he seems just masculine and silly.

VAL: Do you think that's because his father was?

VERA: Yes. You're quite right, it is. I never really cared for Gordon's father, and whenever he kissed me I used to shut my eyes and pretend it was somebody else.

VAL: Who? Clark Gable?

VERA: No...just anybody... Jenny and Esther's father was different. (*She sits left of table.*) Do you know, I really loved my divine Lyndon, Val! (*She sighs.*) But he left me. And I'm all alone now with no one to love. And he went abroad with that awful woman. Do you think one day she'll die, and then he'll come back to me? He might, you know. Look, I'm crying, Val. And I haven't got a hanky. (*She wipes her eyes with her hand.*) Oh, dear. Come and kiss me.

(*VAL gets up and does so.*)

I don't know what I should do without you.

(*VAL sits again.*)

VAL: (*Suddenly.*) Vera – do you know why I'm so horribly miserable, and why everything seems to go wrong? I'm in love with Esther.

VERA: Yes, I know.

VAL: What shall I do? I know she sort of hates me.

VERA: I wish you could make her love you. It's awful to see her all suppressed and nebulous.

VAL: Being a typist's not too inspiring.

VERA: (*Getting up and crossing to divan.*) Her vibrations are all wrong. Look at Jenny, she's happy and perfect. Her vibrations are in tune, you see. It's staggering, Val, I'm sure neither of my daughters have ever been kissed. Properly. In spite of the fact that I've always told them if they want to be successful they must be kissed – properly. (*She sits on divan.*)

VAL: (*Getting up and walking round table.*) What am I going
to do about Esther, Vera? Don't you think it's wrong
for me to love her? I mean, she's so sort of young and
I – I'm sure I don't love her in the real pure sort of way.
I – oh, it's so difficult. Do help me. (*He kneels beside
VERA.*)

VERA: I wish you'd have something to eat.
(*GEORGE starts strumming again.*)

VAL: (*Rising and running in the direction of GEORGE's room.*)
Shut up!
(*After a second, GEORGE appears at his door.*)

GEORGE: Here, steady on, man. What's the excitement?

VAL: I thought Vera told you not to make that disgusting
noise.

VERA: I did, you know, George. (*She gets up from the divan.*)
(*ESTHER, a girl of seventeen, lets herself in at the front
door. She is carrying an attaché case.*)

GEORGE: (*Leaning against his door.*) Well, look here, Mrs
Lyndon, it's a bit thick when I can't play as softly as that.
I thought you wouldn't hear.

VERA: (*To ESTHER.*) Hullo, Esther darling!

ESTHER: Hullo! It's cold tonight. (*She sits down on chair left
of door, placing the case on her knees.*)

GEORGE: Good evening, Miss Lyndon.

ESTHER: Hullo!

VERA: (*Going towards the kitchen.*) Food, darling?

ESTHER: I've had some, thanks.

VERA: Oooh, I've still got this awful tray. I'm divinely
hungry, thank God. (*She takes up the tray and goes towards
the kitchen, calling out.*) Come in the kitchen and I'll cook
you some tomatoes, Val and we'll have a lovely time!
(*Exit VERA and VAL up left.
GEORGE strums a few chords.*)

ESTHER: What's that?

GEORGE: A ukelele.

ESTHER: Oh!

GEORGE: (*Leaning against wall above upstage door right.*) Do
you go to many parties?

ESTHER: No, I don't really.

GEORGE: Don't get much time, I suppose?

ESTHER: Oh well, I...is my sister in, do you know? (*She turns round and calls in the direction of the staircase.*) Jenny! Jenny!

(*There is no answer.*)

She's writing, perhaps. (*Pause.*) Do I look very silly sitting here like this? I'd give anything if my hat and coat could be taken off and my case put away.

GEORGE: (*Stepping to her.*) You are a chump. Why don't you take them off then?

ESTHER: No, I feel like a statue. I'd just like not to move and nothing ever to happen.

GEORGE: You'd soon start moving when you wanted a spot of food, old thing.

ESTHER: (*Looking at him.*) Old what?

GEORGE: What?

ESTHER: Old what? No, it's all right, nothing. Don't continue the conversation. It's silly. Oh well, I suppose I must move some time. (*She gets up and starts to take off her hat and coat.*) Hang them up for me, will you?

(*She hands them to him. He hangs them on hall stand up right.*)

GEORGE: I say, aren't you cold without a fur or anything, this weather?

ESTHER: Of course I'm not – (*She hesitates for a second, wets her lips with her tongue, and then continues.*) Besides, I – I wouldn't – don't ever wear skins of little tortured animals round my neck.

(*GEORGE turns round and gapes.*)

GEORGE: ...What?

ESTHER: (*Coming down centre.*) They're caught in traps that gradually bite through their legs, and they cry all night, and sometimes they gnaw away their own legs to escape, and worse than that even –

GEORGE: But – they're only animals.

VERA: (*Coming out of the kitchen with frying pan.*) Esther darling, if you have a crumpet *with* a poached egg it gives you a lovely gooey feeling in your inside.

VAL: (*From kitchen.*) Quick, the kettle's boiling over!

VERA: (*Running into kitchen.*) Oh!

(*GEORGE and ESTHER continue looking at each other.
At last ESTHER says:*)

ESTHER: I can't argue tonight. But when people talk about furs I feel it's my duty to tell them, because they don't know. Oh dear! (*She sighs.*) It'd be much easier not to care about anything.

GEORGE: (*Coming down to above table.*) I say, Miss Lyndon, let me give you – er – a piece of friendly advice. Don't get mixed up with any of these cranky movements, they don't do anybody any good.

(*ESTHER sits left of table and says nothing. GEORGE strums and sings: 'Make Yourself a Happiness Pie'.
FREDA, a girl of about twenty-five, ordinarily attractive, with a slightly common voice, comes in at the front door. She goes straight to the stove, feverishly pulling off her gloves.*)

FREDA: (*Pushing ESTHER out of the chair and taking it herself.*) Let me get to the stove. It's terrible. (*Putting her gloves on top of the stove.*) I've never known such a winter. My fingers feel as if they'll drop off. There's no warmth in this stove at all.

ESTHER: (*Crossing to the bookcase left and taking up a war book.*) Hullo, Freda.

FREDA: Hullo, Esther, where's your mother?

ESTHER: She's in the kitchen, cooking something for Val. (*She sits on end of divan.*)

GEORGE: Weather's enough to give you the pip, isn't it? Pretty stiff work down at the film studio, eh?

FREDA: Don't talk to me about the studio. Waiting about all day in the broiling heat, then coming out into the icy cold. I thought I was going to faint about six times. Please, please, would you mind not playing that thing, my head's splitting. Please!

(*GEORGE finishes a phrase hurriedly and stops.*)

I've got to be made up and on the set by nine tomorrow morning. The damn stove's not giving out any heat. Vera might get something to eat for me when I come in. It is mean of her. I can't stand fussing about getting myself food when I come home done up and fagged out. What is the good of being alive? I ask you. There's grease or something spilt on this stove. It's all over my gloves now…

(*She furiously rubs the gloves, muttering at the same time. VERA and VAL come in from the kitchen. They are both eating raw tomatoes, and carry a plate each.*)

VERA: (*To FREDA.*) Somebody must have sneaked the crumpets. I'm really going to have a key to the cupboard and lock them up.

GEORGE: (*Right of table.*) All right – landlady.

FREDA: Look at my gloves. Absolutely ruined.

VERA: (*Taking them.*) Where? I can't see anything.

FREDA: Oh, give them back, you'll spill tomato on them. (*She snatches them away.*)

VERA: Esther, don't read those terrible war books, you'll only be sick. You know what happened the last time you read one.

ESTHER: (*In rather a shaky voice.*) Are you getting all maternal in your old age, darling?

VERA: Well, why be sick when there's no need to? It only makes extra work for me. (*She sits on right side of divan.*)

ESTHER: Because it's silly not knowing what life's really like. One – one might as well know. There's no sense in living in a fool's Paradise.

VAL: (*By the chest of drawers.*) Why not? It might be rather a relief, as a sort of rest.

ESTHER: No, it's wrong. (*She returns to the book.*)
(*There is a pause.*)

FREDA: I don't understand these people who read these awful books. Surely everything's quite miserable enough without reading about horrors.

GEORGE: (*Seated on table.*) That's because you're not a highbrow. (*He lights a pipe.*)

VERA: Oooh, be quiet, you awful boy.

FREDA: (*Getting up and taking off her coat.*) What a life! Can't anybody introduce me to a rich old peer, who'd only want me to sit on his knee and call him 'Daddy.'

VERA: There's something the matter with your vibrations, Freda. I'd be divinely happy if I were you.

FREDA: Why? (*She puts her coat over the back of the chair.*)

VERA: You're young; you could make yourself into a perfect little cutie if you wanted, and get divine parts on the pickshers, and you have the best room in the flat ten shillings cheaper than it ought to be.

FREDA: Divine parts. Don't make me laugh. Maids. I never have a single line to say. (*She sits again.*)

VERA: Too much verbiage distracts attention.

GEORGE: What?

VERA: Too much verbiage distracts attention.

(*VAL laughs and chokes over a tomato.*)

GEORGE: Oh!

(*VAL comes down and sits on divan left by ESTHER.*)

FREDA: (*Starting to comb her hair.*) Such a peculiar thing happened to me on the way home. Quite a well-dressed old woman asked me if I could give her sixpence for a cup of tea. I felt such a fool. I just stuttered something and ran off, and a little while later I saw the same woman coming along with a policeman clutching her arm. It just shows, doesn't it? (*Rising and putting her coat round her shoulders.*) And she was quite well-spoken, too.

ESTHER: What does it just show?

FREDA: Not to give anything to a beggar. I mean they're only kind of crooks really.

ESTHER: (*Jumping up angrily.*) How dare you say that!

FREDA: What? (*She takes a cigarette from a case in her handbag.*)

ESTHER: I wonder what you'd do if you'd gone on and on trying to live and keep – respectable – until you – you hadn't got a penny left in the world – and no friends – and you were old, and there was just nothing! (*She sits again and pretends to read.*)

GEORGE: Oh, but some of these chaps make eight or ten pounds a week, you know.

VERA: Oh, isn't poverty devastating. But it's no good minding about it. Everyone finds their own level. It's all vibrations and Karma.

VAL: There's a marvellous idea for a story in that, you know. The sort of respectable girl brought up in a country vicarage, and sort of marrying the wrong man.

FREDA: (*To GEORGE.*) Give me a light.

(*GEORGE does so.*)

ESTHER: If Freda'd given her something she wouldn't have been arrested. Why is everyone so callous and heartless?

FREDA: All this sentiment is very tiresome. I wish you'd keep quiet about it.

ESTHER: I suppose I'd better, because whatever anybody said you'll always go on being selfish and callous and stupid. (*She shouts the last few words, and makes a pretence of returning to her book, but her mouth is trembling.*)

FREDA: (*Coming centre and speaking to ESTHER.*) Can't you even have an argument without insulting people? It's awful. I told you my head was splitting. Talk about selfish! I'm going to lie down. (*She goes to her room, saying.*) The room'll be as cold as hell, I suppose. (*Her door slams. GEORGE plays the chords which mean 'How's your Father – All Right'. VERA goes into gusts of laughter, her whole form shakes.*)

VERA: Oh, you awful boy. Freda really is rather terrible. She'll have to go. Now who's going to help me do some washing-up? Come on, George, you've been doing nothing all the evening. (*She collects the two plates and goes towards the kitchen, calling.*) No rubbish now. We all have to do the mucky bits sometimes.

GEORGE: I'm damned if I'll do the washing-up for her.

VERA: (*In the kitchen.*) Come along now.

(*He goes. A pause. ESTHER is still reading. VAL hums 'Make Yourself a Happiness Pie'. After repeating the same phrase two or three times, he says:*)

VAL: Oh, curse! I've got that rotten thing on the brain.

ESTHER: You'll have to get another song on the brain instead. It's the only cure.

VAL: (*Lying on divan, head down stage.*) I can't think of another one.

ESTHER: (*Seated left of him.*) Neither can I. (*A pause.*) Was it very childish of me losing my temper with Freda? But

what can you do? Everybody seems the same. Nobody
cares about anything. Even you.

VAL: Oh yes, I do, but what's the good? We can't change
anything.

ESTHER: I know, but...we mustn't all think that. Nothing
would ever change. The world would just get fouler than
ever.

VAL: Perhaps it isn't foul, *really.* Perhaps it's only because
we're young.

ESTHER: Because our minds are clear, you mean. Because
they haven't been all clogged up and doped. Look, read
that, Val. (*She passes her book to him.*)

VAL: No, I can't. I'd have nightmares. Besides, it isn't
happening now, the war was all over fourteen years ago.

ESTHER: But everybody's the same still, aren't they? It's
sure to happen again. And everything's crueller and
stupider than ever.

VAL: I suppose I feel the same underneath, hut I just won't
let myself think about it. (*He lies face upward on divan.*)

ESTHER: No, that's wrong. That's the easy way. I feel one
must try and cope with life, fight all the wickedness in it
and in oneself.

VAL: Yes, but how? Is one to go tub-thumping in Hyde
Park or stamp envelopes for the League of Nations!

ESTHER: It seems the only thing to do, and yet you get the
feeling that that's all –

VAL: Sort of – fusty-musty.

ESTHER: Yes – as if you're a funny old lady waving an
umbrella.

VAL: Yes.

ESTHER: I don't know. (*All at once she starts to cry.*) I feel so
sick and sick of thinking about everything... I almost
feel that I'll give it up altogether and just...let myself be
doped.

VAL: (*Sitting up.*) Don't – don't care about things so much,
Esther dear. It isn't worth it. Make yourself not care.

ESTHER: I can't – it's wrong.

VAL: Perhaps you're right. (*He lies down again on his stomach.*)

(They lapse into silence. Not a lull in the conversation, but a silence of thoughts arising out of it. Unconsciously VAL hums the tune of 'Happiness Pie'. ESTHER interrupts him with:)

ESTHER: What'll you do when the next war comes, Val?

VAL: I don't know. I try not to think about it, or pretend it won't.

ESTHER: *(Rising and speaking to him.)* That's no good. You must face things... When I read a lot of these books I dream that it's happening again, and wake up shivering. And I think – well, when it comes I'll just take poison. But that'd be not coping, wouldn't it? *(She lies on divan beside VAL.)*

VAL: I shall do that, anyway – being an effete young man. What ought one to do?

ESTHER: Stand on soap-boxes and be stoned by the populace, I suppose.

VAL: Perhaps we could stand together and they'd throw the big stones at me.

ESTHER: Mm.

VAL: Esther, if we were in sort of love with each other, do you think you'd come away into the country with me and live in a little cottage with two trees and honeysuckle over the door? Would we be happy? I wonder! *(He lies flat and turns his head to her.)*

ESTHER: I've never been in love, so I can't tell. And anyway, there'd sure to be a farm next door, and I should hear the pigs being killed. *(She sits up.)*

VAL: *(Sitting up.)* Esther, listen. I – I think I'm in love with you. No, don't say anything, let me go on. I know you're not in love with me. You see, I don't believe in sort of D H Lawrence and all that, because I suppose I'm a bit sort of effete or something, and I think if – if you could help me, I could sublimate my love into something quite spiritual, and then we could help each other, and well, you do see what I mean, don't you?

ESTHER: Not quite.

VAL: Well, we could sort of tell each other all our troubles, and if you must stand on a soap-box, I really will come and stand with you. But if I sort of get trying to kiss you,

you mustn't get fed up, but just give me a swipe and tick
me off good and proper until eventually I don't try any
more – will you?

ESTHER: I don't quite know about that. It'd be nice to help
each other, Val. (*She puts her hand on his.*)

VAL: (*Pushing it away, jumping up and going to centre.*) No,
that's just what you mustn't do!

(*LAURA and JIMMIE come in by the front door. They are
both young and both good-looking. JIMMIE is holding a
wrapped-up bunch of daffodils. LAURA has a gramophone
record in a paper bag.*)

JIMMIE: (*Waving the daffodils.*) Look, aren't these
wonderful? Quite cheap, too. All the way from the Scilly
Isles.

VAL: Winter must be nearly over. (*Going up to them.*) They're
the first I've seen.

ESTHER: (*Rising, going to right of divan and speaking
simultaneously.*) Let me smell.

LAURA: (*Coming down to ESTHER.*) Jimmie's been most
gloriously extravagant and naughty, haven't you, darling?
Cartloads of flowers when our others aren't dead yet. And
a record. Look, here it is. (*She holds it up.*) Delius. You
shall hear it in a minute. (*She gives record to VAL.*) And
we've been to *the* perfect pantomime this afternoon.
Wasn't it, darling?

JIMMIE: It was. *The* perfect one. Come along and get
warm at the stove, darling.

ESTHER: (*Smelling the daffodils.*) Aren't they lovely!

JIMMIE: I really got them because they match Laura's
complexion.

LAURA: (*Seated by stove.*) Yellow and green?

JIMMIE: Silly baby. You know what I mean. (*He holds them
against her face and then kisses her.*)

LAURA: Silly pet.

VAL: (*Seated below table with record.*) Well, tell us about the
pantomime.

(*ESTHER is standing left centre.*)

JIMMIE: It wasn't one of those awful West End ones, but
right in the suburbs –

LAURA: We hunted all over the place for it, but it really was the best thing I've ever seen. The Fairy Queen came on and said –

JIMMIE: Oh yes, she waved her wand and –

LAURA: No – you're sure to tell it all wrong. Let me, Jimbo darling.

JIMMIE: You – you behaved abominably. She was jumping up and down in her seat all the time, and when the Dame came on and said, 'It's only the hairs on a gooseberry – '

LAURA: That stop it from being a grape – '

JIMMIE: She laughed so much that the woman in front turned round and said she'd have her put out.

LAURA: But you haven't told about the Fairy Queen, darling.

JIMMIE: Oh no – she was old and knobbly – you know – pink tights and a nightie. She waved her wand in the air and said, 'Ah, what is this I see approach?
(*There is a crash off left.*)
It is Cinderella's electrically lighted Fairy Coach.'
(*VERA comes in up left, followed by GEORGE with a teacloth.*)

VERA: It's no good, you'll have to pay for the plate, you awful boy.

GEORGE: (*At head of divan.*) But, look here, Mrs Lyndon...

VERA: All men are the same, quite unevolved and utterly incompetent.

JIMMIE: Now, children – no quarrelling.

VERA: Go back and pick up the pieces.
(*GEORGE goes.*)

LAURA: Anyway, Jimmie's got an inspiration for a Laura Knighty picture out of it, haven't you, darling?

JIMMIE: Yes, pantomime dames resting, I expect.

LAURA: Well, why not, if someone'd buy it?

VERA: Oh, what divine daffodils. Let me hold them, quick. Oooh, how marvellous. They're too heavenly. (*She takes a tremendous sniff at them.*) Oooh, how wonderful. All I want is some marvellous music and I shall pass right away. (*She comes round right of LAURA to divan with daffodils.*)

LAURA: But we've got some. Here you are. The world's loveliest record.

VAL: Yes, *Paradise Garden.*

VERA: No! No, it's too much. I really can't bear it. We must have it at once. Go on. Put it on the gramophone. (*She sits on the divan.*)

LAURA: All right. Come on, Jimmie beautifuls.

JIMMIE: Half a mo, baby. I won't let that woman confiscate your daffodils.

(*He crosses to VERA.*)

VERA: (*Hugging them.*) Oh, no! Oh, no! I've got to smell them all the time.

LAURA: Well, you must give them back.

(*She and JIMMIE run into their room.*
ESTHER and VAL are over at gramophone.)

VERA: Oh, this is too divine. It's just what I wanted. Flowers and music. Oh, isn't it devastating to be so highly evolved?

(*GEORGE enters from the kitchen and drops the pieces of broken plate into the chest of drawers.*)

GEORGE: What's this record that all the excitement's about? Classical music, eh?

VERA: Really, you know, Laura and Jimmie are so soft and sweet and all loovin'.

GEORGE: (*Coming down left of divan.*) Bet you five bob it doesn't last another fortnight.

VERA: Oooh, go away, you awful boy. All this cynical rubbish isn't a bit clever. Hurry up with the gramophone, you awful children.

(*VAL puts on the gramophone.*)

Oooh, aren't these flowers divine?

(*LAURA and JIMMIE come in again. They are giggling helplessly.*)

VAL: If you've found something funny to laugh about, don't keep it to yourselves, share it with the form.

VERA: Put it down there.

(*FREDA comes in up left.*)

FREDA: What's all the noise? It's not a bit of use me trying to rest.

VERA: Lovely moosic, Freda. Come and sit down.

GEORGE: Join the merry throng.

(*LAURA and JIMMIE are still giggling.*)

LAURA: Jimmie's thought of a sublimely funny word.
Preposterous. (*She goes into shrieks of laughter.*)

VAL: Preposterous?

VERA: Preposterous?

JIMMIE: No, you have to say it like this. (*He mouths it.*)
Preposterous.

(*They all giggle.*)

VAL: How preposterously preposterous.

(*FREDA positively shrieks with mirth. Everyone repeats the word in different tones and accents, until they are all out of breath with laughter. They then subside.*)

VERA: Preposterous – I don't call that funny. Be quiet, I want to listen to the music. Somebody turn the lights out.

(*VAL turns out the lights at the switch up right, so that only the standard lamp up left remains alight. He then comes down and opens the gramophone doors.*)

Now we're all perfect.

(*The others have seated themselves on the divan, on chairs and cushions on the floor. The music is soft and plaintive. VERA sniffs the daffodils ecstatically. GEORGE, standing centre, tries to be funny, pretending to play the piano, rolling his eyes and throwing imaginary locks of hair from his forehead. No one takes any notice, so he desists and goes and sits on the chest of drawers and reads a magazine. FREDA, sitting centre above stove, listens soulfully. VAL and ESTHER, who are sitting near each other on the end of the divan, unconsciously lean nearer. He puts his arm round her, but almost immediately jumps up and goes and stands by the door down right. LAURA and JIMMIE, seated on the floor up stage, are happily cuddling, with occasional kisses. VERA beckons to ESTHER and points to her hair. ESTHER obediently goes and runs the tips of her fingers through it. The front door opens and JENNY, a slight girl of nineteen, comes in. The others 'shush' and VERA motions her to join them, but JENNY shakes her head and goes towards the stairs. ESTHER leaves her mother and goes to JENNY. She whispers.*)

ESTHER: Something's the matter, darling.

JENNY: No there isn't. (*Her voice is strained.*)

ESTHER: There is. I could tell it directly you came in.

JENNY: It's nothing.

(*A pause.*)

ESTHER: I don't believe you.

JENNY: I'm only tired. Truly. (*A pause.*) Idiot!

(*JENNY kisses her sister and runs up the stairs. The door of the room shuts. ESTHER stands where she is. The music stops. For a few seconds there is silence, then JIMMIE says:*)

JIMMIE: Rather good, isn't it?

VERA: Oooh, I think it's too wonderful.

FREDA: (*Yawning.*) I always love classical music. It's infinitely better than jazz. (*She rises and crosses to chair below table.*)

GEORGE: But there's no tune in it. (*He rises from chest-of-drawers and sits in the armchair up centre.*)

VERA: (*Calling out.*) Jenny – come down and have some fun.

ESTHER: No, don't call her. She's got a being alone mood, I think. (*She sits on the stairs.*)

VERA: Oh, all right.

FREDA: Jenny's very unsociable. She's always shutting herself in her room.

ESTHER: Well, perhaps she wants to work.

FREDA: Has she had many stories published lately?

VERA: Two. But that's very good for nineteen, you know.

ESTHER: I should think so.

VAL: I like Jenny's stories. There's a sort of truth in them.

FREDA: (*Sitting on chair below table.*) I hate tales like that, they're so depressing.

VAL: Is truth depressing?

ESTHER: Yes, extremely.

LAURA: (*Rising.*) I want to smell my daffies. Come on, Vera, you've sniffed them quite long enough, and you look awfully silly sitting with them like that. Get them for me, Jimmie.

(*JIMMIE runs to VERA.*)

VERA: No, you're not to have them. They're mine. You must buy some more.

(*JIMMIE struggles with her. In the excitement they both fall off the divan. As they are picking themselves up, GORDON, a young man of about twenty-four, lets himself in at the front door. GEORGE, who has been looking bored during the previous conversation, says loudly:*)

GEORGE: Hullo, Gordon. How's it going?

GORDON: (*Coming down and putting his case at back of table.*) Pretty good, thanks. Jimmie, what on earth are you and mother up to?

VERA: Hullo, my son. Don't call me mother. No, you can't have them.

(*The struggle recommences with scufflings and gigglings.*)

VAL: I sent a novel in to your firm the other day, Gordon. Do you know if it's been sort of read yet?

GORDON: What's it called?

VAL: *Nowhere to Go.* (*He puts the record in its case.*)

GORDON: Oh yes, I've seen it lying about.

VAL: If you have to read it, say it's good, won't you?

GORDON: Not if it's not. (*He takes his hat up to the hall.*)

VERA: Let's toss for them. Yes, you must. Come on, George, where's a penny.

(*GEORGE rises, comes down to her, and gives her a coin.*)

FREDA: Don't you get terribly bored having to read all those awful novels that people send in? I should.

GORDON: Well, you don't read them if you don't like them. And if they're very bad, you get a good laugh.

FREDA: Oh, I see.

VERA: (*After spinning the coin.*) Tails! They're mine!

(*GORDON sits above table and settles to work.*)

LAURA: What!

VERA: Never mind, you awful child, you shall have them. There!

(*She hands them over. LAURA kisses her.*)

Oooh, wasn't it divine listening to the music and smelling them. That's what I call happiness.

FREDA: You're *very* easily pleased.

JIMMIE: She's a sensualist.

(*JIMMIE and LAURA are seated below divan. LAURA on the floor.*)

VERA: What's your idea of happiness, then?

JIMMIE: Being in love with Laura.

VERA: Oooh no, love's awful, it's like a crab clawing at your vitals.

(*GEORGE and GORDON roar with laughter.*)

FREDA: If some nice old man would present me with a million pounds that's about the only happiness I can think of.

VAL: (*In chair next to FREDA.*) Anyway, I don't think there is such a thing. We all sort of look for it, but never find it because it isn't there. My God, I hope that's not the sort of thing I put in my novels.

ESTHER: I don't think anybody'd ever be happy if they troubled to think of all the misery in the world, except through feeling they'd done something to lessen it.

FREDA: We've got quite enough of our own troubles without worrying about other people's.

VAL: (*Getting up and sitting on the table.*) No, really though, don't you think the gift for being happy is something you're born with, the same as a long nose. And if you have it, there it is, and whatever sort of happens to you it still stays there the same as your long nose?

GORDON: You're on the ink-pot, old man.

(*VAL jumps up. FREDA gets up and wipes ink from his trousers.*)

GEORGE: Look here, old man, that's silly. If I were to take a knife and cut your nose off, your nose wouldn't stay there and neither would your happiness. Ha, ha, ha, ha, ha! (*He crosses into the hall.*)

VERA: Oooh, go away, you awful boys.

GORDON: (*Seated above table with despatch-case.*) Well, I don't believe in happiness or misery either. Always be comfortable, that's the thing to cultivate. Keep to yourself and don't worry much about anything. It's no good falling in love. After all, if you're never particularly happy, you can never be particularly miserable. It stands to reason.

LAURA: (*On floor below divan.*) I think both Val and Gordon are right. There isn't such a thing as perfect happiness,

anyway, you think you've found it, but in spite of
everything you do, it's very near to perfect misery. I've
got as near to it as anyone can get in being in love with
Jimmie and him loving me, but when one's so very
happy there's a kind of under-current – that makes you
frightened. Terribly frightened of the future and –

JIMMIE: Well, it makes you feel you almost wish there
wasn't one at all.

GEORGE: Oh, Gawd!

(*He turns the lights on. The others look up in surprise.*)

VERA: Why did you do that, you awful boy?

GEORGE: (*Coming down.*) That red light's not good for
highbrows, it makes you all get dopey.

VERA: Well, come along, let's hear some of your ideas.

GORDON: Don't embarrass him. He hasn't any.

GEORGE: (*Above table.*) Well, you know – I'm always pretty
bright and cheery. I'll tell you what. When I stay with some
friends of mine – got a little place down in the country
somewhere – we have a great time. Thumping good ride to
hounds in the morning, thundering good meal afterwards.
There you are, what more does anybody want?

ESTHER: (*Bottom of stairs.*) Are you really one of those
people who think it amusing to chase a terrified little
animal for hours and then watch it torn to pieces? I've
always wanted to meet one.

GEORGE: (*Standing above stove.*) No, as a matter of fact, I'm
hardly ever in at the kill.

ESTHER: It's all the same. You can't see anything wrong in
it. (*She moves to him.*) I suppose you believe in capital
punishment, too?

GEORGE: Well, as a matter of fact, I do.

ESTHER: (*Stepping nearer.*) And what else? I suppose you
think war's damn good fun, and you're looking forward
to the next one?

GEORGE: Well, I don't know about that, but, well, it does
give a chap a chance of seeing life.

ESTHER: (*Up to him. The others all look at her.*) And you
believe in starving miners, don't you? And cutting up
animals alive? And that men are much better than

women and they're the – the lords of creation, I suppose? I hate you! You're a foul, horrible menace! There! (*She hits him in the face with all her force, bursts into floods of tears and rushes to her room.*)

VERA: I told her not to read that awful book. (*She picks it up where ESTHER has dropped it and hides it under the divan.*)

FREDA: Silly little fool.

GEORGE: Good lord! I say, that is a bit thick, isn't it? Hitting a chap like that. You may have your views, but you don't go hitting people. (*He sits in the chair above the stove.*)

VAL: Oh, shut up! (*He goes round to head of divan.*)

GEORGE: (*Jumping up.*) Who are you telling to shut up?

GORDON: Don't be silly, old man, it's no good losing your hair.

VERA: Leave Esther alone, Val! Aren't men awful? Do have some tact.

(*LAURA and JIMMIE are doubled up with laughing.*)

VAL: Can't I even knock at the door?

VERA: Don't be a boring ass.

FREDA: Of course, my head could be falling off for all anyone would care.

VERA: Oooh, this is too terrible. (*She shouts.*) Be quiet! This is my room.

(*There is sudden silence. They all look at each other.*)

(*Firmly.*) George, put something funny on the gramophone.

GEORGE: What? Jazz?

VERA: Yes, of course. We're going to have a dance.

(*GEORGE obeys. The gramophone starts playing 'Happiness Pie'. JIMMIE and LAURA hold each other and wriggle in time to the music. GEORGE jerks his shoulders.*)

GORDON: You can't dance here. There's no room. Besides, I'm trying to work.

VERA: (*Rising.*) Then we must use Freda's room.

FREDA: (*Rising.*) No you mustn't. I've got a headache. I keep telling everybody, but nobody takes any notice. And I haven't any Aspros. (*Moving up centre and round below the table.*)

VERA: Well, if we can have the room, I'll give you some.

FREDA: Oh, all right.

VERA: Here you are. (*She takes Aspros from drawer and gives them to FREDA.*) Perhaps we'll make some tea on Freda's gas-ring.

(*All with the exception of GORDON make for FREDA's room.*)

(*At the door VERA turns.*) Aren't you coming, Gordon?

GORDON: No.

VERA: Well, you can't have all the lights on. Put them out, George.

(*GEORGE turns off the gramophone and then puts out the lights up right. VERA retires. GEORGE follows her. The others by now have all gone into FREDA's room. Somebody shuts the door. The music of a gramophone and the murmur of voices can be heard through the closed door. GORDON, who is still in his coat, rises, takes it off, and hangs it on a peg in the glory-hole under the stairs. He then sits above the table again. JENNY comes out of her room. She comes a few steps down the stairs and then stops as she sees him.*)

JENNY: Hullo, Gordon.

GORDON: (*Breezily.*) Hullo. What've you been doing all the evening?

JENNY: (*Leaning over the balustrade.*) Nothing much. No, as a matter of fact, I've been walking about half the evening and weeping the other half.

GORDON: What, is anything the matter?

JENNY: (*After a long pause.*) Yes.

GORDON: Can I – help? (*He rises and moves over to above divan.*)

JENNY: (*Her voice breaking.*) Oh, Gordon dear, it's rather awful. I – I'd meant not to tell anyone, but –

(*She comes down the stairs and stands just two steps above him. The light from her room shines down on them.*)

GORDON: What is it? I'll do anything I can.

JENNY: No, you can't do anything. It's mean of me to tell you, but... Gordon, we don't know each other very well, do we...?

GORDON: I suppose not – really.

JENNY: Not as well as Esther and I know one another?

GORDON: No.

JENNY: That's why I feel it doesn't matter so much telling you. I saw the doctor again this evening about those pains I've been having in my eyes – and he said – well, it's rather involved – but anyway – I shall soon be blind. (*A pause. GORDON can think of nothing to say. The door of FREDA's room opens and LAURA and JIMMIE come out, shutting the door quietly. They run across to their own door before speaking. They whisper.*)

LAURA: Jimmie!

JIMMIE: I can't stand being in a crowd any longer.

LAURA: You look so handsome tonight, Jimbo. I do love you so.

JIMMIE: We mustn't have that frightened feeling any more, darling. Life's always going to be like this. Nothing will ever go wrong.

LAURA: I'll always be frightened, Jimbo.

(*They kiss. A calm secret kiss, and go to their room with their arms round each other.*

JENNY and GORDON have stood without moving. JENNY is crying a little now. GORDON makes a movement towards her, but she brushes his hand out of the way and comes down into the room.)

GORDON: Jenny!

JENNY: Don't be sympathetic – please be hard and awful. (*She sits left of the table.*)

GORDON: (*Coming to her.*) But can't this doctor chap do anything? I shouldn't believe him, Jenny. Go to a specialist.

JENNY: He is one.

GORDON: What did he say? Will it happen gradually?

JENNY: No, it's a – kind of abscess affair behind my eyes, and one day it'll just go pop, and that'll be that. There won't be any warning, it'll just happen.

GORDON: (*Turning away.*) What can I say, Jenny?

JENNY: It's only a matter of getting used to the idea. Please, you will promise not to tell Vera or Esther. Not to tell a soul?

GORDON: But suppose…

JENNY: You must promise.

GORDON: I promise then. (*He sits on the divan.*)
  (*JENNY sighs. Her body seems to relax. There is a pause.*)

JENNY: It's a vile thing to happen, isn't it? So unnecessary somehow.

GORDON: (*Rising and moving down left.*) Oh God, Jenny, it's beastly. Why couldn't it have happened to Freda or someone like that? I wouldn't have cared then.

JENNY: I've just got to get used to it. Perhaps – everything will be much lovelier. I'll be able to see anything I want to, glowing and vivid, like when you're going to sleep at night…
  (*GORDON moves up left of divan. JENNY pauses and then says in a low, hard voice:*)
  I don't believe it, really. I've got to face it. I shan't be able to see, that's all. I shall have four senses instead of five. (*Desperately.*) Why is it the best one, though? The one I care about most?

GORDON: But it may not – perhaps the doctor – Sorry, Jenny, I feel so helpless though. (*He sits on the divan, facing left.*)

JENNY: You poor sweet. Don't worry about it. There's my work; I can still do that. Dictate to Esty, p'r'aps. And I may be like a canary who sings *better* when its eyes are put out. It is a canary who does that, isn't it?

GORDON: I don't know.

JENNY: (*Rising.*) Yes, you do, silly. (*She moves to divan, sits and kisses him.*) Anyway, Gordon, I've made up my mind on one point. The doctor says it'll probably be a few weeks before the abscess thing breaks. I'm going to live as deeply as I can for that time. I must. Because afterwards I shan't be able to help being rather boxed up in myself. (*She rises and walks round table.*) And I must *see* all the lovely things I can. See them like anything, so that I'll be able to keep them all stored up with no chance of forgetting. And people. I must see them more than I do. Heavens, I'm going to be so greedy, tearing round and devouring everything with my eyes. (*She sits on table.*)

GORDON: (*Sitting on divan facing her.*) You know what you
said just now about our not knowing each other, Jenny...
It's quite true. I've never thought about it before. Is it
too late to begin now I wonder?

JENNY: When we were kids we knew each other.

GORDON: Do you think we've altered – or just drifted
apart? Or is it because we're only half-brother and sister?

JENNY: We've taken each other for granted too much,
that's what it is.

GORDON: The last few years I've tried deliberately to
keep myself to myself, but – I would like us awfully to
know each other again, Jenny...

JENNY: I almost feel we're being real together new for the
first time since we've grown up.

GORDON: Yes, that's right. We are. I'm being myself now.

JENNY: Aren't you always?

GORDON: No, that's not me. That's only what I try to be
because it makes life easier. The ambition of my life is to
be exactly like George. If only I can be like him I shall
escape everything.
(*JENNY is oblivious of him, staring miserably into her own
future. After a pause she pulls herself together.*)

JENNY: What did you say, dear?

GORDON: (*Rising and moving over to her, left of table.*) Oh
nothing, only a lot of rot about myself, as if –

JENNY: Well, it's no good talking about me. What is there
to say?

GORDON: Don't, Jenny. (*He gets a chair and sits next to her.*)
Listen. When it happens, you must let me help you.

JENNY: Dear Gordon.

GORDON: Not that I can do much, but I'll keep my real
self just for you and nobody else.

JENNY: Perhaps that's the reason for my going blind,
Gordon. Perhaps our friendship will be so wonderful
that'll be the good that comes out of the evil. I've always
believed in that – good out of evil – and it's true. Right
inside me I know it's true.

GORDON: That's what religion means, I suppose. I wish
I had it. I wish poor Esty had it.

JENNY: If you look at it and think about it a lot, like Esty does, I know life and people do seem pretty vile. But I'm sure that's only a half-truth...because we can't see everything as a *whole*. If one could get anywhere near the real truth, one would see the perfect beauty at the bottom of everything. I do believe in that. Am I being very sentimental and wind on the heath, brother?

GORDON: You ought to have lived in Ancient Rome, Jenny, and gone to the lions, faithful and happy.

JENNY: I'm not happy, Gordon, don't be absurd.

GORDON: Well, I don't suppose the martyrs were when they were actually being eaten, but you know what I mean.

JENNY: And I *must* work then. Work. I wonder if I shall ever be able to write stories so true that some of the beauty that I know lies at the bottom of everything would...shine through them. Oh dear, wouldn't it be frightful if I found out that I'd always been wrong – there was only ugliness. (*She shudders.*)

GORDON: You *must* be right. (*The phone rings.*) Oh, go away. (*He rises and goes and sits on the bottom of the divan.*) (*After a minute JENNY gets up and crosses to the phone. As she lifts the receiver, VAL, FREDA, GEORGE and VERA come from FREDA's room. One of them turns the lights on.*)

VAL: Bet you half a crown it's for me.

GEORGE: Bet you it's a wrong number, old scout.

FREDA: (*Shrieking with laughter.*) Oh, my God, that last drink has given me the giggles, I can't stop. (*Up centre.*) Oh, what a scream!

VERA: It's sure to be for George, he always gets rung in the middle of the night. There's my little Jenny. (*Her next sentence emerges from the general noise.*) Be quiet, you awful children, she can't hear. (*She sits on the divan.*)

JENNY: Sorry, I can't hear. Who? Peter? Oh, hullo, Peter. Yes, of course I remember you... Yes, she does. Vera, is there any room? (*VERA nods.*) There is a vacant room. Well, where are you? But how absurd! Come along now, then. Good-bye. (*She puts back the receiver. Coming down centre.*) Somebody wants a room, Vera. What about the one in the corridor, next to Gordon's?

VERA: Is he nice? Is he one of us?

JENNY: Yes, you'll like him, I think.

VAL: (*Seated above table.*) What's he do?

JENNY: He's an artist. (*She goes off into the corridor.*)

VERA: Ooh, how divine!

GEORGE: Another bloody highbrow.

VERA: (*Glaring at him.*) Oooh, be qui...go to bed.

FREDA: I believe I've got the hiccups. Do I look like a ballet dancer? (*She dances round the room singing.*)

VAL: What's the matter with Jenny? She looks all sort of shattered.

JENNY: (*Coming back.*) The room's quite ready?

VERA: When's he coming then?

JENNY: In a minute. He was only round the corner at the call-box.

VERA: Oooh, no, I can't bear this. It's all too sudden. I'm going to bed. (*She rises and goes to the cupboard under the stairs.*)

FREDA: (*Dancing.*) Look, Gordon, now do I look like a ballet dancer? (*She comes down to divan.*)

GORDON: No, not very. (*He rises and moves round divan up centre.*)

FREDA: What a cheek. (*She collapses on the divan, shrieking with laughter.*) I'm Cleopatra. Vamp me, somebody. (*GEORGE sits next to her. They commence a mock love scene.*)

VERA: Will you show him the room and do all the parlezvous, Jenny? I'm divinely tired. (*She yawns.*) Come along. All go away. I'm sick of you all. I want to get to bed. All to your rooms. Come along now.

FREDA: (*Wailing.*) Want to stay up and see Pe-ter.

VERA: How's your headache, Freda?

(*ESTHER looks round from the corridor.*)

ESTHER: Jenny, come and tuck me in, darling.

JENNY: Well, I mustn't be very long – (*She goes. VERA crosses centre.*)

FREDA: Want to see Pe-ter.

VAL: You sound like a couple of cats.

(*VERA starts to pull her dress over her head, speaking at the same time.*)

VERA: Get off my divan, you boring asses. I've got to sleep in it. (*The dress comes off. She drops it on the floor.*)

FREDA/GEORGE: We – want to see Pe-ter!

VERA: (*Pushing them away and sitting down and pulling her stockings off.*) Go away, you irritating fools. You can see the awful man, but you've got to go to your rooms directly after.

FREDA: Anything to oblige.

GORDON: Well, I'm going, anyway.

(*The bell rings.*)

FREDA: Oh, there he is.

(*GORDON opens the door. Outside PETER is standing. He is tall, almost too good-looking. His age might be anything between twenty-five and thirty-two. He wears a shabby old raincoat and is carrying a suitcase.*)

PETER: Oh, thanks.

VERA: Come in.

(*He comes into the hall. GORDON shuts the door, saying:*)

GORDON: It's cold out tonight, isn't it?

VERA: You're very naughty, coming when we're just going to bed. I'm not going to take any notice of you. I always sleep in the hall, it leaves more rooms to let. (*She gets on with it, stripping the cover off the divan, turning back the clothes and arranging the pillows.*)

PETER: I'm awf...well, I – (*He stops, at a loss, catches VAL's eye, and bursts into laughter.*)

VAL: (*Who has risen.*) Don't mind her, she's sweet really.

PETER: (*Putting down his suitcase.*) I won't. (*He comes to centre.*)

FREDA: (*Coming towards him and stretching out her hand.*) Well, as nobody seems to be going to introduce us, my name's Freda.

PETER: Mine's Peter.

(*He holds her hand rather long. They are both looking into each other's eyes. FREDA, slightly flustered, withdraws her hand.*)

FREDA: What a nice name, Peter. Mine's awfully silly. Oh, do you know each other? This is George. And the other one's Val.

PETER: How do you do?

(*He shakes VAL's hand.*)

GEORGE: Oh, all right, thanks. Have you come to join us in this gay abode, then?

PETER: Yes, I hope so.

GORDON: Take your coat off; it's a bit wet, isn't it?

FREDA: Oh, do you know each other? This is Gordon.

(*By this time VERA has got into bed and is making herself comfortable.*)

VERA: Be quiet, Freda. You're talking too much. None of this introduction rubbish.

PETER: (*Coming down to divan.*) Of course, I know who you are, you're Jenny's mother. She's told me about you.

(*VERA, having settled down, turns round and looks at him.*)

VERA: Oh, but you're a beautiful young man. I can't bear to look at you.

(*VERA bellows with laughter and pulls the clothes over her head. The others laugh too. PETER looks at them helplessly.*)

PETER: What is one to do?

(*GEORGE and FREDA are at the head of the divan.*)

VERA: (*Emerging from the bedclothes.*) Do you want the room for long?

PETER: Well, I'm not sure. As a matter of fact I only arrived in town tonight, and I remembered Jenny told me about – (*He stops.*)

(*JENNY has come out of ESTHER's room. There is a tiny pause, a fraction of a second's utter silence, then JENNY's voice drops into it, low and with a sort of shyness.*)

JENNY: Hullo, Peter.

PETER: Jenny!

VERA: Show him his room and everything, darling, and we'll talk about the business bits in the morning. (*She yawns.*) Go away everybody – Good night, Jenny pet. There's a lovely blue divan in your room, Peter. (*She snuggles down.*)

PETER: (*Taking up his suitcase.*) Good night.

FREDA: (*With a special smile for him.*) Good night. (*Going to her room.*) Good night, everybody. I'll show you your room. It's down the corridor next to mine and you'll want to know where the bathroom and things are.

(PETER follows to the corridor. JENNY goes up to her room.)

GEORGE: Oh well, I suppose I'd better turn in. Cheerio, everybody. *(He goes to his room.)*

VAL: Good night.

GORDON: Cheerio, sleep well.

(GORDON turns off the chandelier and follows PETER down the corridor.)

VAL: *(Kissing VERA.)* Good night, darling. *(He turns off the lamp.)*

VERA: *(Mumbling.)* Nearly asleep. Mmmm. Sweet li'l thing.

VAL: *(Meaninglessly.)* Don't call me that, darling.

(He goes into his room.

There is silence, except for VERA's heavy breathing. After a while JENNY comes out of her room.)

JENNY: *(Speaking over the stairs.)* Are you awake, Vera darling? *(She looks in the direction of the corridor. PETER is there. She does not appear surprised.)*

Hullo, Peter!

PETER: *(At foot of stairs.)* Won't you come and talk to me? It's much too early for sleep yet, isn't it? Have the others all gone to bed?

JENNY: Yes.

PETER: *(Coming upstairs towards her.)* Why so early?

JENNY: It just happened tonight, I think.

(Pause.)

PETER: It's awfully good of your mother putting me up on the spur of the moment.

JENNY: Well, it's all business for her, isn't it?

PETER: Yes.

(A pause. VERA's breathing stops for a second, and then commences again.)

JENNY: Sh! Sh! Oh, I thought we'd woken her.

PETER: No, she's quite all right.

(JENNY looks in the direction of the divan.)

JENNY: We were talking very softly, weren't we?

PETER: Yes.

(Pause.)

JENNY: Did you just suddenly decide to come here tonight?

PETER: Yes. I felt lonely – sick of being in the studio by myself...

JENNY: Yes, it must be a bit...
(*Pause.*)
PETER: (*At top of the stairs, taking her hand.*) Are you cold,
Jenny? You're trembling.
JENNY: Am I? No, I'm not. (*She moves away to front.*)
PETER: Yes, I gave up the studio a few days ago. I sold it
all outright. And the new man took possession today.
I was practically turned out...
JENNY: Wasn't it sad, having to leave everything?
PETER: It was. Awfully sad.
(*Another pause. Suddenly he takes her in his arms. They kiss
long and passionately. At last she draws herself away, and
says, shakily:*)
JENNY: This is all terribly strange, isn't it?
PETER: It's not strange, it's wonderful.
(*JENNY comes down the stairs and stays above table.*)
JENNY: It's – it's love at first sight, I suppose.
PETER: (*Coming downstairs and moving over to her.*) I've loved
you from the first moment I saw you.
JENNY: (*Moving round table away from him to down right.*)
It's funny – I hardly thought of you then – I've hardly
thought of you at all until tonight. And then – just
before you rang up, I had a feeling that something was
going to happen, and when I came out of the door and
saw you – I had a funny feeling, here – not quite in my
tummy, but here – and then all my inside seemed to go
like melted butter, and I thought I'm in love, and – it's
never happened before to me. Oh, Peter!
(*She goes to him and he holds her.*)
PETER: You adorable, wonderful child. It's like a dream, all
this. I've never stopped thinking about you ever since
that day I saw your funny little face in the –
JENNY: Oh no, you couldn't have fallen in love in a pub.
(*She sits on right of table.*)
PETER: But I did. My God, how I had to worm my way
through your friends, just to be near you –
JENNY: I was drinking a Gin and It.
PETER: I remember.
JENNY: How did you start the conversation with me?

PETER: Don't know now. Do you remember I showed you some sketches?

JENNY: I've never forgotten them, they were beautiful.

PETER: I've got them still. They're in my bag.

JENNY: Oh! Suppose I hadn't told you about Vera and the flat that night. You might never have come here – this might never have happened.

PETER: But we saw each other other nights.

JENNY: Oh, isn't life funny. It is funny. I never thought then…
(*PETER crushes her to him, pressing his mouth on hers.*)
(*Suddenly frightened.*) No – No…

PETER: Yes. Why not?

JENNY: We'll wake Vera. Sssh! (*She moves round below table to centre.*)

PETER: What's the matter, darling?

JENNY: (*Coming back.*) You frightened me. (*She sits right of table.*)

PETER: (*Seated on table, above her.*) Jenny, I'm sorry. Darling, it's only because I love you.

JENNY: I love you too, Peter. I was silly being frightened. I wonder what'll happen to us both in the end. (*She turns to him.*)

PETER: We love each other, Jenny, and it's going to last. I'll make you so happy.

JENNY: It'll have to finish sadly some time.

PETER: Never.

JENNY: It will.

PETER: Why?

JENNY: I won't tell you. It's nothing. (*She suddenly begins to weep.*)
(*In a moment he has knelt beside her, and puts his arm round her shoulder.*)

PETER: (*Soothing her.*) Don't cry! Don't cry! (*As if to protect and comfort her.*) Jenny… Jenny…darling. (*He draws her close to him.*)

End of Act One.

ACT TWO

The same. Three weeks later. Evening.

The sound of 'Make Yourself a Happiness Pie' can be heard from FREDA's room, and a murmur of laughter, voices and shuffling feet. PETER gets a suitcase out of the glory-hole and puts it up by the front door, concealing it carefully. JENNY, with an exercise-book and pencil in her hand, emerges from her room.

JENNY: I'll be down in a minute, dear.

PETER: Right you are.

JENNY: I'm longing to dance with you some more.

PETER: Well, come on, then.

JENNY: We're all going to the club afterwards, we'll dance then. I'm rather inspired, too. It'd be wrong not to finish it now. I've done such good work since you've been here, Peter. I wish I helped your work, too.

PETER: Oh, nonsense.

JENNY: It quite worries me. I wonder if I hold you back. You've done no painting at all since we've been together.

PETER: (*Crossing left and standing on divan.*) Haven't I? No, I suppose I haven't. I shall feel like it suddenly, I suppose. I've gone much longer than this without working sometimes. But you know what it is, Jenny, these last two or three weeks there's been no room for anything. (*LAURA and JIMMIE have come secretly from FREDA's room. On seeing the other two, they groan in exaggerated disappointment.*)

LAURA/JIMMIE: Oh, oh!

PETER: Hullo, you two, what do you want?

LAURA: Oh, do go away.

JENNY: Why?

JIMMIE: (*With LAURA.*) We want you to go. We can't explain. But we've got a surprise.

LAURA: (*With JIMMIE.*) The whole thing'll be ruined if you see.

JENNY: Oo, what fun. Go along, Peter, we'll hide ourselves.

167

LAURA: Is it a nice party?

PETER: No, dreadful.

(*The others laugh. LAURA pretends to be cross and grabs him, but he eludes her and, laughing mockingly, dashes into FREDA's room and slams the door.*)

JIMMIE: (*At foot of stairs.*) That's one out of the way. Now, if Miss Lyndon at the top of the stairs there will kindly remove herself...

JENNY: Let me stay and share the secret.

(*A pause.*)

LAURA: Yes, let Jenny stay, then.

JIMMIE: All right. Jenny stays.

JENNY: Thank you. Well, what is it?

LAURA: Come down the stairs and we'll whisper.

(*JENNY runs down the stairs. They meet her at the bottom and whisper hoarsely.*)

LAURA/JIMMIE: A wedding cake!

(*A pause.*)

JENNY: A real one?

(*They giggle.*)

JIMMIE: Don't act like a daft girl. Of course it's real.

JENNY: All covered in horrible icing with cupids all round and Queen Victoria on the top?

LAURA: I don't know what you're so surprised about. It's the correct thing to have a wedding-cake after a wedding, isn't it? And we've been presented with a most imposing cocktail set.

JIMMIE: Ssh!

(*FREDA's door opens and GEORGE, who is very slightly drunk, comes into the hall.*)

GEORGE: What cheer, newlyweds!

LAURA: What do you want? Go back.

GEORGE: Look here, d'you mind if I phone up and ask a girlfriend to come round? Perfectly topping girl, only lives round the corner. Name's Sylvia. God, she's marvellous.

LAURA: Go on, then.

(*GEORGE goes to the phone and lifts the receiver. He gets the number during the following conversation.*)

Come on, Jenny, we'll get the cake and the drinks ready, and then march triumphantly in with them.

GEORGE: (*At telephone.*) Shut that darn door, I can't hear a thing.

JENNY: You two must go first with the cake, I'll follow behind.

JIMMIE: (*Shutting the door of FREDA's room.*) It doesn't want three of us to prepare the things. You stay here, and I'll set them out and bring them in. (*He runs across to his room.*)

LAURA: Go on then.

(*He goes.*)

GEORGE: What do you mean – press button A?

LAURA: Jimmie's just like a funny little boy, he adores doing everything himself.

GEORGE: Is that you, Sylvia? – I say, be quiet a minute – Listen, darling. Will you come along here tonight? We're having a party. What? Well, it's not really a party, it's a wedding breakfast. Yes, wedding breakfast. Then we're going on to dance at a club afterwards. Oh, doesn't matter. Evening dress optional. Optional, you knew the word. Something like that. You *are* dressed? I'll be right along now, then. Good-bye, darling. See you in a minute. (*He puts the receiver down.*) She's coming.

LAURA: So we gathered.

GEORGE: (*Crossing down left.*) Well, I call it a damn sauce, listening to a private conversation. (*He takes a scarf from a peg under the stairs, and throws it round his neck.*)

JENNY: (*Crossing centre.*) Come back and put your twopence in the plate, you never do, I'm sure. Poor Vera will be ruined when the phone bill comes in.

GEORGE: (*Crossing back and putting a shilling in a plate full of coppers which stands beside the phone.*) Good lord, yes. Owe it a bob. Damn shame about those phone bills. Post Office is nothing but a ruddy ogpu! (*He goes out by the front door. There is a pause.*)

LAURA: (*Seeing the book in JENNY's hand.*) Are you in the middle of a story now?

(*Both move to above table.*)

JENNY: Yes, I'd meant to write a bit this evening, but I've not done a word yet, my eyes are tired, I think.

LAURA: Be naughty for once; I should.

(*JIMMIE, holding a hammer and a piece of wood, puts his head round the door and says:*)

JIMMIE: Sorry I'm such a time. I'm having a spot of bother with that cake.

LAURA: Let me help, darling.

JIMMIE: No. Do it meself. It won't come out, and there's bits of icing all over the floor like plaster.

LAURA: (*Looking after him.*) Oh, Jimmie. (*She turns to JENNY.*) Do you ever look at Peter and you feel you love him so much you just simply don't know what to do? (*She sits on the table.*)

JENNY: (*Left of table.*) Yes.

LAURA: It's rather awful, isn't it? As if all your inside had turned to pink melted toffee.

JENNY: How funny, that's exactly how I've always felt about Peter. Only I thought it was butter.

LAURA: Do you think one should love so much? Don't you ever think what might happen if the other person died?

JENNY: I don't know. There *are* worse things. You would feel them near you, I'm sure – they wouldn't just stop…

LAURA: If only that were true, Jenny.

(*Pause.*)

I can't ever get the thought of death out of my mind. I care for Jimmie so much – and I think this happiness can't last, something will take it from me. That's why we've married, really – anything to hang on to. But then, I might die and that would be worse even, for Jimmie. There it is at the back of my mind always. However much we love whatever happens to us, it's got to end in death. Do you know every time Jimmie's late home – if he has to go on a long train journey or even when –

JIMMIE: (*Pushing open his door.*) At last. It's ready. Look.

(*He picks the cake off the floor and comes into the room.*)

JENNY: (*Down left of table.*) It's a perfect dream!

JIMMIE: Isn't it? Jolly heavy, though!

LAURA: (*Rising.*) I'll get the cocktail arrangement, then.

JIMMIE: All right, my sweet.

(*LAURA goes to her room.*)

JENNY: But where are the cupids?

JIMMIE: Well, I'm sorry to disappoint you, lidy, but there ain't none.

JENNY: Let me break a little nobbly bit off and eat it.

JIMMIE: Go on, then.

(*JENNY breaks a bit off and puts it in her mouth.*)

JENNY: Mm yum yum yum.

JIMMIE: Have some more?

JENNY: No, spoil the look of it.

(*LAURA comes back, holding the cocktail set.*)

LAURA: Here we are.

JIMMIE: Ah, here we are, now we must all line up for the grand procession.

LAURA: You go first, then.

JIMMIE: With the cake?

LAURA: Yes. Then me with the drinks.

JENNY: And I'll hold up your train.

JIMMIE: Splendid.

(*They line up, JIMMIE centre, holding the cake, the other two behind.*)

LAURA: For God's sake don't drop it.

JIMMIE: Don't you either.

JENNY: (*Holding up LAURA's skirt at the back.*) Do you mind your knickers showing?

LAURA: No, they're pretty.

JIMMIE: Marks and Spencer's, cheap line.

(*JIMMIE, LAURA and JENNY walk up towards FREDA's room. GEORGE comes in at the front door. SYLVIA follows when he beckons. SYLVIA is young and very attractive. She has a West End voice.*)

GEORGE: Good heavens, what's going on?

(*The procession stops.*)

JIMMIE: Just our fun, you know.

GEORGE: Oh, I say, do you know each other? This is Sylvia. The one with the book and the highbrow expression is Jenny.

SYLVIA: (*In hall, right of GEORGE.*) How do you do?

GEORGE: And the one with the drinks – and the dubious expression, is Laura.

SYLVIA: (*To her.*) How do you do?

GEORGE: And the one with the – good lor', whatever's that?

JIMMIE: A wedding cake.

GEORGE: Good lord! Oh well, that's Jimmie.

SYLVIA: (*To him.*) How do you do?

(*A pause. They all laugh rather uncomfortably.*)

(*Walking down centre.*) It's not actually a wedding cake, is it? How quaint. (*She openly examines the hall from floor to ceiling.*)

JIMMIE: We were just going to take it in and give everybody a surprise when you came. Shall we – all proceed together?

SYLVIA: Yes, I'd love to. (*Up centre, right of JIMMIE.*) Are you dancing in there? I worship giving people surprises. Amusing, isn't it? Is George drunk, or only pretending to be?

LAURA: Drunk.

GEORGE: No, I'm not.

SYLVIA: (*Walking down right.*) Oh, yes you are, dear. Don't be silly. What a quaint room this is, isn't it? I love all the little bits of furniture. I'm sure you must all trip about all over the place over them. *Oh*, I'm terribly hot all of a sudden. (*Sitting right of table.*) It's these sleeves, they're so large. I really feel one must wear cool things, don't you think?

JENNY: You're coming on to the club with us, aren't you'?

GEORGE: (*Sitting on table, above SYLVIA.*) Oh, good lord, yes.

SYLVIA: Yes, I'd love to. How amusing. Lovely. Is my hair terribly untidy? (*She looks in the glass in the flap of her bag.*) Oh no, it's all right. Oh, I saw such a sickening film this afternoon, I simply *couldn't* bear it. *How* I suffered though! I always suffer in the pictures. Which club is it? I hope it's not terribly smart. I've got a perfectly sickening dress on.

JENNY: (*Taking a step forward.*) I've been admiring it.

SYLVIA: Have you? It's not bad. (*She rises and moves to below table.*) The line's not quite right here. It's quite Vogue-y though, don't you think? I feel *Vogue* really is one's favourite book, don't you think? People ask me who my favourite author is and I always say the editor of *Vogue*. Awfully the right thing to say, don't you think, rather?

GEORGE: It's a damn good dress.

(*SYLVIA gives him an icy look and speaks to the others.*)

SYLVIA: Well – shall we go in now?

LAURA: Yes, come on.

(*All start to go.*)

SYLVIA: Oh, just a minute (*They come back.*) I must just put my hair straight. I had the most sickening hairdresser the other day. Nothing so sickening as a sickening hairdresser, don't you feel? How I suffered. No one's any idea. You know these beads aren't Chanel at all; everybody thinks they are. I got them wonderfully cheap. But I shan't tell you where, it's a secret. Where's all the fun then? It all sounds terribly amusing. Oh yes, the wedding cake. How quaint.

(*They all go towards FREDA's room, chattering, but with SYLVIA's voice on top. She takes no particular notice of GEORGE, but talks to everyone in general. At the door they stop, and even she is silent for a second. Then they enter. There is a scream of delight from VERA; the gramophone, which has been playing intermittently during the preceding scenes, stops. A babel of voices and laughter ensues. Someone shuts the door, and the noise subsides to a murmur again. The hall remains empty for a second or two, then JENNY comes back, still holding the book and pencil in one hand, but now with a piece of cake in the other. JENNY switches on the standard lamp, then sits in the armchair, sucks her pencil, takes a bite of cake and starts to write. PETER and FREDA come in from up left. JENNY's chair has a high back and is turned away from them. FREDA is saying, intensely:*)

FREDA: But you must, Peter, you must.

PETER: Must – must – mustard. (*He crosses to right.*)

(*JENNY laughs.*)

FREDA: Ooh, you did give me a start.

JENNY: Sorry. (*She kneels on the chair and looks at them over the back.*)

FREDA: No, I think it's very mean, startling people like
    that. It'd be all right if I had a weak heart, wouldn't it?

JENNY: But you haven't a weak heart, dear.

FREDA: I might have. The doctor says I'm to be very
    careful. (*A pause.*) Oh! (*She suddenly turns and flounces back
    to her room.*)

PETER: What a silly girl.
    (*JENNY giggles.*)

JENNY: But what *must* you, Peter?

PETER: (*Walking across to her.*) Oh, nothing. I don't know –
    something quite unimportant.

JENNY: Well, what was it?

PETER: Oh, she – she wanted me to promise to paint her
    picture, and I said I couldn't now, because the mood
    wasn't on me, but she kept insisting, so perhaps I shall.
    It might be interesting, you know. Those eyes...the
    mouth.

JENNY: Yes, I should think she'd be rather...vivid. (*She sits
    down again and opens her book.*) Look, Peter, I've written
    two lines. Come and see them.
    (*He stands at the back of her and mechanically kisses the top
    of her head.*)
    Darling Peter. Give me your hand.
    (*He obeys her, she snuggles it against her cheek.*)
    I think this is such a sweet bit – listen. 'So she lay down
    and looked at a bird which was sitting on a branch of the
    apple tree. Presently it returned her gaze. Its hard,
    metallic little eyes seemed friendly, and she felt warmed,
    comforted.' And that's all I've done.

PETER: (*Seated at the end of divan.*) Clever, adorable Jenny.

JENNY: It's only two lines, but I do love that little bird.

PETER: I've always loved them, too. When I was a child
    I used to strew crumbs about on my window-sill, and
    then hide behind the curtains and watch the sparrows
    come along and eat them up. (*He laughs boyishly.*) Silly,
    wasn't it?

JENNY: No, it shows that nice natures are born, not made.
    Peter, I want to ask you something. (*She rises and sits right
    of him at the end of the divan.*)

PETER: Um?

JENNY: You know what it is. We must go to the country. Please, Peter.

PETER: We're happy as we are.

JENNY: We'd be happier. It isn't just a whim, I swear to you it's much deeper than that. It – it does matter a tremendous lot to me. I know I've been almost a nuisance about it lately, but – it's important, Peter, to go at once. (*Then, hurriedly.*) What objections can you have? There can't be any real objections.

PETER: Well, there's the money.

JENNY: I've got enough.

PETER: Oh! Jenny!

JENNY: Oh, I know it's beastly and hurtful to your pride not being able to do everything for me, but, Peter – you won't be cross at what I'm going to suggest, will you?

PETER: It all depends.

JENNY: Let me give you a present. No, don't be silly.

PETER: Jenny darling, you know I'll pay back every penny you've lent me once I start painting again.

JENNY: I've got – let's see – about twenty pounds hidden away upstairs.

PETER: What!

JENNY: That's from stray earnings and savings. We could almost go to Switzerland for that. Let me give it to you, Peter, then you can just take me away and we'll have a very lovely holiday. Please.

PETER: It would really be that you were taking me, but –

JENNY: No, it wouldn't. It wouldn't. If I give you the money, it's yours. You can do what you like with it, and you choose to take Jenny for a lovely holiday. (*A pause.*)

PETER: All right, Jenny. We'll go. (*He rises and goes up stage round left of divan.*)

JENNY: At once, then. Tomorrow.

PETER: (*Coming down right of divan to her.*) Tomorrow. There. I'll kiss your nose to seal it. (*He kisses her nose, then her mouth.*)

JENNY: Oh, how lovely! We'll get a train to somewhere with an absurd name, and find a cottage to stay in when we get there. Oh, it's exciting, isn't it?

PETER: (*Sitting again, above JENNY.*) The sort of thing that happens in dreams.

JENNY: Is it? But things in dreams always go wrong, or you wake up too soon.

PETER: Jenny – look here, will you give me the money tonight? So that you won't have to give it to me tomorrow. So that – well, by tomorrow, we can forget about your having given it to me and our holiday will be quite idyllic, nothing sordid or anything.

JENNY: (*Rising.*) Oh, all right. I'll fetch it now. (*She goes towards the stairs.*) But I want our holiday to be the sort of dream where we won't wake up too soon and which we can remember.

PETER: (*Rising and going to her at foot of stairs.*) Yes, of course, we must remember it always. A fragrant memory running through our lives.
    (*JENNY laughs.*)

JENNY: (*On stairs.*) Really, Peter, I believe love's making you as completely idiotic as it is me.

PETER: Idiotic? How? What do you mean?

JENNY: Well, darling – fragrant memory.

PETER: Oh! Oh, yes, it is a bit silly, perhaps. I love you so much, though, I simply don't know what I'm talking about sometimes.

JENNY: I hardly recognise myself since it's happened. I'm sure I often behave exactly like a half-wit. Do I?

PETER: You can't help love. That's what it does to you.

JENNY: Perhaps I'm an awful example. There ought to be two pictures – one fairly intelligent and the other completely pop-eyed of me – before and after falling in love.
    (*They both laugh.*)
    Peter – isn't it wonderful about tomorrow? Don't let anything spoil it. Nothing must spoil it. I'm willing things to be as we want them. The sun hot all the time, a perfect cottage, flowers, and little lambs with black

stockings on everywhere, no quarrels at all... What was
I doing? Going upstairs for something... Oh, I know –
the money. (*She continues towards the top of the stairs.*)

PETER: (*As she gets to the top.*) Oh, Jenny –

JENNY: (*Turning to him.*) Yes?

PETER: Perhaps – don't get it now.

JENNY: Why not?

(*He doesn't answer. After a moment's pause, she says:*)
Peter, there's something else I want to get over and
done with tonight, so that we can forget all about it
tomorrow. (*A pause, then, with an effort.*) When the
holiday ends, I want everything to end. I want us to go
our different ways.

PETER: (*At bottom of stairs.*) Why? What's the matter?

JENNY: Nothing's the matter. I'd always meant this, but
I put off telling you. I – I know this sounds like *Peg's
Paper* or something, but it's because I love you so
much... Peter dear. (*She comes down two steps.*)

PETER: You can't love me if you're sending me away.

JENNY: I can't explain, but there's something that would
make everything different, something that wouldn't be
fair on you.

PETER: Let me get this straight, Jenny. You want everything
to finish?

JENNY: Peter! Don't say it like that. Only after the holiday,
only when I'm...
(*VERA bursts in and flings herself on the divan with a loud
'Oooh!'*)
(*At the top again.*) I'll wrap it up in my best silk
handkerchief – and drop it over the banisters. Oh, hand
me my book and pencil, Peter. Look, they're on the chair.
(*PETER gets them from the armchair down left.*)

VERA: Oooh, that awful girl! Why aren't you two in having
fun?

JENNY: George's girl? I thought she was rather amusing.

VERA: Oooh, no, her vibrations are terrible. And she
registers sinister.

PETER: Registers what? (*To JENNY, standing on divan.*) Here
you are, dear. (*He hands her book and pencil up to her.*)

VERA: Sinister. But then so do you, Peter.

PETER: You don't mean that, Vera? Good heavens, me sinister? (*He laughs and gets off divan.*) You're entirely wrong there.

JENNY: Don't you know Vera by now? The only thing is to accept everything she says, and scratch her back.

VERA: (*Wriggling on the divan.*) Oh, how divine.

(*JENNY is just going in her door, when PETER stops her.*)

PETER: Jenny.

JENNY: Mm?

PETER: I don't think I'll come to the club tonight.

JENNY: Why, darling?

(*FREDA comes in from her room.*)

PETER: I'm going to make a sketch for a picture I've thought of.

JENNY: Peter!

PETER: Well, you're always begging me to work, and now I suddenly feel like it –

JENNY: How selfish of me, of course you must work. I am glad, Peter, aren't you? Sorry we shan't dance, though.

PETER: Never mind, the sketch will be something special for you.

JENNY: It's a good omen.

PETER: What is?

JENNY: (*Disappearing into her room.*) The muse coming back to you on the very day I've willed everything to be perfect.

(*FREDA leans behind VERA's divan. VERA starts. PETER sits in the armchair.*)

VERA: Oooh, what's that? Is that that beastly Freda? Hullo – why aren't you in having fun?

FREDA: I've got a headache. It's all very well, the way people use my room for parties. I can never lie down and rest when I want to.

VERA: Why don't you go and lie in the bath? It's quite comfy.

FREDA: (*Behind divan.*) I would, but the cistern makes terrible noises, and you see yourself, all yellow, in the geyser.

VERA: Hang a towel over it.

FREDA: (*To PETER.*) Aren't you coming to the club after all?

PETER: No, I'm going to work.

(*FREDA, who is standing behind VERA, makes signs to PETER that she shall stay as well, but he shakes his head.*)

FREDA: It's just like a tight iron band all round my head. God, I wish I could lie down.

PETER: (*Rising, he crosses to FREDA's door and throws it open.*) Come in here, the whole lot of you, Freda wants her room. The poor darling's got a head! (*He moves back to centre.*)

FREDA: Don't, Peter! *Don't!* I didn't tell you to do that!

JENNY: (*Coming out of her room.*) Peter – catch! (*She throws something down to him which he misses and picks off the floor.*) Butterfingers!

PETER: (*Standing centre.*) Thank you, darling. (*He kisses the little package, throws the kiss to her, and puts the package into a jacket pocket.*)

(*SYLVIA, ESTHER, GORDON, GEORGE, LAURA, JIMMIE and VAL surge into the hall.*)

SYLVIA: (*To GORDON, above the general chatter.*) And we ran over the poor thing. Lots of blood, of course. Positively packets. How I suffered. (*To FREDA.*) Oh, my dear, I'm terribly sorry. Nothing's quite so shattering as a shattering head, don't you feel?

GEORGE: (*At head of divan.*) Rotten luck, Freda. Pretty tough these beastly headaches.

(*VAL comes round and sits on divan. Others join in the commiserations.*)

FREDA: (*Screaming.*) I haven't got a headache. It was Peter being funny. (*She crosses and sits in the armchair.*)

(*There is a momentary silence, then:*)

VAL: Jenny darling! Aren't you sort of coming to the club?

JENNY: I'm just going to make myself pretty.

(*SYLVIA sits above table. LAURA and JIMMIE dance together, humming 'Make Yourself a Happiness Pie'. During the following scene PETER takes the package out of his pocket and counts the money under cover of a book. FREDA watches him all the time, but can't see what he is doing. Occasionally they catch each other's eye.*)

VERA: Val, come and do tiggy in my hair, you sweet little thing.

(*VAL does so, quite mechanically, without even looking at her.*)
Ooh, how divine.

VAL: (*To JENNY.*) Are you putting on yer pink or yer mauve?

JENNY: Me blue! (*She laughs and goes to her room.*)

SYLVIA: Come and sit here, Gordon. Oh, go and get my bag, George, it's in the other room. What was I saying, Gordon? Oh, yes, oh my dear, it really was quite too much of a good thing. Oceans of blood. I screamed, and then I couldn't decide whether it was too spurious to faint, or not.

GEORGE: (*Up left of her.*) Fetch you what?

SYLVIA: Bag, in the other room.

(*GEORGE goes off into FREDA's room.*)
So I really felt perhaps I was being a bit too spurious.
I am terribly spurious altogether, don't you feel?

VERA: Yes.

SYLVIA: What? Still, it is really the perfect thing to be, don't you think?

GORDON: I shall have a fit in a minute.

(*He grabs and kisses her. SYLVIA screams with laughter, then rises and goes right.*)

VAL: (*Who is still tickling VERA's hair, to ESTHER, who is sitting on the other side of her mother, also tickling her hair.*)
Sometimes I think D H Lawrence might be sort of right after all.

ESTHER: I know. I've been thinking that a bit lately. But –

VAL: I don't mind about loving you any more.

VERA: (*Drowsily.*) Oooh, how divine! You're doing it marvellously.

(*SYLVIA has joined LAURA and JIMMIE at the gramophone.*)

ESTHER: I feel I just don't care what's right and what isn't this evening.

VAL: Forgetting all the vileness of the world for once.

ESTHER: You make me sound such a silly prig. Perhaps I've had too much to drink. I hope nothing awful happens tonight. It always does when I'm in a don't care mood.

(*GEORGE enters and crosses to SYLVIA.*)

GEORGE: Is this the bag?

SYLVIA: (*Moving centre.*) Oh, my dear, thanks so much. Perfectly sweet of you. (*She takes it from him, then addresses the room generally.*) You know, I really have got the most disastrous habit of leaving my bags in all the *wrong* places. London's absolutely festooned with bags dropped by me at one time or another. Of course, it's probably a complex, but I do think it's rather a charming one, don't you feel? (*She moves over to right of divan.*)

VERA: (*Pushing ESTHER and VAL away and sitting up.*) I can't stand this any longer. Let's play something.

GEORGE: Esther. What about one of those singing games?

LAURA: Isn't it time to go to the club now?

JIMMIE: We could have one game first.

ESTHER: Something silly!

(*They all begin suggesting games at once, but SYLVIA talks them down.*)

SYLVIA: There's one game that is, of course, the perfect one; it's terribly amusing and not a bit pompous. I simply can't bear games that are pompous, and really it's awfully smart too, one does feel that all the nicest people play it.

VERA: Well, what's it called?

SYLVIA: Rude drawing consequences.

VERA: I knew you'd suggest something like that, directly you came in.

LAURA: It sounds grand, do let's play it.

GEORGE: My God, yes. Pretty hot, eh?

(*ESTHER giggles uncontrollably.*)

VERA: Get off my tummy, you awful child.

GORDON: Come on then, let's play it.

VAL: (*Together.*) Yes, come on.

LAURA: (*Together.*) We mustn't take too long.

SYLVIA: You'll be quite sick with laughter, my dear.

GEORGE: Damn funny this game is. Damn funny.

VAL: We want some pencils and paper, I suppose.

ESTHER: Let's all be absolutely silly.

SYLVIA: George, get some pencils and paper, dear. Now where shall we sit? (*She sits below table.*) Gordon, bring that little table into the corner, don't you think? You can strew yourselves on the floor. That is obviously the right thing to do, don't you feel? I simply couldn't bear it if we looked like a bridge party.

(*GORDON brings the table at head of divan to below table right.*)

GEORGE: I say, this is all I've got. (*He produces a pencil stub.*) Will some stout fellow oblige with a few more?

GORDON: There's a whole lot in the desk in my room, old man.

SYLVIA: (*To GEORGE.*) In the desk in his room, dear.

(*GEORGE goes off up left.*)

Of course, this is *the* perfect game. I play it wherever I go, and I collect the drawings and keep them in an album.

(*LAURA switches on the small standard lamp, then moves to centre. ESTHER and VAL wander over to right. Somebody gets pencils from right-hand drawer of chest of drawers.*)

LAURA: Freda and Peter, aren't you going to play?

FREDA: I don't feel like it much.

PETER: (*Seated on chest of drawers.*) You may not believe it, but I'm putting in a lot of heavy brain work at the moment.

LAURA: Oh, come on, Peter.

PETER: Considering that I hope to devote my evening to sketching something rather beautiful, the sight of your rude drawing consequences might have the wrong effect.

SYLVIA: My dear, they're not really rude – only slightly vulgar. One mustn't overstep the mark, don't you feel?

ESTHER: Is it the game where you draw a face and then pass it on, and then a body, and so on?

SYLVIA: Yes, we'll all be sick with laughing.

VERA: Are you playing something? (*She gets off the divan and joins them.*) I've been to sleep, and I dreamt my divine Lyndon was here, but when I looked closer it was only the milkman.

SYLVIA: How odd.

(*PETER gets up and sits on the divan.*)

VAL: Poor darling, come and sit next to me.

VERA: Dear little thing. (*She crosses to VAL.*)

GEORGE: (*Coming back*.) Look here, there wasn't enough paper so I tore a page or two from the back of that old book on your table.

GORDON: Don't worry, it's only a first edition.

GEORGE: Hard lines, old man, rotten luck, tut, tut! and again tut!

VERA: Oooh, how awful. Come along now. Give me one. (*GEORGE does so. They start their game, all seated at the little table. Some on chairs, but most of them on the floor.*)

FREDA: You are being horrid to me tonight.

PETER: (*Lying on divan.*) Horrid to you, Freddie?

FREDA: (*Sitting in armchair.*) Yes, horrid.

PETER: But you like my being horrid to you.

FREDA: Whatever do you mean?

PETER: Of course you do, you simply adore it.

VERA: What's first – face?

JIMMIE: A hat.

LAURA: I've done mine – it's a riot. (*She giggles.*)

GEORGE: Hurry up.

FREDA: I'm sick and tired of all this deceitfulness. Peter, do you love me? Better than her?

PETER: You know I do. Haven't I told you a thousand times?

FREDA: It's only that I like to hear you telling me. Somehow I never thought anybody'd ever love me properly. Like you do. It's so wonderful. I hate everyone not knowing.

PETER: They will, if you speak any louder.

VAL: Cheat! You're not to look.

ESTHER: Ooh, I didn't!

VERA: Here you are, that's all I can do. It's a bowler thing with two feathers on the top.

JIMMIE: Don't tell. You'll spoil it.

SYLVIA: A face now.

VERA: Oooh, yes, a face.

FREDA: And even if she led you on in the first place.

PETER: Look here, Freddie. I promise you – I swear solemnly I'll have it all out with her tonight.

FREDA: You'll tell her everything?

PETER: Everything.

FREDA: Well, the sooner it's over the better.

PETER: Now stop worrying.

FREDA: All right, Peter dear.

ESTHER: Damn I've done the mouth all wrong.

FREDA: Do you know, I'm sure nobody's ever loved each other like we do.

PETER: Do you ever wish you hadn't fallen in love with me?

FREDA: Of course I don't.

PETER: In spite of everything?

FREDA: I hate Jenny, it's no good pretending I don't. We'd have been married by now if it wasn't for her. (*She rises, comes centre and speaks to the others.*) My head's splitting and I've got to go round the agents tomorrow.

GORDON: The body now, Sylvia?

SYLVIA: Yes, dear, the body.

GEORGE: The good old bod, in fact.

LAURA: Darling pet, so sweet. (*She kisses JIMMIE.*)

FREDA: (*Moving back to him.*) How soon will we get married, Peter?

PETER: Tomorrow, if you like.

FREDA: Be sensible... Of course, I think you should have broken off with Jenny long ago. Directly you found you cared for me.

PETER: (*Rising and sitting in the armchair.*) Darling, you're being awfully silly tonight.

FREDA: You're more sensitive than me, that's what it is. You always want to spare people's feelings. (*She sits on the divan.*)

VERA: I must buy a dream book. Perhaps it meant that Lyndon's coming back to me.

VAL: Get on with the game, darling.

LAURA: (*At left of group, rising.*) It's ten o'clock. We must go now. Don't bother about the legs.

SYLVIA: All show what you've done, then. We'll be sick with laughing. Pass on quickly, and then open. Of course, it really is exactly like George. Look!

(*All rise. She displays it to them. They are sick with laughing.*)

VERA: (*Tearing up the drawing.*) Well, it's all much too much of a good thing. I'm out of tune for it. I think I shall wash my face and go to bed.

(*Several voices say: 'No, you must come, Vera'; 'You'll feel all
right when you get there etc., but she insists on staying.*)
No, I'm going to be mouldy and stay at home.

VAL: You must come, dear.

VERA: Now what are you two beastly creatures doing? (*She
crosses to the glory-hole under the stairs.*)
(*There is sudden complete silence: everyone turns and looks
at FREDA and PETER. JENNY comes out of her room and
runs down the stairs.*)

JENNY: Well, I'm ready. Good heavens, what is going on?
(*Crossing to table.*) I thought you'd all be waiting for me.

JIMMIE: Just been having a bit of rudery, dear. I know,
let's look at them all when we get there. I'll collect the
drawings.
(*The others agree. The group breaks up. LAURA exits to her
room for a shawl. FREDA leaves PETER and goes towards
her room. VERA takes a towel and goes to the bathroom off
up left.*)

SYLVIA: My dear, of course. We can all be sick with
laughing when we get there. Don't lose them, anybody.
Oh, Freda, may I come in with you and tat myself up.
Terribly sweet of you, shan't be a minute, Gordon. Better
get a taxi, George – make sure that it's a new one. Poor
darling, it must be awfully drab for you having these
heads, too much noise I suppose –
(*She disappears with FREDA into her room. GORDON goes
out of front door for a taxi.*)

GEORGE: I say, what about taking the old uke with us?
That's an idea. Good lord, yes. (*He goes to his room.*)

VAL: Wait for me, Esther. I'm just going to put my shoes on.

ESTHER: All right. I shan't be a minute.
(*They disappear into their respective rooms.*)

GORDON: (*Entering again and moving down to centre.*) Hullo,
Jenny.

JENNY: (*Who has been looking at the drawings with JIMMIE
and LAURA, and laughing.*) Hullo, dear. How's things?

GORDON: Ooh, not so bad. So-so and all that. Something
funny's happening to me this evening.

LAURA: Not that poisonous girl?

GORDON: Yes, poison and all. I'm potty. (*He rushes to FREDA's room.*) Can I come in?

SYLVIA: (*Off.*) Yes, do.

(*He does so.*)

LAURA: Well, let's go on, shall we? (*She switches off the standard lamp.*)

JENNY: Yes, let's. Where's Peter?

PETER: (*Sitting in armchair.*) You're very unobservant this evening.

JENNY: (*Going to him.*) Darling, well, fancy hiding away over there. Tch, look at your tie, all crooked. (*She pats it straight.*) That's better.

PETER: No, don't, dear. It was perfectly all right.

JENNY: What's the matter, Peter? Nervy?

LAURA: We'll go and call for a taxi, and wait for you at the bottom. Come on, Jimmie.

JIMMIE: Oh, no. Half a minute. (*He sits on the small table down right.*)

LAURA: Poor little fing. Pain in tummy?

JIMMIE: No, mental pain. I've been wildly gay all the evening, then, all at once, I felt this wasn't happening now, it's only a memory already.

LAURA: Don't, Jimmie! Don't!

JENNY: It's only because it's your wedding day.

JIMMIE: Probably. (*He jumps up and clutches LAURA, and they go towards the front door.*)

LAURA: Bye, Peter. Sorry you're not coming.

PETER: Farewell.

(*They go.*)

JENNY: I don't want to go really, shall I stay with you?

PETER: Of course not. (*He rises.*) Why miss the entertainment?

JENNY: I shall think about you all the evening. And about tomorrow.

PETER: Well, go along, the taxi's probably ticking up like mad. (*He takes her up centre.*)

JENNY: Goodbye, darling.

(*They kiss.*)

Stay awake, won't you? Get back as early as I can.

PETER: I'll still be up, I expect.

(*JENNY kisses her finger, touches the tip of his nose with it, and goes. PETER sighs almost with relief, and goes towards the stairs. As he ascends them, ESTHER comes from her own room and studies herself in a mirror up centre. PETER goes into JENNY's room. ESTHER has dressed herself carefully in contrast to the previous act, when her appearance was nondescript. Now she looks rather beautiful, and is just beginning to be aware of it. She turns, comes down and calls out.*)

ESTHER: Va-al, I'm ready.

(*But receives no answer. GEORGE opens his door. He looks at her for a moment, and then says:*)

GEORGE: Good lord!

ESTHER: Hullo!

GEORGE: You're marvellous.

(*He drops his ukelele on the table, and grabbing her to him, kisses her passionately. She does not resist, but, when he kisses her for the third time, says in a surprised, terrified voice:*)

ESTHER: No, no! Let me go! Please let me go!

GEORGE: (*Releasing her.*) I say, I'm sorry. I... Good God, I'd forgotten all about that taxi.

(*He picks up his ukelele, runs to the front door and goes out. ESTHER stands trembling, and then, going to VAL's room, calls.*)

ESTHER: Val. Val, darling.

VAL: (*Emerging.*) Ready.

ESTHER: (*Taking his arm.*) You have been a time, Val darling. Come on, we...

VAL: You're shaking all over, dear. What's the matter, Esther?

ESTHER: Nothing. I – I'm a bit surprised at myself, that's all. Don't ask me now.

VAL: (*Putting his arm round her.*) Poor lamb.

(*VERA has come in up left in her pyjamas and got into bed.*)

VERA: (*Yawning.*) Oooh, I'm so tired. I wish you'd all hurry up and go.

(*She turns over and goes to sleep.*)

ESTHER: We are. Good night, pet. (*She bends over the divan.*) She's nearly asleep already.

VERA: (*Mumbling.*) 'Night, darling. 'Night, Val, sweet li'l thing.

VAL: Shall I turn the lights out? (*He turns out the standard.*)

VERA: Mm.

VAL: Well, I'll leave one on in the hall, or we'll trip over when we come in.

(*SYLVIA, GORDON and FREDA reappear.*)

SYLVIA: ...so I said it's not a bit of use saying it's not your fault, my...

(*ESTHER turns out the chandelier at the switch up right.*)

VAL: Ssh! Don't make such a row.

SYLVIA: Oh, my dear, I'm most terribly sorry. We'll creep out on our toes.

ESTHER: (*Whispering.*) George has gone for a taxi. It's probably waiting.

GORDON: (*Whispering.*) Well, how many of us are getting into it?

(*They are outside the door by now, FREDA is the last. She turns and calls softly:*)

FREDA: Good night, Peter.

(*But there is no reply, so she goes out and shuts the door. There is a pause – talk and chatter outside, then a door-slam off right. There is no sound now but VERA's breathing, which develops into a quiet snore interspersed with vague murmurings as she talks in her sleep. PETER emerges from the upper room and comes cautiously down the stairs. He has on his hat and is wearing the old raincoat in which he first appeared. There is a suitcase in his hand.*)

VERA: Go back, Lyndon.

(*PETER starts and stumbles on the stairs.*)

PETER: Damn!

(*VERA wakes up.*)

VERA: Oooh, how awful. What are you doing, Peter? Why are you all dressed to go out? I thought you stayed in to sketch.

PETER: (*On stairs.*) So I did, but I found that I hadn't any chalks, and I was just going out to buy some.

VERA: (*Rising.*) What are you doing with Jenny's case? Were you stealing?

(*Without answering he takes up the case and goes towards the door. VERA intercepts him.*)
You needn't run away. I shan't do anything. You're going for good, I suppose? Are you?

PETER: (*After a long pause.*) As a matter of fact, I am.

VERA: Well, I shan't stop you. I never interfere with fate.

PETER: How very wise.

VERA: I've never quite been able to place you, but I understand now. You're quite ruthless.

PETER: Quite ruthless, dear, quite unscrupulous, unmoral in every way.

VERA: Exactly how wicked are you?

PETER: Well, I'll tell you. (*He moves down left of divan.*) To begin with, I've never painted in my life. Those sketches I stole from a friend of mine. I've lived on them and my looks quite comfortably for years. There are lots of girls, like Jenny, who are only too anxious to help a good-looking artist between intervals of inspiration. It's a lovely life. Don't you think so, Vera? (*He lights a cigarette.*)

VERA: Poor little Jenny... Well, it had to happen to her some time. Of course, I admire you, really.

PETER: Oh, but you shouldn't. That's very wicked of you.

VERA: I always admire anyone who has the courage to be entirely evil. (*She switches on the standard.*)

PETER: It doesn't need any courage. I've always been like it.

VERA: Of course you're very highly evolved, really. All in the wrong way. (*She sits on the divan.*)

PETER: (*Sitting on side of armchair.*) Well, Vera darling, why don't you phone up the police and have me arrested?

VERA: It's no good fighting against evil. Besides, what would be the use? It wouldn't help Jenny.

PETER: This is all terribly interesting. How long have you known I wasn't all I appeared to be?

VERA: Well, I've often looked at you, and thought – what does he mean? In spite of his beautiful face, I don't know what he means. And then I've thought – if he is really cruel and ruthless underneath, it's no good warning Jenny. I never interfere with people's lives.

PETER: You're very unmaternal.

VERA: Oooh, no, I'm not. I love my children. I want them to be *happy*, and they can't have *real* happiness until they've come right up against evil and faced it and got over it for themselves.

PETER: You think I've been good for Jenny, then? That's a relief because I've been more *fond* of her than any girl I've done this on before. Do you know, I nearly didn't go tonight. I've enjoyed this affair so much, and Jenny was so charming, I thought, why not prolong it a bit more. But as she herself suggested it should end in a fortnight, I carried on with my original plan. You see, she's not very different from any of these other girls really.

VERA: (*Jumping up.*) Oooh, you're foul and common. I thought you were grandly evil as if evil ever could be grand. It's petty and small, because it's cheating. Get out.

PETER: (*Rising and putting his cigarette out.*) Why this violent change all of a sudden?

VERA: And give me that case! (*She grabs it and tries to pull it from him.*) It's full of stolen things, I suppose.

PETER: Don't be a fool. You're much too fat to do this sort of thing. Fat and ridiculous. You and your precious daughter, a nice sort of mother you are.
(*VERA hits him in the face.*)
Oh dear, she's a temper, hasn't she?

VERA: (*Still grabbing the case.*) You'll be caught one day. You won't go through all your life like this. Everyone finds their own level, and you know where yours is, don't you? You'll land there one of these days, where you belong! In the mud!
(*There is a hurried knocking on the front door, and GORDON's voice 'Vera! Vera!' PETER is so surprised that his hold on the case relaxes. VERA with a triumphant 'Ah!' throws it to the other end of the room.*)

PETER: Oh well, I'm glad of that. I can do quite well without it.
(*He goes up right, grabs at the phone plate, spilling the pennies over the floor, picks up his own suitcase and goes*

out of the door. GORDON, who is standing outside, hardly
seems to notice him.)
Hullo, Gordon, you're back early.
(*He continues down the outer stairs. After a pause GORDON*
pulls himself together and says:)
GORDON: Peter... Peter...
VERA: Let him go.
(*GORDON comes into the room. He stands against the door*
for a minute without saying anything. VERA walks back to
the divan. She says vaguely:)
Pick the pennies off the floor, Gordon. There're all the
phone money. (*She crosses to right of table and sits.)*
GORDON: (*Up right centre.*) Vera... (*After a pause.*) Has
someone told you? Vera. Answer. The others'll be back
in a minute. Do you know?
VERA: Know what, Gordon? What do you mean? What's
the matter?
GORDON: I don't know. I – I thought someone might have
told you...
VERA: Told me what? What is it? (*She looks at him.*)
Gordon... Well, be sensible; don't be silly about it.
GORDON: Jenny was taken ill on the way to the club. Her
eyes. I knew it was coming, she told me about it before.
VERA: Told you what?
GORDON: I promised her not to tell...
VERA: *Go on.*
GORDON: She's had an abscess behind her eyes – the
specialist told her that one day it might burst. Oh Vera –
VERA: Gordon! (*She moans and clutches his arm, shuddering*
with horror.) Where is she? Where have they taken her?
GORDON: Esther and Val – they've taken her to the hospital.
VERA: Oh, Gordon, I can't bear it. Where's Val? Val? What
have they done? Taken her to a hospital? They shouldn't
have gone to a hospital...they should have brought her
here to me.
(*LAURA and JIMMIE appear in the doorway. They come*
slowly into the room. LAURA hesitates. JIMMIE says
dazedly:)

JIMMIE: (*Coming down to table.*) Did you know Peter's gone? We met him – the bottom of the stairs. He said he was going for good. Freda's down there, crying her eyes out.

GORDON: Vera!

VERA: It's perfectly true. He was stealing. He's bogus from beginning to end...

GORDON: What?

VERA: I've always known it.

(*LAURA comes down to JIMMIE and sits left of table.*)

JIMMIE: Can't someone fetch him back? If he knew what had happened he'd...

VERA: Thank God he's gone.

(*There is a long, heavy pause.*)

GORDON: Vera, listen. How can we prevent Jenny from finding out? She believed in Peter. He was everything. She wanted idyllic memories and all that to help her...can't we say he's been called away somewhere...anything...

VERA: I can't think... I don't know any more. I don't know what's right.

JIMMIE: (*Turning up stage.*) There's pennies on the floor.

(*He commences to pick them up.*)

VERA: Don't do that.

JIMMIE: Sorry.

(*The other two just sit. At last GORDON says:*)

GORDON: Listen, Vera, couldn't we tell her he was dead? An accident or something?

VERA: I don't know, Gordon. Can we do things like that?

GORDON: We must. We can't have her whole life ruined by Peter. Jenny's got to stay like she is. It's important, Vera, you must understand.

VERA: You think we ought to pretend he's dead, then?

GORDON: Could we?

(*FREDA comes in, and goes across to her room, sobbing hysterically.*)

FREDA: Peter – Peter!

(*As she gets half-way across the stage, the curtain falls.*)

End of Act Two.

ACT THREE

The same. Some weeks later. Sunday morning.

VERA is seated on the edge of the divan in her underclothes and a dressing-gown, eating toast, drinking tea, and reading the 'News of the World'. A church bell is tolling. ESTHER, who has just come from JENNY's room with a tray containing the remains of her breakfast, is standing on the stairs.

ESTHER: What depressing omelettes this morning, dear. (*She moves down centre.*)

VERA: I know, darling. I thought you'd be too sleepy to notice. Put the tray down, I'll take it to the kitchen. (*ESTHER puts the tray on the table.*) Esther, look, dear! (*She holds out the newspaper.*) Sh! Don't make a noise about it. You see. I told him he'd find his own level. Isn't it a terrible photo, though?

ESTHER: Oh, how awful, Vera! No, I can't bear to read it. (*She snatches the paper and goes to table to read it.*) Do you think the police'll catch him?

VERA: He's so clever, they probably won't. No, let me see again, dear; I didn't assimilate it properly.

ESTHER: (*Crossing and giving the paper back to VERA.*) For goodness' sake be careful, Jenny might come out of her room.

VERA: Everything works out, you see. Going blind has spared her all this. What's he call himself? Captain – *Captain* Mainwaring. Look at the headline, 'High-Priest of Heartbreakers.' Ooh, aren't Sunday papers awful? 'Trail of ruined lives.' 'Highgate victim tells of broken engagement and stolen jewels.'

ESTHER: Do be careful, Vera.

VERA: My dear, I can hear if Jenny's door opens.

ESTHER: But the others... (*She picks up the tray from the table and takes it into the kitchen.*)

VERA: You don't suppose they won't read it for themselves, darling? But it doesn't matter, they've all been very good

and clever since Jenny's been back from the hospital, and
kept up the pretence wonderfully. Poor little Jenny.

(*ESTHER comes back.*)

ESTHER: Oh, it's all too foul and sordid. Sh!

(*FREDA comes from her room. She is attired in a happy-coat.
She carries a bottle of Eno's and a glass of water.*)

VERA: What a nice fluterpush, Freda. Suits you.

FREDA: (*Crossing to above table. Dismally.*) It's a happy-coat.

VERA: Nice brekpups?

FREDA: The omelette was most peculiar. I couldn't possibly
eat it. (*She takes the lid off the Eno's.*)

(*VERA hands her tray to ESTHER, who takes it off to the
kitchen.*)

VERA: Oh well, I made them all in such a hurry, you know.
I wanted to get all the brekbups over and done with.
There's only Laura and Jimmie's now. Boring asses, I've
given up calling them before eleven on Sundays, they
only let it get cold.

FREDA: (*Sitting down above table.*) There's all black things
in front of my eyes, and my head feels as if it'll drop off.
(*She drinks the Eno's.*)

VERA: Well, it's your own fault, sticking in your room day
after day. And you're very silly, Freda, just not bothering
about jobs. You haven't paid me for four weeks.

FREDA: (*Snappily.*) Oh, I'm sorry. I'll pay you in a week or
two. There's been nothing doing lately.

VERA: Yes, there has. But you'll never get cast, my dear, if
you go about looking so drab.

FREDA: Who's that a photo of?

(*ESTHER comes back from the kitchen.*)

VERA: (*Pulling the newspaper away.*) Oh, it's nothing. It's all
very terrible. You don't want to see it.

FREDA: It looked like Peter... Was it?

ESTHER: (*Above divan.*) Yes, it was. Speak quietly. Jenny
might hear.

FREDA: I can't speak any quieter. (*Rising and moving to
divan.*) Let me see it, please.

VERA: (*Rising and moving round left of divan and off up left
with paper.*) No, I can't bear all this persistence. You must

buy a paper yourself. And please don't discuss the subject in the flat. Ooh, this awful washing-up.

(*A pause.*)

FREDA: (*Sitting at end of divan.*) What'd it say in the paper?

ESTHER: (*Standing.*) He's been caught at last, that's all.

FREDA: Have the police got him?

ESTHER: No, they're trying to. He got engaged to some poor girl at Highgate, and stayed with her people, and then went off with the bits of jewellery. It makes me feel sick to think anyone can be so wicked. (*She goes to the table.*)

FREDA: (*Loudly.*) Did it say he'd – he'd done it on a lot of girls?

ESTHER: Sh! Yes, of course. Oh, but what's the good of talking about it. It'll only make it even more difficult for me to try and sound enthusiastic when Jenny talks about him. (*She sits right of table.*) Let's forget it. It's nothing to do with us now.

FREDA: Isn't it?

VERA: (*Coming back with a tray containing tea and toast and the paper.*) Did you see that he...

ESTHER: (*Rising.*) Sh! Vera, do whisper, please.

VERA: Oh, all right, dear. That it was a week ago he ran away from that Highgate girl, and they only just told the police on Friday.

(*FREDA snatches the paper away and sits on small table.*)

ESTHER: Tried to hush it up, I suppose.

VERA: Yes. Esther, take this tray and wake up those lazybones. (*She gives ESTHER the tray.*)

ESTHER: (*Moving to upstage door right.*) Laura! Jimmie! Brekbups. Still asleep.

VERA: (*Sitting on divan.*) Oooh, what awful brutes. Jimmie! Laura! You sweet little things. Esther, open the door.

ESTHER: I can't, I'm holding the tray.

VERA: Put it down, then.

ESTHER: (*Obeying her.*) Jimmie! Laura! (*She turns the door handle.*) It's locked.

VERA: No, it's not, dear. Try again.

ESTHER: It is. Look. (*She pushes against it.*)

VERA: Laura! Jimmie! (*She rises and crosses right.*) Oooh, good heavens, what's the matter, I wonder.

ESTHER: Open the door! Can you hear us? I can't see in the keyhole. It's stopped up.

(*VAL comes out of his room. He is in the middle of dressing and is attired in a shirt, flannels and bedroom slippers.*)

VAL: Whatever's going on?

ESTHER: The door's locked, and they won't answer. You come and try.

VAL/VERA/ESTHER: (*Banging at the door.*) Laura! Jimmie!
(*FREDA rises and crosses to table. GEORGE, holding a ukelele, comes from his room in a dressing-gown.*)

GEORGE: Steady on, man, what's all the fun? (*He moves up to centre of group.*)

VERA: It's no good shouting any more. If they won't hear, they won't. They've probably killed themselves.
(*GEORGE strums.*)

FREDA: Oh, my God! Shut up, George! (*She snatches the ukelele from him and puts it down on the table.*)

GEORGE: (*Going to the door.*) Don't be silly, little woman. Here, I'll try. (*Yelling.*) Jimmie! Laura!

FREDA: (*Clutching her head.*) Oh! Oh! My head!

VERA: Shut up, George. This is all too awful. We must push the stuff out of the lock. Try the pin of this brooch.
(*There is a lot of chatter.*)

GORDON: (*Who has come in during VERA's last speech.*) Won't they answer? What's happened? (*He is up centre.*)

ESTHER: The door's locked. Vera thinks they've killed themselves. Oh, whatever shall we do?

GORDON: Good heavens. (*He comes to the door.*)

VERA: Come on, don't waste time about it.
(*VAL pushes the door ineffectually.*)

GEORGE: Come out of the way. That's no good.

VAL: (*To VERA.*) But, Vera, they can't have sort of killed themselves. What for? They were perfectly happy. It's a joke, perhaps.

GEORGE: Jimmie! Laura!

VERA: Wait a minute, George, be quiet. See if we can smell gas.

(*They all sniff. JENNY comes from her room and feels her way down the stairs. She has her handbag. ESTHER runs to her.*)
Jenny – go back.

ESTHER. You shouldn't come down by yourself, darling. Do be careful.

JENNY You must let me. Don't be irritating. What's happened? (*She sits on the divan.*)

VAL: I believe I can smell something.

FREDA: Oh God!

VAL: It is gas.

GEORGE: You see, they've blocked up the bottom of the door and everything.

VERA: Go on, you fools. Do something. Open it.

GORDON: Have you tried the other keys?

GEORGE: No, that's an idea. (*Going to his door for the key.*) I'll try mine. I opened mine with theirs last week. (*He tries it.*) Good, it fits!

VERA: (*Backing to divan.*) Stand back, Val. It's full of gas. (*She picks up a chemise off the divan and flaps it about.*)

ESTHER: (*At head of divan, nearly in tears.*) Whatever made them do it?

FREDA: Mind the fumes. Don't light any matches. Do mind the fumes.

GORDON: We'd better go in.

GEORGE: Right. (*He takes a handkerchief from his pocket and starts to tie it round his mouth.*)

VERA: (*Crossing right again.*) Mind out of the way. You silly fool. I'll open the window.

(*She goes in calmly. The others hover at the door all talking at once.*)

(*Off.*) Quick! They're still breathing. Go away, George. Gordon!

(*They all rush in to her. JENNY sits where she is, not quite sure what has happened. She says:*)

JENNY: Esty...are they all right? Esty?

(*After a second or two VERA appears behind the others, ushering them back into the hall.*)

VERA: Go along. Go along now, all of you. Out of the room. No rubbish. You've had your excitements.

VAL: But, Vera –

VERA: There's nothing to worry about. They'll soon be better. There was a crack in the top of the window and the air was coming in all the time. Gordon, you stay and help me make them sick. Bring the salt.

(*She shuts the door, leaving herself and GORDON in the bedroom.*

A pause.)

VAL: Poor darlings. (*He sits in the armchair.*)

GEORGE: (*Seated on table.*) But why did they do it, that's what I can't make out. They'd nothing to worry about. Good lord, man, they must be crackers.

VAL: It's a pity they didn't die if they really sort of wanted to. I must work it into a novel.

ESTHER: (*At head of divan.*) I can't understand why they did it.

FREDA: (*Seated on hall chair by telephone.*) They were always so cheerful, weren't they?

JENNY: I'm not very surprised. Things Laura's said to me sometimes.

VAL: They looked so sweet.

FREDA: (*Rising and going to chest of drawers for cigarette.*) God, what a Sunday morning to wake up to. My head was bad enough before, but all that banging on the door and shouting –

JENNY: Well, it saved their lives, didn't it?

FREDA: Oh, I know, I know. (*She lights a match.*) It's all very well for you to – (*Pause.*) What's the matter? Why are you all looking at me like that? (*She burns her fingers with match.*) I shall go mad! Yes, and I know you all think I'm horrible and bad-tempered. I know. But if you had to put up with what I have to put up with, and a lot of sympathy I get, don't? And you're all laughing at me inside, I suppose, but if you knew; if you only knew.

(*She makes hysterical sounds and disappears into her room. The others look at each other in blank amazement. VERA, followed by GORDON, comes into the hall.*)

VERA: It's all right. It's all right. They've been divinely sick.

GEORGE: Thank God.

GORDON: Shut up! There's been a fearful noise going on all the time. Do be quiet, or they'll never get better. (*He sits in chair by telephone.*)

GEORGE: It's only old Freda. She's gone completely crackers.

VERA: (*Crossing left.*) Oooh, she's much too much of a good thing lately. I must do something about it. (*She sits in chair left of table.*)

JENNY: Are they really all right now, Vera?

(*VAL rises and moves over to divan.*)

VERA: Yes, Jenny darling. Look, they left a note. It's so pathetic. (*She reads it out.*) 'Sorry, Vera, we wanted things to stop like they are. The rent's on the mantelpiece. Laura and Jimmie.' (*She folds it up and puts it in her bosom.*) They've got the gas out of them, and I've wheeled the bed in front of the window so that the air will blow over them. They're quite green round the gills, of course, and everything's very suppressed and nebulous, but they'll soon be better with that divine air.

ESTHER: We must be ever so tactful.

VAL: Yes, we must. Do you think we ought to just sort of ignore the subject? Or should we sort of ask them if they feel better? Or would that be rude?

VERA: I'll tell you what we'll do. Rather a divine man at the club won two bottles of gin with some coupons, and as he doesn't drink he gave them to me. Now let's go out until lunchtime so that Laura and Jimmie can be quiet. And then come back to a divine party. We'll have the gin and I'll get something exciting to eat. (*She rises and goes down left.*)

VAL: (*At door of his room.*) But will gin be all right for them?

VERA: It'll cheer them up.

(*VAL exits.*)

GEORGE: By Jove, yes. Well, it's all been damned exciting. (*He picks up his ukelele from the table and starts strumming 'Happiness Pie'.*)

VERA: I won't have this sort of thing.

(*GORDON rises and snatches the ukelele from him.*
VERA is putting on a skirt over her pyjamas down left.)

You must all go for a walk. Go on, George. Into your room, right in; dress yourself, shave yourself and go out. And the same applies to everyone. What are you going to do, Jenny darling? Go for a walk with Esther?

JENNY: I don't know, Vera. Perhaps.

VERA: I'm going to sit with those poor little things for a bit. Will you come with me, darling? I'll read to you if you like.

(*GORDON, who has been walking up and down, suddenly picks up the statuette on the bracket right, and smashes it on the floor. The others stare at him.*)

JENNY: What was that? Someone else getting temperamental?

GORDON: I'm ever so sorry. I forgot about Laura and Jimmie for a moment. I'm in a furious temper. I had to do something. (*He goes to his room.*)

VERA: (*Coming centre.*) Well, I'd have broken it myself one day. Beastly thing. It always registered sinister.

(*JENNY gets up and goes towards VERA. ESTHER attempts to lead her.*)

JENNY: (*Firmly.*) Esty, don't.

VERA: Let her do it by herself, Esther.

JENNY: I must get used to the geography of this room. I walked round it three times yesterday without tripping once. Now, wait a minute. (*She moves forward but trips over a chair above the table.*) Oh damn; well, I could have done it. You must have moved the furniture, the chair wasn't there last night.

ESTHER: Yes, it was moved for breakfast. Oh, Jenny, are you hurt?

JENNY: Well, don't get all tragic, dear. I only knocked my knee.

VAL: (*Who has entered from his room.*) Vera, did you darn my grey socks? Hullo, what's the matter?

ESTHER: Oh, darling, shall I do something? What do you want put on it, butter?

VAL: (*Moving over to JENNY.*) No, sort of steak, isn't it? Tie
a piece of steak on it.
(*They are above the table.*)

JENNY: (*Laughing.*) That's for a black eye, you fool. No, it's
all right. The pain's gone already.
(*She goes towards VERA with ESTHER leading her.*)

VERA: Come along, darling little Jenny. How are they
getting along?
(*ESTHER opens the door and takes JENNY in.*)
Oh, you're sitting up then, you poor little things.

JIMMIE: (*Voice off.*) Hullo, we've been sick!

VERA: What! Again? (*She goes into the room.*)

ESTHER: (*Coming out and shutting the door.*) Every time
I look at Jenny I nearly burst into tears. I mind it all
much more than she does herself.

VAL: (*Left of table.*) Is it right, do you think, all this sort of
fool's paradise business we've pushed her into?

ESTHER: (*Right of table.*) It's against my principles, against
everything I've ever said. But truth isn't always right,
perhaps. If we'd told Jenny the truth about Peter she
might have gone potty. You don't know, all those things
coming at once.
(*A pause.*)

VAL: (*Sitting left of table.*) Where are you going this morning?
Will you come out with me?

ESTHER: I can't. I'm going to an Anti-Cruelty League
meeting.

VAL: You're always going to some sort of meeting the last
week or two, Esther.

ESTHER: (*Sitting right of table.*) I know. It's the only thing,
I've decided. I'll probably be going to them for the rest
of my life.

VAL: You're looking pale and ill. It's all horribly bad for you.

ESTHER: I can't help it. When we're discussing things at
the meeting – things that are too unbelievably vile,
I nearly throw faints, and lately, I never get to sleep at
night – I dream I'm a soldier caught on barbed wire, or
else I'm waiting to be hanged. But when my mind's got

used to things a bit...hardened, I'll be able to fight...
to argue against wickedness without getting hot and
bothered and forgetting what to say. That's all I'm going
to work for now. Anything else seems a waste of time.

VAL: (*Rising.*) It's no good my loving you any more, is it,
Esty? I'm not going to after today. We must try not to
see each other at all. You see, you've got your life work
and I suppose I've got mine. But you're so pretty and
I still want you, and I won't sublimate, oh, and I sort of
hate myself. As soon as I've had one novel published,
I'm going to be a Catholic Priest. (*He sits again.*)

ESTHER: Seriously, Val? Do you really believe in it all?

VAL: (*Defiantly.*) Yes, I do!... Well, I will when I've studied
it properly, anyway. (*He rises.*) What time are you going
to the meeting?

ESTHER: In about ten minutes.

VAL: May I just walk there with you? You know, for the sort
of last time? We won't say anything at all, but just walk.

ESTHER: (*Rising.*) All right, Val dear. Go and get your
things on then.

VAL: Yes, I'd better. (*He goes across to his room. At the door he
says:*) Do you like these bedroom slippers? An aunt gave
them to me.
(*He goes into his room.*)

ESTHER: (*Going to room up right and calling.*) Jenny!

VERA: (*Putting her head round the door.*) Shh, dear! What do
you want?

ESTHER: Only to know if I can get anything for her while
I'm out.

VERA: Be back by one, won't you?
(*JENNY appears behind her.*)

JENNY: Did you type out the next chapter?

ESTHER: Mm, every word.

JENNY: (*Coming into the hall.*) How exciting. Do fish it out
and let me feel it.

LAURA: (*Voice off.*) Give me a hanky, Vera.

VERA: Oooh! (*She goes back into the room, closing the door.*)

JENNY: Do you think it's good?

ESTHER: Yes, I do.

JENNY: (*Walking round below table to left.*) Of course, you can't get the feel of it when you've taken it down from the beginning. It's definitely the best thing I've done, though. I know it is. No, don't go yet, darling, get it in a minute.

ESTHER: (*Who has crossed to JENNY's side.*) I won't. Look, here's the divan. Wait a second while I put the cushion up. That's better.

(*JENNY is now seated on the divan. ESTHER sits beside her on the floor.*)

JENNY: Thank you, dear. If only being blind didn't make me feel like an irritating child. Esther, I wish everyone wouldn't be so suppressed about it. You make a pretence that I'm really the same as all of you. In a way you seem ashamed to admit that I'm blind to me. It makes it worse somehow. I feel if only everyone in the flat would congregate together with me there, and we were all to say 'Blind, Blind, Blind' again and again, it would clear the atmosphere.

ESTHER: I know what you mean, darling, I'm ever so sorry. But we all feel a kind of shyness to you since it's happened. (*She sits up by her on the divan.*)

JENNY: The same thing applies to Peter, too. I do so want someone to talk to me about him sometimes, but no one ever does.

ESTHER: I do, Jenny.

JENNY: I know, but – I never quite feel your mind meeting mine. Is it because you're frightened it will upset me too violently?

ESTHER: I expect so. (*She rises.*)

JENNY: It won't. Because I never really feel that Peter's dead at all. And I never shall feel it. I know now my blindness was providential. It's brought me so close to him. I know the real Peter, the Peter that I loved is as alive as you are, Esty. And if I wasn't blind, I'd never have realised that so clearly. Because, as far as I'm concerned, you're only a little more tangible than Peter is. You're only a presence and a voice. I feel Peter's presence just as clearly as yours, and I can see him clearer than you, Esty. Do you remember that line by Rupert Brooke? 'And see, no longer blinded by our eyes.' I wonder if Peter knew that poem. I hope death is like that, don't you, Esty? Esty dear, why don't you answer? Where are you? Esty?

ESTHER: (*Who has seated herself left of the table.*) I'm... I'm here, Jenny darling.

JENNY: What's the matter? You're crying, dear. Oh, Esty, don't!

ESTHER: No. It's only the poem. That one always makes me cry. (*Pressing her handkerchief to her mouth.*) I'll... I'll get the manuscript now. I've done ever such a lot. (*She rises and goes up stage.*)

JENNY: No, wait a minute, please. You were crying about me, weren't you?

ESTHER: Yes, I was. (*She kneels by JENNY.*)

JENNY: Well, don't, dear. It's awfully silly of you. I'm happy. I'm not minding the blindness so much as I thought I should. It's opening new things to me, exciting things. And I've still got Peter. And we're working very well, aren't we?

ESTHER: Yes.

JENNY: Well, all right, idiot.

(*ESTHER rises.*)

Now go and get the manuscript so that I can – feel it in my hands – and think how clever I am!

ESTHER: (*Drying her eyes.*) Do you want all the chapters from the beginning?

(*GORDON comes in up left. He is fully dressed.*)

GORDON: (*Blackly.*) Has George gone out yet?

ESTHER: No. Ooh, I must hurry. I shall be late for the meeting. (*She goes to her room.*)

JENNY: Why are you livid? I can feel wave upon wave of rage exuding from you.

GORDON: I'm raving mad, that's all. I knew I'd go mad one day, and now I have. Oh, everything's gone wrong,

Jenny. Everything's changed, just when I didn't want it to. (*He sits right of the table.*)

JENNY: Why, Gordon?

GORDON: Because I'm in love –

JENNY: What!

GORDON: With that preposterous Sylvia. I don't want to be. I hate her. (*He rises and walks round the room.*) She gets on my nerves, but I'm in love with her. I can't think of anything else, and now Sylvia's messed up everything. I'd got my life entirely mapped out. Oh...and I promised you something too. (*He comes back to left of table.*)

JENNY: Do you mean about our getting to know each other?

GORDON: Yes... I promised such a lot of things then. I haven't fulfilled any of them.

JENNY: It's my fault too.

GORDON: (*Sitting on divan by JENNY.*) But I did mean them, Jenny. Honestly, I did. I mean them still, but somehow it's not so easy. I can't see anybody except Sylvia – and me. Last night she had a date with me and didn't turn up, and I've found out she was with George. (*He rises.*) Oh, well – I don't know why I should worry you with it all. (*He goes and sits on the chair in the hall, by the telephone, and glares in the direction of GEORGE's room.*)

VAL: (*Coming out of his room.*) Hullo. Where's Esther? (*He goes up left of divan.*)

JENNY: In her room. She'll be out in a second.

GORDON: Oh, Val, I forgot to tell you. Somebody read your novel at the firm and thought it was pretty good.

VAL: (*Going over to GORDON.*) You don't mean it! You're pulling my leg!

GORDON: I'm not. I saw a report on somebody's desk. It sounded quite hopeful.

VAL: Gordon! Do you think they'll sort of publish it? Oh, Jenny, you are sweet. May I kiss you? Esther, do come in here. Isn't it marvellous? How many royalties will they sort of give me? Oh, they must do it. Of course, they won't really, it would be too good to be true. Perhaps they will, though. Do tell me. What did it say on the report? Did it think it was brilliant or only promising? I wonder how *much* I should get. A hundred pounds, do you think? Good heavens, I'll be able to pay Vera at last. Vera! Vera! (*He knocks on upstage door right.*)

GORDON: (*Who has risen and come down to GEORGE's door.*) I want a word with you.

GEORGE: Come in.

(*GORDON goes in to GEORGE's room.*)

ESTHER: (*Coming from up left with the papers.*) I've been sorting out the top copies from the carbons. Here it is, darling.

JENNY: Ooh, quick! Let me feel! (*She takes the papers from ESTHER.*)

VERA: (*Appearing.*) Sh! They've just gone to sleep. Hello, you sweet little thing. What do you want?

VAL: Oh, nothing. It's a bit silly. Of course they won't do it. Good lord! What a fool. And who'd understand it if they did? (*He sits above table.*)

(*GEORGE and GORDON start quarrelling off.*)

VERA: Be quiet, you awful boys. What's the matter with everyone this morning? (*She crosses to JENNY and then to the glory-hole for her cloak.*)

JENNY: Look, I've dictated all that to Esty in ten days. Is that hard work, or isn't it?

ESTHER: (*Moving up to front door.*) Goodness, I must fly. It's nearly one already. Come on, Val.

VAL: (*Jumping up.*) I'm waiting. (*He goes up to her in the hall.*)

VERA: Don't be late.

ESTHER: I shan't. It's only a tiny meeting.

JENNY: Good-bye. 'Bye, Val.

ESTHER: 'Bye, darling. Be caref – 'Bye, Vera.

VERA: Sweet little things.

VAL: 'Bye, Jenny darling. (*He blows a kiss to VERA.*) Did you hear about my novel? Gordon said there's a chance it might be sort of...

(*They go.*)

JENNY: What do you think of it, Vera?

VERA: (*Who has been reading the typescript.*) I don't know yet. I'm not sure it registers quite right.

JENNY: Funnily enough, it's come awfully easily. Vera, can you understand this? I'm sure Peter helps me to write it. When I get hopelessly stuck on occasions, I swear I can hear his voice telling me where I've gone wrong, or what the next sentence should be...

(*During this VERA has put on her cloak.*)

VERA: (*Quickly changing the subject.*) Oh, Jenny, there's a Queen's Hall Symphony concert this afternoon, shall we go? Now where did I put that gin? (*She goes on her hands and knees and retrieves two bottles of gin from under the divan.*)

JENNY: Do let's, Vera! How exciting! What is it?

VERA: Ah, here it is. Now how shall we get these open? I haven't seen a corkscrew for months. I'll put them here.

JENNY: What are you putting where?

VERA: (*Above table centre.*) Gin on the table. We'll have to have cups; there aren't enough glasses to go round. (*She goes to the kitchen, and comes back with cups.*)

JENNY: It never tastes so good.

VERA: Never mind. I'll get some sandwiches from one of those funny shops if they'll let me have them. Divine party. Freda'll probably spoil it. (*She gives a wry look at the Eno's bottle which FREDA has left on the table.*)

JENNY: She is rather a trial. Oh, I think I'll go and practise writing in Esty's room till one, then. Will you help me, Vera? I've done enough tripping about for one day.

VERA: (*Going to below her.*) Come on, you darling little thing. (*They begin walking off up left.*)

JENNY: It's incredibly difficult to know where the end of the page is. I often go right over it and begin scribbling on the table. Are we in the passage yet?

VERA: Just.

JENNY: There you are, I knew.

GEORGE: (*Following GORDON out of his room.*) That calls for an apology. (*He has forgotten that he has no trousers on, and is wearing only a shirt and short pants.*)

GORDON: Does it?

GEORGE: You'll damn well apologise or I'll knock your block off.

VERA: Ooh, my God, aren't men awful? (*She comes centre.*)

GORDON: Oh, shut up, Vera.

GEORGE: I'll give you a damn good hiding if you're not careful.

GORDON: That'll be nice.

GEORGE: Who met her first, anyway? Did I bring her here or did you?

GORDON: I don't care who brought her here first. That's no excuse for...

VERA: (*Stepping in between them and shouting them down.*) Go and have a fight in the street. We're not used to this nonsense in my flat.

GORDON: (*Together.*) Look here, Vera, I was to meet Sylvia last night –

GEORGE: (*Together.*) Look here, Mrs Lyndon, I brought Sylvia here in –

(*JIMMIE appears in his doorway with a pale reproachful face.*)

JIMMIE: (*Going round left of GORDON, wearily.*) For God's sake! Don't you know we're ill?

(*He returns to his room again. There is a pause.*)

GEORGE. (*Together.*) I put it to you, Mrs Lyndon, how would you like it if –

GORDON: (*Together.*) Vera, I wish you'd ask George to –

VERA: I don't care what either of you do as long as you go out this minute. (*She starts pushing them towards the front door, then runs into GEORGE's room for his trousers.*) Go on. Go along.

GORDON: Stop all this pushing. I'm going, anyway.

VERA: And George too. You can fight outside if you like. And I hope Gordon knocks you out, and both be back at one for the party. And here are your trousers. (*She throws him his trousers.*) My God!

(*She hurries them out of the front door, bangs the door on them and turns back into the room. JENNY bursts into laughter.*)

JENNY: Poor Gordon! That's really a case of poetic justice. Still, I hope he gives George a black eye, or something –

VERA: (*Seated on chair below telephone.*) You know, Jenny, the flat wants weeding out. There are two people in it who are becoming a nuisance.

JENNY: Who's the other – Freda?

VERA: Yes, she's worse than ever lately. Perhaps there's something wrong with her vibrations.

JENNY: Perhaps there's something wrong with her mind.

VERA: As for George. Do you know, Jenny, I really think it's positively old-fashioned to be a man. And in a few years there won't be any left. They'll all go right out of fashion.

JENNY: Well, good-bye, dear. I'm going to work. (*She goes off up left.*)

VERA: (*Rising.*) Will you be all right by yourself, darling? I'm going to buy some sandwiches, and I haven't any money. I'll have to borrow from the phone.
(*JENNY shuts herself in. VERA goes to the phone-plate, takes a handful of coppers and goes towards the front door. But she stops and calls out:*)
Oh, Freda, Freda!
(*FREDA comes from her room. She looks as if she has been crying.*)

FREDA: Yes?

VERA: Will you give me something off your rent, please. I'm very hard up this week and nobody seems to be giving me any money.

FREDA: Well, if nobody's giving you any, why do you pick on me especially?

VERA: That's nothing to do with it. Besides, the others compensate for their misdoings by being pleasant.

FREDA: Are you insinuating that I'm unpleasant, then?

VERA: You're always going round being rude to everybody, aren't you?

FREDA: When have I been rude? What do you mean? How dare you say that? It's you who are rude. You're always being rude and horrible to me.

VERA: Don't shout. You seem to forget there are people ill in the house.

FREDA: What about me? (*She comes down and sits on the divan.*) Of course, I don't count at all, do I? I could be dying and nobody in this house would give me an ounce of sympathy.

VERA: Well, as you generally seem to be dying every day, we would find it a little difficult.

FREDA: You horrible woman. You pretend to be very grand, don't you, but I know all about you! You were a...

VERA: (*With supreme dignity.*) I was nothing of the sort, Freda. I was simply a highly evolved woman who lived the life I wanted to.

FREDA: (*Laughing hysterically.*) Funny, aren't you?

VERA: Ooh, how awful you are. (*She steps up and away.*) Well, you must clear off tomorrow, rent or no, you don't belong here.

FREDA: (*Rising.*) So you turn on me like that now, do you? After all the months I've been here paying you regularly.

VERA: It's nothing to do with that. It's because you're out of place, out of tune with everybody. We can't cope with you any more. (*She goes to hall.*)

FREDA: (*Following her.*) And suppose I can't cope with you? Suppose I can't cope with you, eh?

VERA: Well – all the better, then you won't mind going.

FREDA: I hate you! I hate you!

VERA: Well, as long as you leave the flat tomorrow, I don't mind.

FREDA. I can't leave. Where can I go? I haven't any money. I haven't got a penny, I tell you.

VERA: Well, that's nothing to do with me. It's your own fault if you've just sulked in your room instead of looking for work. Oh, go away, you make me sick. (*She goes out of the front door.*)
(*FREDA stands shaking all over with rage. She makes one or two inarticulate sounds, and then crosses left and goes three steps up the stairs.*)

FREDA: (*Calling.*) Jenny! Jenny! Miss Lyndon! I want to speak to you.
(*JENNY comes from ESTHER's room and stands in the archway. She carries her manuscript.*)

(*Shouting.*) Peter's not dead at all. We only pretended he is so you wouldn't know he's a cad and a thief and he's wanted by the police.

(*There is a long pause. FREDA has averted her head from JENNY as she shouts her revelation. Now, slowly and with terror, she turns, gazing at JENNY with trembling apprehension. At last she says:*)

Oh, I didn't mean it. I didn't mean it, Jenny. I didn't mean it... (*She commences to sob.*)

JENNY: (*Coming slowly into the room.*) What did you say? Peter's not dead? (*Below chest of drawers.*) He isn't dead?

FREDA: No, no. I didn't mean it. Don't take any notice, I didn't know what I was talking about.

JENNY: Tell me what you said.

FREDA: I can't. I can't.

JENNY: (*Stepping to her.*) Tell me what you said. Do you hear?

FREDA: No, no, I can't. I only made it up. It's not true. I'm mad; I don't know what I'm talking about.

JENNY: You said Peter wasn't dead. I know you said it in a temper, and I shan't blame you, but you can't go back. You must tell me the truth.

FREDA: (*Restraining her sobs a little.*) Please, please, don't ask me to, Jenny. Don't ask me.

JENNY: I am asking you.

(*FREDA makes an effort and controls herself.*)

FREDA: (*Turning away to head of divan.*) It's true, then. He's not dead.

(*After a long pause JENNY speaks, in a strained, unreal, rather high voice.*)

JENNY: Why did you all pretend he was? Where is he? Did you make it up about the accident? Freda? I want to sit down. I can't think what the room looks like.

FREDA: (*Going to her.*) Here's the divan. Here you are. I didn't mean to tell. Really, really, I didn't mean to tell you. (*She sits her on divan.*)

JENNY: What else was it you shouted just now?

FREDA: Oh, Jenny...please...

JENNY: (*Harshly.*) Tell me what you said.

FREDA: I can't. What good can it do?

JENNY: Tell me what you said.

FREDA: (*Above table.*) I – I said that he was a cad and a thief and that the police wanted him.

JENNY: Is that true?

FREDA: Yes. (*She sits above table.*)

JENNY: Why? What did he do?

FREDA: Vera found him going away on that night when you went...when you were taken to the hospital. He had your case.

JENNY: So you all thought I'd be happier thinking he was dead... Whose idea was that?

FREDA: Gordon's, I think... Vera's... I don't know.
(*JENNY sits perfectly still, but very straight and stiff. At last:*)
(*Rising.*) Jenny, Jenny, don't sit there like that. Jenny, do say something.

JENNY: Why did you tell me?

FREDA: (*Through her sobs, working across to armchair.*)
I couldn't help it... I did it without thinking... If you knew what I've had to go through... I was in love with Peter too; he pretended he was with me. When he left you like that, he was leaving me as well. I had to bear it all...and I've had no work, and I'm too ill to go out, and everyone thinks I'm putting it on. You've been happy and I've been miserable, and I hated you... I hated you because it wasn't fair. And I'm getting ugly lately and your mother was beastly to me... (*She sobs wildly in the armchair.*)

JENNY: It's all right, Freda.
(*She still sits stiffly in her chair, a queer, strained expression on her face. The phone rings. FREDA controls her sobs sufficiently to rise and answer it.*)

FREDA: Yes. Yes, it's Freda speaking. (*A long pause while she listens, then:*) Peter? No! No! I can't. I can't meet you. (*She drops the receiver on the table and turns into the room.*) It's Peter. He wants some money. Whatever shall I do? He wants me to meet him outside. The police are after him.

JENNY: Peter's outside... Freda, ask him to come here.

FREDA: No, no, you mustn't.

JENNY: Please do what I tell you.

(*FREDA looks at her and then goes slowly to the phone. She lifts the receiver.*)

FREDA: Are you still there? Come up and see me.

JENNY: Say there's no one here.

FREDA. No, it's all right. Nobody's in. You'll come, then. (*She drops the receiver and turns.*) I don't know what I'll do when I see him, Jenny. I don't know what I'll say to him. I've been hating him so, but I'm so frightened I might start loving him again. That's no good, is it? It's only silly... Neither of us must see him. He mustn't come. (*She opens the front door.*)

JENNY: Will you do something for me, Freda?

FREDA: Yes, I will. Anything!

JENNY: Don't see him at all. Stay in your room.

FREDA: (*Shutting the font door.*) Oh, Jenny, I don't know. Perhaps if he saw me. No, I mustn't. I'll lock myself in. I'll wait till he's gone. (*She crosses left.*)

JENNY: Go now, will you?

FREDA: But, Jenny –

JENNY: Please go. (*She rises.*)

(*FREDA goes to her room. JENNY moves and sits in the chair left of table. She is shivering, and once or twice she moans. PETER appears in the doorway. Finding JENNY instead of FREDA, he half backs out again, but changes his mind and comes into the room.*)

PETER: (*Up centre.*) I thought Freda said there was nobody here.

JENNY: I told her to. I wanted to speak to you.

PETER: (*Coming down.*) Listen, Jenny. I've no time for beating about the bush. You know what I am, don't you? I'm not ashamed of it, and it's your own fault if you were fool enough to believe in me. Well, that damned photo in the paper's done it. My landlady saw it and phoned the police. I heard her and tore out of the house, like a fool, without a penny in my pocket. Can you give me some?

Anything. A pound or two. Ten shillings; enough to get a train to somewhere. Come on, answer me, don't sit like that. You've altered. Why do you look so funny? (*He is right of the table.*)

JENNY: My eyes. I can't see any more.

PETER: Can't see? (*He comes nearer to her.*) Are you quite blind?

JENNY: Yes.

PETER: I'm sorry. (*He backs away.*)

JENNY: (*In terror.*) Please don't come near me. Please.

PETER: I wasn't. (*He goes up.*) Where's Freda? Has she got any money?

JENNY: Just talk to me for a minute or two and then I'll give you some and you can go.

PETER: What do you want?

JENNY: Only to talk a little bit.

PETER: Well? (*He comes back to above table.*)

JENNY: Did you ever care for me at all? Tell me the truth. (*He does not answer.*)
You only wanted to live for nothing, I suppose, and get what you could?

PETER: If you put it like that.

JENNY: I'm not the only one, of course.

PETER: No. That's how I live.

JENNY: Don't you mind what you do to people? They might kill themselves. Anything.

PETER: Oh, rot! The way I look at it is like this. If they're fools enough to be taken in by me, they deserve all they get. Still, I'm sorry, Jenny, that's how it is. Lots of these girls are just out for a hectic affair. You really were in love with me, weren't you?

JENNY: No, I wasn't in love with you. It wasn't you at all.

PETER: Who was it then?

JENNY: Not you. It was someone I imagined. (*For the first time her strained unnatural self-control begins to waver.*) Peter...

PETER: Don't start crying, Jenny. (*He moves towards her.*)

JENNY: Not you!

PETER: Look, where's this money? Give me some money
and I'll go.

JENNY: There's my bag on the table.

PETER: Where? Oh, here it is. How much is in it?

JENNY: A pound or two.

(*PETER takes out the money.*)

PETER: All right. (*Going to the front door.*) Good-bye, then.
(*A pause.*)
Good-bye. Thanks for the money. I'm sorry about...your
being blind. (*He hurries out.*)
(*When the door is shut behind him, JENNY gets to her feet.
She walks forward about three steps and then faints over the
steps leading to the hall. After a minute, FREDA's door slowly
opens and she cautiously puts her head round. Then she sees
JENNY.*)

FREDA: Oh! (*She runs to her and, kneeling beside her, calls:*)
Jenny! Jenny! Oh, whatever shall I do? Laura! Jimmie!
(*Jumping up, she runs to their room. We hear them inside.*)

JIMMIE: What's the matter? We've been to sleep.

LAURA: What? What's that?

FREDA: Do come and help me. Jenny's in a faint. She's on
the floor. What can we do? Where's some water? Quick!

JIMMIE: (*Sleepily.*) Wait a minute.

LAURA: What can we do?
(*VERA comes in at the front door. She hurriedly drops the
boxes of sandwiches which she is carrying, on the telephone
table, and kneels beside her daughter.*)

FREDA: Can't you come without any slippers? Here you
are. Hurry. Oh dear, shall I phone for a doctor? Yes,
that's what I'd better do.
(*She appears in the hall again.*)

VERA: Come and help me, please.
(*FREDA does so, and they help JENNY into a sitting position
in the armchair. Meanwhile, FREDA is saying:*)

FREDA: It wasn't my fault, I swear it wasn't. Peter's been
here. She's found out everything. Oh dear, whatever shall
we do?

VERA: Go and get some water.

(*She bends JENNY forward, so that her head is between her knees, and, for a few seconds, holds her like that.*)

FREDA: I swear it wasn't my fault – If I'd known – I'd never...

VERA: Go and get some water.

(*FREDA obeys. As she is going towards the corridor, LAURA and JIMMIE appear in their doorway, where they stand apathetically.*)

LAURA: Can we do anything?

VERA: No, go to bed again.

JIMMIE: Are you sure?

(*VERA doesn't answer, so they go back to their room, shutting the door.*

JENNY moves, and VERA pulls her back into a normal position supporting her with her arm.)

JENNY What's the matter? Have I fainted? Who's that?

VERA: It's me, darling.

(*Then JENNY remembers. Her face crumples. She whispers.*)

JENNY: Oh, Vera.

(*And, turning to her mother, leans against her, Sobbing quietly. VERA strokes her hair.*

FREDA comes in with a glass of water, but VERA waves her away. For a second or two FREDA hovers about helplessly. Then she bites her lip, and puts the glass down on the table, and goes to her room At last, JENNY says, brokenly:)

I don't want to live any more, Vera.

VERA: (*Her arm round her.*) Sh, darling. Don't say that...you don't mean it, Jenny.

JENNY: Nothing's real now... Nothing... He was there in the room, Vera, but it wasn't Peter. Where is he? He's nowhere! I made him up. Vera! (*She suddenly calls the name as though terror-stricken.*)

VERA: Darling...darling...

JENNY: And it was his voice. I wanted him to put his arms round me, I wanted to touch him, but that wouldn't have been any good... It wasn't Peter. (*Her weeping becomes uncontrolled.*)

(*VERA envelops her in her arms, rocking her, hushing her, almost crooning to her. Not till JENNY's sobbing has abated somewhat does she speak.*)

VERA: In the end, Jenny, you've got yourself. Nothing
anybody can do to you really matters. It's all evolving,
darling. It had to be. When Lyndon went away I didn't
say life was at an end. I said, I've got myself. Nothing
anyone can do to me really matters. And soon afterwards
I got the idea of painting the furniture. And, although
I think about Lyndon and talk about him, I've forgotten
him really... If he did come back, I wouldn't really
care... You'll forget Peter too, Jenny. You'll forget him
soon...

JENNY: Give me my manuscript, Vera. I think I dropped it
when I fell.

(*VERA gets manuscript.*)

It was my fault. I was just an idiotic fool. All my talk
about truth...and I made up pretty lies for myself –
invented a man to fall in love with...

(*Her lip trembles and a few more tears trickle down her
cheeks. Her hand clenches on the sheets of typescript. She
picks them up, and tearing them across twice, drops them on
the floor.*)

That's no good, it's only sentimental. Tosh. Pretty. I must
start all over again. (*A pause. Then she says pleadingly:*) It
was my fault, wasn't it? I should have seen through him.
And it might not have happened. It might have been
someone nice instead of... (*With a tremendous effort she
holds back her tears.*) I've just got to start all over again,
that's all.

(*JENNY stands up. VERA puts out her hand to restrain
her.*)

No, darling, you mustn't keep helping me. I'm all right
on my own.

(*She goes weakly to the stairs and so to her room. VERA
stands staring after her. GEORGE and GORDON burst in
at the front door.*)

GEORGE: I'm ravenous. Where's the sandwiches? Hooray!
Can I open them, Vera? (*Without waiting for a reply, he
opens the boxes and starts to eat.*)

(*VERA crosses to the divan.*)

GORDON: (*Moving down to the table.*) Hullo, darling. Got a headache? Well, you'll be pleased to hear that the Sabbath air has had a beneficial effect on George and me. We've decided to fight a duel, haven't we, George?

GEORGE: Rather. Corking idea. (*He puts the box of sandwiches on the table.*)

GORDON: Give me one, swine.

(*FREDA comes into the hall and runs across to VERA, who is now sitting in one of her favourite positions, cross-legged in the middle of the divan.*)

GEORGE: (*With his mouth full.*) Who are you calling swine? (*He goes into his room for his ukelele.*)

FREDA: Is she better? I am sorry about just now. Please let me stay on. I'll get some work next week, I know I will. (*GEORGE comes out with his ukelele and strums, sitting in the armchair.*)

VERA: If you like, Freda. (*She is almost oblivious to the others, gazing up at JENNY's door.*)

(*LAURA comes out of her room, followed by JIMMIE.*)

GORDON: (*Together.*) Hullo, are you better?

GEORGE: (*Together.*) You've soon got over it.

JIMMIE: We're not really.

LAURA: But we thought the only thing to do was to come and join the party. Is Jenny all right now?

GORDON: (*Seated right of table.*) Why? Has she been ill? (*VAL and ESTHER come in. ESTHER is carrying a bunch of flowers.*)

VAL: (*Coming down to the table.*) Sandwiches (*He grabs one but spits it out again.*) Oh God! Garlic! Everything seems full of sort of omens lately. I bet you they don't take the book after all, Gordon.

ESTHER: (*Standing at the bottom of the stairs.*) Jenny!

LAURA: Jimmie darling, everything's going round.

JIMMIE: Sit down, pet.

(*He turns GEORGE out of his chair. LAURA sits.*)

GEORGE: (*His mouth full.*) What about the gin, Vera?

FREDA: Don't bellow!

(*There is a momentary silence as JENNY comes from her room.*)

ESTHER: What's the matter, darling? I've brought you some flowers. Can you reach?
(*JENNY comes down two steps and takes them from her over the banisters.*)
Got them?
JENNY: (*Sniffing them.*) How lovely. What are they?
ESTHER: Jonquils. They've got little surprised faces. You feel.
(*JENNY touches them with her fingers.*)
JENNY: So they have. (*She gives a little laugh.*)
VERA: Darling? Are you all right?
JENNY: Yes, Vera. I'm all right. (*She smiles as, leaning over the banisters, she drops her mother a flower.*)
VERA: Jenny... You're smiling... (*And she is smiling too a calm, slow smile, almost of beatitude.*)
(*VAL suddenly switches on the gramophone. Everybody but VERA and JENNY start talking at once. The noise swells into a babel of sound as the curtain falls.*)

The End.

BEFORE THE PARTY

based on a short story by W Somerset Maugham

Characters

LAURA WHITTINGHAM
a young widow

DAVID MARSHALL

KATHLEEN SKINNER
Laura's elder sister

SUSAN SKINNER
Laura's younger sister

BLANCHE SKINNER
Laura's mother

AUBREY SKINNER
Laura's father

NANNY

Before the Party was first performed at the St Martin's Theatre, London on 26 October 1949, with the following cast:

LAURA, Constance Cummings

DAVID, Roderick Lovell

KATHLEEN, Judith Furse

SUSAN, Margaret Barton

BLANCHE, Mary Merrall

AUBREY, D A Clarke-Smith

NANNY, Winifred Oughton

The action of the play passes in Laura's room in the Skinners' house in Surrey

Act I: a summer afternoon

Act II: three hours later

Time: the present

ACT ONE

LAURA's room in the Skinners' house in Surrey. A summer afternoon.

The room is a large one on the first floor and has been comfortably furnished to serve both as a bedroom and a sitting-room for LAURA. The door to the landing is centre right of the back wall and when the door is open, part of the balustrade of the stairs can be seen. The bathroom, where the pedestal washbasin can be seen when both doors are open, is directly opposite across the landing. A door approached by two steps across the corner up right, leads into KATHLEEN's room. There is part of a large bay window left, with a balcony overlooking the drive and front garden, and the roof tops of neighbouring houses can be seen in the distance. The fireplace is in the centre of the wall right. There are well-filled built-in bookshelves to the right of the landing door. A small writing-desk with an upright chair to it stands down right below the fireplace. Between the fireplace and the door up right there is a work table. The chest of drawers with a telephone on it, stands left of the landing door with the bedstead to the left of it. There is a wardrobe in the corner up left and a dressing-table above the window bay, where there is an occasional table, an upright chair and a waste-paper basket. Two upright chairs stand to the left of the bed and below the bookshelves, and there is a stool in front of the dressing-table. A chaise-longue or couch stands centre right and a low coffee table down centre. The fireplace has an ornate mirrored overmantel and a large club fender. The floor and landing are carpeted and gay chintz curtains hang at the window. Several pictures and plaques decorate the walls. There are three pairs of electric wall brackets, one pair each side of the overmantel, and one pair over the bookshelves. The switches are left of the landing door.

When the curtain rises, it is a bright sunny afternoon and the window is open. Both doors are shut. LAURA in her underclothes and dressing-gown is seated on the end of the bed, staring unblinkingly, forlornly, in front of her. After a few moments, DAVID calls from the garden off left.

DAVID: (*Off, calling.*) Laura.

(*LAURA looks up, startled and hunted.*)

(*He calls again.*) Laura.

(*LAURA rises, goes to the window and closes it, then moves restlessly about the room, first to the fireplace, then above the chaise to the dressing-table where she pauses, turns and finally throws herself on to the bed. There is a knock at the landing door.*)

LAURA: (*Raising herself on her elbow.*) Who's that?

DAVID: (*Off, calling.*) David.

LAURA: You can't come in.

(*She watches the landing door in silence for a few moments, then it is slowly opened and DAVID enters. He stands in the open doorway looking at her gravely.*)

(*After a pause.*) I said you can't come in.

DAVID: (*Entering and closing the door behind him.*) What's the matter with you? Have you gone crazy?

LAURA: (*Rising.*) David, please go.

DAVID: Where would you like me to go to?

LAURA: (*Moving down left.*) Go back to London – (*She turns.*) and don't ever come here again.

DAVID: (*Moving centre.*) Haven't you forgotten something? We're going to be married.

LAURA: We're not. I told you. I've changed my mind.

DAVID: Apparently you changed it in the middle of kissing me on Broom Hill – and hared off home before I had a chance to answer back.

LAURA: There's nothing to answer. I've changed my mind.

DAVID: (*Moving to right of LAURA.*) Have you? Well, I've not changed mine.

LAURA: David – for God's sake. I don't want to see you any more. I don't want to marry you. I know it must seem very erratic and odd, but leave it at that. I shouldn't have let it go so far.

DAVID: But what have I done?

LAURA: You've not done anything. I ran away to avoid a dreary cross-examination. Now go. Kathleen's probably in her room – she'll hear us.

DAVID: So what?

LAURA: Well – this is my bedroom. (*She crosses below him to centre and turns.*) You've been drinking again, haven't you?

DAVID: I stopped at The Feathers on my way. Any objection?

LAURA: No – it has nothing to do with me.

(*KATHLEEN enters up right. She stops right of the chaise on seeing DAVID.*)

KATHLEEN: Oh – excuse me. There was something I wanted to talk to you about, Laura – something very serious.

LAURA: Later, Kathleen. After the party.

(*KATHLEEN looks from LAURA to DAVID, then turns to the door up right.*)

What's the matter, Kathleen?

(*KATHLEEN stops and turns.*)

Do you object to David coming up here to talk to me?

KATHLEEN: I don't want to criticise, Laura, and I know it has nothing to do with me, but I think you should remember that you're not in West Africa now – you're in Luffingham.

LAURA: (*Moving and sitting on the end of the bed.*) I'm under no misapprehension.

KATHLEEN: Well, you must realise that things that might be all very well on the Gold Coast are looked upon in Luffingham as extremely bad form. Of course, it's nothing to do with me, I know.

DAVID: It's my fault for coming up here, Miss Skinner.

KATHLEEN: I'm not blaming you, Mr Marshall. I know you were in the underground movement in Yugoslavia during the war –

LAURA: I don't see what that has to do with it.

KATHLEEN: (*Ignoring the interruption.*) – and I can well imagine you became accustomed to a different kind of life between the sexes. But that was some time ago now.

LAURA: What do you mean by – 'a different kind of life'?

KATHLEEN: Well – a life without time for social conventions and so on. Men fighting side by side with women – sleeping in the same tents together...

LAURA: I don't think they had tents.

KATHLEEN: Well – next to each other on the grass, then – or whatever it is they do in guerilla warfare. But please remember, Mr Marshall – and I don't mean to criticise, I'm speaking to you as a friend – you're in England now – you're not still in the Resistance – and Laura is not a guerilla.

(*DAVID bursts into laughter.*)

(*Angrily.*) Oh, you know what I mean. How else can one pronounce the word? And I don't think it's very nice, Laura – going on like this while you're still in mourning. (*She turns and exits up right. DAVID is abruptly sobered by her words.*)

DAVID: (*Looking intently at LAURA.*) Is that what's worrying you?

LAURA: What?

DAVID: Mourning. What people will think, and all that.

LAURA: (*Protestingly.*) Oh, David!

DAVID: What then?

LAURA: (*Looking away.*) I – I just thought – I'm not a very good person for you to marry.

DAVID: (*Moving in left of LAURA.*) Can't I judge for myself? (*He kneels on the left end of the bed and kisses her.*)

LAURA: Darling – I'll try – I'll try so hard to be good for you.

DAVID: What are you talking about?

LAURA: I don't know. Nothing.

DAVID: Tell me – is there any insanity in your family?

LAURA: Yes.

(*They kiss again and fall backwards on to the bed. LAURA frees herself and sits up.*)

DAVID: (*Trying to pull her down.*) Hey!

LAURA: No, no, Bruce darling – let me go. She'll come in again.

DAVID: (*Releasing her.*) Did you hear what you said then? You called me Bruce.

LAURA: How extraordinary – yes, I did. (*She ponders a moment.*) Yes, how extraordinary.

DAVID: Who were you thinking of? (*He pauses.*) Laura – did you call your husband Bruce?

LAURA: No, no. Bruce was someone I knew years ago before I married. I certainly wasn't thinking of him consciously. (*She studies DAVID's face and runs her fingers through his hair.*) You are a bit like him, though, now I come to think of it.

DAVID: Were you in love with him?

LAURA: Yes. I was very young – it was ten years ago. Really, that *is* odd, my suddenly calling you Bruce.

DAVID: What's happened to him?

LAURA: Bruce? He was killed in the war – so Nanny told me. I never saw him again after I went to Africa. (*She pauses.*) (*DAVID sits up.*) (*She rises with a sigh.*) I *must* start getting ready for the Bishop. (*DAVID rolls over and lies face downwards on the bed, with his head at the downstage end and his feet on the pillow.*)

DAVID: Is that what you were always saying to this character – 'No, no, Bruce darling, let me go'?

LAURA: (*Laughing.*) Not at all, David. (*She moves to the wardrobe.*) You've got your boots on the bed. (*DAVID rolls over on to his back.*) Oh, it doesn't matter – leave them there. (*She opens the wardrobe and takes out a clothes hanger.*)

DAVID: (*After a pause.*) What's this about getting ready for the Bishop? I thought it was the Canon's garden party.

LAURA: (*Moving right of the dressing-table.*) It is, but the Bishop's coming – the Bishop of Capetown.

DAVID: That's Armstrong – isn't it?

LAURA: Why, do you know him?

DAVID: My father did. (*There is a pause, during which LAURA picks up her black suit from the stool, and hangs it on the clothes hanger.*)

LAURA: He's giving an address this afternoon – on missionary work on the Gold Coast.

DAVID: Will there be anything to drink?

LAURA: (*Picking up a clothes brush from the dressing-table.*) Yes – lemonade and iced coffee. (*She brushes the suit.*) And they're having ices sent in from Boddy's in the High Street.

DAVID: What a prospect! (*He sits up, swings his feet off the bed and sits on the right edge of it.*) Can't we go to the party and then quietly disappear?

LAURA: (*Replacing the brush and moving to the wardrobe.*) I don't want to spoil Mother's afternoon. (*She hangs the suit in the wardrobe.*) I know she's planning to show me off to the Bishop. (*She moves to the stool, sits and manicures her nails.*) She thinks we must have lots in common because we've both been to Africa.

DAVID: (*Lying back on the bed with his head on the pillow.*) When are you going to tell her – and your father – about us?

LAURA: (*After a pause.*) After the party perhaps.

DAVID: (*After a pause.*) I *must* get a job with better pay. (*He sits up.*)

LAURA: Stick to the one you're in for the moment, David.

DAVID: (*Swinging round and sitting on the end of the bed.*) I wish to God I could find a job that interests me.

LAURA: Do you think you ever will, while you know that whatever you do, it's only marking time?
(*SUSAN enters from landing with a rush. She is an intent-looking child of twelve.*)

SUSAN: (*As she enters.*) Laura... (*She stops short on seeing DAVID.*) Oh, sorry. (*She closes the door.*)

LAURA: Just a minute, Susan, we're talking.

SUSAN: (*Moving down centre.*) I want to tell you something.

LAURA: Not now, dear. Come back in a minute or two. And don't listen outside the door.

SUSAN: As if I would.

LAURA: I thought it was your favourite occupation.

SUSAN: Just because I happened to hear Nanny and Logan talking about something they shouldn't.

DAVID: What was that, Susan?

SUSAN: Working out how many American babies there were in Luffingham. I only happened to be doing up my shoe outside the door. They shouldn't have been talking about it.

DAVID: And how many were there?

LAURA: Don't encourage her, David.

SUSAN: Sixty-two – but Logan says they're nearly all Poles.

LAURA: Well, go away, dear – come back in five minutes.

SUSAN: (*Moving to the landing door.*) I might just as well have told you what I was going to while we were standing here gossiping.

(*She exits, closing the door behind her.*)

DAVID: Laura – shall I make an all-out effort to ingratiate myself with the family?

LAURA: Why?

DAVID: To make it easier for you – if you're going to tell them today.

LAURA: I shouldn't bother. Susan likes you, anyway.

DAVID: She won't be much help. Has Nanny any influence?

LAURA: Nanny's always spoilt me; she'll be the only one who won't say I might at least have had the decency to wait another four months.

DAVID: Why four months?

LAURA: So that a year will have passed since Harold's death. A tribal custom. (*She rises and moves to the wardrobe.*) David, look out of the window while I change.

DAVID: (*Rising and easing up to the landing door.*) Shall I go outside?

LAURA: (*Taking a bright frock from the wardrobe.*) No, I want to talk to you. (*She moves below the bed.*)

DAVID: (*Crossing to the window.*) Don't forget you're not in West Africa now. (*He gazes out of the window.*)

LAURA: (*Placing the frock on the bed.*) Kathleen should go and live in West Africa for a few months before being superior about it. (*She takes off her dressing gown.*) The white residents have extremely high moral standards. Their hypocrisy is an example to the world.

(*DAVID turns and looks at her, then recollects himself.*)

DAVID: (*Turning again to the window.*) Sorry, I'm looking.

LAURA: (*Picking up the frock.*) David – do you think – before we're definitely engaged – (*She slips the frock over her head while she continues speaking.*) – that I ought to tell you a great deal more about myself?

DAVID: A great deal what?

LAURA: (*Her head emerging.*) A great deal more about myself before we definitely become engaged. (*She moves to left of the bed.*) You can look round now.

DAVID: (*Turning.*) You've told me about this Bruce character in your life. Are you bent on going through the whole list?

LAURA: (*Sitting on the stool.*) There weren't any others. No, I meant about my life with Harold.

DAVID: You can tell me if you want to, but what's the point?

LAURA: Well – (*She glances quickly at him.*) – perhaps it's best for us to know more about each other. (*She picks up the bottle of nail varnish.*)

DAVID: Are you working up for a probe into my past?

LAURA: No, no, no. I only said that about Harold, because... (*She breaks off and puts down the bottle of varnish.*) Oh, I shan't varnish my nails, I can't be bothered. (*She stretches out her hand to DAVID.*) They look all right, don't they?

DAVID: No, they're chipped. You'd better fix them.

SUSAN: (*Off, calling.*) Can I come in now?

LAURA: (*Calling.*) Yes, if you like.
(*SUSAN enters, closing the landing door behind her.*)
You've come back very quickly.

SUSAN: (*Easing to right of the bed.*) I wasn't listening, if that's what you're trying to say.

LAURA: (*Rising.*) I should think not, as you said you wouldn't – (*She crosses to right of the chaise.*) – or did you have your fingers crossed?
(*DAVID moves to the stool and sits.*)

SUSAN: Well, I did as a matter of fact, so that I could have listened if I'd felt like it.

LAURA: You leave nothing to chance.

SUSAN: It's best to be prepared in this life.

LAURA: I dread to think what you'll be like at my age, Susan.

SUSAN: I won't be like anything. I'm going to take poison before I get old.

(*DAVID and LAURA laugh.*)

DAVID: What was the great news, Susan?

SUSAN: (*Bouncing herself on the end of the bed.*) I saw a pig being killed.

LAURA: You didn't stop and watch, did you?

SUSAN: Yes, I did. (*She sits on the end of the bed.*) I was passing the farm, and the gates were open. They stuck a knife into its throat and all the blood was pouring out and it was screaming like anything.

LAURA: You disgusting child.

SUSAN: Why? The man who stuck the knife in was disgusting. I was sorry for the pig. (*She pauses.*) Anyway, you had bacon for breakfast.

LAURA: So did you.

SUSAN: Yes – but I hadn't seen then. I'm going to consider not eating it any more.

LAURA: Is that the dress you're wearing to the party?

SUSAN: Yes, why?

LAURA: You know Mother told you to wear your blue. You'd better change it.

SUSAN: (*Indicating LAURA's frock.*) Are you really going to wear that?

LAURA: Yes, of course.

SUSAN: Oh well, I shan't change then. Mother'll be so upset at your wearing pink instead of mourning, she won't notice what I've got on.

(*LAURA sits on the chaise, facing the fireplace, takes up the copy of 'The Tatler' and looks through it.*)

DAVID: Susan, tell me – you're an expert on these things. What's the best way of getting your mother to view you in a favourable light?

SUSAN: Do you mean me or you?

DAVID: I mean me, really.

SUSAN: Well, I have all sorts of ways, but they wouldn't be any good for you. Having clean nails and not sniffing, for instance.

(*DAVID looks at his nails and makes a slight grimace.*)

Not wolfing meals and not shouting about the house.

LAURA: Every one of them applies to David.

SUSAN: He doesn't sniff.

LAURA: (*To DAVID.*) I don't know why you should worry about what they think of you, but if you really want to please Mother, tell her how young she looks in the new hat she's got for the garden party.

DAVID: And I suppose I should pay more attention to – (*He lowers his voice.*) Kathleen.
(*LAURA shrugs her shoulders.*)
And what about your father?

SUSAN: I know what he ought to do, Laura, he ought to call Daddy 'sir'. (*To DAVID.*) Daddy loves younger men to call him 'sir'.

LAURA: Yes, you could throw in a few more 'sirs' when you're talking to him. I think he misses the deference due to his years and lack of experience. But I shouldn't bother.

SUSAN: (*Rising and moving right of the bed.*) If I said Daddy lacked experience, you'd be furious.

LAURA: Well, I'm allowed to say things you can't.

SUSAN: Why?

LAURA: Because I'm grown up.

SUSAN: I don't see what difference that makes. The fact that you were born before me is purely accidental.
(*BLANCHE enters through landing door. She is wearing her dressing gown and a hat decorated with veiling and ospreys. DAVID rises. She closes the door behind her and poses with a roguish expression for them to admire the hat.*)

BLANCHE: Well? (*She notices DAVID, and her face falls.*) Oh, hello, Mr Marshall, I didn't know you were here.

DAVID: (*Breaking to the window and turning.*) I came up to talk to Laura.

BLANCHE: (*Moving centre.*) Excuse my being in my dressing gown. I wanted to ask Laura about my hat. (*To LAURA.*) Why didn't you take Mr Marshall into the garden, dear? (*She turns to SUSAN.*) Susie, go and change, there's a good girl.

SUSAN: I have changed, Mummy.

BLANCHE: That's not the dress I told you to wear. (*To LAURA.*) It's the most awful nuisance, we'll have to start off much earlier than I planned.
(*SUSAN sprawls on the bed, her head at the downstage end.*) There's not enough petrol to get to the party. (*She crosses to the dressing-table.*) I do think the Government might allow one special concessions for occasions like this. (*She examines the effect of the hat in the mirror over the dressing-table.*) It's nothing but lack of imagination. I'm sure Sir Stafford Cripps has never had to arrive at a party with skirts splashed with mud, and laddered stockings. (*She sits on the stool.*)

LAURA: (*Putting the magazine down on the chaise.*) It was January, Mother, when that happened to you. There's no mud on the roads now.

BLANCHE: There would be I'm sure, if the Government could arrange it.
(*LAURA rises.*)
Laura – you've tried on your new frock. Let me see, darling.
(*LAURA moves below the chaise. DAVID sits on the chair in the window bay.*)
Yes, it's quite well cut – but I do think it foolish of her, don't you, Mr Marshall, to buy new clothes now instead of waiting until she's out of mourning and can wear them?
(*LAURA sits on the chaise, leans back, and puts her feet up.*)
In four or five months' time, skirts may be long again, and coupons are so expensive, too. One used to be able to buy one's charwoman's coupons for two and six each, but now they want three shillings for them. It's always the same with that class of person – the moment you try to help them, they take advantage of you.

SUSAN: We don't have to have clothes coupons any longer, Mummy.

BLANCHE: Oh yes, that's right. I was thinking of chocolates. But you must all tell me what you think of this hat. (*She looks in the mirror and adjusts the feathers and veiling.*) Did you go for a nice walk, Susie, after your rest?

SUSAN: I saw a pig being killed.

BLANCHE: That was nice... (*It dawns on her what SUSAN has said, and she turns sharply.*) *What* did you say?

SUSAN: They stuck a knife in its throat and all the blood was spurting out.

LAURA: Oh, don't keep *on* about it.

BLANCHE: Now, Susan, if you ever stop and look at anything like that again, I shall take you straight to a psychiatrist. It was very ill-bred of you to watch. Thank goodness I've never seen anything like that, or I'm sure I should never eat meat at all. They say those stock yards in Chicago... What was that book that created such a scandal before the last war, exposing all the horrors of the corned beef factories? *Greed*, that's what it was called – by Sinclair Lewis. Mrs Baxter – you know, the woman on the Committee of the Institute with me – she was telling me how they make *foie gras*. It's horribly cruel, she said, forcibly feeding the geese or something – just as they used to do with suffragettes – she a Theosophist – but I absolutely refused to listen. Heaven knows, I said, we have little enough pleasure allowed us with this awful government, but I happen to have a jar of *foie gras* sent me from America. I've been looking forward to it as a treat, and you mustn't spoil it for me by telling me how it's made. (*She adjusts her hat again in the mirror.*) If there's one thing I cannot stand, it's cruelty to animals. (*She turns to display her hat.*) Well, shall I wear it, or not?

(*There is a pause.*)

Don't you like it?

LAURA: It's not bad.

BLANCHE: Is that all? Why? Is it too young-looking?

DAVID: Oh no, certainly not. You look a bit like Hedy Lamarr in it.

(*SUSAN giggles.*)

BLANCHE: (*Scrutinising herself again in the mirror.*) La Marr? She's on the films, isn't she? Stop giggling, Susan. (*She turns.*) I was mistaken for Lily Elsie once, when

I was a girl. Of course, talking of corned beef factories,
I really oughtn't to wear ospreys. I wouldn't dream of
buying them myself.

SUSAN: (*Eagerly.*) Do they pull them out of the birds alive?

BLANCHE: Susan, I don't like the way your mind's
developing at all. But my poor son-in-law brought them
for me, Mr Marshall, the last time he was home on leave.
(*She turns to LAURA.*) By the way, Laura, Harold's
photograph's disappeared from the drawing room. You
haven't taken it, have you?

LAURA: Yes. I put it away.

BLANCHE: I should have thought you'd like to have it out
(*She pauses.*) It was so nice of him, too – before he'd
started to get so fat. (*Hastily.*) Not that I minded him
getting a bit stout, dear. I thought it made him so jolly-
looking, poor boy. (*She indicates the framed photograph on
the dressing-table.*) That's awfully good of dear little
Jeremy, too, isn't it? Hasn't he got his father's eyes...?
Darling, why don't you put his Daddy's picture next to
him – they'd look so nice together?

(*There is an awkward pause.*)

(*Her eyes wander to the window.*) I wonder if they'll have
the same ices that we had for our party last year –
they're awfully good – really creamy. But I have to be so
careful, Mr Marshall, only the simplest food.

(*KATHLEEN enters up right.*)

KATHLEEN: (*Moving above the chaise.*) Do you know where
the Flit is, Mother? My room's full of mosquitoes. I've
been bitten on the elbow.

BLANCHE: The Flit?

SUSAN: Nanny's got it in the nursery.

DAVID: (*Rising.*) Can I get it for you, Miss Skinner? (*He
crosses to the landing door.*) Yes, do let me. The nursery –
that's on the next floor, isn't it? Yes, I know.

KATHLEEN: Well, you'll never find it.

DAVID: Yes, of course I will, Miss Skinner. I insist. (*He exits.*)

KATHLEEN: (*Breaking to the fireplace and turning.*) What's
come over Mr Marshall all of a sudden?

SUSAN: Is that how Harold got malaria, Laura – through a mosquito bite?

BLANCHE: You're a thoughtless little girl – you don't want to upset poor Laura, do you?

LAURA: What makes you think I'm so easily upset, Mother?

SUSAN: (*Kneeling upon the bed.*) Well, that is how you get malaria. Miss Trotman's brother was in India, and he got bitten and he was dead in a week – all through going out in the afternoon with his knees showing.

KATHLEEN: Susan, is this your idea of how to dress for a garden party?

SUSAN: I've no ideas about it.

BLANCHE: Don't be pert, darling.

KATHLEEN: You know perfectly well that it is not the dress that Mother told you to wear. And look at your hair, too. You might be one of those dreadful William's children from Elm Tree Cottage, instead of a girl from a decent home. Go and change at once.

(*There is a pause as SUSAN reluctantly gets off the bed and exits through landing door.*)

You'd think she had no pride. She might take some trouble not to let the family down at the party. She knows Sir Arthur and Lady Boot will be there, and their children are always so beautifully dressed. And Mother, Laura's set such a bad example to the child. I don't want to interfere, but...

BLANCHE: Now, children, don't quarrel and spoil everything.

KATHLEEN: Perhaps you can say something to stop Laura behaving like a housemaid. Not only does she ask that uncouth Mr Marshall into her bedroom, but she's obviously changed in front of him, too.

BLANCHE: Oh, Kathleen, I don't think that's so terrible. Everybody's more free and easy than before the war. It's all the result of everybody sleeping on top of each other in air raid shelters.

LAURA: (*Rising and moving below the bed.*) You must remember to tell that to the Bishop.

KATHLEEN: Laura twists everything one says into something dirty.

BLANCHE: Why, what did I say?

LAURA: Excuse me, Mother.

BLANCHE: (*Rising and easing below the bed.*) Sorry, dear.
(*LAURA moves to the wardrobe and takes a gay hat from the hat box. KATHLEEN stares at her in horror.*)

KATHLEEN: (*After a pause.*) Mother, I didn't want to say anything until I was certain, but it's obvious that Laura intends to go to the party in that dress.

BLANCHE: (*With overwhelming reproach and appeal.*) Oh, Laura, you don't! (*She pauses.*)
(*LAURA moves and places the hat on the dressing-table.*)
Do you?

LAURA: (*Sitting on the stool.*) Yes.

BLANCHE: It's not very nice or feeling of you, is it, dear, only eight months after poor Harold passed away.

LAURA: I'm sure Harold wouldn't want me to wear mourning indefinitely.

BLANCHE: But darling, what will people think if the sister's wearing mourning and the widow's dressed in pink?

LAURA: (*Laughing.*) Oh, Mother, that's a perfect jingle!

KATHLEEN: Well, whatever Laura may do – *I* shall wear my black chiffon.

BLANCHE: (*Sitting on the end of the bed.*) Laura, what's the matter with you? I've not said anything before, but you've been most strange ever since you came back from Africa – hasn't she, Kathleen? It's like – it's like having a stranger in the house.
(*There is a long pause, during which KATHLEEN gazes intently at LAURA.*)

KATHLEEN: There's something which I think Laura ought to know. I was playing golf with Gladys Benson this morning.

BLANCHE: Gladys Benson? Is she that woman who's related to Sir Arthur Boot?

KATHLEEN: (*Quickly.*) Only by marriage. Lady Boot is her aunt, that's all.

BLANCHE: Oh yes, of course I know her – Gladys Benson – she was elected Honorary Secretary of the Golf Club

239

this year, and you were so disappointed because you didn't get it again.

KATHLEEN: I was *not* disappointed. Everyone knows I didn't want another year of never-ending work, or they'd have voted for me.

BLANCHE: Yes, of course, dear.

KATHLEEN: They only voted for Gladys because of her aunt. You know what snobs some of them are at the Club. As if titles meant anything these days.

BLANCHE: Well, I consider we're a much better family than half the people with titles round here. Families like ours are the backbone of England, your father always says. What were you going to say about Gladys, dear?

KATHLEEN: She was dining with the Canon last night, and the Bishop was there. He's been to the Gold Coast, and he knows a good many people that you know, Laura.

BLANCHE: Oh, how interesting, Laura. That is nice. (*To KATHLEEN.*) Did he know poor Harold?

KATHLEEN: Yes, he remembers him very well. He says he was shocked to hear of his death. (*She pauses.*)
(*LAURA opens her jewel case and takes out a pair of earrings.*)
Laura, why did you tell us that Harold died of malaria?
(*LAURA looks at KATHLEEN's reflection in the mirror over the dressing-table for a moment, then slowly commences to screw on an earring.*)

BLANCHE: What do you mean, Kathleen?

KATHLEEN: The Bishop says Harold committed suicide.
(*BLANCHE gives a startled cry.*)
Is it true, Laura?

LAURA: Yes.

BLANCHE: But, Laura darling, why didn't you tell us?
(*LAURA pauses for a moment, then methodically screws the second earring into place.*)

LAURA: I thought it better for Jeremy to think that his father died of fever. I didn't want him to know anything about it.

BLANCHE: Poor Harold. (*Tears trickle down her cheeks.*) He was always a good son-in-law to me. Whatever induced him to do such a dreadful thing? (*She pauses.*) I understand about Jeremy, of course dear – but surely you could have told *me* the truth?

KATHLEEN: You might have known it was bound to come out.

LAURA: *(Turning.)* Why? I didn't expect a gossiping old parson to have nothing better to talk about than me.

KATHLEEN: When the Bishop said he'd been to the Gold Coast, it's only natural that Gladys should ask him if he knew you and Harold. It put me in a very awkward position with her. Now she'll tell everybody we hushed it up because we were ashamed, and it'll be all round the Golf Club in no time.

BLANCHE: But Harold always seemed so jolly – and so normal. And he had dear little Jeremy and a very good position in the Civil Service. And he always seemed to like the life in West Africa, in spite of the snakes and natives. *Whatever* made him do it, Laura?

LAURA: The climate.

BLANCHE: Poor boy, how dreadful! And he kept it all to himself so as not to worry you, I suppose? He never said a word to us when he came home on leave. What a terrible shock it must have been for you. How did it happen, Laura?

LAURA: Kathleen can probably tell you.
(KATHLEEN hesitates, then decides to speak.)

KATHLEEN: *(Moving centre.)* The Bishop says Harold cut his throat.
(BLANCHE gasps.)
He says that Laura had been away with Jeremy, and when she came back she found poor Harold dead on the bed.
(BLANCHE begins to sob and rises.)

BLANCHE: *(Moving to LAURA.)* Laura – my poor child.
(She puts her arm around LAURA.)

LAURA: *(Pulling herself free.)* Please don't fuss me. I can't stand being mauled about.
(BLANCHE moves and sits on the end of the bed.)

KATHLEEN: *(Moving to BLANCHE.)* Don't cry, Mother. *(She lays her hand gently on BLANCHE's shoulder.)* It'll make your eyes look red, and people will think it so funny.

(*BLANCHE makes a successful effort to control herself.*)
Now you know the truth, Laura *must* wear mourning to
the party, mustn't she? It would be bad enough wearing
pink if poor Harold had died a natural death – but with
the Bishop and Gladys Benson knowing what really
happened – and they've probably told everybody by now
– people will think it very funny indeed.

LAURA: They'll probably think it even funnier when they
hear that David and I are going to be married.
(*There is a long pause. BLANCHE and KATHLEEN stare
at LAURA.*)

BLANCHE: To be married, Laura?

LAURA: Yes – quite soon.

BLANCHE: You're not serious, are you? (*She pauses and
looks helplessly at KATHLEEN.*) But, Laura, you can't.
What would people think?
(*KATHLEEN breaks up centre right.*)
Only eight months after this terrible tragedy with
Harold. Why, we don't know anything about this Mr
Marshall. And what does he earn? Six pounds ten a
week, or something. It's out of the question.

LAURA: Six pounds and commission.

BLANCHE: Why, you wouldn't have enough to eat. Why
don't you say something, Kathleen?

KATHLEEN: (*Breaking to the fireplace.*) I've nothing to say.
(*She sits on the downstage end of the chaise.*)

BLANCHE: Oh, I'm beginning to feel a hard lump in my
stomach. It's always the same if I'm worried after a meal
– the nerves in my inside get tied into a knot. If I'd
known this was going to happen, I'd have had toast and
Bovril for lunch instead of goose.

LAURA: Shall I get you some bicarbonate, Mother?

BLANCHE: (*Pressing her diaphragm.*) No, no, I'll be all right
in a minute. (*She pauses.*) I don't know how I'm going to
get through the party.

KATHLEEN: I hope Laura doesn't expect us to congratulate
Mr Marshall.

BLANCHE: Let's not say anything about this idea of yours
yet, Laura. I'm sure after you've thought it over, you

must see how impossible it is. And, Kathleen – Laura, don't mention anything of this to your father yet. You know he has to go up before the Central Conservative Committee on Monday.

LAURA: What's that got to do with it?

BLANCHE: He mustn't be worried, Laura. I think he's supposed to make a speech – a sort of sample speech – in front of them before they accept him as a candidate for the By-Election. It would be a tragedy if he was so distracted by all this, that he forgot what he was going to say. We'll have a serious talk after the party, Laura – just you and me.

KATHLEEN: (*Rising and moving to the fireplace, in an undertone.*) I think I hear Mr Marshall coming back.

BLANCHE: (*Rising and moving to the window, loudly.*) Oh, I'm so glad Gladys Benson can come. Did you win your game with her, dear?

KATHLEEN: No.

LAURA: The news about Harold's death must have put you off your stroke.

BLANCHE: (*In a shocked whisper.*) Laura, how can you? (*DAVID enters from landing. He carries a Flit sprayer.*)

DAVID: (*Moving centre right.*) I was going to ask you, Mrs Skinner, what was that first course we had for lunch? It was absolutely pre-war – better than anything you get in black market restaurants.

KATHLEEN: (*Moving to right of DAVID and taking the sprayer from him.*) Thank you. I'll do it. (*She moves to the door up right.*)

BLANCHE: (*Abstractedly.*) We've only had Cook two weeks. We got her over from Austria.

(*DAVID perches himself on the head of the chaise.*)

KATHLEEN: (*With a significant glance at BLANCHE.*) Do you go to black market restaurants, Mr Marshall?

DAVID: If anybody asks me. I can't afford them myself.

KATHLEEN: (*Spraying violently towards the ceiling.*) I've never been in one, and I'm sure I don't want to. I wouldn't even know where to find one. (*She stands gloating over the death of a fly.*)

DAVID: You ought to try the Roumanian Restaurant in Greek Street, and the Château de Madrid. You get the most terrific steaks there.

KATHLEEN: Do you? (*The interest in her voice is unmistakable.*) Really thick, pre-war ones?

DAVID: (*Measuring with his hands.*) Porterhouse – like that.

KATHLEEN: Really? But isn't it full of the most dreadful black market types?

DAVID: The two occasions I was there, it was full of duchesses and peers.

KATHLEEN: Really? Where did you say it was?

(*AUBREY enters through landing door. He is heavy with sleep after his afternoon nap. He wears a dressing gown over his shirt and trousers.*)

AUBREY: (*As he enters.*) Blanche! (*He leaves the door open.*)
(*DAVID rises and moves to the fireplace.*)
Will you please go and see what's happening in the kitchen? (*He stares at DAVID, resentful of his presence.*)

BLANCHE: Why? What's the matter?

AUBREY: I cannot see why this house can't be run smoothly like other houses. I can't even rest in the afternoon. What am I to do? Close the bedroom windows and suffocate, or leave them open and have shouting and clamouring in the kitchen?

BLANCHE: (*Moving centre.*) I'll go and see what it is. Laura, you come with me, dear, you're so good with the servants. What was the matter, Aubrey?

AUBREY: Some dispute between Muriel and the cook. (*He turns and goes out on to the landing, leaving the door open.*)

BLANCHE: Laura, couldn't you go and settle it, dear?
(*LAURA rises and crosses to the landing door.*)

AUBREY: (*Turning and re-entering, sharply.*) Don't shirk your responsibilities, Blanche.
(*LAURA exits, leaving the landing door open.*)
Why don't you exercise authority in your own home, instead of leaving it to your daughters?

BLANCHE: Oh, I haven't any authority. I never had. (*She moves to the door.*) I haven't the personality for it.

(*She exits, closing the landing door behind her. AUBREY sits on the right edge of the bed.*)

KATHLEEN: (*Moving in pursuit of a fly above AUBREY's head.*) Excuse me, Father. (*She sprays violently, then moves below the bed.*)

AUBREY: (*Waving his hand in front of his face.*) Kathleen, I've *begged* you not to bring that stuff near me. You know it affects my sinus. (*He presses his hands to his head.*) I've been in agony since lunch time. I can hardly see with pain.

KATHLEEN: (*Spraying towards the floor.*) I must finish him off.

AUBREY: (*Groaning.*) You won't deny yourself a moment's pleasure.

KATHLEEN: (*After a pause.*) I get little enough, goodness knows. (*She crosses to the door.*) Will you ask Laura not to wear that pink dress to the party, Father? – it really is such bad form – whatever her future plans may be.

(*She exits abruptly up right, closing the door behind her.*)

AUBREY: (*Looking up.*) What's that, Kathleen? (*He sees she has gone, then looks at DAVID as though seeing him for the first time.*)

(*DAVID takes his pipe tobacco and matches from his pocket and proceeds to fill and light his pipe.*)

How long are you staying with us, Marshall?

DAVID: Till Monday morning.

AUBREY: Oh. I thought you were going back Sunday night.

DAVID: No, Monday morning – the seven forty-five. It just gets me there in time for the office – sir.

AUBREY: I thought you'd given up your job?

DAVID: No. That was the last time I came down. I've got another now – just as uninteresting – but I daresay I'll stick it out for a few weeks.

(*AUBREY shakes his head. His attention is caught by some marks on the counterpane.*)

AUBREY: Look at this. (*He rises and brushes the counterpane vigorously with his hands.*) Somebody's been lying on the counterpane with their dirty boots.

DAVID: (*Crossing to the foot of the bed.*) Where, sir?

AUBREY: It will have to go to the cleaners now.

DAVID: Perhaps one of the dogs has been up here.

AUBREY: The dogs aren't allowed in the bedroom. (*He puts his hands over his eyes.*) Do you mind if I ask you not to smoke a pipe, Marshall?

DAVID: (*Crossing to the fireplace.*) Not at all, sir – sorry.

AUBREY: Sorry to appear inhospitable, but I am already suffering from my daughter's thoughtlessness with the Flit. (*DAVID knocks out his pipe against the side of the fireplace.*) If you don't mind, Marshall, please!
(*DAVID stops his knocking.*)
Thank you! Against the white paint!

DAVID: Sorry, sir – I didn't think.

AUBREY: (*Moving to the window.*) You know it's a funny thing, Marshall – but everybody in this house is always telling me they 'didn't think'. If only they'd realise how much unpleasantness could be saved by a little forethought. (*He opens the window and contemplates the garden.*) This man, Logan, for instance – I pay him three pounds ten a week and his keep, to look after the garden and drive the car occasionally. He knows how much petrol the government allows us, but he keeps no account of how it's used, and chooses to tell me, an hour before we're due to set out for the Heywood's party, that every drop of our allowance has been consumed. (*He turns.*) Of course, it doesn't make any difference to *him* that I shall have to walk three miles in this blazing heat, thanks to his thoughtlessness.

DAVID: Couldn't you get out of going?

AUBREY: (*With an air of resignation.*) I wish I could. I'd far rather have tea in my own garden. But the Beeders will be there – Sir Willlam and Lady Beeder, you know – and the Bishop of Capetown and the Boots.

DAVID: (*Moving and sitting on the left edge of the chaise.*) Who, sir?

AUBREY: The Boots – Sir Arthur and Lady Boot – he's on the Central Committee, you know.

DAVID: Oh, yes.

AUBREY: (*After a short pause.*) They're all the same, that class, I'm afraid. If one's stupid enough to treat them fairly, they take advantage of it.

DAVID: Boot's not so bad, I believe – but I've always heard
Beeder's a terrible crook.

AUBREY: I was talking about Logan, the gardener. I meant
the servant class. (*He picks up 'The News of the World' from
the table.*)

DAVID: Oh sorry, sir, I thought you meant the Beeders and
the Boots.

(*AUBREY signs and makes a gesture with the newspaper.*)

AUBREY: I've absolutely forbidden this paper in the house,
for instance – but one of the servants (*He moves centre
left.*) has brought it in, and it must have been lying about
here since last Sunday – full of the most intimate details
of divorce cases. Supposing Susan picked it up and read
it. Frankly, some of these cases I wouldn't care to think
of Laura or Kathleen reading – or even Mrs Skinner.

DAVID: Don't you ever handle divorce cases?

AUBREY: (*Tapping the paper.*) Not this type. I try to confine
myself to clean ones. Cruelty, lunacy or drunkenness for
instance – something I would not be ashamed of my
daughters hearing in court. The only sexual divorces we
handle are where the misconduct has been performed
purely as a formality. (*As he speaks he moves above the chaise
to the fireplace, and stands with his back to it.*) Of course,
occasionally a client comes to me with something that
isn't quite nice, but I always tell him Skinner and
Weatherby don't care to undertake that sort of thing.
I generally pass him on to some other firm. (*He glances at
some headlines.*) But few of the old – established firms
keep to any decent standards nowadays. (*He taps the
paper.*) Here's a reputable people like Godden and
Stapleton for instance, acting for the defendant in a most
unsavoury case of rape.

DAVID: (*Stretching out his hand for the paper.*) May I see, sir?

AUBREY: (*Handing the paper to DAVID.*) Please destroy it
when you've read it.

DAVID: Yes, of course, sir. (*He becomes absorbed.*)

AUBREY: You should read the leading article, it's
surprisingly sane and reasoned for a paper of that type –
exactly what I've been saying myself about this attempt

to abolish capital punishment. Why should the State provide criminal murderers with food and lodging for the rest of their lives, instead of putting them out of the way? Leading sheltered existences, free from responsibilities, they may live to be eighty or ninety, doing nothing to justify themselves, and costing the taxpayers fifty-four shillings and sixpence a week each. (*He pauses.*)

(*DAVID, still engrossed in the paper, becomes suddenly conscious of the silence, and looks up to find AUBREY staring at him.*)

DAVID: Fifty-four shillings and sixpence each, sir? Er...do you think that's profiteering?

(*AUBREY glares at him.*)

Sorry – I didn't quite catch what you said.

AUBREY: I wish you'd throw that paper away, Marshall.

DAVID: (*Rising.*) Look, sir, if you're worried about getting to the party – I can fix it for you. Why don't you let me run the car down to the garage opposite The Feathers – I know the chap who owns it. He'll give me all the petrol I want.

AUBREY: Thank you – no.

LAURA: (*Off left, calling.*) David.

DAVID: (*Crossing to the window and calling.*) Yes?

(*KATHLEEN enters up right and crosses to the dressing-table.*)

LAURA: (*Off, calling.*) Come down into the garden.

DAVID: (*Calling.*) Have you made peace in the kitchen yet?

(*He places the newspaper on the table.*)

AUBREY: Oh, this shouting!

LAURA: (*Off, calling.*) Come down – I want to tell you something.

DAVID: (*Turning.*) Excuse me, I'm going down to the garden, sir. (*He crosses to the landing door and pulls the handle. The door sticks.*) What's the matter with this thing? (*He tugs at the door and the handle comes away in his hand.*) God damn it! Sorry, sir. It's all right – I'll fix it.

AUBREY: (*Moving in to right of DAVID.*) Give it to me, Marshall – I'll do it myself.

DAVID: It won't take me a minute.

AUBREY: (*Taking the handle from DAVID.*) No, leave it, please.

DAVID: It must have been loose. (*He hesitates, then gripping the metal bar which the handle has left exposed, turns it with difficulty and opens the door.*) Sorry.

(*He exits.*)

AUBREY: It's like having an ape in the house. (*He searches about on the carpet.*) What's happened to the screw now?

KATHLEEN: Father, there's something I want to tell you before Mother comes back.

AUBREY: Just a minute, dear. See if you can find it while I put the handle on. (*He puts the handle on its bar.*) There was something I wanted to ask you – let me see, what was it now?

KATHLEEN: I think you ought to know...

AUBREY: Just a minute – just a minute, Kathleen. I'm trying to remember. Oh, yes. Do you think there's going to be a collection after the Bishop's address?

KATHLEEN: (*Kneeling with one knee on the left edge of the bed.*) I shouldn't think so. It would be rather bad form.

AUBREY: (*Looking up from the door handle.*) Well, I'd better be prepared. If there is one, I'd better give for all of us. I was wondering if ten shillings would be enough, or if I should give a pound?

KATHLEEN: I think a pound would look better.

AUBREY: I don't want to give less than anybody else, but on the other hand, I see no reason to give more than I need. Can't you find the screw?

KATHLEEN: No, I can't see it.

AUBREY: We'll have to open the door carefully. I'll get Logan to mend it afterwards. (*He feels the handle.*) I think that should hold. (*He turns to KATHLEEN.*) Now – what was it you were saying about Laura's having made plans? (*The door handle is pulled from the outside and the inner handle falls to the floor. There is a faint cry.*)

BLANCHE: (*From landing.*) Oh! The handle's come away.

AUBREY: (*Calling.*) Why don't you take more care, Blanche?

(*The outer handle is pushed through its hole in the door, the door is opened and BLANCHE enters. She is now dressed for the party, in semi-mourning, and carries her gloves and handbag.*)

BLANCHE: (*Moving to the chaise.*) Kathleen, get me some bicarbonate, will you, dear? (*She sits on the left side of the chaise.*)

(*KATHLEEN crosses to the door and exits, leaving it open. AUBREY replaces and fiddles with the handle.*)

(*To AUBREY.*) What do you think Cook was wicked enough to do? You know it's Muriel's day off? Well Cook's locked her in the kitchen cupboard. Muriel's been having hysterics down there. We had to give her brandy to bring her round.

AUBREY: (*Moving centre.*) Brandy? What brandy?

BLANCHE: I took if off the sideboard, dear.

AUBREY: (*Sitting on the end of the bed.*) Oh, good heavens! The Courvoisier. You know it's to be kept for special occasions.

(*KATHLEEN enters up right. She has a glass of bicarbonate and water, which she is stirring with a spoon.*)

BLANCHE: Well, with Muriel being shut in the cupboard and having hysterics and threatening to leave – I thought it was a special occasion.

(*KATHLEEN hands the glass and spoon to BLANCHE, then eases down right.*)

AUBREY: I shall have to lock it away.

(*BLANCHE sips the bicarbonate gratefully, occasionally patting her diaphragm.*)

Did you try slapping her face and throwing water over her?

BLANCHE: Oh, but Aubrey – she was threatening to leave.

AUBREY: What had she done to Cook?

BLANCHE: (*Rising.*) I'd better get Nanny to tell you. (*She moves towards the landing door.*) She knows exactly what happened.

AUBREY: (*Rising quickly and moving to the landing door.*) I'll call her. You'll only have the handle off again. (*He carefully opens the door and calls.*) Nanny, Nanny – Nanny.

NANNY: (*From landing, calling.*) Just a minute.

(*BLANCHE moves and sits on the left side of the chaise.*)

AUBREY: (*Moving to left of the bed.*) Muriel must have done something to offend Cook. (*He sits on the stool.*) No one's going to lock a woman in a cupboard without some sort of reason.

(*NANNY enters from landing, closing the door behind her. She is a dignified woman in her early sixties. She carries a small bag of sewing.*)

NANNY: (*As she enters.*) She's calmed down a bit now – I gave her another good dose of that brandy.

AUBREY: You had no right to do so, Nanny, without asking permission. Sit down and let us have the facts.

(*NANNY sits on the end of the bed and gets on with her sewing.*)

Is it true that Cook locked Muriel in the kitchen cupboard?

NANNY: In the boot cupboard.

AUBREY: In the boot cupboard, then. And why did Cook lock Muriel in the boot cupboard?

NANNY: Because Muriel's a Jewess.

AUBREY: Is Muriel a Jewess? Had you any idea she was a Jewess, Blanche?

BLANCHE: No, I hadn't – her nose is rather turned up.

KATHLEEN: (*Turning the chair down right and sitting.*) But, Nanny, it is her uncle who keeps the farm, isn't it? He's certainly not a Jew.

NANNY: No, he's Wesleyan or something like that. It's her mother who was a Jewess.

KATHLEEN: She is one, then. (*To BLANCHE.*) She might have told you when you engaged her.

AUBREY: The girl was under no obligation to disclose her parents' race or religion.

KATHLEEN: It is the limit though, the way they worm themselves in everywhere. We've even got one at the golf club now.

BLANCHE: Who's that, dear?

KATHLEEN: You know that Scottish woman, Mrs Burns, whom you thought so charming? Well, we'd never have known she was a perfectly awful Jewess if Gladys Benson hadn't found out her name was really Bernstein. I've been very cold to her ever since.

AUBREY: Never mind about that now. (*To NANNY.*) What is the reason for Cook's extraordinary behaviour? Is she an ex-Nazi Fascist?

NANNY: Yes, of course she is. She gets a paper sent her every week with a picture of that Oswald Mole-sey on the front, and what's more, she started telling me something about we fought on the wrong side in the war. We ought to have fought side by side with Hitler, or some such nonsense.

AUBREY: (*Rising.*) She can leave this afternoon.

BLANCHE: Oh, Aubrey!

AUBREY: You can give her a fortnight's wages, and she can catch the first train up to London.

NANNY: Quick march at the double.

BLANCHE: But, Aubrey dear...

AUBREY: Blanche, please understand, if there's any chance of my representing Luffingham, my household must be above reproach. (*He moves down left and turns.*) I cannot have it said that I allow a Jew-baiting fascist to cook for me.

KATHLEEN: You're making a mountain out of a molehill, Father. It's not as if she were a Communist.

(*SUSAN enters from landing. She has changed into her party frock.*)

NANNY: Oh, there's a pretty girl – come and show Nanny – in her new party frock.

(*SUSAN crosses to left of NANNY, with an ill grace.*)

BLANCHE: Aubrey, it really is rather drastic, dear, telling Cook to go today.

KATHLEEN: I don't know where we're going to find anybody else like her. And what about supper tonight?

AUBREY: We can finish the goose.

BLANCHE: There's not nearly enough.

KATHLEEN: Mr Marshall had three helpings.

BLANCHE: And there's not a bit of stuffing left.

AUBREY: Then we can open a tin of corned beef. I will not allow a Hun and a Nazi under my roof, after six years of fighting them.

BLANCHE: It wasn't only because of Muriel's being half a Jewess, was it, Nanny?

AUBREY: Oh? Now what is the truth about this? (*He moves to the stool and sits.*)

BLANCHE: Well, Nanny tells me Cook said that Muriel was nothing but a... (*She breaks off.*) Susan, go outside – you don't want to hear this.

SUSAN: Oh, I'm not listening, Mummy, I'm thinking.

NANNY: Out you go now, quick march – at the double.

AUBREY: Go outside the room when your mother tells you. (*SUSAN sighs and crosses to the landing door.*) And the handle's loose so don't pull it off. (*SUSAN exits, closing the door behind her.*)

BLANCHE: Put this glass down, Kathleen. I shall have to take some Bisodol tablets to the party with me. (*KATHLEEN rises, takes the glass from BLANCHE, places it on the coffee table, then resumes her seat.*)

AUBREY: You can't say I didn't warn you, Blanche. You insisted on a second helping of that rich goose.

BLANCHE: Oh, don't browbeat me, Aubrey. I'm nearly out of my mind with worry. How could I know I was going to have all these upsets?

AUBREY: What upsets? There's only this trouble with Cook, isn't there? Or is there something else? (*He pauses.*) Blanche, answer me. What's the matter with you?

KATHLEEN: As a matter of fact, Father...

BLANCHE: Be quiet, Kathleen. (*To AUBREY.*) Why, it's nothing – nothing, dear. Nanny, tell Mr Skinner what it was Cook said.

NANNY: She said Muriel was nothing but a prostitute, or something of that, and everybody in the village knew about her goings on when the American soldiers were here – hanging around the camp every night – drinking gin and limes with them, and singing disgusting songs.

KATHLEEN: It doesn't surprise me in the least.

AUBREY: What is Muriel's answer to these allegations?

NANNY: She says if the Americans came back, she'd do the same again.

KATHLEEN: Oh, no! Really!

BLANCHE: I'd never have believed Muriel was that sort of girl. Would you, Kathleen?

AUBREY: (*Rising briskly and breaking down left.*) She can pack her bags too – and quick about it.

BLANCHE: Oh, Aubrey, please be reasonable. You know you can't get servants nowadays.

AUBREY: I will not countenance immorality under my roof. A nice thing, isn't it – a kitchen full of prostitutes and Nazis. I'd feel I couldn't go before the Central Committee on Monday, Blanche, knowing I willingly employed such people.

NANNY: Quite right, Mr Skinner.

BLANCHE: Well, I don't know if you realise it, Aubrey, but it's entirely through Muriel that we're able to get all that butter and fresh meat. You know it's her uncle that has the farm, and I'm sure if we give Muriel notice like that, he won't go on supplying us and risking enormous fines if he's found out.

AUBREY: (*Pressing his hands to his forehead.*) I don't want to hear all this. I have quite enough to contend with. The feeding of the household is your department.

BLANCHE: Yes, Aubrey. (*She pauses. In a subdued tone.*) Anyway, I should be ill if I lived on the rations. The doctor told me only the simplest food – underdone steaks and chops – lightly boiled eggs and farm butter.

AUBREY: Well – thank you, Nanny. At least we know where we are now. (*He picks up the 'News of the World' and browses through it.*)

NANNY: (*Collecting her sewing together and rising.*) I'll be glad to see the backs of both of them.

BLANCHE: What are you making, Nanny?

NANNY: A nightdress for Miss Laura. (*She displays the garment.*) It's a lovely shade, isn't it? What would you call it now – duck egg blue or something of that?

KATHLEEN: (*Rising and moving to the fireplace.*) Why have you suddenly decided to give a present to Miss Laura, Nanny? It's not her birthday.

NANNY: (*Placing the nightdress in her sewing bag.*) Well, birthdays aren't the only times you give presents, are they, Miss Kathy? There's other occasions besides birthdays. (*She notices AUBREY with the paper.*) Tch! (*She moves to AUBREY.*) I've been looking for that everywhere – somebody must have borrowed it from my room. (*She holds out her hand for the paper.*)

AUBREY: (*Drawing the paper out of her reach.*) You know quite well, Nanny, I will not have this paper in the house.

KATHLEEN: I don't know why you want to read those awful murder and divorce cases, Nanny.

NANNY: Well, I like to know what's going on in the world.

AUBREY: A great many sordid and disgusting things happen, Nanny, about which there's no need for decent people to concern themselves. (*He crumples the newspaper, moves and puts it in the waste-paper basket.*)

NANNY: I'm very sorry, Mr Skinner, I'm sure, but I have quite enough of fairy tales in my job. When I'm by myself I like to read a bit of real life for a change. (*She moves to the landing door.*) I can't spend the whole time in rosy spectacles with my head in the clouds. I'm very sorry, I'm sure.
(*She exits with an air of resentful martyrdom, closing the landing door behind her.*)

BLANCHE: Now you've upset her, Aubrey.

AUBREY: (*Moving centre.*) What did she mean about a special occasion for giving Laura a present?

BLANCHE: Oh, I never know what Nanny's talking about. Aubrey, don't be too hasty with Muriel and Cook, will you, dear?

AUBREY: Does that mean you expect me to take on all the unpleasantness of dismissing them?

BLANCHE: I really don't feel up to it. But please don't forget – I can't manage the housekeeping without Muriel's uncle at the farm.

AUBREY: I shall not be unfair to the girl, Blanche. (*He breaks down left and turns.*) After all, she may have adopted an attitude of bravado to annoy Cook further –

I quite appreciate that. But whatever happens, that German woman must not stop another night under my roof. (*He moves towards the landing door.*)

(*SUSAN enters, closing the landing door behind her.*)

BLANCHE: (*Rising and intercepting AUBREY at centre.*) And, Aubrey, do you think it's all right for me to wear this hat?

KATHLEEN: I think the ospreys are rather bad form. (*She picks up the copy of 'The Tatler' and stands idly glancing through it.*)

SUSAN: (*Moving to the coffee table.*) Mr Marshall said Mummy looked like a film star in it. (*She sits on the coffee table, with her back to the audience.*)

BLANCHE: Oh yes – he did. He said I looked like Barbara la Marr.

SUSAN: *Hedy* Lamarr, Mummy.

BLANCHE: I don't think I've seen *her*. (*To AUBREY.*) Well, are the feathers bad form or not?

AUBREY: You haven't got it on straight.

BLANCHE: (*Moving to the stool and sitting.*) Wait a minute – I'll put it on differently. (*She adjusts the hat in the mirror over the dressing-table.*)

KATHLEEN: Mr Marshall was only trying to flatter you, Mother. You don't look in the least like Hedy Lamarr.

SUSAN: Yes she does – a bit. It's the shape of her eyes.

AUBREY: (*Easing to the landing door.*) Hurry up, Blanche.

KATHLEEN: Don't interfere, Susan – you've never even seen Hedy Lamarr.

SUSAN: (*Rising.*) Yes, I have – with Charles Boyer in *Algiers*, where he cuts his wrists at the end because she goes off with another man. (*She moves and sits on the downstage end of the chaise.*)

AUBREY: (*Moving centre.*) Blanche, you oughtn't to take the child to see that sort of picture.

BLANCHE: I haven't taken her to see it. You know I can't stand things like that.

AUBREY: Well, who did take her?

KATHLEEN: I certainly didn't.

AUBREY: (*Moving to left of SUSAN.*) When did you see this film, Susan? Are you lying about it just to show off?

SUSAN: No.

KATHLEEN: It was on at the Classic in Godalming last week.

AUBREY: Is that where you saw it, Susan?

SUSAN: Yes.

AUBREY: Whom did you go with?

SUSAN: Nobody.

AUBREY: I've told you before, and so has your mother – you're not permitted to go sneaking off to cinemas on your own.

KATHLEEN: She must have gone with somebody, Father. Children aren't allowed in to that sort of film unaccompanied.

AUBREY: (*Crossing to the chair down right, sitting and facing SUSAN.*) If you're telling lies, Susan, you can stay at home instead of going to the party. Now – who did you go with to see this disgusting film?

SUSAN: It wasn't disgusting.

BLANCHE: Don't answer your father back like that, Susan – of course it was disgusting. A man cutting his...

AUBREY: You haven't answered my question, Susan. Whom did you go with?

SUSAN: Tommy and Joyce Williams asked me to go with them.

BLANCHE: (*Rising and moving centre.*) Oh, Aubrey – that's those dirty children from Elm Tree Cottage. I've told her never to speak to them.

SUSAN: They aren't dirty, Mummy – they're the most intelligent children I know.

AUBREY: Don't answer your mother like that, Susan. How did you get into the cinema if unaccompanied children weren't allowed?

KATHLEEN: They're the *most* dreadful people, Father – the husband's an artist.

BLANCHE: And I'm sure Mrs Williams never washes her hair.

AUBREY: Well, Susan?

SUSAN: Well – Mrs Williams was with us. She took us as a matter of fact.

BLANCHE: Oh, Susan, you didn't let her take you? It would be a nice thing, wouldn't it, if poor Daddy lost his chance of entering Parliament because of you? Supposing Lady Boot had seen you, and told the Committee what sort of people Mr Skinner's little girl went about with. They'd say we don't want Luffingham represented by the father of a child who mixes with the dirty Williamses.

AUBREY: If you've quite finished, Blanche. (*To SUSAN.*) You haven't answered my question, Susan. Did you allow this woman to pay for you?

SUSAN: Well, she asked me to go with them.

AUBREY: You mean to say you had so little pride... (*He pauses.*) Did you let her pay for you?

SUSAN: I suppose so. (*She pauses.*) No – I didn't.

AUBREY: And how much was it?

SUSAN: I've forgotten. I think – I think it was about a shilling.

AUBREY: What do you mean – about a shilling?

BLANCHE: Susan, you didn't sit in the cheap seats? Nobody goes in them, Aubrey. You don't know what she might have picked up there.

SUSAN: (*Wearily.*) I went in the two and threes.

AUBREY: Where did you get two and three from? Have you ever given her two and three to go to the cinema, Blanche?

KATHLEEN: Of course Mother hasn't.

BLANCHE: (*Sitting on the end of the bed.*) Oh dear, first Laura and now this.

AUBREY: Where did you get that two shillings and three pence from, Susan?

SUSAN: I don't know – it was in my purse.

AUBREY: I don't want any more lies from you.

SUSAN: I'm not lying – it *was* in my purse.

BLANCHE: Don't answer your father like that, Susan.

SUSAN: How can a person defend herself except by answering?

BLANCHE: (*After a pause.*) Don't be such a wicked child.

AUBREY: Susan – I'm asking you – *how came that money in your purse?* Are you a thief as well as a liar?

SUSAN: I'm not – I'm not a thief. It was some change I had from getting Kathleen's shoes from the menders.

AUBREY: So you did steal it.

SUSAN: It wasn't stealing.

KATHLEEN: I'd like to know what else it was, then.

SUSAN: I was going to save up and give it you back.

AUBREY: I want no more lies from you, Susan.

BLANCHE: It means we can't believe a word you say, now, Susan. We'll have to take her to a psychiatrist, Aubrey – it's the only solution.

SUSAN: I won't be taken to one. I'd rather kill myself.

AUBREY: (*Rising and moving to centre.*) Don't talk such exaggerated nonsense. Go to your room at once – and you can take off your party frock.

SUSAN: (*Rising and moving to right of AUBREY.*) Oh, but Daddy – there are all sorts of people I promised to meet at the party. Please let me go.

AUBREY: It's no good pleading with me, Susan; I don't want to see you – you're too much of a disappointment to me.

BLANCHE: Oh well, Aubrey – perhaps we ought to let her come this once, as the Heywoods are expecting her.

AUBREY: And what sort of impression would that give the child, Blanche? She's got to understand quite clearly that I will not countenance lies and dishonesty. Go on, Susan, go to your room, and don't pull the handle off the door.
(*SUSAN moves to the landing door.*)
I shall discuss with your mother later, what's to be done about you.
(*SUSAN exits, closing the door behind her. There is a pause in which they all look at each other.*)

KATHLEEN: (*Moving and sitting on the downstage end of the chaise.*) You see – she's an absolute born liar.

AUBREY: What is the good of my being firm with her, Blanche, if you chip in with stupid remarks.

LAURA: (*Off left, calling.*) Daddy.
(*AUBREY exchanges a glance with BLANCHE, shakes his head, and with hand to his forehead, crosses to the window.*)

AUBREY: (*Speaking through the window in a restrained voice.*)
Must we always have this shouting? If you want to speak
to me, Laura, come inside.

LAURA: (*Off, calling.*) Why don't you let David take the car
down and get some petrol. I don't want to walk all that
way to the Heywoods in this heat.

(*BLANCHE rises and breaks left to AUBREY.*)

BLANCHE: (*Eagerly.*) Oh, could he really get us some
petrol? Do ask him to, Aubrey.

AUBREY: (*Turning from the window.*) If you want it to be all
over the village that we have dealings with the black
market.

KATHLEEN: Everybody else round here does. The Boots
and the Beeders always have all the petrol they want.

AUBREY: (*Crossing to centre.*) We are not the Boots or the
Beeders.

BLANCHE: Oh, Aubrey, dear, please. It's as if all the
nerves in my stomach were tied in a knot – I couldn't
face that long walk in this heat.

AUBREY: Don't shout at me.

BLANCHE: I wasn't shouting, Aubrey.

AUBREY: You've no idea what my head's like with my
sinus. I wash my hands of the matter. How many times
must I tell you that I won't be dragged through all these
household arrangements. I don't want to know anything
about it. (*He moves to the landing door, opens it and turns.*)
But I do beg of you, if Marshall is going to obtain this
petrol, tell him he must not bring my name into it. Let
him walk into the village with a can – or a couple of
cans. He'll find some in the right-hand corner of the
garage – behind the lawnmower. And ask him not to pay
any fantastic prices – not more than double the standard
rate.

(*He exits, closing the door behind him. BLANCHE sits on
the stool. KATHLEEN rises and crosses to the window.*)

KATHLEEN: (*Calling off through the window.*) Mr Marshall –
will you do that for us about the car, after all?

DAVID: (*Off left, calling.*) How much do you want?

KATHLEEN: (*Calling.*) I wonder if you'd mind getting two cans out of the garage, and carrying them down. It won't take you long – only Father doesn't want the car used yet.

DAVID: (*Off, calling.*) I'll take three if you like.

BLANCHE: Oh, do ask him to get three, Kathleen, then I can go up to town on Wednesday and get my hair done.

KATHLEEN: (*Turning to BLANCHE, in a fierce whisper.*) No, no, he can't, Mother. (*She calls through the window.*) Just two cans, thank you, Mr Marshall. It is nice of you. Thank you so much. I'm sorry you have to walk all that way in this heat.

DAVID: (*Off, calling.*) That's all right.

KATHLEEN: (*Turning to BLANCHE.*) I can't help it, Mother – I can't stand him. (*She crosses to right of the bed.*)

BLANCHE: I don't know what your father's going to say about it all. (*Her eyes wander to her reflection in the mirror, then she turns dramatically to KATHLEEN.*) Kathleen – don't you think it's most extraordinary that the first time I put on these ospreys poor Harold gave me, I should hear this terrible news about him? Are they supposed to be unlucky?

KATHLEEN: (*Sitting on the end of the bed.*) Do be sensible, Mother. What are we going to do about Laura? He hasn't even got a proper job.

BLANCHE: Yes, what *is* his job? Selling something on commission, isn't it?

KATHLEEN: He's practically a commercial traveller. It really is a bit much.

BLANCHE: Your uncle Vernon's a commercial traveller, dear.

KATHLEEN: Yes, Mother – but we're not talking about uncle Vernon. And incidentally, I wish you wouldn't.

BLANCHE: I'm sorry, dear. What were you going to say?

KATHLEEN: Where does Marshall get the money to dress so well always, and to pay for hired cars to drive about in? I think there's something fishy about him.

BLANCHE: Do you, dear?

KATHLEEN: Besides, he's two years younger than she is.

She's going on in just the same way she did with Bruce Fraser, when she was eighteen. I'm beginning to wonder if she isn't man-mad. God knows what poor Harold may have had to put up with in Africa, in the tropics.

BLANCHE: Of course, I know this has nothing to do with it, but Nanny did say Mr Marshall did very well in the war. Mr Partridge from The Feathers told her he'd been specially decorated by Marshall Tito.

KATHLEEN: Marshall Tito? I don't think that's anything to be proud of.

BLANCHE: Well, he *was* fighting on our side, then, dear. (*She pauses.*) Wasn't he?

KATHLEEN: Anyway, these foreign decorations are ten a penny. As a matter of fact, I think we should tell Father the whole thing now.

BLANCHE: Oh, do let's leave it till after the party, dear.

KATHLEEN: He'll be much more furious if he finds out we've been keeping it back from him.

BLANCHE: We'll have to start going soon.

KATHLEEN: (*Rising and moving to the landing door.*) I'm going down to tell Father we want to see him. It's all been so upsetting for you, I don't see how telling him can make it worse.

BLANCHE: (*Plaintively.*) Very well, dear, if you really think it best.

(*KATHLEEN tries to open the door and pulls the handle off.*)

KATHLEEN: Damn!

BLANCHE: (*Weakly.*) Don't swear, dear. (*She closes her eyes as if in pain.*) And bring my Bisodol tablets, will you? They're on my bedside table.

(*KATHLEEN replaces the handle and exits, closing the door behind her. BLANCHE sighs heavily, looks in the mirror, powders her nose with LAURA's powder, then rises, moves to the window, takes the newspaper out of the wastepaper basket and starts to glance through it. She suddenly glances towards the landing door and quickly replaces the paper in the basket. As she does so, she sees the pieces of torn photograph in the basket, retrieves them and laying them on the dressing-table, pieces them together. As she stares at them, disconcerted, LAURA enters from landing, closing the door behind her.*)

LAURA: (*Moving left of the chaise.*) Fascism's been routed and immorality condoned. Father's sacked Cook and given Muriel the benefit of the doubt.

BLANCHE: (*Tragically.*) Laura – I've just found Harold's photograph.

LAURA: (*Crossing to the dressing-table.*) I wish you wouldn't poke about in my room, Mother. (*She picks up the pieces of photograph.*)
(*There is a pause. BLANCHE looks at LAURA, speechless.*)
Don't you think it's nice of David, struggling down to the garage and back with the petrol cans to save Father's face? I hope you all appreciate how nice he is.

BLANCHE: (*Sitting on the stool.*) Laura, whatever your feelings about Mr Marshall may be, I shall never, never understand how you can treat poor Harold's memory in this shameful way.

LAURA: (*Moving and dropping the pieces of photograph into the wastepaper basket.*) If you'll never understand, then there's no point in worrying about it, is there?
(*AUBREY, followed by KATHLEEN, enter from landing. KATHLEEN closes the door carefully, then stands leaning against the chest-of-drawers.*)

AUBREY: (*Moving centre.*) Is this true, Laura – what Kathleen tells me?

LAURA: (*After a slight pause.*) That David and I are going to be married? Yes, it is. (*She moves to the dressing-table.*) Excuse me, Mother.
(*BLANCHE rises and eases down left.*)
I want to get a handkerchief.

AUBREY: And there's something else, Laura – something very shocking, which puts your decision in an even more impossible light.

LAURA: (*Picking up her handkerchief and sprinkling it from the scent bottle.*) You mean – Harold's killing himself?
(*BLANCHE draws in her breath sharply.*)

AUBREY: Yes, I mean Harold's having committed suicide.

LAURA: (*Sitting on the stool.*) Mother, I wish, if you use my powder, you'd put the lid back. (*She picks up the pair of gloves.*) Look, there's powder all over my gloves. (*She picks up the clothes brush and brushes the gloves.*)

BLANCHE: I'm sorry, dear.

AUBREY: (*Moving to right of LAURA.*) Laura, I'm speaking to you on a very serious matter. You don't help the situation by an affectation of unconcern.

LAURA: (*Putting down the gloves and brush.*) I don't see that there is a situation. You know now that I'm going to marry David, and I suppose you want to say you don't approve of the idea. But I might as well tell you, Father, that nothing you say will make any difference to me. I don't mean it rudely. I'm simply trying to save a lot of unpleasantness.

AUBREY: You should have thought of that long ago, if you wanted to save unpleasantness.

LAURA: I meant – before the party, Father.

(*There is a pause. AUBREY crosses to the fireplace, suppressing his anger.*)

AUBREY: Why don't you sit down, Kathleen? Surely there are plenty of chairs in the room.

(*KATHLEEN sits on the right edge of the bed.*)

(*To LAURA.*) Of course I disapprove of such a marriage. I think you must have taken leave of your senses. The news about Harold will be enough of a scandal, and now this. Who is this Marshall, anyway? He's certainly not a man I should care to introduce as my son-in-law. Who are his friends around here? A garage proprietor who keeps a pub and sells black market petrol, and the local Toms, Dicks and Harrys whom he drinks beer with in the public bar at The Feathers.

LAURA: Jim Partridge at the garage was in the paratroops with him, and David happens to find his friends there pleasanter company than the Boots and the Beeders. (*She pauses.*) Why don't you say what you really mean, Father – that you don't like David because he has a job as a traveller and only earns a few pounds a week. It's too despicable. I won't even discuss him with you.

BLANCHE: (*Crossing to left of the chaise.*) Laura, how can you say your father's despicable after all he's done for you?

AUBREY: Very well, Laura, but don't imagine you'll get any more help from me if you marry this man before you're decently out of mourning.
(*BLANCHE sits on the downstage end of the chaise.*)
Or afterwards. That's all I have to say. You might show some thought for me, also. A fine chance I shall have of representing Luffingham, if you create a first-class scandal in the constituency. Everything that any of you do now is going to reflect on me, don't forget.

BLANCHE: And it's so insulting to the memory of poor Harold, Laura. (*Tearfully.*) He was such a fine man, and so fond of you, too.
(*LAURA looks from BLANCHE to AUBREY with a cynically ironic expression which masks a cold anger, but she says nothing.*)

AUBREY: Even if you've no consideration for me, Laura, you might consider the effect on your son of giving him a feckless good for nothing to take Harold's place.

BLANCHE: Well, we can only hope that wherever poor Harold is now, he won't be able to look down and see the way you're treating him.

KATHLEEN: And I might tell you, Laura, by hiding the truth about Harold, you've started all sorts of malicious gossip.

AUBREY: What gossip?

KATHLEEN: Well, you know what Gladys Benson is – she's certainly not reliable – but she said that when the Bishop and the Canon were discussing Harold's death, the Bishop said he believed that Harold drank.

BLANCHE: Oh, my dear, what a shocking thing to say!

KATHLEEN: Of course, I told her it was completely untrue.

AUBREY: This is what comes of making a secret of things. It's always the same. If you try to hush a thing up, all sorts of rumours get about which are ten times worse than the truth.

KATHLEEN: The Bishop said there was even a rumour going round the Gold Coast that Harold killed himself while suffering from delirium tremens. I think for all our sakes you ought to deny that, Laura.

BLANCHE: It's such a dreadful thing to have said about anyone who's dead. And it'll be so bad for Jeremy when he grows up.

AUBREY: It's quite bad enough for me now, Blanche.
I suppose Sir Arthur was present when this conversation took place?

KATHLEEN: Yes, Father.

LAURA: What does it matter? Do you think the Committee will turn you down because of some gossip about your son-in-law?

AUBREY: What is the foundation of this story, Laura? Harold was very abstemious.

LAURA: (*After a pause.*) Here.

AUBREY: Did he drink?

LAURA: Like a fish.

(*AUBREY, BLANCHE and KATHLEEN look startled.*)

BLANCHE: (*After a pause.*) Laura! How can you talk like that about Harold, now that he is dead? I could never have believed a girl of mine...

AUBREY: Never mind about that, Blanche, we can go into all that later. I don't know how far what the Bishop has been telling people coincides with the facts, but if you take my advice, you'll tell us everything. It will make it easier for all of us if we, at all events, know the truth.

LAURA: (*After a pause.*) I don't think you'll much like the truth if I tell it to you. But in view of your attitude to David, I think you should hear it.

BLANCHE: I don't see what our attitude to Mr Marshall has to do with it, Laura.

LAURA: As you're all so concerned with preventing my marriage to David, I think it will be good for you to learn the truth about the man you pushed me into marriage with, whom from the very start I never even liked.

BLANCHE: (*Indignantly.*) I...

(*AUBREY silences BLANCHE with a rapid gesture.*)

LAURA: I was twenty-one and still tied to your apron strings. The fact that Harold was nearly twice my age didn't matter to you, did it? All you cared about was that he had a good position, and you jumped at the chance of getting me off your hands.

AUBREY: That's a most unfair statement.

BLANCHE: (*Dolefully.*) I see now why you tore up the photograph.

KATHLEEN: Don't, Mother.

LAURA: (*Rising and breaking down left.*) Do you know why Harold married me? (*She turns.*)

BLANCHE: Why he married you? Because he – he fell in love with you, of course.

LAURA: Harold came to England for the sole purpose of marrying someone. He didn't much mind who it was. Do you remember how you both went out of your way to catch him for me? (*She turns and faces the window.*) You needn't have taken so much trouble.

BLANCHE: (*Stiffly.*) I don't know what you mean, Laura. I saw he was attracted to you.

AUBREY: You're trying to put your mother and me in an unpleasant light. Why should we have schemed to 'catch Harold', as you call it?

LAURA: (*Turning.*) Because you were impressed by his being a District Commissioner. (*She crosses to right of KATHLEEN.*) And you thought it a good idea to get me married off quickly to someone you approved of before there was another episode like the one with Bruce Fraser.

KATHLEEN: I don't see why you have to drag that in.

LAURA: Don't you, Kathleen? Why? Are you ashamed of having helped Mother and Father to spoil everything between Bruce and me, because his father was a bankrupt, and they lived in Union Lane? (*She crosses to the window.*)

KATHLEEN: I don't know what you mean.

AUBREY: Your mother and I have always tried to act for the best for you.

BLANCHE: You're being very unkind, Laura.

KATHLEEN: It's all very well for you to try and blame everything on Mother and Father like this, but you always seemed eager enough to marry Harold.

AUBREY: You needn't have accepted him. I don't see why you did, if you disliked him as you say.

BLANCHE: Quite right, Aubrey.

LAURA: I was pushed into it by both of you. But at least I was grateful for the chance to get away from home.

AUBREY: I've worked hard all my life to bring you girls up in luxury, to give you the best possible background. I'm sorry to find I might just as well have saved myself the trouble and expense.

KATHLEEN: *I'm* not ungrateful, Father.

AUBREY: No, I know you're not, dear.

LAURA: You killed my chance – you and Mother between you – of enjoying my youth with someone of my own age, someone I could laugh with – someone... (*She breaks off and pauses.*) Do you expect gratitude for that?

BLANCHE: (*Endeavouring to restrain her tears.*) We did our best, Laura, I'm sure. You don't realise what sacrifices your father and I have made. (*Her tears get the better of her.*) You couldn't, or you'd never say such wicked, cruel, ungrateful things.

KATHLEEN: (*Rising, moving to the chaise and sitting on it above BLANCHE.*) Mother, don't start crying when we have to go to the party.

BLANCHE: I'm not crying. I admit I did want Laura to marry Harold, and I didn't put any obstacles in the way. I thought it was all for the best.
(*LAURA moves left of the bed.*)
How was I to know he drank?
(*LAURA sits on the left edge of the bed and faces the window.*)
And even if he did come to England with the intention of marrying, I don't see there's anything very bad in that.

LAURA: He married me because he wanted a keeper. (*She turns and faces front.*) He was a confirmed drunkard. His friends used to take bets on how long I'd make him stay sober. He used to go to bed every night with a bottle of whisky and finish the lot. The Chief Secretary said he'd give him one more chance, and he gave him leave to come to England and find a wife who could look after him.

BLANCHE: But he was in love with you. When you were having Jeremy, he wrote me such a lovely letter about you.

LAURA: That was after I'd made a scene one day when I'd found him dead drunk at the Court House – administering

justice to the natives. I told him I was going to have a
child, and he wept and gave me his word of honour he'd
go 'straight', as he called it.

AUBREY: Why didn't you write to me, Laura, and explain
the situation?

LAURA: What good would that have done?

BLANCHE: Well, your father – your father might have
written to him – he could have appealed to his honour as
a gentleman.

(*LAURA laughs sarcastically.*)

LAURA: He'd given me his word of honour. I don't see
what difference a letter from Father would have made.

AUBREY: Didn't he even attempt to keep his promise?

LAURA: Oh yes, for a few months – before I went away to
have Jeremy. When I came back – we were going up the
river by motor launch – he could hardly keep his
balance on the landing stage, he was so drunk. I knew
I hated him then. I could have killed him.

BLANCHE: Oh, Laura, don't say that. Don't forget he's
dead, poor man.

(*LAURA looks at BLANCHE, and her expression darkens.
AUBREY moves uneasily.*)

KATHLEEN: Wasn't he ashamed of himself, Laura?

LAURA: Ashamed – oh yes, I dare say he was ashamed. But
he had another attack of DTs within three months.

KATHLEEN: Why didn't you leave him?

AUBREY: From what you tell us, I find it most extraordinary
that he wasn't dismissed the service.

LAURA: Oh, he wasn't drunk all the time. Sometimes he'd
go for two or three weeks without drinking. Besides,
nobody knew – we were so isolated there.

BLANCHE: But, Laura, when you came home on leave,
Harold certainly wasn't drinking then.

LAURA: No, I threatened him; I threatened him; I told him
if he ever let Jeremy see him drunk, I'd take the child
away for ever.

KATHLEEN: Didn't that have some effect on him?

LAURA: Yes, it did. He did actually keep sober for nearly
six months – until I left him for a week to take Jeremy

to the sea. Harold's assistant had to go up country to arrest a woman who'd murdered her husband, and Harold was by himself for about three days. Only three days, and when I got back, the bungalow was littered with empty bottles. (*She rises and eases left.*) He must have started almost as soon as he was alone in the place. He'd just sat there, drinking and drinking, pouring the stuff down his throat.

BLANCHE: Oh, Laura dear, don't go on with it. (*She rises.*) I'm quite upset enough. (*She moves to the landing door.*) I shall go out of the room.

(*She hesitates, right of the bed, and cannot resist remaining as LAURA continues her story, hardly conscious of the interruption.*)

LAURA: If I'd left him, or if Jeremy had died – if something terrible had happened to him in the past which he'd wanted to forget, there would have been some excuse. But there was none – none. He couldn't be left alone even for three days. I'm not sorry – he deserved it – I still say he deserved it. It was only luck that Jeremy wasn't with me when I found him. I was so beside myself – I can't say exactly what happened even to this day. There was a knife on the wall beside the bed where he was lying – it was above the table which had empty bottles on it, and glasses knocked over – and suddenly the blood spurted out from his throat – there was a great red gash across it.

KATHLEEN: (*Rising.*) Laura – what in God's name are you saying?

(*BLANCHE stands staring with startled eyes, her mouth open.*)

LAURA: The knife wasn't on the wall any more. It was on the bed.

AUBREY: (*After a pause.*) I don't understand. (*He moves below the chaise to left of it.*) How can he have committed suicide if he was in the state you describe?

KATHLEEN: (*Crossing to LAURA and shaking her.*) Laura, for God's sake explain.

LAURA: (*Releasing herself.*) The knife wasn't on the wall.
I told you. I don't know what happened. There was all
the blood. He never spoke. He died almost at once.
(*There is a pause.*)

AUBREY: But you wicked woman, it was murder.

BLANCHE: (*After a pause.*) Laura, you didn't do it, did you?

LAURA: I don't know who else did. (*She sits on the stool.*)

AUBREY: My God!
(*NANNY, followed reluctantly by SUSAN, enter from landing.*)

NANNY: (*As she enters, over her shoulder to SUSAN.*) Come
on – in you come, quick march at the double – and tell
them what you've done.

KATHLEEN: Not now. Don't interrupt us now, Nanny.

NANNY: (*Moving right of the chaise.*) In you come, miss.
(*SUSAN closes the door and moves to right of BLANCHE.*)
That's the second time this week I've found her listening
outside the door.
(*There is a pause. All stare at SUSAN.*)
Aren't you going to say you're sorry? No good standing
there like a misery on a mopstick.

BLANCHE: (*Faintly.*) Susan, you weren't listening outside
this door, were you?
(*There is a pause.*)

AUBREY: (*Sharply.*) Answer your mother, Susan. How long
had you been there?
(*SUSAN bursts into convulsive sobs, runs across to LAURA
and kneels at her feet.*)

SUSAN: Oh, Laura.

LAURA: Don't. Don't go on like that, Susan.

AUBREY: (*Hurriedly.*) Nanny, go outside. Leave us, will you?

BLANCHE: Yes, you'd better go – you'd better go, Nanny.

NANNY: (*Moving to the landing door.*) Very well, I'm going.
I don't want to hear any secrets. (*She pulls at the door and
the handle comes off.*) Oh, drat the thing. (*She fumbles and
tries to replace the handle.*)

AUBREY: Susan!

LAURA: Now, Susie. Susie, dear – what is it? It's all right –
I promise you it's all right, darling.

SUSAN: Oh, Laura, I heard you – I heard you. You said you killed Harold – he didn't die, you killed him. You said you cut his throat with a knife.

BLANCHE: (*With a cry.*) No!

KATHLEEN: (*Moving to SUSAN and shaking her.*) Be quiet, Susie, be quiet.

LAURA: Don't do that to her, Kathleen.

(*SUSAN rises.*)

NANNY: Dratted handle! (*She succeeds in refixing it.*) Have to get Logan to see to it.

(*She exits, closing the landing door behind her.*)

LAURA: I didn't say it, really I didn't, Susie. You must believe me. It was a misunderstanding. You must put it out of your mind.

AUBREY: Susan, you'd better sit down and calm yourself.

BLANCHE: (*Crossing to SUSAN.*) Yes, dear. Come and sit down, and don't be such a silly girl, upsetting us all like that over nothing. (*She leads SUSAN to the bed and sits her on the end of it.*)

SUSAN: It wasn't nothing.

BLANCHE: (*Right of the end of the bed.*) Yes, it was. Just because Laura had been telling us a story – the story of something she'd seen on the pictures. And you thought it was real – you silly girl – you couldn't hear properly through the door, and you imagined things. She's too vivid an imagination, that's what it is, isn't it, Aubrey?

AUBREY: You'd better take her to the nursery, Blanche.

(*SUSAN stops crying and her expression becomes hard and set.*)

KATHLEEN: You do imagine things, Susan.

BLANCHE: Now, I'll tell you what, dear. Go into Mummy's room, and in the top right hand little drawer of the dressing-table, you'll find a lovely box of chocolates. Go along, dear, there's a good girl, and don't let your imagination run away with you in that silly way again.

AUBREY: That's right, Susan. Now go and do what your mother tells you.

SUSAN: (*After a pause, with a baleful and reproachful look at BLANCHE.*) Why do you want to give me a present?

BLANCHE: (*Helplessly.*) I... Oh, don't ask silly questions, Susan. Surely you'd like some nice chocolates, wouldn't you?

SUSAN: No, I don't want any.

(*She rises suddenly, and without looking at any of them, moves to the landing door and exits, closing the door behind her.*)

BLANCHE: What are we going to do? (*She sits on the end of the bed.*) What *are* we going to do?

KATHLEEN: Ssh, Mother – she's probably still listening.

(*AUBREY moves quickly to the landing door, opens it, peers out, then closes it quietly.*)

AUBREY: (*Turning and moving above the chaise.*) She's gone upstairs.

KATHLEEN: (*Moving down left.*) Do you think Nanny heard?

AUBREY: I don't see how she can have failed to.

BLANCHE: She was fiddling with that lock – I don't think she was listening.

KATHLEEN: She's probably told Cook and Muriel by now. It'll be all over the village by this evening.

LAURA: I don't know why you have such a poor opinion of Nanny. I'm not worried about her, so I don't see why you should be.

AUBREY: Perhaps I'd better speak to her.

LAURA: Do nothing of the sort, Father. It's my business. If anybody's going to speak to Nanny, I will.

BLANCHE: She's a bit deaf, you know. I don't think she heard. (*Hysterically.*) Oh, Aubrey, how can we all be so calm?

AUBREY: (*Moving to left of BLANCHE.*) It won't help us by losing your head. And the more normal we appear, the better it will be for Susan.

KATHLEEN: Yes, Father, quite right We must keep to Mother's story – (*She crosses to the fireplace.*) that Laura was telling us a scene from a film. It's our word against hers, and after a time she'll come to believe it. She's only a child after all.

BLANCHE: Oh, it doesn't seem possible, that we're sitting here talking like this. It's like some dreadful dream. What's going to happen to us?

LAURA: Nothing at all, Mother. If you're worried about my being found out, that's all been looked after a long time ago.

AUBREY: What do you mean, 'looked after'?

LAURA: I'm not going to be found out. I wrote a letter to Mr Simpson – Harold's assistant – and told him everything.

AUBREY: You told him everything?

LAURA: I said that when I got home, I found Harold with his throat cut. By the time Mr Simpson got back, he'd been buried for two days. You know in the tropics you have to bury people quickly. I told him I'd found the knife in Harold's hand. I showed him the empty bottles. The servants said he'd been drinking hard ever since I left. Everyone was very kind, and the government granted me a pension. So there's no question, Mother, of my being found out.

(*There is a long pause.*)

AUBREY: (*Pulling himself together.*) I am a member of the legal profession. (*He breaks down centre right and turns.*) I have certain duties. We've always had a most respectable practice. You've put me in a monstrous position – monstrous.

LAURA: Well, what are you going to do about it?

AUBREY: It was murder, that's what it was. Do you think I can possibly connive at that?

BLANCHE: Oh, Aubrey, what on earth are you saying?

KATHLEEN: Don't talk nonsense, Father. You can't possibly give up your own daughter.

AUBREY: (*Looking at LAURA.*) You've put me in a monstrous position. This is the end of all our hopes, Blanche. How can I even think of entering Parliament now?

LAURA: Rubbish. You made me tell you. And I've borne it long enough by myself. I'm only sorry for poor Susan.

DAVID: (*Off left, calling.*) Laura, I've got the petrol. Two cans. Shall I fill the car up and bring it round?

(*LAURA rises and moves to the window.*)

LAURA: (*Calling through the window.*) Yes, please, David. We'll come down.

BLANCHE: We can't go to the party now. How can we face the Heywoods? And the Bishop will want to be introduced to you.

(*LAURA makes a gesture of indifference. Her eyes still hold
their ironical expression.*)

KATHLEEN: We must go, Mother. It would look so funny
if we stayed away. And Susan had better come too – it'll
help to take her mind off things.

BLANCHE: Oh yes, we mustn't let her start thinking.

KATHLEEN: (*To LAURA.*) You've told Mr Marshall the
truth about Harold, I suppose?

LAURA: That is entirely my affair.

KATHLEEN: You'll have to tell him. You couldn't possibly
marry a man under false pretences like that. And we'd be
wicked if we allowed you to...

LAURA: If you dare say a word about it to David, I – I'll
kill you.

BLANCHE: (*With a cry.*) Laura! For God's sake don't say
things like that.

AUBREY: (*Moving above the chaise.*) Oh, you take things too
literally, Blanche.

KATHLEEN: It's Laura's duty to tell Mr Marshall, isn't it,
Father?

AUBREY: I don't know – I really don't. We'll talk about
that later, Kathleen.

BLANCHE: But we can't – we can't go to the party, Aubrey.

AUBREY: I'm afraid we must, Blanche.

BLANCHE: And with those ospreys in my hat, that Harold
gave me with his own hands...

LAURA: You'll get used to it, you know. At first I thought
of it all the time, but now I forget it for two or three
days together. It's not as if there were any danger.

(*KATHLEEN moves to the landing door and opens it.*)

AUBREY: (*Moving left of the chaise, then below it to the
fireplace.*) I ought never to have been told. I think it was
most selfish of you.

KATHLEEN: (*Calling off.*) Susan? Are you ready? We're
going now. Hurry up. (*She turns.*) Your coat needs
brushing, Father. (*She moves to the door up right.*) Wait a
minute.

(*She exits up right.*)

BLANCHE: (*Rising and moving to the dressing-table.*) Oh dear, do I look all right? (*She looks in the mirror.*) I don't look as if I've been crying, Laura, do I?

LAURA: You look perfectly all right, Mother.

(*KATHLEEN enters. She carries a clothes brush.*)

KATHLEEN: Here you are, Father, turn round. (*Standing up right of the chaise, she brushes AUBREY's shoulders.*)

AUBREY: What is that child doing? (*He eases towards the door and calls.*) Susan.

BLANCHE: Oh, I shall have to change my stockings.

(*KATHLEEN exits up right with the clothes brush.*)

Look at this ladder. When did I do that? Oh dear, oh dear.

LAURA: (*Moving to the chest of drawers.*) Here you are, Mother. Take these. (*She takes a pair of stockings from the drawer and gives them to BLANCHE.*)

(*BLANCHE sits on the bed, takes off her shoes, and changes her stockings. LAURA moves to the dressing-table, and puts on her hat. SUSAN enters from landing, closing the door behind her.*)

SUSAN: I don't want to go to the party, if you don't mind.

(*KATHLEEN enters. She carries her hat and gloves.*)

BLANCHE: Of course you're coming to the party, Susan.

SUSAN: I'd rather not.

BLANCHE: Now, Susie, dear, don't be difficult. You're coming out to enjoy yourself and have a lovely time, isn't she, Kathleen?

KATHLEEN: Of course.

(*The sound of a car arriving and stopping is heard off left.*)

LAURA: (*Moving to the window.*) David's bringing the car round.

KATHLEEN: (*Moving to SUSAN.*) Come here, Susan. I don't like the way you've got your sash. (*She adjusts SUSAN's sash.*)

(*AUBREY moves to the door, tries to open the door and pulls the handle off. The outer handle falls on to the landing.*)

AUBREY: Confound it. I told everybody to be careful with the door. Someone must have pulled the handle out on the other side.

BLANCHE: Oh dear. (*She calls.*) Nanny, Nanny.
(*Three blasts of a car horn are heard off left.*)
LAURA: (*Calling through the window.*) David – we're locked
in. The handle's come off the door.
DAVID: (*Off left, calling.*) Hold on, I'll come up.
AUBREY: (*Holding his head.*) Oh, this shouting! Why can't
we walk out quietly through Kathleen's room?
NANNY: (*Off, calling.*) What's the matter?
BLANCHE: Here's Nanny.
KATHLEEN: (*To SUSAN.*) Now run and dab your eyes with
cold water. You don't want people to see you've been
crying. (*She moves to the fireplace, puts her gloves on the
mantelpiece, and puts on her hat.*)
(*SUSAN exits up right. NANNY opens the door and enters.*)
AUBREY: Thank you, Nanny.
(*He exits through landing door.*)
NANNY: What time will you be back to dinner? Cook's
leaving on the seven thirty – five. Shall I tell Muriel to
open some corned beef? (*She moves down centre left.*) Or
there's a tin of that American tongue – you could have
that with the salad.
BLANCHE: (*Fastening the last suspender.*) Oh, I can't say
now, Nanny. Let's leave it till we come back.
KATHLEEN: (*Calling.*) Hurry up, Susan.
(*AUBREY enters from landing. He carries a carnation.*)
AUBREY: (*Easing right of the bed.*) Do you think I should
wear a buttonhole, Blanche?
BLANCHE: (*Putting on her shoes.*) Yes, I think so.
KATHLEEN: I shouldn't. I don't think it's awfully good
form.
(*DAVID enters from landing. SUSAN enters up right.*)
DAVID: (*As he enters.*) Oh, Nanny's rescued you. Everybody
ready?
AUBREY: I think so. Come along, Blanche.
BLANCHE: (*Rising.*) I haven't got my Bisodol tablets. (*She
retrieves her handbag and gloves.*)
KATHLEEN: (*Moving to the door.*) I'll get you some. Go on,
Mother, I'll bring them down.

BLANCHE: Yes, wear a buttonhole, Aubrey.

KATHLEEN: (*Turning in the doorway.*) I shouldn't. You'll find only clerks and people like that will wear them. The Heywoods have had to ask everybody, you know.
(*She exits up right.*)

AUBREY: (*Moving to NANNY and handing the carnation to her.*) Put that in water, will you? We'll be back about half past six.
(*He turns, moves to the landing door, and exits. NANNY crosses and puts the carnation on the table in the window bay.*)

BLANCHE: (*Moving to SUSAN.*) Have you got a clean handkerchief, Susan?

SUSAN: Yes, Mother. It's all wet, though.

BLANCHE: Never mind, I've got a spare one. Come along.
(*She turns and exits through door. SUSAN glumly follows her off. NANNY commences to tidy the room. LAURA moves to the dressing-table and picks up her gloves and handbag. DAVID moves to LAURA.*)

DAVID: What's up with you? Not another family row?
(*LAURA nods.*)
The sooner you're out of this hell-hole, the better.
(*KATHLEEN enters up right. She carries her handbag. She glares resentfully at DAVID and LAURA for a moment, then moves to the mantelpiece, picks up her gloves and puts them on.*)

KATHLEEN: We're terribly late.

DAVID: Shall I drive, Miss Skinner, or would you rather Logan did?

KATHLEEN: (*Moving to the door.*) I think it'll look better if Logan drives, thank you – and anyway, he's put on his chauffeur's cap.
(*She exits to landing. DAVID follows her off. LAURA moves to the door. Then hesitates, turns and looks at NANNY.*)

LAURA: Nanny... (*She pauses.*)
(*NANNY, busily engaged picking up the tissue paper from the floor left, does not hear her. After a moment, LAURA turns and exits, closing the door behind her. Voices are heard off left, accompanied by the slamming of car doors and the starting of the car engine. NANNY moves to the window and looks off through it.*)

KATHLEEN: (*Off left, calling.*) Good-bye, Nanny.

AUBREY: (*Off.*) Good-bye, Nanny.

BLANCHE: (*Off, calling.*) Good-bye, Nanny.

DAVID: (*Off, calling.*) Good-bye, Nanny.

NANNY: (*Calling.*) Enjoy yourselves – that's right. Have a nice time. (*She moves from the window and continues to tidy the room.*)

End of Act One.

ACT TWO

The same. Three hours later.

Before the curtain rises, voices are heard.

KATHLEEN: Wait a minute, Susan, don't get out that side.

BLANCHE: Go straight up and change your shoes and socks, Susie. Ask Muriel to bring out an umbrella – or Nanny, if Muriel's out. No, wait a minute. Logan, you go and get an umbrella.

AUBREY: What a fuss, Blanche, about a few drops of rain. We don't need an umbrella, Susan.

(The curtain rises. The landing door is open, and the window is shut. The sky is yellow and lowering, and rain pours steadily. The door up right is shut.)

KATHLEEN: (*Off left of landing door, calling.*) Oh, do come on, Mother.

AUBREY: (*Off left of landing door, calling.*) Susan, come back and wipe your shoes. What do you think the mat's there for?

BLANCHE: (*Off left of landing door, calling.*) Give me the rug, Logan, thank you. Aubrey, mind that puddle by the door, dear.

(KATHLEEN crosses the landing from left to right.) Oh dear, I'm in one myself.

(NANNY appears on the landing and leans over the bannister. SUSAN crosses the landing from left to right.)

I should take off your wet things at once, Aubrey. Oh, hullo, Nanny. Fancy it turning out like this.

NANNY: Yes, isn't it a shame? Poor Mrs Heywood, she will be upset – and the Canon. Did you have a nice time?

(BLANCHE appears on the landing. The ospreys in her hat are sagging damply and her stockings are splashed.)

BLANCHE: Yes, thank you. It was bad luck for her, wasn't it, after all that trouble and expense.

AUBREY: (*Off left of landing door, calling.*) Don't stand about gossiping, Blanche, in your wet shoes.

BLANCHE: (*Entering the room.*) I wonder if Laura's back yet. (*She looks around.*) Oh, she's not back. Nanny, I would like a nice cup of tea now. (*She moves to the door up right and calls.*) Would you like some tea, Kathleen?

KATHLEEN: (*Off up right, calling.*) No, thank you, Mother. (*BLANCHE moves to the chair down right and sits. Aubrey enters from landing.*)

AUBREY: (*As he enters.*) I shouldn't have any tea, Blanche, after what you ate at the party. I thought your stomach was supposed to be upset.

BLANCHE: (*Wearily.*) Oh, don't browbeat me, Aubrey. Surely I know what's best for myself.

AUBREY: I don't think you do.
(*He turns, goes out on to the landing, then exits right, leaving the door open.*)

BLANCHE: Very well, I – won't have any tea, then – although it's the one thing that'll calm my nerves. (*She calls to NANNY.*) No tea, thank you, Nanny.

NANNY: (*On the landing.*) I'll get you some if you like.

BLANCHE: (*Taking off her hat.*) No, thank you. (*She stares sadly at the ospreys.*) I should never have worn them again, anyway. (*She calls.*) Kathleen.
(*AUBREY appears on the landing, looks reproachfully at BLANCHE, sighs, and without entering, closes the door. BLANCHE throws her hat on to the chaise, and sits waiting. After a moment, KATHLEEN enters up right. She is wearing a dressing-gown, which she fastens as she enters.*)

KATHLEEN: (*Moving to the fireplace.*) Well, have you thought of what to do?

BLANCHE: I don't know. I really don't know what to do for the best.

KATHLEEN: Well, it's done now, we can't get out of it.

BLANCHE: Yes, I know. (*She pauses.*) Couldn't we open the tin of tongue, and give them a nice salad? And open that tin of sardines for hors-d'oevres?

KATHLEEN: Think how superior Gladys Benson would be. (*BLANCHE takes off her shoes and stockings, and is in her bare feet until her next exit.*)

BLANCHE: Well, I'll tell you what. Supposing I open two tins of salmon, and make some fish cakes with the cold potatoes.

KATHLEEN: Oh, Mother, we cannot ask the Boots and the Bishop to dinner, and then give them fish cakes.

BLANCHE: (*Placing her shoes and stockings on the floor beside her chair.*) Well, I could do them with a white sauce. Oh, it's daddy's responsibility. He'll simply have to get Cook to stay. (*She rises, moves to the landing door, opens it and calls.*) Aubrey – come here a minute, will you? (*She turns to KATHLEEN. In a subdued voice.*) Why did Laura leave suddenly like that?

KATHLEEN: I think she quarrelled with Mr Marshall.

BLANCHE: What about, I wonder?

KATHLEEN: I wish I knew.

(*They glance at each other, and look away. They both have the same thought.*)

BLANCHE: (*Moving and sitting on the downstage end of the bed.*) The Bishop seemed to know him, didn't he?

KATHLEEN: I don't think so. He was merely being polite.

BLANCHE: He asked after his father. I distinctly heard him.

KATHLEEN: I hope they have quarrelled.

BLANCHE: Don't say that, dear – it seems so unkind.

KATHLEEN: You know what I mean, Mother.

BLANCHE: (*After a pause.*) I dread going into the drawing room now, I really do. We shall have to take them down.

KATHLEEN: Take what down?

BLANCHE: (*Closing her eyes.*) Those knives on the wall. Assegais, or whatever they call them. (*Her lips tremble.*)

KATHLEEN: Now, Mother.

BLANCHE: (*After a pause.*) Kathleen, wait a minute. (*She rises, moves to the landing door, and calls.*) Nanny. Nanny. (*She closes the door and turns. Quietly.*) See if you notice anything strange in her manner – you know what I mean. I'm sure if she really heard anything she wouldn't be able to meet our eyes, or something. (*She moves and sits on the downstage end of the bed.*) I don't think she heard, do you?

KATHLEEN: I don't know.

BLANCHE: (*Her eyes filling with tears.*) Oh, Kathleen, isn't
it awful? Whatever shall we do?

KATHLEEN: (*Crossing to the window.*) It's no good going on
like this.

BLANCHE: (*Pulling herself together.*) You know, dear, I was
thinking. Something's occurred to me – it's my opinion
Laura didn't do what she said she did, at all.

KATHLEEN: (*Turning.*) What on earth do you mean?
(*The rain ceases.*)

BLANCHE: Ssh!
(*NANNY enters from landing. KATHLEEN sits on the chair
in the window.*)
Nanny, we're in the most awful predicament.

NANNY: (*Easing centre, evenly.*) Yes, I know you are, Mrs
Skinner.

BLANCHE: (*Glancing at KATHLEEN, hurriedly.*) Sir Arthur
Boot is coming to dinner, and the Bishop of Capetown
and Miss Benson, and we don't know what to do about
the cooking as Cook's going.

NANNY: I'll help, if you like, providing you don't want
anything too fancy.

BLANCHE: Well, Nanny, what do you think we could
have?

NANNY: Let's see, now. I think there're some sausages –
I could do you a toad-in-the-hole, and then you could
have a canary pudding, or a nice bread-and-butter
pudding – that's quick. Or we could always open a tin of
pears.

KATHLEEN: Mother, we can't give them that sort of meal.
(*AUBREY enters from landing closing the door behind him.*)

AUBREY: I've been thinking it over, Blanche. We must ask
Cook to stay tonight. I don't see there'd by any great
harm.
(*NANNY eases down right.*)

KATHLEEN: Thank heavens you're being sensible about it,
Father.

AUBREY: We can't have people like Sir Arthur and the
Bishop to dinner, without offering them a decent meal.
It's most unfortunate, but there it is.

BLANCHE: I wish you hadn't asked them, Aubrey.

AUBREY: I had no choice. I couldn't help myself.

KATHLEEN: It was the Bishop's fault.

BLANCHE: How can it be his fault, Kathleen?

KATHLEEN: I've never heard broader hints for an invitation, and insisting on seeing our Gold Coast collection.

AUBREY: Even then, Kathleen, I don't see why you had to chip in and include Sir Arthur and Miss Benson.

KATHLEEN: Well, considering I did it entirely to help you, Father. I'm not interested in Sir Arthur Boot. I only suggested him coming because he's on the Central Committee.

AUBREY: (*Easing centre.*) Don't take that tone with me, Kathleen. I still don't see why Miss Benson had to be asked.

KATHLEEN: Anyway, they were all at the party together – one couldn't very well ask one without the others.

BLANCHE: It makes so many for dinner. Cook will refuse to stay, that'll be the next thing.

AUBREY: I'll see about that, Blanche.

NANNY: (*Picking up BLANCHE's shoes and stockings.*) I don't think she will stay, Mr Skinner.

KATHLEEN: What do you mean, Nanny?

NANNY: Not after being told to take a minute's notice like that. She's very independent. (*She picks up BLANCHE's hat from the chaise.*) Do you know what she had the impertinence to do, Mr Skinner? She came into my room when I was trying to have a nice quiet cup of tea, and started running down the government. Well, nobody minds that, but Socialists or not, I won't stand for that sort of thing from a German. 'Go on now,' I said, 'you'd better go right back to Germany, quick march at the double, and take Sir Oswald Mole-sey with you'.

AUBREY: Don't let's go into all that now, Nanny, there isn't time. I'll go down and talk to her.

NANNY: Oh, then she started a proper carry-on about the Socialists and the Jews.

(*SUSAN enters from landing, closing the door behind her.*)

BLANCHE: (*To SUSAN.*) Yes? Do you want anything, dear?

SUSAN: Can I speak to Daddy for a moment?

BLANCHE: Yes, dear. Of course, dear.

AUBREY: What is it you want, Susan?

(*The mournful but determined look in SUSAN's eye causes AUBREY to turn hurriedly to NANNY.*)

Nanny, I think you'd better go down and have a word with Cook. Tell her she can take a week's notice, and I'll pay her the extra week's salary if she'll stay tonight.

(*NANNY hesitates, her lips pursed.*)

Hurry up – hurry up, now. Or she'll be leaving the house.

SUSAN: She is leaving the house.

AUBREY: What?

SUSAN: She was just going out when I came down.

AUBREY: Why didn't you say so, Susan?

KATHLEEN: (*Rising and opening the window.*) There she is – she's just going down the drive. (*She calls.*) Mrs Kunstler. Mrs Kunstler.

BLANCHE: (*Rising, moving to the window below KATHLEEN; calling.*) Cook. Cook.

(*SUSAN sits on the downstage end of the bed.*)

AUBREY: (*Crossing to the window.*) Oh, Blanche. (*He interposes himself between BLANCHE and KATHLEEN, leans from the window and speaks off left in a restrained and persuasive tone.*) Just a moment, Cook.

(*BLANCHE moves below the dressing-table.*)

Would you wait a minute? Please come back into the house. I think there's been a misunderstanding.

(*KATHLEEN resumes her seat in the window.*)

Nanny will explain. Ja! (*He turns.*) That's all right. Go on, Nanny, I'll be down in a few minutes.

NANNY: (*Moving to landing door, muttering.*) Well, I don't know, I'm sure. I don't know whether I'm on my head or my heels in this house.

AUBREY: (*Moving centre right.*) That's quite enough, Nanny, thank you.

NANNY: I've mended the door handle for you. It's quite firm now, look.

(*She opens the door and exits to landing, taking the shoes, stockings and hat with her. There is an uncomfortable pause. AUBREY, BLANCHE and KATHLEEN look at SUSAN, then at each other. SUSAN avoids looking at any of them. BLANCHE moves uneasily.*)

AUBREY: Yes, Susan, what is it?

SUSAN: Can I speak to you alone, Daddy?

BLANCHE: You can speak to me too, Susie, can't you?

SUSAN: I'd rather speak to Daddy alone.

BLANCHE: (*Moving up to landing door.*) Apparently I'm no comfort to my children at all, as none of them seem to come to me if they're in trouble.

SUSAN: I'm sorry, Mummy, I didn't mean anything.

BLANCHE: That's quite all right, Susan.

AUBREY: Don't pad about in your bare feet like that, Blanche, you'll tread on a tack. We've quite enough trouble as it is.

BLANCHE: Do you think the water's hot enough for a bath, Kathleen?

KATHLEEN: I don't know, Mother.

(*BLANCHE sighs and exits to landing, closing the door behind her.*)

AUBREY: (*To SUSAN.*) Now you've made your poor mother unhappy. (*He pauses.*) Well, leave us alone, Kathleen, if the child has something to say to me.

KATHLEEN: (*Rising and crossing to the door up right.*) I hope you're not going to add to Father's worries, Susan. He's got quite enough to think about with the by-election.

SUSAN: (*Doggedly.*) I want to speak to Daddy, please.

(*KATHLEEN sighs deeply, gives a significant glance at AUBREY, then turns and exits up right.*)

AUBREY: Now, Susan, what's troubling you? I haven't a great deal of time.

(*There is a pause, then SUSAN speaks with difficulty, and in a small voice.*)

SUSAN: I'm not so silly as you all seem to think. It wasn't something Laura'd seen on the films. She really did do what she said, didn't she?

(*She pauses. Until now she has avoided looking at AUBREY, but at this moment, she turns her eyes on him, imploringly, accusingly.*

AUBREY does not answer immediately, but paces down right, turns, paces centre, then stops and looks at SUSAN.)

AUBREY: No, Susan. You misunderstood what Laura said.

SUSAN: (*After a pause.*) I'm not trying to say you're a liar, Daddy. I know everybody's supposed to be silly until they're grown up – but, Daddy, you needn't worry about me knowing what Laura did, because I'm just as bad really. At least, it's only luck that I'm not.

(*There is a pause as AUBREY swallows and crosses to the window.*)

AUBREY: (*Gazing out of the window.*) Susan, I tell you you must accept our word about this matter. (*He pauses, then turns.*) What do you mean – you're just as bad, really?

SUSAN: Well, when Eileen Richards, at school, had been making fun of me, I hated her so much, I wanted to kill her, and when she was coming down the stairs, I waited round the corner at the bottom with a boot brush, to hit her on the head with it.

AUBREY: (*Moving to left of SUSAN.*) That was most un-English of you, to waylay a defenceless girl, like that.

SUSAN: I was only telling you to show that I understand that if you hate someone, you want to kill them. But actually, Daddy, Eileen wasn't defenceless at all, she was coming from the art class with a bust of Apollo, and I missed her, and she snatched the brush from me and *she* hit *me* with it, and kicked me, too. Look, I can show you the bruise. (*She holds out her leg and examines it.*) It's nearly gone now, but you can just see where it's yellow.

AUBREY: All right. Well, run along now, Susan. And don't let me ever hear of you doing anything like that again. (*He presses his thumb and third finger on the bridge of his nose.*) I'm in great pain with my sinus today. (*He moves down left.*)

SUSAN: (*Rising.*) But, Daddy, I haven't asked you what I wanted to, yet.

AUBREY: (*Turning and lowering his hand.*) Before we go any further, will you give me your assurance that you accept what I tell you – what we all tell you, about this unfortunate – (*He searches for the right word.*) misunderstanding, and give me your word of honour that you will never mention it, or think about it again?

SUSAN: How can I give my word of honour not to think about something?

AUBREY: Well – if you train your mind to exclude certain thoughts, you'll find that after a time – automatically – they cease to present themselves.

(*There is a long pause. AUBREY turns and gazes out of the window.*)

SUSAN: Daddy? Is the Bible true?

AUBREY: (*Turning.*) I *really* can't go into all that now, Susan. You must choose a better time to ask such questions, or discuss it with your teacher who gives you scripture lessons.

SUSAN: Well, she seems to think it's true, and she's quite intelligent.

AUBREY: (*Crossing to landing door.*) Now, Susan, I have to go and speak to Cook. Ask me about it some other time.

SUSAN: (*Moving quickly to AUBREY, catching his arm and turning him round.*) No, no, Daddy, please, just a minute. I asked about the Bible because if it's true, then it's true about Hell, isn't it?

AUBREY: Susan, I tell you, I can't go into these questions now.

SUSAN: (*Desperately.*) But, Daddy, please, I *must* know. If the Bible's not true, it doesn't matter, but if it is, it means that if someone's done something awful, they'll burn alive for ever and ever, with shrieking and gnashings of teeth.

AUBREY: These matters are very deep, Susan. When you're grown up you'll understand better, but at the moment there's no need to think of such things.

SUSAN: Do *you* believe in the Bible, Daddy?

AUBREY: Naturally I do.

SUSAN: (*In anguish.*) But then, if you believe in the Bible,
you must believe it's true that they will burn for ever, if
they've done something awful.

AUBREY: No, no, that's not true. You mustn't think of that.

SUSAN: You don't believe in the Bible, then?

AUBREY: (*Moving above the chaise to the fireplace.*) Of course
I believe in it. Why don't you discuss it with the Vicar?

SUSAN: (*Moving down centre right.*) What's the good of that?
He's no good.

AUBREY: I've told you before, Susan, you are not to
discuss your elders and betters. (*He moves to SUSAN and
leads her to the bed. He sits her on the downstage end of the
bed, then sits right of her.*) Will you do something for me,
Susie? Will you try to put these matters right out of
your mind until you're old enough to understand them?
I don't think you have enough outdoor exercise. If you
had some little friends round here you'd soon forget all
these difficulties after a nice day in the open air. Why
don't you go on a picnic with somebody, and finish up
with a good game of rounders? But not with the
Williams' children.

SUSAN: (*With weary impatience.*) Oh, Daddy!

AUBREY: Don't shrug away from me like that. Any girl
becomes morbid and imagines things if she doesn't play
enough games and take enough exercise. That's what's
happening to you, Susan – *Mens Sana in Corpore Sano.* Do
you know what that means, Susan?

SUSAN: (*Flatly.*) A healthy mind in a healthy body.

AUBREY: (*With false cheeriness.*) That's right. I'll get your
mother to speak to your headmistress tomorrow, and
suggest that as soon as possible you join the Girl Guides.
(*He pauses.*)
(*SUSAN is lost in gloomy speculation.*)
Come on, now.
(*There is an awkward pause.*)
(*He pats her shoulder.*) Well, cheer up now, like a good
girl, and try and be extra nice to Mummy. You hurt her
very deeply just now.

SUSAN: Daddy, please let me ask you just one more question.

(*LAURA enters from landing, leaving the door open.*)

LAURA: (*Moving to the fireplace.*) I do wish I could have some privacy sometimes. (*She is distracted and unhappy, but makes an effort to conceal it.*) What's the matter, Susie?

SUSAN: Nothing. Could I speak to you for a minute?

(*AUBREY rises, pulls SUSAN to her feet, and leads her to the landing door.*)

AUBREY: No, you can't, Susan – come along now.

LAURA: (*Crossing below the chaise to the dressing-table.*) A little later, dear. (*She puts her handbag on the dressing-table, removes her hat and places it also on the dressing-table.*) Do you know if David's back yet?

AUBREY: (*Sternly.*) I've not seen him.

SUSAN: Neither have I. (*She crosses to the door up right and opens it.*) I'll ask Kathleen.

AUBREY: Susan, I told you to come along.

SUSAN: (*Calling off up right.*) Have you seen Mr Marshall, Kathleen?

(*KATHLEEN enters up right. She is brushing her hair.*)

KATHLEEN: Didn't he come back with you, Laura?

LAURA: (*Removing her gloves.*) No, he went on – he felt like walking. The Margetsons gave me a lift. (*She puts her gloves on the dressing-table.*)

KATHLEEN: I don't see how he could have got here before you, then.

(*LAURA sits on the chair left of the bed, and changes her shoes. She moves to the fireplace.*) I thought perhaps you'd had a quarrel or something.

LAURA: Susie, get me a glass of water, will you? I want to take some aspirins. (*She lies on the bed.*)

(*SUSAN exits up right.*)

AUBREY: (*Calling.*) Susan, I told you to come along.

(*BLANCHE enters from landing. She wears her dressing-gown and slippers, and is carrying a bath towel.*)

BLANCHE: (*Moving centre.*) Oh, Laura, how did you get back, dear? Are you very wet?

LAURA: No, I got a lift.

BLANCHE: Wasn't it a shame, the party turning out like that – poor Mrs Heywood – and the Bishop got soaked.

AUBREY: It was the greatest mistake asking those people to dine. I wish you wouldn't be so impulsive, Kathleen. (*He turns and exits to landing, closing the door behind him.*)

KATHLEEN: (*Indignantly.*) Well, really he's never stopped telling us how useful Sir Arthur Boot would be to him. (*She sits on the right edge of the chaise.*) I really think – (*SUSAN enters up right. She carries a glass with a little water in it.*) – Father's the most unfair man who's ever lived.

BLANCHE: Don't say things like that in front of Susan. (*SUSAN crosses to the dressing-table.*)

KATHLEEN: (*To SUSAN.*) Go along, dear, you'd better go and change.

SUSAN: (*Placing the glass of water on the dressing-table.*) Why? Am I coming down to dinner tonight?

KATHLEEN: I don't know. Should she, Mother?

BLANCHE: I don't know. What do you think, Kathleen?

KATHLEEN: I think perhaps she shouldn't.

SUSAN: Oh, why?

BLANCHE: Do you particularly want to, dear?

SUSAN: Yes. I – I haven't met the Bishop properly yet I'd like to speak to him.

KATHLEEN: Don't be so stupid. What can a little girl like you have to say to a Bishop? I don't think she'd better come down, Mother.

BLANCHE: Well, go on, Susie dear, we'll see.

SUSAN: What does it depend on, then?

BLANCHE: I don't know, dear. Don't ask such silly questions.

SUSAN: (*Crossing to landing door.*) Well, I'll change, anyway. (*She exits to landing, closing the door behind her. LAURA rises, moves to the dressing-table and takes an aspirin.*)

BLANCHE: (*With a frightened glance at LAURA.*) What are you going to wear, Kathleen?

KATHLEEN: (*Rising.*) I thought I might wear that dress that Mrs Hardwicke altered. I certainly don't want to look over-dressed like Gladys.

BLANCHE: And *did* you see Lady Beeder's hat?

(*LAURA gives an exasperated sigh, moves and sits on the left side of the bed, leaning her head against the upstage end. KATHLEEN exchanges a glance with BLANCHE, sighs, shrugs, then exits up right, closing the door behind her. BLANCHE stares with a scared expression at LAURA, who, after a moment, without moving her head, looks at BLANCHE.*)

LAURA: (*Wearily.*) So Father's begging Cook to stay now?

BLANCHE: (*Her voice constricted.*) Well, he had to, dear, with the Bishop coming and everything.

LAURA: (*Ironically.*) Yes, of course.

(*BLANCHE misses the irony, sniffs, her lips tremble, she moves to the chaise, sits on the left side of it, and starts to weep.*)

BLANCHE: Oh, Laura – Laura, I can't help it. I can't go on like this. What are we going to do?

LAURA: Have a good cry and get it over, and then try not to think about it.

BLANCHE: (*Through her sobs.*) I was going to have a hot bath and shut myself in the bathroom – I don't want to make it worse for everybody – but the water's cold. Cook's used it all.

LAURA: (*Rising and moving centre.*) I shouldn't have told you, I know, you're too defenceless. But I'm not sorry about Father and Kathleen. Not in the least. I think it'll do them good. (*She turns, crosses to the window and glances out.*)

BLANCHE: (*Looking up, her tears momentarily arrested.*) That's not them, is it?

LAURA: (*Turning.*) No, no, I heard a car. I thought it might be David.

BLANCHE: Come here, dear, I want to speak to you.

LAURA: (*Moving centre.*) If it's about Harold, there's no point going over it. I told you what happened.

BLANCHE: (*With a determined and dramatic air.*) Laura – you didn't do it.

LAURA: (*Shaking her head and sighing.*) Oh, Mother.

BLANCHE: Listen – no, listen, darling. Come and sit down. (*LAURA moves to the chaise and sits on it, above BLANCHE.*) I've been thinking. You told us when you found poor Harold – in that state you had what they call a mental blackout, and then you came to, and found him lying there. Well, haven't you ever thought what might have happened, with all those natives about? I'm absolutely convinced that one of them crept in while you were unconscious – somebody who had a grudge against Harold – you know what they are, they all have grudges against their masters – against the whites, and he, or it may have been she, it may have been the nurse for instance, must have done away with him, and placed the knife in your hand, and when you came to, naturally you thought that...

LAURA: No, no, Mother, no. It's not true, I'm afraid.

BLANCHE: Yes, it is. It is, Laura. (*She starts to cry again.*) It must be. I can't go on if it's not true.

LAURA: (*Sympathetically.*) I'm sorry, Mother.

BLANCHE: (*Endeavouring to control her tears.*) You know, darling, whether it's true or not – don't forget you are my child, and whatever's happened I still love you, you know.

LAURA: (*With tears in her eyes.*) Oh, Mummy, don't. You may be right – yes, perhaps you are. You may be right.

BLANCHE: (*Blowing her nose and wiping her eyes.*) Of course I am, dear. I know no girl of mine would ever have done a terrible thing like that. You're too good, Laura dear, that's what it is. It was the same when you were a schoolgirl, always ready to take the blame for other people. Well, thank God I've found out the truth at last. You do agree with me, darling, don't you?

LAURA: It could have happened. Anything's possible, I suppose.

BLANCHE: It did happen. It did. You must get those other dreadful ideas out of your mind. I'm right, Laura, aren't I dear? Tell me I'm right.

LAURA: All right, Mother, if you like.

BLANCHE: (*Rising and crossing to the dressing-table, sighing.*)
Now I can face them all tonight. I don't know how
I could have gone through with it, otherwise. (*She looks at
herself in the mirror.*) Oh, my dear, my eyes must be quite
puffy. I think we'd better light the candles for dinner, and
not put on the centre light. (*She wipes her eyes carefully,
then uses LAURA's powder.*) I wish I hadn't eaten those
little pastry things this afternoon. What do you think was
in them? I thought it was some sort of French cheese, but
your father said it was curried fish.
(*KATHLEEN enters up right. She is wearing her dress for
the evening, and is adjusting the zip fastener. She looks
curiously from LAURA to BLANCHE.*)

KATHLEEN: (*Moving right of the bed, casually.*) Mother, I've
had an idea. Couldn't Cook make one of her vol-au-vents,
and use the goose in the filling?

BLANCHE: (*Turning, in a strained voice.*) A vol-au-vent.
Yes, dear, she does those awfully well.

KATHLEEN: And has Muriel's uncle sent the eggs this week?

BLANCHE: Three dozen, yes – they came on Thursday.

KATHLEEN: Then why not get her to do a cheese soufflé,
like the one she did when the Heywoods came the other
day?

BLANCHE: Yes, that would be nice, we could have the
soufflé first, then the vol-au-vent, with peas and mashed
potatoes.

KATHLEEN: (*Correcting her.*) *Pommes purées.*

BLANCHE: *Pommes purées,* then. The only thing is,
I shouldn't be able to eat any of it, it's all too rich.

KATHLEEN: You could leave the pastry, couldn't you?
And the peas and potatoes wouldn't hurt.

BLANCHE: I can't have nothing but peas and potatoes for
dinner.

KATHLEEN: There's always the inside of the vol-au-vent.

BLANCHE: Well, perhaps just a taste of the pastry wouldn't
matter if I ate it carefully. I wonder if it'd be better to
have French beans instead of peas, Kathleen. Beans and
peas are both starchy, aren't they?

LAURA: (*Rising and moving to the fireplace.*) My God! Can this family *never* stop talking about food?

BLANCHE: Well, I don't know that we're so different from other families, dear.

KATHLEEN: (*Sharply.*) Someone has to arrange the dinner. You're always quite willing to eat it, I notice.

BLANCHE: Now, children, don't, please.

KATHLEEN: (*Sitting on the left side of the bed.*) Mother, you've been crying again.

BLANCHE: (*Lowering her voice.*) Laura? You wouldn't tell Kathleen what we've just been discussing, would you, dear? Please? (*She pauses.*) Oh, well. I'll leave you two together and go down and discuss the dinner with Cook. (*She moves to landing door.*) Now, let me see – soufflé first, then the vol-au-vent with peas or beans and mashed *pommes purées* – no, we'll have the soufflé as a savoury with chocolate instead of cheese – then it would be a sweet.

(*She exits to landing, closing the door behind her.*)

KATHLEEN: (*After a pause.*) What *did* you tell Mother?

LAURA: I didn't tell her anything. *She* told me that a native crept into the bungalow and killed Harold, while I was having a mental blackout.

KATHLEEN: What *do* you mean?

LAURA: That's what Mother's decided, and if it makes life any easier for her, I think it's best to let her go on believing it.

KATHLEEN: At least, then, you do see how selfish you were to insist on telling us about this dreadful thing that you've done.

LAURA: (*Breaking down right.*) *Insist* on telling you? (*She turns.*) It was you who insisted. You wanted the truth and you got it. Only it was just a little more scandalous than you'd bargained for.

KATHLEEN: It's no good losing your temper, and being sarcastic.

LAURA: I'm not losing my temper, but I wish you'd all leave me alone. I'd rather not discuss it any more.

KATHLEEN: (*After a pause.*) Will Mr Marshall be in to dinner?

LAURA: Naturally he will, as he's staying with us. Why do you ask?

KATHLEEN: Oh, I thought he mightn't be. I had the impression that you'd quarrelled with him at the party, and that he'd gone off by himself. I wondered if it was because you'd decided to tell him about Harold after all.

LAURA: That's what you'd like to have happened, isn't it? Why can't you be more frank?

KATHLEEN: I'm speaking to you for your own good, Laura. God knows it's bad enough what you've done – but you can't – you simply cannot marry a man without telling him the truth about yourself. Haven't you any sense of decency – or fair play?

LAURA: I don't follow your reasoning – perhaps you'd like me to tell Jeremy as well?

KATHLEEN: That's not the same at all. But surely, Laura, you must see – that a woman who's done what you've done – has no right to marry again.

LAURA: You hate the thought of my being happy, don't you?

KATHLEEN: I know you won't believe me, but I'm thinking of you, only of you, Laura. You are my sister after all, however much we may have quarrelled. There's such a thing as right and wrong, and I cannot stand by and see you plunging further into – downright wickedness. Can't you see that I'm frightened of what may happen to you?

LAURA: Rubbish!

KATHLEEN: Oh, very well, if that's all you can say when I'm doing my utmost to help you.

LAURA: Yes, in the same way that you always have. When you found out about poor Bruce's father – and you couldn't wait to let Daddy know about it.

KATHLEEN: It was my duty to tell him.

LAURA: (*Moving up right.*) Even when we were at school and you told Mrs Morrison I'd got Valerie Webster to finish my homework for me, you were doing it to help me, I suppose – for the good of my soul?

KATHLEEN: Yes, I was. And how can you be so petty as to bring up something that happened all those years ago?

LAURA: (*Crossing to the window.*) All my life, Kathleen, except when I was in Africa, I've suffered from your determination to 'help' me. I don't believe one word of what you say about your concern for my moral welfare. Even though you may believe it yourself. You want David to leave me, because you're jealous of me, as you always have been. I do believe you were even jealous of Harold, when you thought I was happy with him.

KATHLEEN: (*Rising and moving centre.*) I really think you must be mad. Do you really think you can hurt me by saying things like that? Why should I be jealous of you? All right, marry this man whom you hardly know, and who's years younger than yourself – it doesn't matter to me. If you're so fond of him as you say you are, I wonder you don't hesitate before trapping him into marriage with a...

LAURA: Yes, go on, Kathleen, go on. There's no need to mince words.

KATHLEEN: (*Moving and sitting on the left side of the chaise.*) No – there are some things I can't say. You can be as cruel to me as you like – I can't. (*She pauses. Dully.*) They'll be here soon.

LAURA: It's half past seven.

KATHLEEN: In half an hour, then.

LAURA: (*Glancing out of the window.*) The rain's stopped. (*She pauses, then turns.*) Kathleen, can't you recognise the truth in what I say, and leave me alone? You're not a happy person. I think you're disappointed with life, and something in you makes you resent the idea of my being happy.

(*There is a pause as KATHLEEN revolves these remarks in her mind.*)

KATHLEEN: (*Heatedly.*) You're speaking as if this were a perfectly normal situation. I've never heard that people who've done what you've done, should expect to be happy for the rest of their lives.

LAURA: (*Moving centre.*) All right. Now I know exactly where I stand with you. You think I've no right to happiness – you've as good as said it. But I say I have as much right as you have – and I'll not let you interfere between David and me, Kathleen, do you hear – I will not let you.

KATHLEEN: (*Rising quickly.*) I've had enough of your sneering at me because I've never been married or engaged. It may surprise you to know that there's a drawer full of love letters in my room, yes, and poems too – sonnets – written to me when I was a girl of eighteen.

LAURA: (*Sitting on the end of the bed.*) They were from Millie Jarvis when she was still at school. You showed them to me and pretended they were from Roger Lubbock, and I pretended to believe you.

(*KATHLEEN breaks below the chaise to the fireplace and musters what dignity she can.*)

I've had other letters, too, that you don't know about. (*She pauses. Suddenly.*) Let me tell you, I've had as many chances as you have, and if I had married, I wouldn't have made a mess of it as you have, and dragged us all into it with you. But, unlike you, I wasn't interested in being pawed about by men, and I'm not now. (*She moves above the chaise.*) You think I don't know what went on between you and Bruce Fraser. Perhaps you've forgotten one afternoon when you thought everybody was out, and you were alone in the house. It was *disgusting* – absolutely disgusting.

LAURA: I always wondered if you went about spying on me.

KATHLEEN: Spying or not, now perhaps you know why I did what was only my duty, and told Mother and Father.

LAURA: Yes, I think I do know now, Kathleen – I think you did it because you were in love with Bruce yourself. And I think you'd like David for yourself, too.

KATHLEEN: (*Moving in to right of LAURA.*) That's a lie – a bloody lie – and you know nothing, less than nothing – about me.

(*She turns and exits angrily up right, closing the door behind her.*)

DAVID: (*From landing, calling.*) Laura, can I come in?

LAURA: (*Rising, moving to landing door, and opening it eagerly.*) Yes, come in, David.
(*DAVID enters from landing. He wears a wet raincoat.*)
Where were you? (*She closes the door.*) Where did you get the raincoat?

DAVID: (*Removing his raincoat and putting it over the head of the bed.*) I borrowed it from Jim Partridge at The Feathers. (*He lowers his voice.*) Was that Kathleen shouting?

LAURA: (*Moving centre.*) Oh, it's nothing, nothing. Just a family row.
(*DAVID moves to left of LAURA, and they gaze at each other for a moment.*)

DAVID: Laura. I'm sorry.

LAURA: I'm sorry, too. But you rushed off like that – you wouldn't let me explain.

DAVID: There's no point in explanations, darling, but I just wanted to get away.

LAURA: I know I should have told you before, but – David – I did start to this afternoon, before the party, and you said you didn't want to hear.
(*The sound of sobbing is heard off up right.*)

DAVID: What's that?

LAURA: (*After listening for a moment.*) Oh, it's Kathleen crying. Don't take any notice – she'll be all right in a minute. David, you did say that, didn't you?

DAVID: (*Sitting on the end of the bed.*) What made me feel so bad Laura, was this. I didn't mind your not having told me the truth about Harold, but I can't understand why you had to tell *me* he'd died of malaria.

LAURA: Oh, I know, it was stupid of me.

DAVID: You see, you made me feel that all our relationship together, which I thought was completely open and honest – no secrets from each other and all that sort of thing – couldn't be quite what we'd pretended it was.

LAURA: But there was no pretence – there isn't now. Don't – don't, David darling, think anything like that.

DAVID: Well, but I mean it made me feel you couldn't trust me when I found you'd been holding back on me about Harold's death.

LAURA: (*Crossing to the dressing-table.*) I suppose it was a sort of habit. It was what I told everybody – that he'd died of malaria.

DAVID: Why, do you think I'd have minded that he committed suicide? The idea would certainly never have occurred to me that you'd driven him to it. Was that what was worrying you, Laura?

LAURA: (*Sitting on the stool.*) Yes, I daresay it may have been.

DAVID: (*Rising and easing centre.*) And then coming out casually in conversation like that, with old Strong – naturally it was a bit of a shock. (*He moves to right of LAURA.*) And who was that awful bitch with him, who kept dragging the conversation back to suicide and trying to make you feel uncomfortable?

LAURA: Gladys Benson. (*Before he can comment on this news, she rises quickly and throws her arms around him, tears in her eyes.*) Oh, darling. (*She kisses him.*) David, darling.

DAVID: Don't worry about it. It's just one of those things.

LAURA: Do you know, David, since you left me at the party – and this may sound exaggerated – but I know now something of what I shall feel if you die before me, or if you ever leave me.

(*They kiss.*)

DAVID: Let's forget about it. I have forgotten about it. I feel fine now. I had three doubles with old Jim Partridge. (*The sound of sobbing is heard off up right.*) Listen. Oughtn't we to do something?

LAURA: (*Sighing.*) Only leave her alone.

DAVID: What was it all about?

LAURA: David?

DAVID: Darling?

LAURA: I wish you wouldn't drink so much.

DAVID: (*Moving and sitting on the end of the bed.*) Why not? You say I'm always restless – a drink or two helps me to relax.

LAURA: Harold drank, you know.

DAVID: Good heavens, you don't think I'm like him because I knock back a few Scotches or pints occasionally. He used to have DTs, didn't he?

LAURA: Frequently.

DAVID: I've never suffered anything worse than a bad hangover in my life. Laura, was that how he came to kill himself?

LAURA: How?

DAVID: In a fit of DTs?

LAURA: Yes.

DAVID: Listen, darling. I've got a plan for tonight. Oh, wait a minute. By the way, I've got a present for your father.

LAURA: A present for him?

DAVID: I thought it might please the old boy, and persuade him to view me in a more favourable light. (*He rises, moves to the head of the bed and extracts a bottle of whisky from the pocket of his raincoat.*) White Horse – pre-war.

LAURA: Where did you get it?

DAVID: (*Moving down centre.*) Old Jim Partridge let me have it. Not too steep, either – two pounds ten.

LAURA: Darling, you can't afford it.

DAVID: I didn't pay. I've got an account with him. He knows I'll pay up sometime.

LAURA: Oh, David. I wish you wouldn't run up enormous debts.

DAVID: They're not enormous. What about us both having a shot now? Got any glasses up here? (*He crosses to the dressing-table and picks up the glass.*)

LAURA: No, you can't give Father a present, and then drink it yourself.

DAVID: (*Indicating a section of the bottle.*) We'll only have that much – and then fill it up with water.

LAURA: You can if you like – I don't want any. But don't fill it up with water, David. Tell Father you've had a drink out of it.

DAVID: (*Moving and sitting on the end of the bed.*) All right. (*He opens the bottle.*) I'll tell you what we're going to do, then – we're going straight down to The Feathers for dinner. (*He pours some whisky into the glass.*)

LAURA: No, I must stay at home tonight. You don't want all that, do you? Don't drink it neat, I'll get you some

301

water. (*She takes the glass from him, moves to landing door, opens it and crosses the landing into the bathroom, leaving both doors open.*)

DAVID: (*Rising.*) Okay, but don't let me down with old Jim. (*He puts the bottle on the dressing-table.*) I've got it all planned. (*He moves to landing door.*) Some of the chaps who were in Yugoslavia with us have come down for the weekend. They're crazy to meet you.

(*LAURA turns from the wash-basin, crosses the landing and re-enters the room, closing the door behind her. She carries a glass of whisky and water, in place of the glass of whisky which she has left in the washbasin.*)

LAURA: I'd love to, but we've got these boring people coming to dinner. (*She hands the glass to DAVID.*)

DAVID: (*Taking the glass and moving centre.*) Thanks, darling. Can't you make an excuse?

LAURA: But I must stay for Mother's sake.

(*DAVID drinks the whisky, emptying the glass.*)

DAVID: All right, then. I won't try to force you. (*He puts the glass on the chest of drawers.*) But if you don't mind, I'll nip back and tell them we're not coming.

LAURA: I shouldn't go all the way back. Why don't you telephone?

DAVID: No, it's all right. I'd like to see some of the fellows and have a drink with them. I can be back by – let's see – a quarter past eight. Is that early enough?

LAURA: I should think so. Don't be later, though. Good-bye. (*They kiss.*)
And, David darling?

DAVID: Yes?

LAURA: I wish you… Oh, nothing – nothing. Don't forget I need you to see me through tonight.

(*DAVID opens the landing door and picks up his raincoat. As he does so, KATHLEEN enters up right. She is rigid and white with controlled emotion.*)

KATHLEEN: (*Moving right of the chaise.*) Mr Marshall, I want to speak to you.

LAURA: Go on, David. For God's sake – don't listen to her.

DAVID: Why, what's the matter?

KATHLEEN: I want to speak to you – I've something to
tell you.

LAURA: Kathleen, will you keep your mouth shut.

KATHLEEN: Laura's a wicked woman, Mr Marshall.

LAURA: Oh, David, please go on. She's hysterical.

DAVID: Sorry, Miss Skinner, I must go – I'm late for an
appointment.

KATHLEEN: Mr Marshall...

DAVID: For Heaven's sake do make it up together – life's
too short.

KATHLEEN: Yes, it is – and some people have found it
shorter than they expected.

DAVID: I don't know what this quarrel's about, but please,
Miss Skinner, it's nothing to do with me.

(*He exits to landing, leaving the door open.*)

KATHLEEN: (*Running towards the door.*) Mr Marshall...

LAURA: (*Intercepting her.*) Kathleen, please, let's try to
understand each other. If I threatened to break up your
life, wouldn't you retaliate? Would you care how unkind
the things you said were? I'm sorry about them,
Kathleen, please believe me, I'm sorry now.

KATHLEEN: Being sorry has nothing to do with it. If I can't
persuade you to tell him, it's my duty – you can't stop me
– it's my duty.

(*BLANCHE enters from landing. She is in her slip.*)

BLANCHE: (*As she enters.*) Oh, children, children –
whatever is it now? Haven't we trouble enough?

LAURA: She wants to blurt out everything to David.

KATHLEEN: (*Breaking to the fireplace and turning.*) I've
given her the chance to tell him herself.

LAURA: (*Crossing to right of the bed.*) She wants to part us,
she's always wanted to.

BLANCHE: (*Easing to left of the chaise.*) But hasn't she told
you, Kathleen? She didn't do it at all.

KATHLEEN: (*Sitting on the club fender.*) All that story about
the native nurse is just your imagination, Mother – Laura
told me so herself.

LAURA: Oh, be quiet, Kathleen.

KATHLEEN: She did, Mother. She said if it makes life easier for you, she'd let you go on believing it.

BLANCHE: How can you say such things? How can you be so cruel?

LAURA: Yes, how *can* you be so cruel?

BLANCHE: Oh, my God, they'll be here in a minute, too. (*She moves to landing door and calls.*) Aubrey. Aubrey.

BLANCHE: (*Moving to right of the chaise.*) Why did you listen to all that scandal of Gladys Benson's, Kathleen? It's all Gladys Benson's fault.

(*AUBREY enters from landing. He has changed into evening dress, except for the jacket of his suit, and is tying his tie.*)

AUBREY: Oh, this shouting! Are we never to have a moment's peace in this house again?

KATHLEEN: I don't see how we can as long as Laura stays here.

BLANCHE: (*Moving to AUBREY.*) How can you speak of your sister like that?

AUBREY: You should never have told us, Laura – you see what's come of it.

BLANCHE: But she didn't do it, Aubrey, I know she didn't. It was that black woman...

AUBREY: Black woman? What's she talking about, Kathleen?

KATHLEEN: It's just a lot of nonsense Mother's made up. She's hysterical.

BLANCHE: I'm not hysterical, Kathleen. It's you who are hysterical. Why should Laura tell Mr Marshall she did that to Harold, Aubrey, when she didn't do anything of the sort?

AUBREY: Blanche, you're deceiving yourself, I'm afraid.

BLANCHE: (*Moving and sitting on the left side of the chaise.*) I'm not, I'm not.

KATHLEEN: Mother, put your dress on, they'll be here in a minute. Father, can't you persuade Laura that she's no right to marry him, or anybody unless she tells him the truth about herself?

AUBREY: I think it would be most inadvisable to tell anybody the truth. The most decent thing in the

circumstances, Laura, would be to break the whole
thing off.

(*LAURA picks up the glass and moves to the dressing-table.*)

BLANCHE: (*Rising.*) Oh yes, yes, Laura dear, I think
perhaps that is what you should do.

LAURA: (*Coldly.*) I wish you'd all mind your own business.
(*She picks up the bottle of whisky.*)

AUBREY: What is that, Laura?

LAURA: (*Pouring some whisky into the glass.*) It's a bottle of
whisky, and I'm going to have some. (*She replaces the
bottle on the dressing-table.*)

BLANCHE: Oh, Laura, Laura darling, don't have any, it'll
only aggravate matters.

LAURA: You're all working me up to such a pitch, I feel
I need something. (*She drinks the whisky, and places the
empty glass on the dressing-table.*)

BLANCHE: (*Sitting on the left side or the chaise.*) You see
what you're doing, all of you, between you, you're
driving her to drink.

LAURA: (*Laughing weakly.*) Mother, don't be so melodramatic.

AUBREY: (*Closing the landing door.*) I think you should keep
a clear brain, Laura, instead of fuddling it with whisky.
We've all of us agreed that it's your moral duty, in view
of what you've told us, to break off your engagement.

KATHLEEN: Or tell him the truth.

LAURA: And if I don't?

AUBREY: I shall not pay one more penny towards Jeremy's
education. You must give up all idea of Malvern for him:
and put Cambridge right out of your head. You'll have to
send him to a council school, and perhaps he'll win a
scholarship from there.

LAURA: (*With bitter scorn.*) That's absolutely charming of
you, Father. To try to blackmail me out of marriage by
threats against Jeremy.

BLANCHE: Oh, how can you use such a word about your
father?

AUBREY: Very well, Laura, this is the finish. After what
you've just said I no longer wish you to remain under
this roof.

BLANCHE: (*Rising.*) Aubrey! Aubrey!

AUBREY: Be quiet, Blanche, for God's sake.

BLANCHE: (*Resuming her seat, wailing.*) Oh, now he's turned on me. What are we going to do? I'd like to kill myself. (*She rises.*) I will. (*She runs across to the window.*) I'll jump out of the window.

(*LAURA grabs BLANCHE. KATHLEEN rises, runs across and also holds BLANCHE by her right arm.*)

KATHLEEN: Mother. Mother.

BLANCHE: Kathleen, let go of me.

AUBREY: (*Moving to BLANCHE.*) Don't be such a foolish woman, Blanche. (*He leads her to the chaise.*) Sit down and take a grip on yourself.

(*BLANCHE sits on the left side of the chaise.*)

KATHLEEN: (*Moving below the chaise.*) This is what we have to thank Laura for.

AUBREY: You see what you've done, Laura. Look at your poor mother. Look at poor Kathleen. Poor little Susan's mind is permanently warped. Do you think we'll ever have a moment's happiness again, Laura, while you are here with us – a constant reminder of this terrible secret you've forced us to share? (*He moves in to right of LAURA.*) What shall I feel when I go to the office? How can I look the Central Conservative Committee in the eye on Monday?

LAURA: As Sir Arthur Boot's dining with you, you'll have to look a bit of it in the eye tonight.

BLANCHE: Oh, Laura, how can you joke?

LAURA: I quite understand, Father, it'll be most unpleasant for you. (*She moves and sits on the chair in the window.*) But as long as you can't see me, that'll make it all right, won't it?

BLANCHE: Aubrey, you can't turn your own daughter from the house. If Laura goes, I shall go too.

AUBREY: (*Sitting on the end of the bed.*) Don't be so stupid, Blanche. Don't add to my difficulties.

BLANCHE: I will leave – I will.

LAURA: (*Rising.*) David and I will be able to manage quite well, Mummy, and you can come and see us sometimes.

You can pretend you're coming up to town to have your
hair done.

BLANCHE: Darling, why don't you give up Mr Marshall?
– then I'm sure daddy will let you stay.

LAURA: (*Picking up the bottle of whisky and the glass.*) Thank
you, I don't want to stay. I prefer to do without his help.
(*She moves and puts the bottle and glass on the chest of
drawers.*) I'm going to make a clean sweep. I shall tell
David the truth, and if he doesn't want to marry me after
that, so much the worse. But whether he does or not,
I shall leave tonight. (*She moves to the desk.*) Now will you
all, for God's sake go away and leave me alone. By the
way, that whisky's yours, Father. David bought it for you
for a present. (*She sits at the desk with her back to the
others.*)

BLANCHE: (*Rising and moving timidly to LAURA.*) Laura,
dear, if you tell Mr Marshall, you will tell him about the
black woman – the mental blackout. You know how
funny men are, you never know how they're going to
take things.

(*SUSAN enters up right.*)

SUSAN: (*As she enters.*) Nanny says Cook says she can't
possibly have dinner ready before nine o'clock. (*She eases
right of the chaise.*)

BLANCHE: (*Moving centre.*) Oh, dear! We'd better ring them
up, Aubrey, and tell them not to come till later.

KATHLEEN: Shall I ring up Gladys?

BLANCHE: No, dear, you go down to the kitchen and see
that Cook's all right. See if you can persuade Muriel to
help her. I'll ring Miss Benson.

(*SUSAN moves and sits unobtrusively on the chair below the
bookshelves.*)

AUBREY: You'd better get dressed, Blanche.

BLANCHE: Yes, and why don't you finish dressing?

KATHLEEN: Yes, Father, do go on. Hurry up.

AUBREY: (*Rising and moving to landing door.*) If you *are*
leaving before dinner, Laura, I'd like to speak to you
before you go.

(*He exits, closing the door behind him.*)

KATHLEEN: It looks rather funny, doesn't it, having dinner so late?

BLANCHE: Oh well, everyone was late back from the party, and they all ate a lot of sandwiches. We're not going to have stuffed tomatoes, Kathleen, Cook's going to open the foie gras instead.

KATHLEEN: Will there be enough?

BLANCHE: Yes, she's thought of a way to make it go round, but I shan't be able to eat any now. (*She moves towards the telephone on the chest of drawers.*) What is Miss Benson's number?

LAURA: Can't you use the phone downstairs, Mother?

KATHLEEN: I don't remember. It's in the address book on the hall table.

BLANCHE: Go on down, Kathleen.

(*KATHLEEN moves to landing door.*)

Oh, you do look pale, dear – put some rouge on first.

KATHLEEN: I should think we all look pale.

(*She turns, moves to the door up right, and exits.*)

BLANCHE: (*After a pause.*) Laura, dear, you don't really mean it that you're going away tonight?

LAURA: Yes, Mummy.

BLANCHE: But where could you go?

LAURA: I shall telephone Anne Wallace – she can put me up. (*BLANCHE sighs, moves to landing door, and exits, closing the door behind her. Neither she nor LAURA have noticed that SUSAN is sitting unobtrusively on the chair below the bookshelves. LAURA takes a sheet of writing paper from the rack, ponders for a moment, then rises abruptly and moves centre. As she does so, SUSAN rises and breaks to the fireplace.*) (*Surprised.*) Oh, Susie – I thought you went with the others. What's the matter, darling?

SUSAN: I'm terribly worried.

LAURA: Worried, Susie? What about?

SUSAN: Christianity. In case what it says is true.

LAURA: (*Laughing, though her eyes are filled with tears.*) Oh, darling. What it says about what?

SUSAN: About what will happen to people, if they've done something wrong.

LAURA: (*Sitting on the coffee table and facing right.*) But everybody's done something wrong.

SUSAN: (*Sitting on the end of the chaise and facing LAURA.*) No, something terribly wrong.

LAURA: Oh – you mean going to hell, and all that sort of thing?

SUSAN: Yes.

LAURA: Susie, look. Think of the person you hate more than anyone else in the world – someone who's done really wicked things, and treated you abominably.

SUSAN: (*After a pause.*) Miss Cudlipp – the maths mistress.

LAURA: Well, whatever she's done to you, you wouldn't want her to suffer for ever for it, would you?

SUSAN: Not more than a few weeks.

LAURA: Of course you wouldn't – you're not cruel enough. So how can you believe that God, who's supposed to be the God of Love, could be crueller than you or me, who are just ordinary human beings?

SUSAN: But suppose he's not the God of Love at all, suppose he's the God of Hate.

LAURA: No, darling, that's impossible.

SUSAN: I don't see why. I mean, how can anybody tell? (*She pauses.*) Do you think then, that people can do just what they like and not be punished for it?

LAURA: You know, Susie, you mustn't worry about me, really, darling. You didn't hear the end of the story. We found out afterwards it was Jeremy's nurse, who had a grudge against Harold. I didn't realise she'd crept into the room. So she's the only one you have to worry about. I swear it, Susie.

(*SUSAN looks at LAURA with sad, reproachful eyes. NANNY enters from landing. She carries her sewing bag.*)

NANNY: Come along now, Susan. Quick march, supper's ready in the nursery. Mummy says you're to have supper in the nursery, and if you're good you can come down for dessert – but only if you're good, mind.

(*SUSAN rises and moves to landing door.*)

Go on, run along now, quick march, at the double.
(*SUSAN exits, leaving the door open.*)
(*She calls.*) I'll be up in a minute, and don't forget to take
your Bemax. (*She closes the door, moves and sits on the end of
the bed.*) Did you tell her it was all sheer imagination?

LAURA: (*Rising and moving above the chaise.*) Something like
that.

NANNY: (*Commencing to work at her sewing.*) That's what
I said, too. Only I wanted to make sure you hadn't said
something different, and made me look a fool.

LAURA: I'm afraid we've all said something different,
Nanny. Anyway, I'm going tonight. Perhaps after a time,
if I'm not here, she'll give up thinking about it.

NANNY: They're turning you out, Miss Laura – is that
what it is – because of what you told them?

LAURA: (*Moving left of the chaise.*) More or less. I knew
you'd heard this afternoon – Mother thought you hadn't.

NANNY: I couldn't help but hear, could I?

LAURA: Nanny, you won't ever discuss it with anyone, will
you?

NANNY: Now, Miss Laura, you know there's no call to say
that to me.

LAURA: (*Sitting on the left side of the chaise.*) No, I know, I'm
sorry.

NANNY: After today, I won't ever mention it to you again
– let alone to anybody else, but while we're talking about
it, I might as well tell you what I think, Miss Laura.

LAURA: Yes, Nanny.

NANNY: (*Looking up from her sewing and gazing at LAURA.*)
You know, you didn't ought to have done a thing like that.

LAURA: No, I know I oughtn't. I was half mad, I didn't
know what I was doing.

NANNY: It's no good making excuses after it's done. We
can only be thankful you weren't ever found out.

LAURA: I know.

NANNY: (*Resuming her sewing.*) Anybody could see that
marriage would never answer. But don't you worry about
it too much, Miss Laura – you're not the only one – you

read the *News of the World*, and you'll find things like that happening on every page every day of the week. I don't know what it was that drove you to it – but after all, it's only what a lot of wives would like to do to their husbands. I'll be bound Mrs Skinner has to hold herself back from braining your father sometimes, I'm sure I do. I daresay it's that heat out there that makes people do things. So you just settle down and be happy with Mr Marshall – the other one wasn't worthy of you, and he never could be.

LAURA: (*Suddenly bursting into tears.*) Oh, Nanny! Oh, Nanny darling...

NANNY: (*Putting down her sewing and rising.*) There, there my pet. (*She sits on the chaise, above LAURA.*) There, my lamb, tell your old Nanny all about it.

LAURA: (*Through her sobs.*) I'm sorry, Nanny. I wouldn't go on like this, but I've just drunk a large whisky.

NANNY: A cup of tea would have done you more good.

LAURA: (*Recovering somewhat.*) Nanny, will you do something for me? I'm writing a letter to Mr Marshall, and then I'm going out. Will you give it to him as soon as he comes in?

NANNY: You're not going to tell him what you did, are you? I shouldn't.

LAURA: Yes, yes, I must. I must.

NANNY: Well, you don't want to frighten him off.

LAURA: (*Laughing in spite of herself.*) Oh, Nanny. (*She blows her nose.*) Better for him to know the truth now, than to find out afterwards, and think that I'd deceived him.

NANNY: Don't you tell him. You know what men are, he might easily take it the wrong way.

LAURA: Anyway, if I don't tell him, Kathleen will.

NANNY: You stand up to her, Miss Laura – you tell her to mind her own business.

LAURA: You know it's no good telling her anything.

NANNY: Well, suppose he doesn't like the idea and decides to leave you?

LAURA: I can manage by myself, somehow. (*She rises and moves to the fireplace.*) I shall tell him if he doesn't want to see me again – just to leave quietly. If he's not here when

I come back – I shall understand. (*Her voice breaks and her emotion gets the better of her.*) At least I suppose I shall understand.

NANNY: I wouldn't give my husband something he could hold against me all my life. I wouldn't put myself in that position with a man.

LAURA: It wouldn't matter, as long as we were together.

NANNY: Well, no good meeting trouble half way. Perhaps he'll take it all in his stride.

LAURA: Oh, Nanny – do you really think he might? No, I don't think he'll take it in his stride at all. I think this'll tear the whole thing apart. All right, let it. That's what they want, all of them. They want me to leave home – they want me to tell him – very well, then, I'll tell him and I'll go. (*She moves to the desk, sits, and picks up the pen.*)

NANNY: Now you're cutting off your nose to spite your face. That's what comes of drinking whisky.

LAURA: Leave me alone now, Nanny – I want to finish this. (*She starts to write.*)

(*NANNY rises, moves to the bed, sits on the end of it and resumes sewing. There is a short pause.*)

NANNY: I hope it's going to suit you, this colour. Still, I don't see much sense in a pretty nightie these days, if you go to bed all covered in face grease, like they do nowadays. If I was you, Miss Laura, I should have a good night's sleep, and think about it in the morning. (*She pauses.*)

(*LAURA, engrossed in her writing, does not reply.*)

You always were hot-headed. After what it led you into, you of all people ought to know it doesn't answer to do something rash on the spur of the moment. But there's one thing I do ask you to do about that letter – you ask him to burn it. It's very foolish for someone in your position to put anything in writing.

(*LAURA completes the letter, and places it in an envelope, which she seals.*)

LAURA: (*Rising and moving to NANNY.*) Nanny dear, give it to him the moment he comes in, will you? (*She hands the letter to NANNY.*)

NANNY: (*Taking the letter.*) All right, very well, then. I'll watch from the nursery window.
(*LAURA moves to the wardrobe, takes out her coat, and puts it on. BLANCHE enters from landing. She is now fully dressed. NANNY quickly conceals the letter.*)
BLANCHE: Oh, Laura... (*She stands by the door, waiting for NANNY to go.*)
NANNY: (*Packing up her sewing.*) Won't be a minute, Mrs Skinner.
BLANCHE: (*Moving to right of the bed.*) It just cleared up too late, Nanny, didn't it?
NANNY: (*Rising and moving to the landing door.*) That's right. It was a shame for poor Mrs Heywood.
BLANCHE: Yes – and, oh, Nanny – Mr Skinner's in the drawing room. Ask him to come up and see me for a minute, will you?
NANNY: Yes, Mrs Skinner.
(*She exits, closing the door behind her.*)
BLANCHE: Laura, dear, Cook's made some of those little anchovies on fried bread to have with the sherry, when they come. You will come down and have one, won't you, dear? It'll help to take your mind off things.
LAURA: Oh, Mother – I'm going for a walk, and then I have my packing to do.
BLANCHE: Darling, for my sake. I'm sure you'll find, dear, your father will change his mind.
LAURA: (*Crossing to landing door.*) I won't change mine, though.
BLANCHE: You don't really want to go for a walk – now, do you?
LAURA: Yes, I feel like it.
BLANCHE: You're not going far, are you?
LAURA: Just down the lane.
BLANCHE: Where's Mr Marshall, dear?
LAURA: He's out. He'll be back at a quarter past eight.
(*She exits to landing, closing the door behind her. BLANCHE moves to the door and re-opens it, as AUBREY enters. He is now fully dressed.*)

313

BLANCHE: Aubrey.

AUBREY: What is it, Blanche?

BLANCHE: (*Moving left.*) Come in, dear, close the door.

AUBREY: (*Closing the door.*) It's not something else, is it? (*He moves centre.*)

BLANCHE: My dear, I rang up Miss Benson, and Mrs Benson answered, and we were chatting together – she really seems quite nice when you talk to her – and Mr Marshall came into the conversation – and she tells me he's a cousin of Lord Wraysbury.

AUBREY: But that's a very old family, Blanche.

BLANCHE: That's what I gathered.

AUBREY: (*After a pause.*) You're sure she said Wraysbury, not Reresbury?

BLANCHE: No, it was definitely Wraysbury. Why, is there a Reresbury, too?

AUBREY: Yes, but Wraysbury had some dealings with me, or rather his solicitors did – Russell, Biggs and Pargiter. The family name is Marshall. (*He sits on the end of the bed.*) It never occurred to me to connect this young fellow with him.

(*KATHLEEN enters from landing.*)

KATHLEEN: (*As she enters.*) I *suppose* dinner will be ready by nine.

BLANCHE: (*Lowering her voice.*) Come in a minute, dear – close the door.

KATHLEEN: (*Closing the door.*) What's the matter? Has she told him? Has she broken it off?

AUBREY: Kathleen, your mother has just heard something about Mr Marshall.

KATHLEEN: (*Moving centre, eagerly.*) What is it? I always knew there was something fishy about him.

BLANCHE: Well, the Bishop told Mrs Benson – I've just been speaking to her on the phone, and she's really quite nice when you talk to her...

AUBREY: (*Interrupting.*) Oh, Blanche, need we go into all that now? (*To KATHLEEN.*) Mrs Benson told your mother that the Bishop told her that Mr Marshall is a connection of Lord Wraysbury's.

KATHLEEN: Lord Wraysbury? Who's he?

AUBREY: Blakiston Hall. You remember – that summer we spent motoring through Derbyshire. Kathleen – wait a minute. Yes, go and fetch *Who's Who* – on the book shelf in my study.

(*KATHLEEN moves to the landing door.*)

BLANCHE: I think Kathleen's got it in her room. Didn't I see it, dear, on your bedside table?

KATHLEEN: (*Turning towards the door up right.*) Yes, I'll get it. (*She exits up right, leaving the door open.*)

AUBREY: (*Calling after her.*) Really, Kathleen, if you wanted to consult *Who's Who*, why couldn't you put it back in my study where it belongs?

BLANCHE: I expect she likes reading it in bed, dear.

(*KATHLEEN enters up right. She carries a copy of 'Who's Who'.*)

KATHLEEN: (*As she enters.*) Don't be so stupid, Mother. (*She moves to right of the bed.*) I happened to be looking up Sir Arthur Boot, and as it happens, Father, he isn't anything so wonderful.

BLANCHE: What was that place in Derbyshire – you were saying, Aubrey?

AUBREY: Blakiston Hall – one of the finest estates in that part of the country. Well, that's Lord Wraysbury's place.

KATHLEEN: (*Turning the pages of the book.*) I really don't see why you should be all het up because Mr Marshall has a title somewhere in his family.

AUBREY: Here, give it to me, Kathleen, I'll find it.

KATHLEEN: (*Handing the book to AUBREY.*) What is he? Third cousin twice removed?

(*AUBREY consults the book.*)

BLANCHE: Yes, he is a cousin, Mrs Benson said. But anyway, it is nice to know, isn't it, dear, that he comes from a nice family?

KATHLEEN: (*Moving to the fireplace.*) Oh, Mother, don't be so snobbish.

BLANCHE: Have you found it, Aubrey? What does it say?

AUBREY: Yes. Wait a minute.

(*There is a pause while AUBREY continues to consult the book.*)

BLANCHE: It doesn't mention Mr Marshall, does it?

KATHLEEN: Oh, Mother, really. As if *Who's Who* would mention somebody's cousin.

AUBREY: (*Looking up.*) There's some very surprising information here, Blanche.

BLANCHE: Surprising, dear? Why?

AUBREY: Here you are. (*He rises.*) You can read it for yourself. (*He hands the open book to BLANCHE.*) He is Lord Wraysbury's heir. (*He breaks to the window.*)

BLANCHE: Oh, my dear. (*She moves, sits on the end of the bed, and reads the reference in the book.*) Good gracious!

KATHLEEN: (*Moving in to right of BLANCHE.*) Show me, Mother.

BLANCHE: Wait a minute, I haven't read it myself yet. Oh, don't look over me, Kathleen, it makes me nervous. Here it is, yes. (*She reads.*) 'Heir – cousin, William, David, Percival Marshall. B. nineteen twenty – two.' (*She looks up.*) What does 'B' mean? Born, I suppose. Well, there you are. (*She looks at AUBREY.*) It must be him. It couldn't be anybody else, could it?

AUBREY: (*Moving to BLANCHE.*) This certainly places Marshall in a very different light. (*He stretches out his hand for the book.*) May I have it, Blanche?
(*BLANCHE hands the book to AUBREY.*)

KATHLEEN: Father, *I* haven't seen it yet.

AUBREY: Just a minute, Kathleen. (*He studies the book for a moment, then looks up.*) And there's a castle in Ireland, too.

BLANCHE: A castle, dear? (*She pauses. Reflectively.*) How old is Lord Wraysbury, dear?

KATHLEEN: I bet he was one of those frightful profiteers who was given a peerage in the first war.

AUBREY: (*Handing the book to BLANCHE.*) On the contrary, Kathleen, it goes right back to the sixteenth century.
(*KATHLEEN takes the book from BLANCHE.*)
The first Lord Wraysbury received a peerage for his part in the sacking of the monasteries.

BLANCHE: How old did you say he was, dear?

AUBREY: It'll give it there, Kathleen.

KATHLEEN: (*Reading.*) 'Born 1883.' (*She looks up.*) What does that make him?

(*BLANCHE counts rapidly on her fingers.*)

AUBREY: Sixty-six.

BLANCHE: Oh, those old-fashioned aristocrats often live to over eighty, don't they?

AUBREY: I think not in this case, Blanche. I've always understood from Biggs of Russell, Biggs and Pargiter, that Wraysbury is something of a dipsomaniac.

BLANCHE: Oh, my dear, how dreadful!

(*There is a pause.*)

AUBREY: (*Stretching out his hand for the book.*) May I have it, Kathleen?

(*KATHLEEN crosses to AUBREY and gives him the book.*)

(*He studies the book for a moment.*) Yes. (*He reads.*) 'Heir, cousin, William, David, Percival Marshall.' (*He puts the book on the table in the window.*)

BLANCHE: You see, it explains his hiring all those cars and being so nicely dressed on so little money. Naturally, he can get credit everywhere if tradespeople know who he is.

KATHLEEN: (*Crossing to the fireplace.*) Yes, but why should he take a job as a traveller?

BLANCHE: Well, he has to do something while he's waiting.

KATHLEEN: I suppose so – but why mix with all those frightful people at The Feathers?

AUBREY: It's always been a tradition with the aristocracy to hobnob with the working classes.

KATHLEEN: (*After a pause.*) I wonder if Mrs Benson told Gladys? (*She sits on the downstage end of the chaise.*)

AUBREY: What does it matter if Miss Benson's been told? We're discussing Mr Marshall. The point is – let us be honest – he gave us a most unfortunate impression.

KATHLEEN: I wonder if Gladys knew who he was all the time, and didn't mention it because she was jealous of us knowing him.

AUBREY: I fail to see why Miss Benson has continually to be brought into the conversation.

BLANCHE: I think we should all agree, Kathleen, that we've been very unkind to poor Laura.

(*DAVID enters hurriedly from landing. KATHLEEN rises and moves to the fireplace.*)

DAVID: (*Standing in the doorway.*) Oh, sorry. Where's Laura?

AUBREY: Come in, Marshall.

BLANCHE: (*Laughing nervously.*) We were just having a little talk.

DAVID: Is she downstairs?

(*NANNY appears on the landing.*)

NANNY: (*Handing the letter to DAVID.*) Excuse me – from Miss Laura.

DAVID: (*Taking the letter.*) What's this, Nanny?

(*BLANCHE rises.*)

NANNY: From Miss Laura. She said destroy it when you've read it. I don't know what's in it – but burn it, I should. (*She exits. DAVID stares at the letter and then at the others, who wait with bated breath, their eyes fixed on him.*)

DAVID: (*Moving to KATHLEEN.*) Where is Laura, then? Has she gone out?

BLANCHE: Yes, Mr Marshall.

(*DAVID starts to open the letter.*) No, no, please don't read it now.

(*DAVID stares at BLANCHE in astonishment.*)

KATHLEEN: Mr Marshall – there's been a misunderstanding. Please throw that letter away.

(*DAVID moves to left of the chaise.*)

If it's what I think it is, I'm sure Laura won't want you to read it.

AUBREY: (*Crossing to left of DAVID.*) Marshall, I think you'd be advised to give it to me, and let me destroy it – Laura's not been herself today.

BLANCHE: We've none of us been ourselves, Mr Marshall. It's this awful damp heat.

DAVID: I'm sorry, Mrs Skinner, but I can't believe Laura would have written me a letter, if she didn't want me to read it. (*With a sudden movement, he tears the letter open and reads it.*)

BLANCHE: No, Mr Marshall, please don't.

KATHLEEN: (*Despairingly.*) Oh, Mother, it's no good now. (*She moves quickly to the door up right, and exits, closing the door behind her. BLANCHE, followed by AUBREY moves quietly to the landing door and they both exit, AUBREY closing the door behind him. DAVID is quite unconscious of them. When he has finished reading, he folds the letter, puts it in his pocket, breaks down right, then turns and moves towards the landing door. As he does so, LAURA enters, closing the door behind her. DAVID moves centre.*)

LAURA: (*Moving and leaning against the chest of drawers, hesitantly.*) David? I'm sorry. I can't go through with what I said in the letter, without even saying good-bye.

(*DAVID glances at her, then looks away again before speaking.*)

DAVID: I see now why you told me he died of malaria.

LAURA: (*Faintly.*) Yes – but then, I went on and let you believe the suicide story. (*She moves down centre.*) I know it was wrong of me to do that. I hated lying to you.

DAVID: What happened, Laura? Why did you do it?

LAURA: Because I loved Harold, and he let me down.

DAVID: (*Moving in to right of LAURA.*) You loved him?

LAURA: Yes.

DAVID: That's something new, too, isn't it? You seem to have been lying to me all the way. I always thought you hated him.

LAURA: David, let me tell you the truth. At first he meant nothing to me, I thought him rather a bore, but I tried to like him. After I found out he drank, I went through hell with him, David – I really did – trying to bring him back to some sense of decency. No, don't take any notice of that, I mustn't say things to try and win sympathy, or show myself as a wonderful character. I want you to know the absolute truth, in the hope that you'll understand. Harold didn't love me when he married me, I know, but when he saw how hard I was trying to help him, he did come to love me. We made up our minds to fight the thing together, and for six whole months he really tried. He was quite different then.

(*DAVID crosses and stares out of the window.*)

He wasn't pompous any more, but quite humble – like a child depending on me. (*She pauses and looks at DAVID.*) (*DAVID remains staring out of the window, with his back to her.*)

David, dear? They all know that I killed Harold, now. But they don't know why. That's only for you. There were some things I couldn't tell them. Shall I stop now? You know what I said in my letter – if you don't want to see me again.

DAVID: (*Turning.*) No, Laura – go on.

LAURA: (*After a pause.*) I don't know what I was saying now about Harold, yes – I remember one night, Mr Simpson, Harold's assistant, was dining with us, and Harold suddenly turned to him and said: 'You know, if it hadn't been for my wife, I'd have been sacked long ago.' And he said I was the best wife in the world. (*She nearly breaks down, but manages to control herself.*) And when I was away from home with Jeremy for a week – I found myself longing to be back with him, and thinking of him – and all at once, I knew that I loved him. Not in the same way that I love you, David, darling, but it was love, all the same. I can't tell you how happy I was when I realised it – I could hardly wait to get home and tell him. (*She breaks off.*)

(*There is a long pause.*)

DAVID: Yes, Laura?

LAURA: When I got back to the bungalow, he wasn't there to meet me. He was lying on the bed asleep. I was really quite amused, because he always pretended he didn't sleep in the afternoon. So I thought I'd have a joke with him. I tiptoed up to the bed and opened the mosquito curtains. He was lying on his back, with nothing but a towel round his waist. He was drunk. It had all begun again. He'd let me down. He'd let me down. I took him by the shoulders and shook him. He hadn't shaved for days, and his face was bloated and purple. And nothing, *nothing* would rouse him. I was determined to make him look at me. I must have snatched the knife off the wall and struck at him. It was only to make him open his eyes. And then he did open them at last, and they were just like Jeremy's. I waited for him to move – to speak to me. And then I saw he was dead, and I knew that I'd killed him. I didn't care – because I hated him. I hated him because for one whole week I'd loved him from the bottom of my heart. (*She is shaken by sobs.*) I'm sorry, David – I didn't mean to cry like this – it's not fair. (*She makes an effort and controls herself.*) If you can't feel the same about me now, David darling, if you can never be happy with me again – say good-bye now. (*She moves and sits on the end of the bed.*) But don't stay because you're sorry for me, I wouldn't want you to do that.

(*DAVID crosses in silence to landing door, then turns, moves in to right of LAURA, and puts his arms around her. She buries her face in his chest. After a few moments she recovers and stops crying.*)

Oh, darling, I couldn't have borne it if you'd gone. I don't think I could have gone on with my life – I really don't. For months, David, until I met you, I used to try and keep awake all night, for fear of dreaming. I'd have put an end to it all long ago, if it hadn't been for Jeremy. (*She pauses.*) Oh, darling, would it have been better if I'd let you marry me, and kept it a secret from you all my life?

DAVID: No, darling. I think if you'd kept it a secret, it might have come between us, but not now – not now that I know the truth.

LAURA: (*Rising.*) They've been frightful today – Father and Kathleen. (*She laughs shakily.*) Father's turning me out into the snow, because of Harold and my wanting to marry you. He says I've no right to marry anyone again, and I'm not fit to live under the same roof with him and Mother.

DAVID: Let's get out as soon as possible, then. Tell him you don't want to stay under his roof, anyway.

LAURA: I have. I'm going to leave tonight.

DAVID: Let's get the next train.

LAURA: (*Moving centre right and drying her eyes.*) Oh, heavens, I've not rung up Anne yet.

DAVID: You don't want to take much, do you?

LAURA: No, I'll pack a suitcase, and get Nanny to send the rest of my things on.

DAVID: (*Moving to left of LAURA.*) All right, now?

LAURA: (*Nodding.*) I feel starving as a matter of fact. (*She leans back against DAVID.*)

DAVID: (*With his arms around her.*) I could do with something myself.

LAURA: I didn't eat anything at the party.

DAVID: Laura, we needn't talk about it again, but I want you to know – when I was in the woods in Yugoslavia for two years, we'd go down into the villages at night, to get whatever food we could lay our hands on. When you're starving, human lives don't mean a great deal. You asked me once why I'd thrown my decoration away. It reminded me of too many things I'd rather forget.
(*LAURA turns suddenly, throws her arms around him, and they kiss. As they do, KATHLEEN enters up right. She sees them and beams. They break and look at her.*)

KATHLEEN: Oh, sorry to intrude. (*She turns towards the door up right.*) I'll make myself scarce.

DAVID: It's all quite respectable, Miss Skinner, we're going to be married.

KATHLEEN: (*Turning.*) *Married.* Are you really?

LAURA: Does it surprise you, Kathleen?

KATHLEEN: No, of course not. Least, it does in a way, but... (*She recovers herself and moves down between them.*) Well, congratulations, Laura. (*She kisses LAURA.*) Congratulations, Mr Marshall. (*She shakes hands with DAVID.*)

DAVID: Thanks.

KATHLEEN: It had better be David now, hadn't it? I must go and tell the family, they'll be so delighted. (*She moves to landing door, opens it, and calls.*) Mother.
(*She exits, closing the door behind her. LAURA and DAVID stare at each other in astonishment.*)

LAURA: What on earth's come over Kathleen?

DAVID: I don't know. They were all behaving rather oddly just now before you came in.

LAURA: In what way?

DAVID: I got the impression they were frightened if I read your letter, I'd call the marriage off.

LAURA: (*Moving to the window.*) A little while ago that was the one thing in the world they wanted.

DAVID: They may have thought twice about it after all. Look at the way your father altered his mind about Cook and Muriel.

(*LAURA's eyes fall on the open book on the table. She picks up the book and glances at the open page. Her attention is caught by some thing. After a moment, she moves to DAVID and hands the book to him.*)

LAURA: There you are, David, that's the answer.

DAVID: (*Taking the book.*) What's all this?

LAURA: You can see where it's open – at the W's. W. R.

DAVID: (*Glancing at the page.*) Oh. They've been looking up poor old Henry. (*He returns the book to LAURA.*)

LAURA: No, David, they've been looking up you. The Bishop must have been gossiping about your cousin. Does it say anything about you there? (*She glances at the page, then throws the book onto the floor.*) How contemptible!

DAVID: Didn't they know about all that before?

LAURA: Darling, let's get away. I feel I can't breathe in this atmosphere. Not one more night, not one more meal under this roof.

DAVID: Okay, let's go. To hell with packing. Let's go.

LAURA: What, now? This minute?

DAVID: Why not?

LAURA: We'd meet them...

DAVID: If we wait, they'll announce it to the Bishop, and the old beggar will try to bless us.

LAURA: That's what the family would like.

DAVID: And I wouldn't. Can't we slip out without being seen?

LAURA: We could go through Kathleen's room, and down the back stairs.

DAVID: All right, let's go.

(*AUBREY enters briskly from landing. He carries a decanter of sherry and two glasses, which he puts on the chest of drawers. He is followed in by KATHLEEN and BLANCHE, who also carry two sherry glasses each, which they put on the chest of drawers. SUSAN enters next, moves to the fireplace, and sits on the club fender.*)

AUBREY: (*Pouring out six glasses of sherry.*) Well, well, Marshall! What a pleasant surprise! Kathleen has just told me. Congratulations, my boy.

BLANCHE: (*Moving between DAVID and LAURA.*) Congratulations, Mr Marshall. (*She kisses him.*) It had better be David from now on. (*She turns and kisses LAURA.*)

AUBREY: Kathleen, go and fetch Nanny.

(*KATHLEEN exits to landing.*)

KATHLEEN: (*Off, calling.*) Nanny.

BLANCHE: I told you Daddy would change his mind.

AUBREY: I thought the occasion called for a little private celebration, Marshall. You know, before the guests come. By the way, I forgot to thank you for the whisky. Very thoughtful of you.

(*KATHLEEN enters from hall, takes a glass of sherry from the chest of drawers, then moves to right of the chaise. NANNY appears on the landing.*)

KATHLEEN: We mustn't be long, Father. The Bishop will be here any minute.

AUBREY: Come in, come in, Nanny.

(*NANNY enters from hall and stands above the chaise.*) We're just going to drink a toast to Mr Marshall and Miss Laura they're going to be married.

NANNY: Oh, yes.

AUBREY: (*Carrying two glasses of sherry to DAVID and LAURA.*) Your mother's been wondering, Laura, whether you'd both like to make your home here with us, for a little while after your marriage. (*He tends the glasses to them.*)

(*LAURA stares at AUBREY with an ironical smile, then she and DAVID ease left. AUBREY moves to the chest of drawers, picks up two glasses of sherry and hands one each to BLANCHE and NANNY.*)

BLANCHE: And, Nanny, if they do come here, we can
make Miss Kathleen's room into a sitting room for them,
and this – (*She indicates the landing and KATHLEEN's
room.*) would be practically a self-contained flat.
(*AUBREY takes his own glass of sherry from the chest of
drawers and eases left of the chaise.*)

NANNY: And where would Miss Kathleen go?

BLANCHE: Oh, she could have the little top spare room.

KATHLEEN: I *beg* your pardon, Mother?

BLANCHE: Oh, dear, Father's going to make a speech.
(*AUBREY raises his glass.*)
Come on, Susie. (*She sits on the downstage end of the chaise.*)
Aren't you going to join in, too?

AUBREY: Well, Laura, here's wishing you health, wealth
and happiness. Success to all your enterprises, Marshall –
peace and prosperity.

BLANCHE: And a long life.

AUBREY: Oh, Blanche. (*He laughs.*)
(*The sound is heard of a car arriving off left.*)

NANNY: Well, chin chin.
(*They all drink except LAURA and DAVID.*)

DAVID: Thanks, sir. (*He drinks.*)

LAURA: (*Raising her glass.*) Thank you, Father. (*She drinks.*)
(*The car stops.*)

BLANCHE: (*Rising.*) Oh, my goodness – is that them? (*She
crosses.*) Oh, yes, it is. Come on, everybody.
(*Voices are heard off left through the window.*)
Do I look all right, Kathleen?

KATHLEEN: (*Moving to landing door and putting her glass on
the chest of drawers.*) Perfectly all right. Do be in the
drawing room to receive them, Mother – quick.
(*BLANCHE crosses to the fireplace, looks in the mirror over
the mantelpiece and parts her hair.*)

NANNY: Not the drawing room. I've put the glasses on the
table in the garden. It's a warm evening.

BLANCHE: Aubrey, don't forget the sherry.
(*KATHLEEN and NANNY exit through landing door.*)

AUBREY: Don't be long, Laura. (*He puts his glass on the
chest of drawers and picks up the decanter.*) Marshall, don't

let her dawdle about titivating. I'd like to announce the engagement. We ought to get a blessing out of the Bishop.

(*The front door bell rings.*)

Come along, Blanche.

(*He exits through landing door.*)

BLANCHE: (*Moving to landing door.*) I'd better take a couple of aspirins, my head's simply splitting.

LAURA: (*Crossing quickly to BLANCHE.*) Mummy?

BLANCHE: (*Pausing and turning.*) What is it, dear?

(*LAURA kisses BLANCHE.*)

You are a funny girl, Laura. Well, don't be long, then.

(*She exits.*)

DAVID: (*Quietly.*) Shut the door. (*He puts his glass on the dressing-table.*)

(*SUSAN remains seated on the club fender. LAURA moves and closes the landing door, then places her glass on the chest of drawers.*)

Have you got everything you want?

(*LAURA snatches her nightdress from under the pillow, then moves quickly to the dressing-table and picks up her handbag.*)

LAURA: Everything.

DAVID: (*Holding out his hand to LAURA.*) Come on, let's go.

(*DAVID and LAURA move towards the door up right.*)

LAURA: All right. (*She sees SUSAN.*) Oh, Susie, you're not still worrying, are you?

SUSAN: No.

LAURA: (*Moving to SUSAN.*) Darling, please don't be unhappy. (*She attempts to embrace SUSAN.*)

SUSAN: (*Pushing LAURA away.*) Oh, don't. (*She rises.*) I hate being mauled about. (*She crosses to the window.*)

DAVID: Come on, darling. For God's sake, Laura.

(*LAURA exits up right, followed by DAVID. After a moment, DAVID re-enters, moves to the chest of drawers, picks up the bottle of whisky, conceals it in his raincoat, and exits with it up right, closing the door behind him. NANNY enters from landing. She is carrying a tray. SUSAN kneels on the chair and gazes out of the window.*)

NANNY: (*Putting the dirty glasses from the chest of drawers, on to the tray.*) What are you gawking at? Haven't you anything better to do?

SUSAN: I can just see them round the corner on the terrace. I can see them all laughing and talking. I don't understand grown-up people, Nanny, do you?

NANNY: (*Moving to the dressing-table.*) You've no call to understand them. (*She picks up the empty glass.*) Time enough when you're grown up yourself.

SUSAN: (*Rising and turning.*) I'd much rather not grow up. I don't think there's any excuse for grown-up people's behaviour.

NANNY: (*Moving to the chest of drawers and putting the glass on the tray.*) Any more talk like that and you go straight to bed.

SUSAN: There isn't. You know perfectly well there isn't. I hate them all. They make me sick.

NANNY: (*Moving centre.*) Very well, miss, that's the finish. Bed. No dessert for you tonight.

SUSAN: (*Calling after her.*) They do, they do. They make me sick. (*Her attention is drawn towards the garden again. She kneels on the chair in the window, cranes out and protrudes her tongue to its fullest extent. She rests her chin on her hands and remains in that position her face screwed up into a mask of bitter resentment and detestation.*)

The End.

THE OLD LADIES

adapted from the novel by Hugh Walpole

Characters

MAY BERINGER

LUCY AMOREST

AGATHA PAYNE

Voice of BRAND,
  Lucy's son

The Old Ladies was first performed on 3 April 1935 at the New Theatre, London, with the following cast:

MAY, Jean Cadell

LUCY, Mary Jerrold

AGATHA, Edith Evans

Producer, John Gielgud

The action throughout takes place in an old house in
Pontippy Square, Polchester.

ACT ONE

An old house in Pontippy Square, Polchester.

Downstage the hall, to the right, and a bed-sitting-room, to the left, are seen. The latter is occupied by LUCY AMOREST. The front door is to the right. Above it a staircase leading upstage. A small window above the foot of the stairs.

Upstage of these rooms the interiors of two other rooms are visible. One, on the right, is a bedsitting-room rented by MAY BERINGER. The other, at centre, is the sitting-room occupied by AGATHA PAYNE.

When the curtain rises MAY BERINGER, a thin, peaked, old maiden lady, in long old-fashioned clothes, is seen descending the stairs. Reaching the hall she crosses to LUCY's room and knocks nervously at the door. There is no reply.

She knocks again. At that moment the front door opens to admit LUCY AMOREST, neat, tidy, white-haired and happy, a cold wind blowing behind her. She shuts the front door quickly to keep out the wind, and crosses towards her room. MAY has turned, and stands facing her, making nervous noises.

LUCY: (*Checking at centre.*) Miss Beringer, isn't it?

MAY: Yes. Oh yes. I had to come and thank you for being so kind. I was just knocking...and to wish you the compliments of the season, of course. (*She gives a nervous titter.*)

LUCY: I'm so pleased. I hoped we'd meet before Christmas Day. (*She goes to the door of her room and opens it.*) Do come in for a moment. (*Turning, at the door.*) I was just going to make a cup of tea. (*Entering her room.*) I do like a cup of tea between breakfast and lunch.

MAY: (*Following her in.*) Thank you so much. I couldn't wait to thank you for being so generous as I'm sure, indeed, you have been, to a perfect stranger, and someone whom you've never seen in your life before, and you've no reason at all to be kind to.

LUCY: (*Who has been taking off her outdoor things and hanging them up.*) Well, after all, I thought to myself when you arrived yesterday, we're going to be such very near neighbours, we must get to know one another a little. You *will* sit down, won't you?

MAY: (*Breathlessly.*) I'm sure that's very kind of you. (*She sits right of the table.*)

LUCY: I'll make some tea, then. (*She comes to the left of the table.*)

MAY: It's so silly. I *know* I sound as though I'd been running up a whole flight of stairs, but it's only my nervousness. I'm always shy of meeting anyone for the first time.

LUCY: Oh, but you mustn't be like that with me. I'm a very unalarming person.

MAY: I've always been so, ever since I was a child. As quite a little girl I was as shy as anything. (*She gives her habitual nervous deprecating laugh.*)

(*A pause.*)

LUCY: Have you met your other neighbour, Mrs Payne yet?

MAY: Mrs Payne? Oh no. She's the lady in the room next to mine, isn't she? The agent, Mr Richards, told me. Oh, yes. Oh, I'm sure I shall be most comfortable here.

LUCY: The house is very rickety, of course, and when the old gentleman who had your room previously left, I did feel quite queer sometimes, alone in the house with Mrs Payne, but I'm sure we'll all be very happy now. Three just makes the difference, doesn't it? (*She fetches the kettle from the fireplace.*)

MAY: Quite, oh yes. I think it does.

LUCY: (*Returning to the table.*) And, after all, one makes one's own room one's little domain. It's quite possible to be very cosy and at home with one's things, in spite of the draughty hall and so on.

(*A pause.*)

I'll see to the kettle. (*She proceeds to fill it from the water jug on her washstand.*)

MAY: (*As LUCY goes up with the kettle.*) I really could have wept when the charlady came in with such a lovely

surprise this morning. It was such a nice thought. I really
could. And it must be months since I had a fried sausage
for breakfast! You left enough for yourself, I hope?

LUCY: (*Moving down with the kettle, now filled.*) Dear me,
yes. More than I could manage, and I thought you might
like one, and then it would be a good way of introducing
myself. (*She puts the kettle on the fire and then, as she sits
opposite:*) Did you have to come far yesterday?

MAY: Not so very far, no. St Lennans. The three-forty-five it
was... I think...or was it the three-forty?

LUCY: I've never *been* there, but I hear it's very bracing.

MAY: Yes, very. The air's wonderful. It agreed with me
splendidly. Splendidly.

LUCY: Were you there long?

MAY: Oh yes, several years, but it had too many
associations for me after my last little dog died, and then
my friend Jane, who married and went to India, she'd
lived there, too... It's too sad, don't you think, living
with associations of things that are past?

LUCY: Yes...in some ways.

MAY: That's why I decided to live in Polchester, but I'm
sure I shall like it here. The Christmas shops and
everything were so gaily decorated I noticed as I came
along, it quite reminded me of Exeter.

LUCY: Do you know Exeter well?

MAY: Dear me, yes. My home was there. I'm very fond of it
– Exeter. Even when I was by myself I still lived there
for quite a long time. Oh yes, nice, very nice. I was just
saying – the shops at Christmas time – the butcher, you
know, used to have quite a little tableau in the window.
Quite a little tableau. Very bright lights, and there were
six little pigs with hats on, all sitting round to Christmas
dinner. It was quite beautiful.

LUCY: Good gracious! (*She cannot help laughing.*)
(*A pause.*)

MAY: There's a very fine view of the cathedral from your
window, I notice. Is it far away?

LUCY: Oh, no. Quite a short walk. I always go to the
services there.

335

MAY: Do you?... I...er... I was thinking, I'd very much like
to go tomorrow to attend a service... I wonder...of
course, I don't *know* that I shall be able to find the way,
but... I'm so silly at asking...and...

LUCY: Why don't you come with me?

MAY: (*Suddenly, pathetically excited.*) Oh, may I really?
I would like to so much! It's so very nice of you! I don't
know why you should bother, I'm sure! It's really
something to look forward to.

LUCY: (*Warmly.*) I'm so glad, Miss Beringer. It is for me,
too. Of course, I know we're all alone here, you and
I and Mrs Payne, but there's no reason why we shouldn't
have quite a happy little Christmas.

MAY: None at all.

LUCY: To tell you the truth, I'd been wondering whether
I might have a tiny party this evening. Needless to say,
there would only be ourselves.

MAY: *A party!* Oh dear.

LUCY: Well, it wouldn't be a real party. Just tea and cakes,
but – I've got a little surprise. It suddenly came upon me
to buy it on my way home this morning. I thought how
jolly it would be to have a Christmas Eve celebration for
once, and perhaps actually stay up till twelve o'clock.
What do you think?

MAY: Oh, I think it sounds wonderful. And we could lie
late tomorrow morning. Oh dear, yes. The other lady
will be here, of course?

LUCY: Mrs Payne, oh yes, though I haven't asked her yet.
(*A slight pause.*)

MAY: Does...er... Mrs Payne attend at the cathedral, also?

LUCY: No, oh no, she doesn't go about much. She's getting
a little past it, I think.

MAY: (*Nodding her head.*) Quite. Quite.

LUCY: And I have rather an idea that she's a Roman
Catholic.

MAY: You *don't* say so! Tch! Tch! Tch! Oh, dear! So, of
course, she *wouldn't* go to the cathedral. Quite. I've
always had a feeling, you know, that there's something

rather frightening about Roman Catholicism. I remember my father was even diffident about attending Roman Catholic patients. But, luckily, there weren't a great many where he practised – in Exeter, of course.

LUCY: But I don't think our Lord really minds what form the expression of our love for Him takes. (*Almost with a laugh.*) He knows how different we all are.

MAY: Quite. Quite.

LUCY: What *is* happening to the kettle? Perhaps the fire's not hot enough just there. (*She rises and moves the kettle to a better spot.*)

MAY: Do you manage to get about much?

LUCY: Well, I do my shopping, and I go to visit my cousin sometimes, which is rather a tiring walk, but – oh, I don't do so badly. (*She returns to her chair.*)

MAY: I've had a strange pain in my knee today. I think it must be the frost. As a rule there's nothing the matter with me at all.

LUCY: I've always found that rubbing in a little Ellimans' last thing at night is quite wonderful.

MAY: Yes. Ellimans'. I must remember that. Ellimans'.

LUCY: It's quite easy to remember.

MAY: Yes. Ellimans'. (*A pause.*) Did you go far in your walk this morning?

LUCY: Well, right over the bridge past Seatown. And I must admit that by the time I arrived at my cousin's I did feel rather tired. But then it may have been through carrying the picture, because otherwise I've been very sprightly lately.

MAY: Oh, a picture?

LUCY: Well, I couldn't make up my mind what to give him. It's so difficult to know what to give a man, isn't it? Oh, there, the kettle's beginning to boil, and I've nothing ready. (*She rises and, going to the sideboard, produces a crocheted table-cloth and tea-things, which she lays on the table.*) Yes, it's so difficult to know what to give for Christmas to a man like my poor cousin Francis, who's confined to his bed all day and hasn't very long to live. So, in the end, I thought a picture would be nice.

MAY: Yes, a picture's always nice, isn't it? Yes.

LUCY: (*With a glance at her.*) Well, perhaps not *always*. They have some very funny pictures nowadays.

MAY: Yes. Oh dear, yes. I saw some extremely odd ones in a shop at St Lennans once. I don't know *what* they could have been.

LUCY: (*Moving up to the sideboard.*) Would you like a biscuit with your tea, Miss Beringer?

MAY: Oh no, really. I couldn't manage a biscuit, not after the sausage.

LUCY: Are you sure? I...believe... (*Peering in the sideboard.*) there are some here. They're not too crisp, I'm sorry to say. Still, they might as well be put out.

MAY: Not for me, really. Please, don't. Oh, well, perhaps – are you going to have one?

LUCY: Yes, I think I will.

MAY: Will you, really?

LUCY: I think so.

MAY: Then perhaps I will, then.

LUCY: Do.

MAY: (*Finally.*) Well, then, I will.

> (*LUCY brings the biscuits to the table with the crockery. Then she goes, teapot and caddy in hand, to the kettle and makes the tea.*)

LUCY: (*As she crosses.*) Will two be enough? Or do you prefer it stronger?

MAY: No, no, thank you. Not for me. That will do beautifully. Oh dear, we are cosy in here.

LUCY: I'd better let it stand for a moment. (*She places the pot on the table.*)

MAY: (*Rising.*) May I look round your room? You've got such lovely things, if you don't mind my saying so. Oh dear, yes. (*She moves about the room.*)

LUCY: Yes, do, please. (*She sits left of the table.*)

MAY: (*Going to the bookshelf.*) What a nice lot of books you have. I do like reading, don't you?

LUCY: Well, Mrs Henry Wood, of course – she writes *good* stories, I think – and Sir Walter Scott. My husband used to say that Sir Walter Scott had the true romantic spirit.

Although a little old-fashioned. But then my husband was more modern than I was. Yes, my husband was a writer. He wrote plays and poetry, and was very well known in his time. Very well known, indeed. You'll see one of his books there.

MAY: Really? How very interesting. That *is* interesting.

LUCY: Two plays in one volume. *Tintagel* and *The Slandered Queen* by Ambrose Amorest. Can you see it?

MAY: Oh, yes. (*She takes the volume out.*) I should love to read them. I really should. Do you think I might?

LUCY: Why certainly, Miss Beringer.

MAY: Thank you so much. Yes, I really must read them! (*But she puts the volumes back and passes on to the mantelpiece, where she examines a photograph.*) This is your husband, I suppose?

LUCY: Yes. That is my husband.

MAY: What a fine face. A fine face. A fine man he must have been. And how well the cloak becomes him. (*She turns to the other photograph.*) And is this your little boy?

LUCY: (*Speaking with a pride which she is unable to conceal.*) Yes, that's Brand.

MAY: He is a nice little boy. Is he...I...er...

LUCY: He's a grown man now, of course. He lives abroad. I write to him every week.

MAY: Every week? Yes? And which part is he?

LUCY: I...I'm not quite sure. He was...in America when I heard last.
(*A tiny pause.*)
Milk and sugar?

MAY: Oh, if you don't mind. Two. (*She goes back to her seat.*)

LUCY: Yes, he's a sturdy little chap in the photograph, isn't he?

MAY: Yes, very. Very. (*She takes the proffered cup.*) Oh, thank you. That's beautiful, thanks.

LUCY: He was just off to football.
(*Her eyes wander away into the past. She is thinking of BRAND. MAY drinks her tea. She speaks after putting her cup down.*)

339

MAY: That's very odd now, but I have a brother who went abroad when he was young, and lost touch with the family. He may be alive somewhere, one never knows.

LUCY: (*Meaninglessly.*) Yes.

(*A pause.*)

MAY: One gets great companionship from dogs, don't you think? This is the first time I've been without one. Ever since my friend Jane went to India, I've never been without a dog. Never.

(*LUCY, who has not heard a word, brings herself back to earth.*)

LUCY: What a neglectful hostess I am. Do have another biscuit, will you?

MAY: I don't *really* think I could manage one.

LUCY: Oh, but they're nothing.

MAY: Well – perhaps. Are you really going to have one?

LUCY: Yes, I think I will.

MAY: Then perhaps I *really* will, then.

LUCY: Do.

MAY: Thank you. I shouldn't, of course. I'm nothing but a glutton. (*She takes one and eats it. They are very small, thin biscuits.*)

LUCY: Mrs Payne's the one for sweet biscuits.

MAY: She's fond of them, is she?

LUCY: She has quite a passion for sweet things.

MAY: Really? Chocolates?

LUCY: No. Nougat she likes – and sticky things. Queer, isn't it?... And raspberry jam.

MAY: Oh, dear.

(*They both laugh a little.*)

I was very fond of sweet things myself as a child – we were all children together in Exeter, you know. And the times we had, and the things we got up to – when we were all children together in Exeter, you know. There was a little rhyme we used to say – I'm afraid you'll think it awfully silly of me remembering it – oh dear, yes, you will think I'm silly, (*She is giggling nervously through her words.*) ...but it was this:

'Okey pokey, penny a lump,
The more you eat, the more you jump.'
Oh dear, now, I don't know what it could have meant!
(*They both laugh, but a sudden thud on the ceiling causes
them to start and look upwards. There is silence for a moment.
In the room up centre, a bulky sleeping figure, vaguely
discernible until now in a rocking-chair, has heaved itself up
and, in doing so, knocked over a small table. Now it shuffles
to the door, and goes out.*)
What was that?

LUCY: Oh, nothing. Mrs Payne, I expect.

MAY: Oh.

(*A pause.*)

LUCY: She must have knocked something over.

MAY: It gave me quite a start.

(*AGATHA PAYNE appears on the stairs, which she commences
to descend. Large, stout and shapeless, her soiled red wrapper
clutched about her, a jewelled comb in her black tumbled
hair, she is like an old gypsy woman, or at least one of gypsy
blood. MAY and LUCY go on talking.*)

LUCY: Mrs Payne often startles one like that. She sleeps a
lot, you know, and then she probably wakes up suddenly
and moves about without being properly awake.

MAY: I hate anything giving me a start. There's really
nothing I hate more. My heart's not at all good. The
slightest shock and it jumps up and down in such a wild
manner. I can feel it now. And what is worse, it will miss
a beat. Most alarming!

LUCY: I don't think that's anything to worry about, Miss
Beringer.

MAY: Oh, but it is. You've no idea how alarmed I get. I don't
know what I should have done sometimes without Pip –
I don't really.

LUCY: Was that your last little dog?

MAY: Yes. Pip. A little fox-terrier he was.

LUCY: Did you have him long?

MAY: Oh yes. He was quite old when he passed away. And
just like a human being. Jane – my friend Jane – gave him
to me as a gift. Pip first, she gave me, and then the amber.

LUCY: The amber?

MAY: Yes. My most treasured possession – a most beautiful piece of amber. I must certainly show it to you.

LUCY: Do, please, I'd love to see it.

MAY: I do think there's nothing like a gift, is there? Well, I've often thought since – when Pip died it was doubly sad – doubly dad, yes – not only losing him, but something from my best friend as well.

LUCY: But at least you've got this amber; you'll always have that, won't you?

MAY: Yes. I'll always have that.

(AGATHA has now reached the door of LUCY's room. She knocks. MAY draws in her breath and puts her hand to her heart, but LUCY whispers.)

LUCY: It's only Mrs Payne. *(She calls brightly and hospitably.)* Come in!

(AGATHA pushes the door slowly open, and enters. MAY rises to her feet and stands, trembling. She had not expected AGATHA to be quite like this.)

We were just having a cup of tea. Miss Beringer, this is Mrs Payne, who shares the house with us here.

(AGATHA comes forward. MAY giggles nervously.)

AGATHA: *(In her deep, thick voice.)* I'm glad to meet you.

LUCY: You *will* have some tea? I'll get another cup. It won't be very fresh, I'm afraid. *(She moves to the sideboard.)*

(AGATHA sinks into the vacant chair, after peering at an open letter on the mantelpiece. MAY sits, also.)

AGATHA: Not for me, Lucy.

LUCY: Are you sure?

AGATHA: You know I don't like tea. There's no richness to it. A nice cup of cocoa with plenty of sugar, that's a different matter.

LUCY: But I'm afraid I haven't any cocoa.

AGATHA: That's all right, I've had three cups this morning. But tea – I like it about as much as the Devil likes dill-water.

MAY: *(In a voice which is trembling with nerves and with a face which is meant to have an appearance of brightness.)* But do you find cocoa as stimulating as tea when you're tired, Mrs Payne?

AGATHA: (*Ignoring this.*) Have you been out this morning, Lucy?

LUCY: Yes. I met Miss Beringer just as I came. And we've got to know each other in no time. (*She sits in the wing-chair.*)

AGATHA: I heard you laughing. It woke me up. What were you laughing about?

MAY: I can't remember now. Can you, Mrs Amorest? What *was* it?

AGATHA: (*To LUCY.*) And where'd you been?

LUCY: I went and paid a visit to my cousin, just to take a little present.

AGATHA: A present! I wouldn't give him a present. Rich as he is, and does nothing for you. I'm sorry for you, Lucy, with no relations but an old skinflint like him, unless you count your boy. But he might as well be dead for all you see of him.

LUCY: Oh, no, Agatha.

AGATHA: He's been gone for years now. No one knows where. If he is alive he doesn't care about you. I'm glad my child died. She'd only have been a grief to me.

LUCY: He'll come back – Brand, I mean. I feel tonight as though everything's going to turn out well. Don't you feel that sometimes? I'm sure *you* do, Miss Beringer.

MAY: Oh yes, I do, indeed. Often. Don't you, Mrs Payne?

AGATHA: Brand. So that's your boy's name. Queer name.

LUCY: It was my husband who wished it. I think it's a nice name.

MAY: Oh, very nice. Very.

AGATHA: Well, I don't think much of your Brand. Why doesn't he write and tell you what he's doing? Perhaps he *is* dead.

LUCY: I know he's not dead. Brand wasn't the kind of boy who would ever own that he was beaten. It was always the same, in cricket and football. He'll tell me where he is when he's made his fortune. I'm expecting to hear any day now.

AGATHA: You've been expecting to hear any day since I've known you. You're a patient woman.

(*A long pause.*)

MAY: One would never think it was Christmas Eve, would one?

LUCY: Oh, Agatha, I felt I simply had to do something this Christmas. We've just done nothing these last two Christmases, and it did seem too bad. I bought a little surprise for us all, on my way back. I simply couldn't resist it. You will come down tonight, won't you, and I'll have cakes and tea – no, cocoa, I'll remember to get cocoa for you – and we can have quite a little party. But the surprise is the thing. I'm sure you'll like it, dear.

AGATHA: How can you afford a party, Lucy?

LUCY: Well, if one always stopped to think what one could afford one would never do anything.

MAY: No, one wouldn't do anything at all.

(*A pause.*)

AGATHA: What's the matter with you? You've had some good news. The cards last night said there was good news on the way.

LUCY: Well, in a sense I have. And yet it's not news exactly. My cousin spoke to me in a very kindly manner this afternoon.

AGATHA: Did he say he'd leave you something in his will?

LUCY: He did say something. Of course, he may have meant nothing by it. I certainly mustn't rely on it.

AGATHA: Nonsense. (*She leans forward.*) What did he say he'd leave you?

LUCY: Well... (*She turns to MAY before she answers AGATHA.*) Do forgive us, Miss Beringer, but after all, as we're going to be such very close neighbours, there's no harm in knowing about each other's affairs.

MAY: Quite. Not at all. I don't mind a bit.

LUCY: Well, he said a thousand pounds a year!

AGATHA: (*Sitting back.*) A thousand pounds! A thousand pounds a year! Why, Lucy, that's a fortune.

(*A pause.*)

MAY: Yes, it is. Quite a fortune, isn't it? Oh, dear, you must be feeling happy, Mrs Amorest.

LUCY: You're quite right, Miss Beringer, I am. But, after all, it's foolish of me. I shouldn't rely on it. I've only what he said to go on.

AGATHA: Was there anyone else there when he said it?

LUCY: No, there wasn't. We were quite alone, and he was very kind, indeed. I've never known him so nice.

AGATHA: (*Slowly staring at her.*) So *you're* going to get a thousand pounds.

LUCY: It's only what he *said.*

MAY: You never can be sure of anything, can you?

AGATHA: What could *you* do with a thousand pounds?

LUCY: Well, Agatha, I could find my boy and we'd live together again.

AGATHA: Is that all you'd do?

LUCY: That's all I'd want.

AGATHA: You'd have plenty over, wouldn't you? What would you do with that? Wouldn't you buy anything? Wouldn't you buy any jewels or trinkets? Any coloured things? Silks and jewels? No – nothing like that you wouldn't buy, would you?

LUCY: (*Half laughing.*) No, I can't say I would, Agatha.

AGATHA: (*Slowly looking at her with a concentrated stare.*) No. (*There is a little pause. Then AGATHA sits back once more.*)

MAY: Well, I'm afraid there isn't anybody who's likely to leave *me* a thousand pounds. (*She giggles.*) I wish there were. (*She giggles again.*)

LUCY: Anyway, he probably won't leave it to me at all. Do let's talk of something else. It doesn't seem right to be talking of money like this when it comes through someone's death. Shall I take your cup, Miss Beringer?

MAY: Oh, yes. Thank you. Lovely cup of tea it was. I much prefer Indian to China. Except sometimes one doesn't feel like Indian, and then one prefers China. Which do you prefer, Mrs Amorest?

LUCY: Oh, Indian.

MAY: Yes, Indian.

AGATHA: I'll be going, Lucy. And you're quite right. Don't count on the money. You come to me and we'll talk it over. There's nothing like a little plan. Nothing. (*She commences to heave herself up.*)

LUCY: (*Politely.*) Oh, don't go yet.
(*AGATHA does not reply, but, having got to her feet, moves slowly to the door, where she turns.*)

AGATHA: Would you lend me some of the money?

LUCY: Lend you some? Why, of course.

AGATHA: You're a good creature, Lucy. I'd do the same for you. And, after all, you must be pretty sure of it. You wouldn't go spending money on parties and surprises else. You've only got ten pound four in the bank and nothing coming in.

LUCY: (*Springing to her feet in shame and agitation.*) Whatever gave you such an idea? You're quite wrong, Agatha – you are, really! What *could* have put such an idea into your head?

AGATHA: I saw the letter from the bank. 'Twas on the mantelpiece. I didn't really mean to read it.

LUCY: Oh, but you shouldn't have. What were you thinking of? I assure you it's a mistake! The letter was a mistake. You shouldn't have said such a thing…
(*There is a loud knock at the front door. LUCY pauses. They all look questioningly at each other. She contrives to recover her composure.*)
It's for me, I think, I'll go. I won't be a moment. Only stay in here, will you both? You mustn't see before tonight or everything will be spoiled. I won't be a minute.
(*She hurries into the hall, shutting the door of her room. AGATHA, on the other side, stands against it, listening. MAY remains seated; she, too, listens. LUCY holds her skirts down as she pulls the front door open and the wind tears round the hall. On the threshold is a Christmas tree. A sudden peal of bells rings out from the cathedral. It seems to fill the whole house as the curtain falls.
The curtain remains down for two or three minutes, during which the chimes continue, and rises again to the sound of children's voices singing:*)

'No-el, No-el,
No-el, No-el,
Born is the Ki-ing of I-is-ra-el.'
The old ladies are each in their rooms. MAY and AGATHA
are putting the finishing touches to their party best. LUCY,
already attired for the party, is putting finishing touches to
the tree. It stands enshrined in an aureole of golden splendour
at the centre of the room. Father Christmas triumphs at the
peak. Chains of frosted silver, balls of fire, emerald and ruby,
amethyst and crystal are shining and flashing from its boughs.
On either side of the tree are two small tables, with white
cloths. On one are some parcels, tied with coloured ribbon, on
the other cakes and sweets, tea in a pot, cocoa in a jug, cups
and saucers. LUCY sits down and surveys her work. A smile
plays on her lips. Upstairs, AGATHA, in her dark purple
old-fashioned dress, her black hair brushed and her red slippers
on her feet, picks up from where it sits on her work basket a
large doll in a green frock. She looks at it with affection,
pulls the dress straight, and places the doll in a more elegant
position. After this, she gathers up some playing cards from
the table, collects them into a pack, turns down the lamp, and
goes out. A second later, MAY, in an orange silk dress, does
the same. AGATHA has reappeared and descended half way
down the stairs before MAY appears behind her. AGATHA
does not even turn round, but continues her descent. MAY,
suddenly alarmed at seeing her, retreats, to reappear a second
or two later, catching her up just as she reaches LUCY's
door.)
MAY: (*Very breathless.*) Oh...er...good evening, Mrs Payne.
(*AGATHA turns and surveys her.*)
AGATHA: And how are you tonight?
MAY: I'm so excited. I don't know when I've felt so excited.
(*She giggles.*)
LUCY: (*Calling out.*) Come in.
(*AGATHA opens the door. The carol finishes. LUCY has risen*
to her feet. The two ladies stand amazed, gazing at the tree.
They can hardly believe their eyes.)
MAY: (*At last.*) Oh dear! Dear me! Dear me!
(*A pause. AGATHA says nothing, she just stares.*)

LUCY: Was it very silly of me? I hope you won't think so. But I simply had to do it. I do hope you don't mind.

MAY: Mind? Why, Mrs Amorest, it's lovely. It's the loveliest thing. Why, I can't speak... I can't, indeed. Words won't come. I can't say anything at all.
(*A pause.*)

LUCY: Well, sit down, both of you. And, dear me, there's quite a draught. I'll shut the door.
(*MAY goes to a chair and sits. AGATHA, without taking her eyes off the tree, moves as though in a trance to another chair. She sinks into it and goes on staring as though hypnotised. Her lips move. LUCY turns from the door and stands there. The silence remains unbroken. She waits for them to speak, in vain.*)
(*After a minute, with a tiny note of alarm in her voice.*) Oh, do say something, Agatha. I shall begin to feel you don't like the tree.

AGATHA: Don't like it? I can't tell you what I feel about it, Lucy; you wouldn't understand.

LUCY: I think I would.

AGATHA: No. You don't love beauty. Nobody loves beauty like I do. It's beauty and colour – the tree there. That's why I'm the only one that understands it. (*She relapses into her contemplation.*)

MAY: (*Suddenly bursting out.*) Oh, Mrs Amorest, I *wish* I could tell you what I feel. It makes me think of all the Christmases I've ever spent!

LUCY: (*Taking the remaining chair.*) I'm so glad you like it. It's nice, isn't it, to think of all the other trees there are tonight in everybody's homes, and the children sitting round them, and the presents... (*She breaks off.*)

MAY: Oh, it's wonderful. Simply wonderful.
(*A little nearer now, the children's voices commence another carol; the bells peal softly beyond the window; the fire crackles. In a row sit the three old ladies, gazing at the tree. After a little while LUCY bestirs herself. She rises, and moves to the table.*)

LUCY: Oh, I'm forgetting all about the tea. You will have some, won't you, Miss Beringer, and Agatha will have some cocoa, I know. With lots of sugar in it. I got the cocoa specially for you. (*By this time she is at the table, pouring the beverages out.*)

MAY: (*With a sudden rush.*) I remember once when I was a little girl – when we were all children at Exeter, you know – we had one Christmas time a really lovely fairy on top of the tree. Oh, it was lovely. I wish you could have seen it, Mrs Amorest. And then, of course, Gertrude – my sister Gertrude – was given it, but she didn't like it somehow, and she gave it to me. I can't think – I can't remember now why she didn't like it. Oh, but *I* did. I really loved that fairy, Mrs Amorest. I wish you could have seen it, you know how silly children can be. Well, anyway, I came into the nursery one day – we had a big fire going, you know – my mother believed in big fires in the nursery, and there was the fairy, Mrs Amorest – I'd put it in front of the fire because I thought it was feeling cold – there was nothing left but the clothes. It was made of wax and had melted right away.

LUCY: Indeed, that was curious. But quite a little tragedy. You do take sugar, don't you?

MAY: Oh yes. Yes, please. And then I remember there was one thing at Christmas that I never could bring myself to like. I don't know what it was, you know, but there was something about the turkey, or it might be the goose, as it lay on the table waiting to be carved, that always seemed slightly...er...well, *vulgar.* Jane always used to laugh at me about this.

AGATHA: (*Taking the cup which LUCY is offering to her.*) Thank you, Lucy.

LUCY: And you must help yourself to cakes and sweets. Look, I'll put them where you can both reach them.

AGATHA: Thank you, Lucy. That's fine. (*She drinks her cocoa in silence – eyes fixed on the tree. One hand stretches mechanically forth at intervals and, taking a sweet, drops it into her mouth.*)

MAY: Oh, thank you. That's such a good idea, isn't it, and saves running about. Do sit down, Mrs Amorest, and

349

enjoy *yourself* a bit. I'm sure you deserve it, you do, indeed. I've never seen such a beautiful Christmas tree, never.

LUCY: (*Seating herself and taking a cake.*) You're perfectly right, Miss Beringer. I can't help admitting I think it's beautiful myself. All the afternoon I've kept wondering – well, is it silly of me? I don't know, I couldn't make up my mind, but in the end, it looked so lovely that everything seemed to be justified.

MAY: Quite, quite. A thing of beauty is a joy for ever as the poet says.

LUCY: More cocoa, Agatha?

AGATHA: (*Shaking her head.*) No. (*Another sweet is dropped into her mouth.*)

MAY: Oh, and I remember one Christmas party we had at Exeter. Everybody was there, and Gertrude – my sister Gertrude, you know – this was when we were young girls – oh, quite grown up, we were, too – she was lovely looking, she was looking lovely, Mrs Amorest, I wish you could have seen her, and mother had lent her her pearl brooch for the evening, in fact they were all looking lovely, even mother herself. And the men were so dashing. They were very dashing in those days, don't you think, Mrs Amorest – much more so than nowadays, we did have a gay time. And witty, the people seemed to be so gay and witty then. Of course, I was never very good at parties – although I enjoyed them. I always *felt*, you know, that I could be quite clever and amusing, if only I could put my ideas in order. Jane – when she and I were in St Lennans, you know – used to tell me that I could if I'd only try, but somehow, I've never been able to. Something unfortunately always seems to get in the way. And then my brother Rupert, you know, always used to overeat himself at Christmas dinner – oh yes – sick – he often used to be sick afterwards when he was a boy. And then Miss Marchmont, she was our governess. I remember her as if it were yesterday – I wish you could have seen her, Mrs Amorest, she had a very long nose with a flat piece at the end, and we used to call her Miss Rembrandt – I can't remember why, but, of course, people are often called by very odd names. I remember once I was walking along the front at St Lennans with Jane, and a group of young people who were going by looked at me and said, 'There goes the Grenadier' – I've often wondered why they called me the Grenadier, because I'm sure I don't look like a Grenadier – but anyway, what was I telling you, oh yes, about Miss Rembrandt well, we were having a very gay party once, at Exeter of course, and Miss Rembrandt insisted on reciting, and we all began to laugh and titter, you know how silly young people are – we were properly in disgrace. Hm. (*She clears her throat.*) Oh, dear, I hope I'm not sickening for tonsillitis. My throat's quite sore.

LUCY: Have some more tea, Miss Beringer, then you'll feel all right.

MAY: Oh, thank you, yes. But not another cup, no. I'll just finish what I've got. (*She does so.*) Yes, that is better. Perhaps it was through talking such a lot. I do hope that I haven't bored you, Mrs Amorest, but you know how one can get carried away thinking of old times.

LUCY: Not at all. Only too well. I've loved hearing you, I really have. But you must eat a piece of plum cake, or I shall be most upset.

MAY: Why, yes, of course – beautiful it looks. (*She takes a piece and bites.*) Delicious, delicious.

LUCY: There's quite a likelihood I should have been talking of old times myself, if I hadn't been too busy eating.

MAY: Oh, dear!

(*They both laugh.*)

LUCY: Are you going on quite well, Agatha? Some more cocoa? (*She takes up the jug.*) Oh, I'm afraid there isn't any more, only a drain.

AGATHA: That's all right, Lucy.

LUCY: Are you quite sure? Well, then, we'll go on to the next part of the programme. (*She crosses to the table on which are the parcels.*) You mustn't laugh at me, please. They're just little tiny things that I got. The chief part of a present, I always think, is that it should be wrapped up in paper – don't you?

(*She hands them the gifts. There is a pause while they open them up. MAY with trembling excited fingers; AGATHA, lethargically. Nevertheless hers is undone first.*)

It's more than silly of me, isn't it? But I was certain you'd like a new dress for that little doll of yours, and I couldn't resist the blotter because I thought you'd like the colour.

AGATHA: Thank you, Lucy. Yes, I did want a new dress for Miranda. That makes four she's got now. The green, the purple, the ruby, and now the blue. Yes, the room'll look nice when I put the blue on her. Thank you, Lucy. (*She wraps up the dress with the blotter and sits holding them staring once more at the tree.*)

MAY: (*Shrilly, having unwrapped hers.*) Just what I wanted. Dear me. Dear me!

LUCY: I'm so glad you like them. It was so difficult to know what you'd like.

MAY: (*Holding up the book.*) The Light of Asia by Sir Edward Arnold. I've always wanted to read that. Always. And the little scissors in the case are so useful. Oh dear, I shall be able to do lots of sewing now. Lots. Thank you, Mrs Amorest. Well, that *is* a nice surprise.

LUCY: (*Resuming her seat.*) I'm so glad you liked them.

MAY: Oh I do, indeed!

(*A pause. AGATHA is beginning to fall asleep.*)

I don't know when I've felt so happy. I don't think I've felt so happy since Jane gave me the amber.

LUCY: I feel happy, too. If only I thought my boy were coming home I wouldn't mind anything.

MAY: Oh, dear yes. I expect you had lots of fun at Christmas with him. Did he get up to many pranks?

LUCY: Well, I remember one Christmas his father gave him a new kind of top that flew up in the air if it was spun in a certain manner. We were having a dinner-party, and

Brand was allowed down to dessert. Well, he spun the
top, and if it didn't go right up in the air and come down
on Mr Horland's head.

(*MAY clicks her tongue. They both laugh.*)

Mr Horland was the husband of a lady novelist. He was
most upset. My husband used to ask quite a lot of those
sort of people to stay – but, tell the truth, I always thought
the kind of books they wrote were quite horrible.

MAY: Quite. Quite.

LUCY: I wrote to Brand today. But… I can't be sure he gets
my letters… I write, you see, to the address from which
I last heard. Two years ago it was now.

(*She suddenly starts. MAY starts, too. AGATHA is fast asleep.
The parcel has fallen from her hand.*)

MAY: Oh! Oh! I wish she wouldn't do that.

LUCY: She's fast asleep.

MAY: Is she? Are you sure?

LUCY: Quite.

(*A pause. Then MAY leans forward.*)

MAY: (*Hoarsely whispering.*) Oh, Mrs Amorest, I don't like
her at all. Do you like her? Don't you think there's
something queer? There's something very odd about her
indeed.

LUCY: Sh! No, I don't think so. She is a *little* queer perhaps,
but she doesn't mean anything – any harm.

MAY: Doesn't she?

LUCY: No. She's old and all by herself. We ought to be kind
to her.

MAY: Oh, I don't think I can be kind to her. I don't like her
at all – I really don't.

LUCY: But what should you be alarmed about?

MAY: Oh, Mrs Amorest, *you* should understand. Her
manner to you earlier today – about your cousin, I mean
– was *most* alarming.

LUCY: Well, poor old thing, she's so much alone. Perhaps
she doesn't know what she's saying. And tonight – it's
so late for her to be up, and she has this passion for
colours – the tree fascinated her. I often think that in all

probability she comes from gypsy ancestors. And –
well, that would make her a little different.

MAY: Very likely. Very likely.

LUCY: But it's no good alarming yourself about her, is it?

MAY: All right, Mrs Amorest. I'll try not to.

LUCY: That's right.

MAY: And I must really buy myself another little dog.
Perhaps that's what's the matter with me – being without
a dog.

LUCY: I'm sure they must be a great comfort.

MAY: Yes… I've been wondering now. May I ask your
advice, Mrs Amorest? I shouldn't think it would be very
difficult in Polchester to find some sort of a – *position*.
Would you?

LUCY: What kind of position?

MAY: Well, I wondered whether, later perhaps, I couldn't
find a position as a – a – companion perhaps – or where
I could arrange the flowers.

LUCY: I don't *think* such positions are too easy to come by.

MAY: Oh, but Mrs Amorest – you don't mind my telling
you, do you – only I'm sure you'll understand. You see,
I must get a position soon, because at the end of six
months I won't have any money left.

AGATHA: (*In her sleep.*) Give that to me… (*She mumbles for
a second or two.*) It's mine! I'll kill you if you touch it.

MAY: Oh! Oh!

LUCY: She's having a nightmare. Here, Agatha. (*She gives
AGATHA a little push.*) Agatha, wake up! You're dreaming!

AGATHA: What? What's that? (*She wakes up.*) Dreaming?
That's right, Lucy. I was dreaming about that husband of
mine. I dreamed I tried to kill him. Well, he's dead now
and can't do me any harm. No more than I can do him
any. But I could have killed him once. I could have
killed him all right when he threw my hat on the fire. A
fine hat it was – but too gay for him. Can you believe
that, Lucy? I was a young girl then, and prettier than
most of them – 'My Gipsy Queen' he'd call me when we
were courting. My Gipsy Queen. But after that – when

he'd got me – no life, no gaiety then – not even a gay hat. No. So into the fire he threw it. Well, I got my own back. Yes. I can't tell you *how*, because you and Miss Bering – what's her name – Miss Beringer here are too lady-like. Yes. And he didn't know *how*, to his dying day. I used to lie awake after he threw my hat in the fire, thinking what I could do to him. And I read a book about China once – just certain parts of it, you know – I could never read a book right through. But it told you how they'd tie up prisoners with wire, and then they'd get a rat...

MAY: (*Springing to her feet.*) Oh, please! Please don't! I can't bear it! I really can't! I shall have to go.

LUCY: Miss Beringer, you mustn't get in such a state. Agatha, don't go on. Let's talk about something nice.

AGATHA: I was only telling you what I read in the book.

LUCY: (*To MAY.*) Please sit down again. It would be such a pity to end the Christmas party like this. And I believe it's nearly twelve o'clock, too. Christmas Day

MAY: I can't help it. My heart's bad, and my nerves are quite on edge. But I will try. I'd do anything for you, Mrs Amorest. I'd hate to spoil the party. I... (*She sits down.*)

LUCY: That's right. Now...er... Oh, Agatha, why don't you put the new little dress on the doll? I'm quite longing to see what she looks like in it.

AGATHA: I'm too tired, Lucy. If I go upstairs again to get Miranda, I shall stay there and go to bed.

LUCY: It is late, of course, but...

MAY: Let *me* get it for you. Oh, *do* let me, please. I won't take a minute to run upstairs. May I?

AGATHA: Please yourself, I don't mind.

LUCY: I shouldn't trouble, Miss Beringer.

MAY: (*Moving to the door.*) But I'd love to. I... I so want to see Mrs Payne's doll. I... Where will I find it, Mrs Payne?

AGATHA: You can't miss her. She's a big doll. You'll see her all right.

MAY: Thank you, I... I'll get her, then. Oh, this is fun. And...and, Mrs Amorest...?

LUCY: Yes?

MAY: Would...would you like to see my piece of amber that Jane gave me?

LUCY: Yes. Very much.

MAY: I'll bring that down, too, then, shall I?

LUCY: Yes, indeed.

MAY: All right. Bye-bye, then. Bye-bye for the present.

> (*She goes into the hall, and immediately on shutting the door, drops her false brightness and leans for a few seconds against it, her face in her hands. Then, pulling herself together, she goes up the stairs to AGATHA's room, looks round it fearfully, takes Miranda and, going to her own room, lifts reverently from its place of honour on the mantelpiece a lovely piece of carved amber. She then returns to the stairs.*
>
> *During the above the following piece of dialogue has taken place between the two old ladies in the room below.*)

AGATHA: (*Mimicking MAY's last words.*) Bye-bye! Bye-bye! Idiot!

LUCY: Why don't you like her? Poor old thing.

AGATHA: I don't mind her. She irritates me, that's all. What's she so frightened of everything for?

LUCY: You must admit, Agatha, you are a little alarming sometimes.

AGATHA: Me, alarming? Nonsense! Bye-bye! I like people to have *gumption*. Wants to see the doll, does she? Wants any excuse to get away from *me* for a moment, because I frighten her. Bye-bye!

LUCY: I think you're very unkind, Agatha.

AGATHA: Nonsense. She's frightened of everything. You can see that. You and I, Lucy, *we're* not frightened. I like you for that, Lucy. I respect you. You've got independence. But her! Look at her! She's not worth talking about. You're quite right. Poor old thing. She's never known what it is to live. Brrrr. (*She shivers.*) It's cold, the fire's going out, and I'm going to bed. (*She commences to heave herself out of the chair.*) Help me up, Lucy.

LUCY: (*Doing so.*) Must you go now?

AGATHA: Yes, I must. Bed's all I want. And you'll have to help me up the stairs. My legs are funny tonight.

LUCY: Wait a moment. I'll turn the lamp down. It might catch the tree or something terrible.

(*One arm round AGATHA, she turns the lamp down with her free hand. The fire has nearly died down now. In the dim lamplight, the tree, too, looks dead. Glamour has flown.*)

AGATHA: And thanks for the party, Lucy. I enjoyed the tree. Thanks.

(*LUCY smiles at her, and they go into the hall. By this time MAY has nearly reached the foot of the stairs. On seeing them, she stops.*)

MAY: Oh dear, are you going to bed now? Look, Mrs Amorest, I've brought the amber. It's pretty with the light shining through. Look.

(*The street lamp shines brightly through the window behind her. She suddenly holds the amber up, and the light shines through it. Shaped square, like a block of wood, and this block surmounted by a carved red amber dragon – the little ornament glows with the light.*)

LUCY: Oh, what a lovely thing! It's like a piece of fire. And all the colours in it.

(*AGATHA removes her arm from about her, and walks with slow, steady steps to the bottom of the stairs. The amber seems to have hypnotised her as, a little while ago, she was hypnotised by the tree. MAY regards her approach with nervous eyes. Having reached the stairs, AGATHA stops.*)

AGATHA: That's a beautiful thing you have there.

MAY: Oh yes. It is, isn't it. It's my most precious possession. It was given me, years ago, by my dearest friend. I'm so glad you like it.

AGATHA: (*Breathing deeply and advancing one step up.*) I do like it.

MAY: I'm so glad you do. It's been much admired. Everyone likes it. It's worth a lot of money, I believe.

AGATHA: Do you think you'd sell it, if you were offered a large sum? (*She heaves herself up another step.*)

MAY: Oh dear, no. Nothing would induce me. The greatest friend of my life gave it to me. I'd never sell it. Nothing would induce me.

AGATHA: May I look at it closer?

MAY: Why, certainly, do.

(*A pause.*)

AGATHA: May I have it in my hands for a moment?

(*She stretches up for it greedily, but MAY pulls it away.*)

MAY: Oh dear! I feel terribly ill! I'm very sorry. My head's bursting. I must go to bed, You must excuse me. I can't... I...

(*She turns and runs to her room.*)

LUCY: Oh, now, Agatha. You've frightened her again. Poor old thing, she's in such a state of nerves. I'd better go and see if she's all right.

(*AGATHA doesn't answer. She stands leaning against the banisters, breathing heavily. LUCY hurries past her and goes to MAY's room. MAY sits trembling by the side of her bed. During the scene that follows, AGATHA remains where she has been for a few seconds, and then goes slowly, muttering, to her room.*)

MAY: Oh, Mrs Amorest, please don't be cross with me. I'm sorry to have spoilt the party, I really am. But she frightens me. She really does. The queer way she looked at the amber. And the way she looks at me.

LUCY: (*Sitting beside her.*) But Agatha always looks a little strange – she has those big black eyes.

MAY: It wasn't only those eyes. No, it certainly wasn't those eyes. I'm sure she's going to do me a mischief. I'm sure she is. And the way she stretched out her hand for the piece of amber. Just as though it was hers. I'm sure she'll steal it from me.

LUCY: (*Placing her hand on MAY's.*) Dear Miss Beringer, please don't disturb yourself. I know Mrs Payne is a good woman. I've known her a long time. There's nothing to be afraid of.

MAY: Oh, I don't know, I'm sure. I'm sure I don't know. I've always been afraid of something all my life. It seems to be my destiny. It's my fate to have something to be afraid of. I'm sure I don't like being under the same roof with her. She'll do something to me in my sleep.

(*A long pause, during which LUCY pats MAY's hand soothingly. But at last she stands up.*)

LUCY: Now, don't you worry, dear. Have a good rest and you'll find you'll have forgotten all about it in the morning. Good night, my dear. And a happy Christmas.

MAY: Good night.

(*LUCY bends down and, kissing the other's withered cheek, goes from the room. MAY falls face downwards on her bed in a passion of noiseless sobbing. AGATHA, in her room, has dropped into the rocking-chair, and now, staring grimly in front of her, rocks backwards and forwards. As LUCY reappears on the staircase, a bell from the cathedral chimes the first stroke which heralds midnight and Christmas Day. She listens for a second and then continues down the stairs and across to her room. Turning up the lamp, she takes the photograph of her boy from the mantelpiece and kisses it. Then she kneels down and says her prayers. The last stroke of midnight dies away as the curtain falls.*)

End of Act One.

ACT TWO

The same. A few days later.

When the curtain rises AGATHA is in her rocking-chair eating nougat. She is half asleep. LUCY, in her room, is writing. The Christmas tree has been pushed into a corner. MAY comes in at the front door. She finds a letter on the mat and, picking it up, goes towards LUCY's room, and knocks at the door.

MAY: May I come in, Mrs Amorest?

LUCY: Yes, do.

   (MAY comes in.)

   Have you been out? I was just writing to Brand.

MAY: Did you see this letter?

LUCY: *(Taking it.)* Oh, thank you. Dear me, it's typewritten. Will you excuse me a moment. Sit down, dear, will you?

MAY: Yes. Certainly. Thank you so much. I've had that pain in my knee again today. *(She sits by the meagre fire.)*

   (LUCY opens the letter. Her hand trembles as she reads.)

   Oh, I hope it isn't bad news.

   (A slight pause.)

LUCY: No. No. It isn't bad news. It's from the lawyer. I...he wants me to call on him.

MAY: Oh, Mrs Amorest. I do hope it's something nice. It will be so nice if it's something nice.

   (The letter has put LUCY in a great state of nerves, but she tries not to show it.)

LUCY: Yes... Oh dear. *(Her hand goes to her forehead for a moment.)* It's made me feel quite flustered. I... I'd better go and see him this morning. Yes, I certainly had. I wonder... Now what's the time? I really think I'll go almost at once.

MAY: Is it about your cousin?

LUCY: Oh yes, of course, it must be. There's nothing else it could be, is there? I...oh...well, I'll finish the letter to Brand when I come back, then I can tell him everything. Unless, of course...it doesn't... Oh,

I mustn't think about it. (*She collects the notepaper together and puts the stopper in the ink.*)

MAY: No, it doesn't do to think about a thing like that. I mean one way or the other, does it? But I hope, I do sincerely hope for your sake, Mrs Amorest, that your cousin's kept his promise. Oh dear, dear. Now you'll think I'm impertinent.

LUCY: Not at all, of course I won't. But still I think it's better not to talk about it. Anyway, I'll soon know. What an untidy mess the table's in. (*She commences to clear away the remains of her lunch – a coffee cup, a tumbler, a plate with crumbled biscuits and a half-empty sardine tin.*) They're so convenient for lunch – sardines don't you think?

MAY: They save a lot of trouble. Yes.

LUCY: Now I ought to turn the remaining ones out, I suppose.

MAY: Indeed you ought. It's extremely dangerous to leave them in a tin. One's liable to get some odd sort of poisoning – ptomaine, isn't it? – if one leaves them in the tin. Or so I've always heard. Here, let me do it for you, Mrs Amorest, while you're putting the other things in the cupboard.

LUCY: No, don't worry, dear.

MAY: Yes. I insist. (*She is already at the table, scooping the rest of the sardines on to a plate.*)

LUCY: (*At the cupboard.*) I had such a curious sensation during Cousin Francis's funeral the other day. I knew, of course, it wasn't poor Cousin Francis *himself* there, but... I don't know...it somehow seemed that it *was*, and that he'd be feeling cold and lonely. I must have been in a morbid state. I don't generally feel things like that.

MAY: (*Into whose eyes has come a look of terror.*) You must have been overwrought... It wouldn't do if we really believed those sort of things, would it?

LUCY: No, it wouldn't do at all. (*She comes back to the table again and changes the cloths.*) I certainly never believed it at the time. I knew it was just a feeling.

MAY: (*Helping her.*) When poor little Pip died I felt like that. But then, of course, they say that animals don't go to Heaven. Nevertheless I... I feel certain I shall be seeing him again. I...can't help feeling it.

LUCY: And I'm sure you're right. (*She takes the white tablecloth and folds it over her arm.*) Our Lord must be fond of dogs. I'm sure He is. And I'm sure He's got a sense of humour, too.

MAY: Oh dear, dear. Well, I've never heard that point of view before. (*She sits down, absorbed in the conversation.*)

LUCY: When you think of it – He must have. Otherwise – without a sense of humour – how could He endure the...self-absorption and conceit, and everything else...of human beings? Ourselves and...everybody? (*She, too, sits down, momentarily forgetting the tablecloth.*) I don't know. It seems to me sometimes that I attach far too much importance to myself and what becomes of me.

MAY: It's very difficult not to. But I'm sure one does. Oh yes. I used to have philosophical discussions with Jane sometimes at St Lennans. Not often, of course. Oh, no, Jane was such a jolly person. But still, we used to talk very seriously sometimes. Oh, yes. It's a very good thing, I think. And helps one to understand people.

LUCY: Yes, it does. Certainly. But on the whole, I think, people are very simple, don't you? More so than one admits.

MAY: Oh, I don't know. No, I don't think they are. People seem very strange to me. But then, I never have been able to get really *near* people, *know* them, if you know what I mean. Dogs, yes... I can feel I know them, but people... I remember once when I was a girl, I found my mother crying in her bedroom. And I wanted so much to put my arm round and comfort her. But I... I couldn't think what to say. And even now I don't know why she was crying... (*Her voice tails off.*)

(*A pause. LUCY sighs, gets up, puts the cloth away, and bangs the drawer in.*)

LUCY: Well, I think I'll be getting off, now. (*Going to the wardrobe, she puts out her hat and coat.*)

MAY: Have you noticed a new picture postcard of the King and Queen in Becroft's window? It's extremely good of them – extremely good.

LUCY: Really?

MAY: Oh, yes. They do work so hard, poor dears, don't they? I'm sure the dear Prince is overworking himself.

LUCY: Do you think so?

MAY: Oh, I'm sure he is. I only hope he won't knock himself up.

LUCY: Listen! Was that Agatha's door banging?

MAY: Oh, dear, I hope not! Why?

LUCY: I believe it was. That means she's coming down. She's always coming down lately. I wonder if I can get out before she arrives.

(In point of fact, AGATHA has left her room, and now appears at the head of the stairs, down which, in slow stages, she commences to totter. LUCY hurriedly gets into her hat and coat.)

MAY: Oh, let me help you. *(She does so.)*

LUCY: No, listen.

(They stand still for a second, listening.)

It's no good. I can hear her on the stairs. Oh, well, poor old thing, there's no harm, after all, in my talking to her for a few moments.

MAY: Oh, *I* shan't stay. *I* shan't stay.

LUCY: Now you *must*, dear. You *must* get over this feeling about her. It's nearly all imagination.

(She sits down and taking MAY's hand compels her to sit also.)

MAY: It isn't. You know it isn't. Otherwise, why should *you* not want to talk to her?

LUCY: Only because she annoys me by not knocking before she comes in. She's very, very friendly. She's been more friendly than ever since Christmas Eve. And you remember how you felt then. She hasn't done you any harm since, has she? In spite of what you thought.

MAY: *(Breathlessly.)* Oh, but she has, Mrs Amorest. I've never told you before, because you'd think it silly of me, but she has.

LUCY: What has she done?

MAY: She taps on my wall at night. She won't let me sleep. All night she taps on my wall.

(*MAY stops abruptly as AGATHA enters the room. A pause.*)

LUCY: Would you mind, dear, knocking before you come in? It's pleasanter, don't you think, for both of us?

AGATHA: Why it's Miss Beringer. How are you today, Miss Beringer? You're not looking so well. That's a pity.

MAY: (*Rising.*) I'm very well, thank you. Very well. But I was just going to my room, if you'll excuse me. Have you a book, Mrs Amorest? I'd like a nice book to read this afternoon.

LUCY: Why, certainly, dear. Which would you like?

MAY: Oh, it doesn't matter. Any one will do. I'll take this. (*With dignity she takes a book and goes to the door.*) Bye-bye. Bye-bye for the present.

LUCY: Good-bye, dear. I'll see you soon.

(*MAY shuts the door behind her. During the scene that follows she goes to her room, and after putting the kettle on and getting the tea things out, wraps a green shawl round her, pulls her chair to the fire, and starts to read.*)

AGATHA: (*When the door has closed.*) 'Bye-bye! Bye-bye!'

LUCY: Oh, don't be so stupid, Agatha. I dare say you say things just as annoying. I'm going out almost at once.

AGATHA: (*Turning to left of table, to face LUCY.*) Have you heard anything about the money yet?

LUCY: No, not exactly. Well, no – I haven't.

AGATHA: (*Sitting.*) Do you think he's left it to you?

LUCY: Oh, dear, I really can't say. I wish I hadn't told you about it.

AGATHA: Well, you'll be in a fine hole if he hasn't. What are you going to do if he hasn't?

LUCY: I don't know, dear, but I'm sure our Lord will care for me in the same way that He always has.

AGATHA: Cared for you – when He's left you all alone?

LUCY: How can I be alone when He's with me?

AGATHA: Tcha! Do you really believe that?

LUCY: Of course I do.

AGATHA: You're a fool, Lucy. Have you heard from your boy?

LUCY: No.

AGATHA: Your cousin did promise you the money, didn't he?

LUCY: Well, yes.

AGATHA: He said that when he died...

LUCY: Agatha, don't you think there's something rather dreadful in our talking about money like this when we're so old?

AGATHA: (*Hoarsely.*) We can have twenty years yet. You're strong and I'm strong. I knew a little girl who died when she was five. What's the good of thinking about it?

LUCY: (*With vigour.*) We ought to think about it. Not in an unwholesome way, of course. But as though we were going from one country into another. And we must give an account of ourselves. And why shouldn't we think about God's love? It's very nice to think about it.

(*There is a short silence between them, which is broken by AGATHA.*)

AGATHA: That's a fine coloured piece of Miss Beringer's, isn't it?

LUCY: Yes, I've told her how greatly I admire it.

AGATHA: I don't know what an old woman like her's doing with it. She can't appreciate it.

LUCY: She likes it because her best friend gave it to her, and that's a very good reason.

(*A pause.*)

Well, I'm going now, or I shall be late. You will excuse me, won't you? (*She starts to pull her gloves on.*)

AGATHA: Where are you going to?

LUCY: Oh, nowhere much.

AGATHA: (*With awakened interest.*) Nowhere much? What do you mean?

LUCY: If you must know, Agatha, I'm going to the lawyers. I heard from him.

AGATHA: (*Galvanised out of her chair.*) What? A letter? Why didn't you tell me? Why've you kept it a secret?

LUCY: Because you will talk about it so much, Agatha, and I don't like it.

AGATHA: What does he say in the letter? About the money.

LUCY: He simply says that I'm to go and see him. It may not be about the money at all. Good-bye, dear. Stay down in my room, if you like. If you're feeling tired. (*She goes to the door.*)

AGATHA: No, I'll see you out of the front door. (*She follows LUCY.*) Well, I never, aren't you in luck? Whatever will you do with it all?

LUCY: Oh, don't, Agatha.

(*She continues through the hall. AGATHA totters behind. As LUCY opens the front door, AGATHA speaks.*)

AGATHA: Well, good-bye, dear, and take care of yourself.

LUCY: (*Going out.*) Good-bye. I shan't be long – it's only round the corner.

AGATHA: And, Lucy...?

LUCY: Yes?

AGATHA: I should like to know what he says to you.

LUCY: (*Brightly.*) Oh, I dare say that it won't be anything at all.

(*She is gone. AGATHA shuts the door, and stands meditating for a moment, breathing heavily. A sudden gleam comes in her eye, she smiles, goes to the stairs, and climbs them a little more lightly than usual. Meanwhile MAY's kettle has boiled, and she is making the tea. As she fills her cup the door opens and AGATHA is there.*)

AGATHA: Come in and have a little talk with me, will you, Miss Beringer? (*Leaving MAY's door open, she goes to her own room, seating herself in the rocking chair. Nothing happens. She calls out.*) Why don't you come in? You'll be warmer in here.

MAY: (*At last.*) I... I'm having a cup of tea.

AGATHA: Well, have it in here. What's the matter, Miss Beringer? You're not frightened of me, are you? (*A pause.*)

MAY: No, I'm not. (*MAY braces her shoulders, tightens her quivering lip and goes in.*)

AGATHA: Do sit down, Miss Beringer. Make yourself comfortable. That's right. Are you enjoying your tea?

MAY: (*Sitting very gingerly on one of AGATHA's chairs.*) Thank you. Yes, very much, thank you.

AGATHA: Now, tell me. I don't want to be impertinent, but what of your plans?

MAY: Oh, I don't know. I really don't know. It's so difficult to say, isn't it? How can one truly know? I hope to find some work very soon.

AGATHA: What kind of work?

MAY: Companion to some lady, perhaps. Some old lady, you know, who can't look after herself. Someone too old to really care for herself.

AGATHA: But such jobs are rather hard to find, you know, and you're not as strong as you were.

MAY: No, that's quite true, but I'm very hale and hearty still. Still quite strong. If the work were not too arduous...

AGATHA: Would you sell the piece of red amber you have if things went badly? I'm expecting to get a bit of money soon.

MAY: Oh, no, I shouldn't like to sell that. I shall never sell it. It was given to me by my best friend. My best friend gave it to me.

AGATHA: But if you had to sell it...

MAY: I would rather starve, I would, indeed. I'd rather die of hunger.

AGATHA: It's certainly a beautiful piece.

MAY: Yes, isn't it? But it's because my great friend gave it to me that I value it. If she hadn't given it to me I wouldn't value it so much.

AGATHA: No, I dare say not.

(*A pause.*)

You lived in Exeter, didn't you, in your youth?

MAY: Yes... I was very fond of Exeter.

AGATHA: I wouldn't like to live in Exeter. Too sleepy.

MAY: Oh, it wasn't sleepy all the time. Not sleepy at all. No, indeed. There was so much going on. All sorts of things were always happening.

AGATHA: (*Ironically.*) Really? I wouldn't have thought it. What sort of things?

MAY: Oh, I don't know. Meeting one's friends, and concerts, and in the summer we had picnics.

AGATHA: (*Scornfully.*) Picnics!

MAY: Yes, beautiful picnics they were, too. We used to have the moors so close to us, and you could see for miles on a fine day.

(*There is a long pause. AGATHA's eyes are fixed upon MAY persistently. MAY has put her cup down by now. After a few seconds she drops her head and looks at the floor, to get away from that terrifying gaze.*)

AGATHA: Do you know when you're going to die?

(*MAY starts, becomes fully aware, and stares at AGATHA.*)

MAY: To die? Oh, no!

AGATHA: Do you want to know?

MAY: No, I don't. I don't want to think about it.

(*AGATHA gets out of her chair and totters over to the card table, where she sits. The cards slip through her fingers.*)

AGATHA: Ah, you're a coward.

MAY: (*Nearly in tears.*) No, I'm not. But I don't want to think of it. It's not a thing you want to think of.

AGATHA: Why not? It's coming some time. That's certain. It's better for many. Take yourself now. When your money gives out, and you don't get a job, what are you going to do?

MAY: I don't want to think of it. Indeed I don't.

AGATHA: But you ought to think of it. You ought to make provision. Who will you leave your things to?

MAY: My things?

AGATHA: Your odds and ends. That piece of amber, for instance. If you sold it beforehand, you wouldn't have to bother who to leave it to.

MAY: I hadn't thought of it like that.

AGATHA: Haven't you made a will? (*She shuffles the cards.*)

MAY: No, it didn't seem worth while.

AGATHA: Well, I should make a will at once. You never know what will happen.

(*A pause.*)

You'd better know when you're going to die. Try the cards. They'll tell you.

MAY: Oh, no! (*She shrinks back in her chair.*) I shouldn't like that, at all. I shouldn't approve of that. I don't think we're meant to know.

AGATHA: Oh, yes, we are. Here, draw up the chair by the table, I'll show you.

MAY: I'd really rather not, thank you. I've rather a headache. If you'll excuse me.

AGATHA: Nonsense. It will interest you. Come and have a look. You've never seen the cards done the way I do them.

MAY: I'd really rather not.

AGATHA: Come along now.

    (*MAY, as though drawn by AGATHA's eyes, rises mechanically and finds herself sitting up, straight and stuff beside the table.*) There's nothing to be frightened about. What are you looking so frightened for? Miranda can see you. (*She jerks her head towards the doll, which is against the wall opposite MAY.*) Miranda's never looked so frightened as you do, and she's seen lots in her time. (*She deals out the cards, scrutinises them, sweeps them up, shuffles and deals them again.*)

    (*MAY stares with agonised intensity.*) There they are. Six of Clubs. Queen of Spades. Four of Diamonds...! This is you...just as I thought. Eight of Spades.

MAY: Why am I Eight of Spades?

AGATHA: It isn't *you* who are Eight of Spades. It's the combination with the other cards. You're in danger...

MAY: In danger?

AGATHA: Yes, they show it quite distinctly. I'll deal some more. (*She does so.*) Four of Hearts. Five of Diamonds. Knave of Clubs – yes – there you are...don't you see? Ten of Spades – the ten with the Knave of Clubs and the Five of Diamonds. You're threatened with something very serious indeed.

MAY: (*Drawing back from the table.*) Oh, dear! This isn't right. Really, it isn't. I think I'll go to bed if you don't mind.

    (*AGATHA puts her hand on her arm.*)

AGATHA: Wait a minute. We're just coming to the exciting part. (*She makes a little pile of the cards then deals out another six.*) There you are. Isn't it extraordinary? You're in luck tonight. They're coming out well. Now, let's see. (*She takes a card from the pile, then another – and yet another. She strokes her lip.*) All black. That settles it.

MAY: Settles what?

AGATHA: Of course, there may be nothing in it. Still, it's an odd thing, you know. You're very foolish not to sell the amber. You should certainly make your will – you should, indeed. All black.

MAY: (*Nearly in tears.*) It's wicked! You should not do such things, Mrs Payne. They're against religion.
(*AGATHA ignores this outburst and gathers up the cards complacently. She slaps them on to the table and looks up.*)

AGATHA: Yes, all black. You must come to tea another time, Miss Beringer, and we'll do the cards. Makes a nice change for you.

MAY: (*Ashamedly attempting to recover her composure.*) Yes...thank you... I... I... I'm afraid, though, I'm not used to these sort of things. I forget it's only in fun.

AGATHA: (*Jovially.*) Have a piece of nougat? (*She stretches out for the bag.*)

MAY: No, thank you.

AGATHA: Don't you like nougat?

MAY: I – I don't fancy it.

AGATHA: There's none here, anyway. That's a pity, no nougat. Perhaps I'll go out and get some. Yes, I certainly will. It's a long time since I've been out, and I'm wonderfully light on my feet today. (*She has raised herself from her chair and now moves ponderously to her wardrobe.*) Wonderfully light. Don't know why it is. Like a young girl. Yes. Mm. Shop's nearly next door. Shan't wear my best hat.

MAY: (*Uncomfortably.*) I hope you enjoy your little outing, Mrs Payne. And thank you very much for a pleasant afternoon. I...
(*She makes a tentative movement to the door, but stops as AGATHA continues.*)

AGATHA: Of course, I don't get out much, but there's
nothing that does you more good than a minute's walk
when you're feeling light on the feet. Come here, Miss
Beringer, and tell me which you like me in. (*She produces
an assortment of monstrous hats.*) They don't make hats like
this nowadays.

MAY: (*Who, against her will, has returned to the table.*) Yes, the
modern style is not at all becoming. These girls one
sees...so severe.

AGATHA: They won't get the fellows after them like that.
A real man, a man who's worth your while, likes a bit of
beauty, bit of colour. (*She holds up a hat, gazing.*) You can't
beat fruit.

MAY: Yes, the...er, the old ideas are always right.

AGATHA: Nonsense, of course they're not right. What's the
matter with some people is that they've never been
young. I'd get on well enough with the young folk
nowadays, given half the chance. I'd have a rare old
time. Got a cold, Miss Beringer?

MAY: A cold? No. Why?

AGATHA: You look as if you'd got a cold.

MAY: I'm not well, of course. My knee, I...

AGATHA: (*Putting down the hat and picking up another.*)
Your knee? It was your head just now. Or've you got a
headache in your knee? (*She laughs uproariously.*) Wouldn't
suit you, would it – this hat?

MAY: No... I... it's rather... I wear a different style. (*With a
flash of defiance.*) Certainly I would never choose a hat
like that.

AGATHA: No. Grey you'd wear, wouldn't you? Grey. (*She
keeps out the fruit-decked hat and replaces the rest in the
wardrobe.*) Hurry up, Miss Beringer. You haven't got your
coat on yet. I don't like to be kept waiting, you know.

MAY: Oh, dear, I... I didn't say I was coming with you.
I couldn't really, I...

AGATHA: (*Grunting as she changes from her slippers into a
pair of black old shoes with paste buckles.*) We'll get some
barley sugar and a new pot of raspberry. She hasn't
brought me my raspberry lately – Mrs Bloxham. That'll

give her a surprise in the morning, when she finds I've been out and got it myself. (*She looks up.*) What's the matter, Miss Beringer? Why don't you get your coat? Coming without it? *I* shouldn't. You shiver enough in any case.

MAY: I'm sure I don't shiver. It's nerves. I feel a bit nervy sometimes.

AGATHA: Perhaps the cards meant that. Perhaps you'll go out without a coat and catch your death! (*She gets to her feet.*) You can have a piece of nougat on the way back. Hurry up, dear.

MAY: I... I really...

(*She turns round and hastens into her own room, where she sits trembling and listening apprehensively. AGATHA, a smile on her face, dons her hat and coat, tapping playfully on the wall once or twice.*)

AGATHA: Ready? I'm waiting for you, Miss Beringer... I can't wait much longer... I shall have to come in and see how you're getting on. (*She suits the action to the word, leaving her room.*)

(*MAY hurriedly, guiltily, pulls on her hat and coat. AGATHA reappears, opening the door of MAY's room, and entering.*) What a long time you've been. I believe you've just sat on the bed without moving. (*Her eyes rest on the amber for a second or two.*)

MAY: No, I er... I couldn't think where I'd put my things for the moment.

AGATHA: (*Her gaze returning to MAY.*) That's a thin coat for the winter. Well, no one could say we don't dress in different styles.

(*Drawing on her gloves, she exits to the stairs. MAY follows. They reappear a moment later and commence their descent.*)

MAY: Oh! I wonder what it is with my knee.

AGATHA: Best thing in the world for bad knees, a walk.

MAY: Is it far to the...er...confectioners?

AGATHA: About three houses. Only a minute when you're in good health, and the wind's behind you.

(*They are near the foot of the stairs now. MAY stops.*)

MAY: Oh! Mrs Payne – do you mind? You're leaning so heavily – my shoulder. I can't go another step like it.

AGATHA: Very well. You needn't think I can't move without your help. Not at all. I didn't ask you to come. (*She completes the descent alone and goes out of the house without another word. MAY sits on the stairs, leaning her head against the rails. A loud knock brings her to her feet.*)

MAY: Oh! Oh!

(*She clutches at her heart and, staggering down to the front door, opens it fearfully. AGATHA is revealed.*)

AGATHA: (*Smiling broadly – some grasses in her hat blowing in the wind.*) Bye-bye! Bye-bye!

(*She turns, and goes off down the street. MAY shuts the front door again, and, coming into the hall, leans against the stair head, exhausted. There is an even louder knock at the door.*)

MAY: Oh! I can't stand it! I can't stand it! I'll have to lie down...have to...

(*Dragging herself across the hall and into LUCY's room, she lies on the bed. After a little while the noise of the front door opening causes her to start up. LUCY comes in from the street. Looking forlorn and sick, she sinks into the hall chair, centre right. MAY rises, and hurries out to her.*)

Mrs Amorest, I must apologise. A most unpardonable thing. I was lying on your bed.

(*A pause.*)

LUCY: (*Forcing a smile.*) That's quite all right, dear. You know I don't mind... Do...use my room...when you like.

MAY: I felt so unwell – the stairs...

LUCY: Yes, of course.

(*A pause.*)

Have you been out?

MAY: No. No. I was going out with Mrs Payne, but...but I didn't.

LUCY: Has *she* gone out?

MAY: Yes, to buy some sweets...or something.

LUCY: She's not been out for a long time.

MAY: No.

(*A pause.*)

Did you see the lawyer?

LUCY: Oh, yes. Yes, thank you.

(*A pause.*)

MAY: One gets very tired walking, doesn't one? (*She half giggles involuntarily.*) You must be worn out.

LUCY: Yes.

(*A pause.*)

MAY: Would you like me to help you off with your coat?

LUCY: Thank you. (*But she makes no movement.*)

MAY: It's quite slippery underfoot, I suppose.

LUCY: Yes, it *is* rather slippery, but so long as one takes care.

MAY: Quite, quite. A pair of woollen socks is a good thing for slipping... I should say, for *not* slipping. Goloshes, I think, prevent one from getting chilblains. Yes...but then, of course, they're more slippery. One could wear the woollen socks over the goloshes.

LUCY: Yes, what a good idea.

(*A long pause. MAY moves closer to LUCY, and then says, with a touch of embarrassment.*)

MAY: Mrs Amorest. Would you – why don't you lie down, and let me make you a cup of tea?

LUCY: (*Pulling herself together.*) No, thank you. It's a little too soon after lunch. But don't worry, dear. I can't think why I've been sitting here like this.

(*A gust of wind warns them of AGATHA's return. She enters, banging the door hurriedly on seeing LUCY. She is holding a large bag of sweets.*)

AGATHA: Lucy. Hullo, Lucy. Haven't you been? What's happened? Aren't you well? (*She glares at LUCY, getting her breath.*)

(*MAY, having withdrawn downstage, looks on with anxious eyes.*)

LUCY: Well...? Yes, I'm all right, thank you. (*Wearily.*) I just felt a little tired.

AGATHA: Didn't you see him?

LUCY: Who?

AGATHA: Why, the lawyer, of course. The lawyer you were going to see.

LUCY: Oh, yes, I saw him.

AGATHA: Is it all right?

(*She receives no reply.*)

The money your cousin left you?

LUCY: I'm afraid I was wrong about that, Agatha.

AGATHA: Hasn't he left you any?

LUCY: He didn't do what he said he would, that's all. I was silly to believe in it.

AGATHA: He's left you nothing?

LUCY: Something of his to remember him by. Mr Agnew, the lawyer – wanted me to go to his office to choose something. But I didn't feel well enough. Tomorrow, perhaps. He says there's a very nice little writing desk I could have.

AGATHA: And that's all?

LUCY: Yes. Why should he have left me anything else? I was only his cousin. It was very kind of him to think of me.

AGATHA: Then he cheated you.

LUCY: Oh, no! I cheated myself. It was only one day he was feeling kindly. I happened to be there. He would have said it to anyone else who was kind to him.

AGATHA: (*Her voice hoarse with anger.*) I say he cheated you. He said he'd give it to you. He made a solemn promise. May he rot in hell, I say.

LUCY: It's kind of you to be interested, Agatha. But there's no more to be said. It was only an idea that I had that he might leave me something. I shouldn't have spoken to you about it.

(*She rises and crosses towards her room, but turns as AGATHA speaks.*)

AGATHA: (*Turning savagely upon her.*) No, you should not. Making me believe things that weren't true. It's wicked – a wicked shame. And you'll pay for it. No one's deceived me yet and not paid for it. You just wait.

(*She throws up her head as though to spit upon LUCY, then half lurches, half stumbles up the stairs, taking no notice of MAY, who cringes back to let her pass. LUCY turns towards her door, but checks as MAY speaks.*)

MAY: Mrs Amorest! (*She hesitates, then comes a step or two towards LUCY.*) I… I'm so sorry about your disappointment. I… I…
(*She stops suddenly and runs off up the stairs. LUCY enters her own room, closing the door. MAY reappears in her own room and paces up and down in anguish of mind, going over the two scenes in which she has just taken part. AGATHA has already reappeared in her room, from which, occasionally, strange sounds cause MAY to listen fearfully at the wall, or even put her head round the door. LUCY, for her part, after picking up the unfinished letter to BRAND and dropping it back on the table, puts on the kettle for tea and sits before her fire, too listless even to remove her hat and coat. AGATHA, meanwhile, is in a fine frenzy.*)

AGATHA: I'll teach her to take me in like that! Blasted milk-faced old fool! I'll teach her! Pretending this and pretending that just to make herself more important! (*She picks up anything she can lay her hands on and flings it to the floor.*) I knew there was no money coming to her. Talked like that to amuse herself I suppose! Amuse herself! I'll amuse her before I've done with her! (*She sweeps the cards off the table and, with trembling knees, flops into the chair on the right of the room. She finds herself facing Miranda.*) Don't look at me like that – d'you hear?
(*Her hand goes out and grasps Miranda. She, too, is thrown to the floor. AGATHA is silent for a few moments, rocking frenziedly backwards and forwards. Then she begins to mutter – her muttering resolving into definite sentences.*)
Well…if there's to be no money, I'll get it the other way. The amber. Why did I ever think of buying it? She stole it from me, the Beringer woman. It's always been mine. Mine! Before she was born or thought of it was mine. Long, thin old fool. Old maid. Stealing it from me. You've only got to speak and she's frightened. She'll give it back all right. She'll give it back to me whether she wants to or no – if I have to wring her neck to get it. (*Pacified now, she heaves herself from the chair, goes to the wall, and taps.*)

(*On the other side, MAY stops her perambulations and stands, stricken. AGATHA chuckles and taps again. After that, still chuckling to herself she goes into the passage. A moment later, she knocks on MAY's door.*)

MAY: (*In a little whisper of a voice.*) Come in.

(*AGATHA pushes the door open and enters.*)

AGATHA: Well, Miss Beringer, it's very disappointing for poor Lucy about the money, isn't it? (*She moves into the room, pulls the armchair down a little, and plumps into it, her eyes fixed on the mantelpiece, where the amber is.*) And how do you find yourself now?

(*A pause.*)

MAY: (*Breaking out hurriedly.*) Mrs Payne – tell me, why are you persecuting me like this? Why do you come to my room? Why do you knock at my wall? I haven't done anything to harm you. I never saw you before I came here. I never interfered with you. I know it's silly of me to go on like this, but I haven't been sleeping. (*The tears, which she has been struggling to keep back, now break through the hands that she presses to her face.*) But won't you leave me alone? I've done you no harm.

AGATHA: Perhaps I thought you were lonely.

MAY: (*Excitedly.*) I'm not lonely. I'm not at all. I don't want anybody. I want to be alone. But you want to tease and frighten me. And you want something else. You want my piece of amber.

AGATHA: (*Quietly.*) Who says I want it? You have strange ideas in your head. You should see a doctor. You're ill. The cards said you would be.

MAY: That's it. Of course, I'm ill. I know I'm silly if you put ideas into my head, I always was as a girl. I've been like that ever since I was a child... I am not going to die! I'm not going to die! (*Her voice has risen to a scream now. She makes a great effort to control herself.*) I do ask you not to come here. It's my room. I forbid you to come any more.

AGATHA: Well, if you'll give me that piece of amber, I won't come any more.

MAY: (*Snatching the amber from the mantelpiece.*) Nobody shall have it. It's the only thing I've got.

AGATHA: (*Rising and crossing to the door.*) We'll see...we'll see...

(*She gives MAY another penetrating glance and goes out, reappearing in her own room a moment or two later. Immediately the door closes MAY becomes frenziedly active. In great agitation she walks up and down, looks at her precious amber, listens to hear any sounds that may be coming from AGATHA's room, and then, making a hurried decision, pulls an old Gladstone bag from under the bed, and feverishly commences to fill it with her belongings. LUCY, meanwhile, has made her tea, and is drinking it, while AGATHA has put the water on to boil for her cocoa, and is again in her rocking-chair, making plans for the night. When her bag is half filled with things MAY has a new impulse and, running from her room and down the stairs, calls.*)

MAY: Mrs Amorest?

(*LUCY does not hear. MAY comes down another step and calls again.*)

Mrs Amorest!

(*LUCY puts down her cup, rises, and comes, questioning, into the hall.*)

LUCY: (*Near the door of her room.*) Yes? What is it, dear?

MAY: Oh, please, Mrs Amorest, will you come up with me a minute? Do forgive me, please, when I know you've got your own worries, but if you could only come for a moment.

LUCY: (*Coming a little towards her.*) What's happened?

MAY: I can't tell you now. Please. Please come to my room.

LUCY: (*Beginning to cross the hall.*) All right, dear. Of course I'll come. Whatever is it?

(*MAY turns and disappears up the stairs to her room, which she enters, and stands breathing heavily, waiting for LUCY. LUCY follows her, and a moment later is seen entering the room.*)

MAY: Shut the door, quick, please.

LUCY: (*After closing the door.*) Why, you're packing your bag.

MAY: Yes. I can't stand it any longer. I really can't. I'm
going. But I don't know about the trains. If only I could
know about the trains. Do you know where there'd be a
timetable?

LUCY: Well, I don't know. I don't think there's one in the
house. But you can't go running off like this, just when
we're getting so used to each other.

MAY: Oh, I know. It's terrible to have to go when you've
been so kind to me. But I can't stand it. I really can't.
I must go away. I must go away at once.

LUCY: But what's happened? Is it Agatha? What's she been
doing? Miss Beringer, dear, do try and control yourself.
Here, I'll put the things in, if you *must* pack.

MAY: Oh, thank you. Just a few things will be enough.

LUCY: But you must tell me what's happened. I mean, it's
so distressing for you to be in such a state.

MAY: No, not now. I can't. I couldn't go over it. There's no
time. I only want to get out of the house.

LUCY: But you're not well, dear. You can't go now. And
where are you going to?

MAY: It's all right. It is, really. It's perfectly all right. I'm
going to St Lennans. I'm going to friends.

LUCY: But what can you do about your things – your
furniture? You can't leave them behind.

MAY: I'll send for them. I'll give you an address to send
them to if you'll be so kind as to send them on to me.
But please, please couldn't you get me a timetable? You
must please get me one.
(*She takes her coat out of the almara, and starts to put it on,
with violently trembling hands. LUCY helps her.*)

LUCY: Well, I know about the trains, dear. I remember.
There's always one at four-thirty, and it's a quarter-past
three now.

MAY: Oh, hurry! Hurry! Where's my hat? I mustn't miss it.
Don't know what I should do if I missed it.

LUCY: Why don't you wait a little, dear, and get the next
one? You mustn't go while you're like this.

MAY: I can't help it. I shall be all right when I'm outside.
When I'm at St Lennans I shall get better. The pain in

379

my back will get better. I shall buy another little dog like Pip, and everything will be all right again. Look – (*She takes some money from her handbag.*) here's some money for the charlady. Please give it to her. Oh, and thank you for being so good to me.

(*She suddenly collapses on the bed, and sits with an ashen face, her hand to her heart. LUCY puts her arm round her.*)

LUCY: There, what is it? You must take things more quietly. You mustn't excite yourself so much. Is it your heart?

MAY: Yes. Yes, it's my heart. It stopped then. And now it's going so fast. I'm ill.

LUCY: Well, you're too ill to go out, anyway. Certainly too ill to go to St Lennans.

MAY: No. I must go. I can't stay here. It's only my heart. It's been like this before.

(*A pause.*)

What was that? She's outside the door. She is, I'm certain. She's listening.

LUCY: (*Rising.*) Who? Agatha? Nonsense. Of course she's not. Well, we'll see, if you like.

(*She goes to MAY's door and opens it. AGATHA is there.*)

AGATHA: Hullo, Lucy. What are you both doing? I was coming in to see what was going on. (*She moves into the room.*)

(*MAY has risen. Before they have time to realise what is happening, she has picked up her bag and rushed past them from the room. LUCY hurries after her.*)

LUCY: (*Heard in the landing.*) Come back! Please come back! You can't go out like this...

(*MAY reaches the stairs and descends them, panting as though she had run a mile. LUCY appears and comes down to her.*)

You're not in a fit state, you're not, really. It's a bitter day, too. Here, let me take the bag. If you stay only till tomorrow, then you can catch a nice train. But you mustn't really go like this...

MAY: (*At the front door.*) No, it's no good. I can't stay here another minute. I want to be at St Lennans. I want

St Lennans. I hate this house. I hate this town. I hate it all. Ah...

(*With the handle of the door in her grasp she gives a long, terrible sigh, and rolls into a faint. LUCY kneels beside her. AGATHA appears at the head of the stairs. She smiles at what she sees and commences slowly, but inexorably, to descend.*)

AGATHA: What's the matter? Aren't you well, Miss Beringer? You'll have to stay in bed, then, won't you? But never mind – I'll be with you. I'll see that you are all right. You won't be lonely now...

(*She continues her descent as the curtain falls.*)

End of Act Two.

ACT THREE

A few hours later. Dusk, and the lamps are lit.

When the curtain rises AGATHA is sitting at the table, playing cards. MAY's room is empty. MAY herself is downstairs in LUCY's bed, propped up with the pillows, asleep. LUCY is sitting between the bed and the fire with one eye on MAY, the other on a saucepan which is beginning to boil. She is sewing. MAY opens her eyes.

LUCY: Are you awake, dear?

MAY: Yes.

LUCY: Lie still then. I'll give you some nice beef tea in a minute.

MAY: Have I been asleep long?

LUCY: Quite a long time, dear, yes.

MAY: Is it nearly night, then?

LUCY: Oh, no, the last post hasn't been yet. I always count the beginning of night-time from when I hear the postman go by. It's still the evening now.

MAY: You're not going, are you?

LUCY: No, dear, don't worry. I'll get the beef tea. (*She puts her sewing down and, taking the saucepan from the fire, pours the contents into a cup.*)

MAY: In the morning I'll be able to go to St Lennans, won't I?

LUCY: Yes, dear.

MAY: Will you come and visit me at St Lennans? I'll show you the places Jane and I used to go to. And where I used to take Pip for walks.

LUCY: Oh, yes, I certainly will. Here you are now, drink it up and it will do you the world of good.
(*MAY takes the tea and drinks it apathetically.*)

MAY: Thank you. Sit closer, will you? Next to the bed, do you mind?

LUCY: Why, certainly, if you wish. (*She pulls her chair close to MAY and resumes her sewing.*) Is the bed fairly comfortable? I always find it so. It makes a great difference, I think, if the mattress is turned every morning. Now, would you like a little bread with the beef tea?

MAY: Is that my bag over there?

LUCY: Where? Oh, yes. Do you want something from it?

MAY: My amber. My amber's in it. Will you give me my amber?

LUCY: Now, dear? Do you want it now?

MAY: Yes, please.

LUCY: But...

MAY: Please give me my amber.

LUCY: Very well. As long as you don't get excited. (*She gets up and goes over to the bag.*) Where would it be? Underneath the other things?

MAY: Yes, it's at the bottom because I put it in first. Can you feel it?

LUCY: Ah, yes, there it is. *What* a beautiful thing. There. Now don't drop it in the bed and fall asleep, or you'll be like the princess and the pea, most uncomfortable.

MAY: (*Taking the amber.*) Thank you. (*She puts it under the pillow and settles back more peacefully.*)

LUCY: You've not finished, have you?

MAY: I couldn't drink any more.

LUCY: Oh, do try. Just the last little drain. There's all the goodness at the bottom.

MAY: I don't think I can.

LUCY: Then you won't be able to go to St Lennans tomorrow. Drink it up.

(*MAY does so.*)

That's right. You'll feel a different woman in no time. (*She takes the cup and puts it on the table.*)

MAY: Hold my hand, will you? Do you mind holding my hand? Do tell me if you mind.

LUCY: (*Obeying her.*) But of course not. (*They sit silently for a moment.*)

MAY: I'll tell you now why I decided to go away. May I?

LUCY: I can guess what happened. Agatha frightened you again I suppose?

MAY: Speak softly. She can hear what we say.

LUCY: But, of course, she can't. She's in her room.

MAY: No, but she can.

LUCY: (*Smiling and patting her hand.*) Now that's really nonsense. You've had ideas about Mrs Payne since you first saw her. Of course she's very odd and alarming, but I'm certain she doesn't really mean any harm. She helped me carry you in when you fainted and everything, and she even offered to help take you upstairs, but I wouldn't hear of it. After all, I've lived in this house for months and months with her, and she's never done me any harm.

MAY: That's because you haven't got anything that she wants.

LUCY: What do you mean?

MAY: It's my piece of amber she wants, and she's not going to have it.

(*LUCY leans forward and strokes her friend's forehead.*)

LUCY: Now, dear. You mustn't imagine things like this. It's only because you're not well.

MAY: I don't imagine it. She came into my room after you'd come back from the lawyers and said she wouldn't leave me alone unless I gave it to her.

LUCY: What? She must be mad! Mad and wicked, too. Why, that's as bad as being a thief!

MAY: She *is* a thief. She'd take it at once if I were alone in the house. She *is* a thief.

LUCY: I can't understand anybody wanting anything like that. Of course, I like to have nice things... Why, it's truly wicked! And that's only a bit of stone or something. It isn't as though it were alive. What is it made of; really?

(*MAY takes it from under the pillow, placing it on the counterpane, and regards it tenderly.*)

MAY: I don't know. I think the Chinese find it on the seashore or something. But I'm not certain about it's not being alive. When you've put a lot of feeling into something, don't you give it a sort of life? It may be grateful, you know, for your being so fond of it. Of course that's very fanciful and perhaps it isn't very religious. Jane said, when she gave it me, that it had some of her heart in it, and I think perhaps it has.

(*She sits propped up in bed gazing down at it. LUCY continues her sewing. After a little while she looks up, inclining her head towards the door.*)

LUCY: Listen...there is the post coming down the street. Can you hear him?

MAY: It's the night, then.

LUCY: Yes.

(*A pause.*)

MAY: You're not going, are you?

LUCY: No, dear, of course not. What would you like?
Would you like me to read you something?

MAY: Yes, please.

LUCY: (*Putting down her work and moving to the bookcase.*) Let's
see what there is. Mrs Gaskell. Do you like her? Or a
story from the *Cornhill Magazine*? Or Tennyson? I think
he's very nice, don't you?
(*As she takes the volume down there is a knock on the door
and a letter drops through into the box.*)
Oh, I wonder what that is. We very seldom get anything
by the last post. A circular, probably. I'll see. (*She hurries
out into the hall.*)

MAY: You're coming back? You're not going, are you?

LUCY: (*From the hall.*) Of course not, dear.
(*She reaches the front door and, taking up the letter, examines
it; but the light is too weak for her old eyes, and she has to
take it back to her room before deciphering anything.
AGATHA, meanwhile, has emerged from her lair and has
reappeared on the stairs, peering over the balustrade. She
remains for a few moments alone on the stairs, then she turns,
goes along the landing, reappears in her room, and resumes
her card playing.*)
(*As she crosses the hall.*) I can't make it out in this light – it
seems to be covered in stamps and addresses. What is it?
What's it say here? 'Not known', is it? (*She shuts the door
and then, going to the lamp, holds the letter underneath. When
she recognises the writing her body trembles all over and she
sinks into the chair left of the table. Her voice seems to come
from far away.*) It's from my son, Miss Beringer. At last.
After all these months.

MAY: (*Turning herself round in the bed.*) Your son? Oh, Mrs
Amorest.
(*LUCY, after gazing at the envelope for quite a little while,
tears it apart. She takes the letter out.*)

LUCY: A whole year. Where can the letter have been? And he's sent a photograph. (*She commences to read the letter.*) 'Dear Old Lady, I can't pretend to have been much of a letter-writer during the last year and I'm ashamed of myself. The truth is that I'd made an oath to myself not to let you know anything until I'd brought a deal off here...' I always thought it was something like that. '...What I wanted to do was to make my pile, turn up unexpectedly in Cheltenham, give you the fright of your young life, and then make you a duchess as you ought to be... (*She breaks off, making a queer sound between a laugh and a sob.*) Oh, dear! (*She wipes her eyes and resumes again.*) 'But I've had the worst of bad luck over and over again. I was on to a wonderful thing three months ago, but then what did I do but tumble down with diphtheria...' Oh, what a terrible thing!

MAY: He must be better or he wouldn't be writing.

LUCY: 'But I'm all right now...' Yes, you see. '...and there's some land prospecting down south that promises fine. Hold on for a while yet, and I'll astonish you still one fine morning. I don't like being beaten...' It's quite true, he was always the same. 'I'm enclosing a photograph I've had taken here. You'd hardly recognise your promising son, would you? I'm as fit as anything now, and it may not be long before you see me...' (*She takes the photo and gazes at it for several seconds before handing it to MAY.*) There he is, Miss Beringer.

MAY: Oh, yes. Oh dear, yes. He's very handsome. And such a nice expression. It's a splendid photograph.

(*LUCY takes it back, has another little gaze, and then continues.*)

LUCY: '...I am pleased to see from your last letter that you are keeping well and happy. The address on your paper is Polchester. Don't know the place, but gather you are still living in Cheltenham. Isn't Polchester the place where there are some cousins of ours? Perhaps you are staying with them. You don't say. Glad you're stopping at Cheltenham where you've got plenty of company. Don't be lonely, old lady. So long for the present, and look out for me any day now. Your loving son, Brand.' (*She sighs deeply when she has finished it and, folding it up, places it in her bosom. The photograph and the envelope she keeps in her hand.*)

MAY: How wonderful. How happy you must feel to get a letter like that.

LUCY: You see, I didn't want him to think I'd left Cheltenham. It might have fussed him. And I was thinking then, I might return any time. I left them this address in the post office there. I don't know wherever this letter can have been. (*She examines the writing on the envelope.*) It must be because he's written the address so badly. Careless boy. But I knew he hadn't forgotten me, whatever they might say.

MAY: Will you let me meet him when he comes back, Mrs Amorest? I'd love to meet him. Is he fond of dogs?

LUCY: Brand? Oh, yes – very.

MAY: He'd have loved Pip, then; and Pip would have loved him, I'm sure. Not that Pip liked everybody, no. Oh, no. He'd go for Mrs Payne if he were here. I'm sure he would. You know, Mrs Amorest, she made me faint before I could get away. She's bad. You don't know how frightening she can be when she looks at me with those awful eyes and smiles.

LUCY: Now you mustn't get excited. It's nearly time to go to sleep. (*She rises.*) *I'm* going to sleep upstairs tonight.

MAY: Oh, Mrs Amorest…

LUCY: I'll just take my things up, and when I come down I'll read you something till you go to sleep.

MAY: Promise not to be too long.

LUCY: You're not feeling worse, are you? Is your heart bad still?

MAY: Yes, my heart. Put your hand here, and just see how it jumps.

(*LUCY puts her hand against the other's breast.*)

LUCY: Well, you must let me get a doctor in the morning. I insist on a doctor. I know a very nice one here. I insist on your seeing a doctor.

MAY: I don't believe in doctors. I had a doctor once in Exeter, and he said I must wear spectacles, and so I did for two years, and there wasn't anything the matter with my eyes at all. They're all humbugs, if you ask me.

LUCY: Well, we'll see how you are in the morning.

(*She bends down and kisses her, then going to the mantelpiece, places BRAND's photo on it. MAY's eyes follow every move. LUCY turns at the door.*)

MAY: Mrs Amorest, you're so good to me. I'm sure I don't know why.

LUCY: Nonsense.

(*Shutting the door behind her she goes up to AGATHA's room. It is not long before MAY is fast asleep. LUCY finds AGATHA still sitting at the table, playing cards. AGATHA does not look up when the other woman enters, but her lips move and her hand, holding a card, hangs, hovering over the table.*)

Excuse me, Agatha, I want to speak to you a moment.

(*AGATHA takes no notice. She bends forward, touching the cards as they lie on the table. LUCY comes further into the room. She repeats.*)

Excuse me, but I *must* speak to you. It's something important.

(*AGATHA lays the card in her hand carefully on the table, and then looks up.*)

AGATHA: What is it?

LUCY: I have been seeing Miss Beringer. You know, of course, that she's ill, but I don't think you realise that she's very seriously ill indeed.

AGATHA: Well, I helped you take her into the room, didn't I? I can't help her illness. What have I to do with her?

LUCY: You have this to do with her. You were the cause of her running away in such a state, and that brought on her heart attack. You'd been in there and said something that frightened her. She is easily frightened and her heart's very bad. You must leave her alone, or I'll have a doctor here who'll make you.

AGATHA: Indeed. Who says I've frightened her?

LUCY: She says so herself. She has an idea that you want to steal something of hers. I can't believe that of you, but

sick women have strange fancies. She's done you no
harm – why don't you leave her alone?

AGATHA: Leave her alone! (*She laughs.*) The silly old fool!
Silly old fools, both of you. A pair of sentimental old
women. You with your precious boy, and her with her Jane
and her dog. (*She turns contemptuously back to the cards.*)

LUCY: You leave my son alone. And you leave Miss
Beringer alone, too. From what she tells me you're no
better than a thief.

AGATHA: Thief is it? Now you leave me alone, Lucy
Amorest, and mind your own business, or it will be the
worse for you.

LUCY: It *is* my business. The poor woman's sick, and has
no one to care for her. If you go and frighten her again
or, in fact, go near her at all, I'll – I'll call for the police!

AGATHA: (*Laughing.*) You will, will you? And what have the
police to do with it? You'd look fine and silly with the
police coming in. You'd have them arrest me, I suppose?
And what for? Now, look here, Lucy Amorest, you mind
your own business. I've stood you long enough, poking
your nose in where you're not wanted. I've not interfered
with you, have I? Well, then, leave me to myself.

LUCY: You may say what you like to me. I'm not afraid of
you. But that poor woman's life is in danger. She's old
and ill and penniless. Give her another fright, and with
her heart as it is, anything can happen, and then you'll be
a murderess as well as a thief!

(*She pauses, her breast heaving with indignation. AGATHA
seems to quieten. She stares beyond LUCY into the corner of
the room.*)

AGATHA: She's as bad as that, is she? Well – what does it
matter? We're old and penniless, too. Three penniless old
women. The Beringer woman, she's always complaining,
and crying. It would be a kindness if I were to go now
and put my hand round her neck and choke her.

LUCY: How *can* you talk of her like that? It's only because
she's got something you want – a piece of coloured stone
that is nothing – nothing at all.

AGATHA: Speak of what you understand. What do
you know of lust or desire for anything? You've never

felt passion, with your milk and water religion and sentimentality. If I were to know that I had only half an hour more to live, I would want the sensation of owning that beautiful thing. Beauty! You don't know the meaning of the word.

(*She slumps back into her rocking chair with her back to LUCY and rocks, kicking her shoe in the air.*)

LUCY: You must leave her alone. Whether I'm sentimental or not, I'll see to that.

(*During the latter part of this scene MAY has woken up in a cold sweat of terror, and now running out into the hall shivering in her nightdress, she calls.*)

MAY: Mrs Amorest! Mrs Amorest!

(*LUCY hurries out. AGATHA returns to her cards.*)

Mrs Amorest! Oh, please come. I'm so frightened. I'm so frightened.

LUCY: Why, whatever is it? (*She hurries down the stairs.*) You'll catch a death of cold coming out into the draughty hall like that. Go back at once, Miss Beringer. You mustn't be silly. Come along, now, I'll stay with you – you mustn't, really. (*As she speaks she is manoeuvring her friend back to bed.*)

MAY: I couldn't help it. I felt so horrible. Oh, I had such an upsetting dream… I couldn't really tell you how upsetting it was.

LUCY: But, my dear, you mustn't come out in your nightdress and get so distressed, just because you have a silly dream.

MAY: Oh, but I couldn't help it. It was a real nightmare, worse than anything I've had for years. My nerves are in such a state I don't know what to do.

LUCY: Now you get into bed. It won't do any good your sitting shivering on the edge like that.

MAY: I know how stupid you must think I am, but what could it have meant? Do you think dreams mean anything?

LUCY: Well, just get into bed, dear, and then you can tell me all about it.

MAY: (*As she gets into bed.*) It was so vivid – as if it really
    happened. There was this road stretching for a long, long
    way ahead – and the wood to one side, yes, and there was
    a wind – a bitter biting wind blowing. And I had to go on
    to meet this terrible something. I didn't want to, but
    I couldn't stop myself – the wind it must have been that
    was driving me. Yes, that's what it was. And I thought, if I
    can get into the wood, it will be all right, but I couldn't
    stop or run away. I just went on faster and faster. Then,
    as I got nearer, I could see the cross-roads in the
    moonlight, and so real it looked, just as if it were true, and
    there was this someone waiting for me. Oh, it was terrible,
    Mrs Amorest – I can't tell you how terrible, and two
    hands seemed to be coming out to take me by the throat. I
    had to come out and call you. Do forgive me, please.
LUCY: There's nothing to forgive. I was only thinking of
    your making yourself worse by coming into the hall.
    Pull the clothes up. There, that's right. Now you're nice
    and comfortable. Well, I gave Agatha a proper talking to.
    She won't annoy you any more, I'm certain of it.
MAY: You spoke to her? Oh, you shouldn't have! Oh, dear.
    What did you say? Whatever did she do?
LUCY: I told her if she went near you again I should call
    the police. So you're not to worry about her. I'll look
    after you, dear. (*Rising, she goes to the bookcase, her back to
    MAY.*) And I'll leave the door open upstairs, then I can
    hear if anybody moves about.
    (*MAY starts up in bed at this; her mouth falls open, but she
    says nothing.*)
    Oh, here's the Tennyson. I was going to read you some
    Tennyson, wasn't I? Would you like that?
MAY: (*Faintly.*) Yes, please.
LUCY: (*Seating herself by the fire.*) He's such a noble poet,
    I always think. Perhaps a little *too* noble sometimes.
    Don't you think people can be *too* noble, just now and
    again?
MAY: Yes.
LUCY: (*Turning the pages and yawning.*) Dear me, I can't stop
    yawning. This will never do. Well, now. *The Idylls of the*

King. Do you like that? Guinevere. That's a beautiful tale. It's very long, though. I shan't be able to read it all tonight. (*She smooths the pages out and begins.*)
'Queen Guinevere had fled the court, and sat
There in the holy house at Almesbury
Weeping, none with her save a little maid,
A novice. One low light betwixt them burned
Blurred by the weeping mist for all abroad,
Beneath a moon unseen, albeit at full,
The white mist, like a face-cloth to the face,
Clung to the dead earth, and the land was still.'
(*She pauses for a few seconds, struggling against sleep, and then continues with an effort.*)
'For hither had she fled; her cause of flight
Sir Modred; he, the nearest to the King,
His nephew like a subtle beast
Lay couchant with his eyes upon the throne,
Ready to spring...'
(*A long pause.*)

MAY: Mrs Amorest...please don't leave me tonight... I'm sure you could make yourself comfortable with the armchair and the other chair. I'll never forget it if you stay. Only for tonight. Please, please don't leave me alone.
(*But LUCY has not heard. She is dozing. The book falls to the floor.*)

LUCY: (*Waking up.*) Oh, I must have fallen asleep while I was reading. I'm afraid I can't go on. I'm so tired. We'll read it tomorrow, shall we? I don't know why I should be so tired. It's not at all late. But I think an early night and a good sleep would do us both good. I'm so sorry about not reading to you, but my eyes just won't keep open.

MAY: Don't you think...

LUCY: What is it, dear?

MAY: ...you could make up the fire a little before you go?

LUCY: Why, of course I will. (*She makes up the fire, pats the pillow, then kisses MAY.*) Now you're sure you're comfortable? Your heart isn't troubling you so much, is it?

MAY: Oh, no. No. (*She puts out her hand and draws LUCY to the bed.*) Do stay with me a moment longer. I don't want you to go.

LUCY: Why, of course I will, dear.

MAY: You don't think me foolish, do you?

LUCY: Of course not.

MAY: I am foolish and frightened. A silly old woman. But you've been so kind to me. There's one thing I'd like to do.

LUCY: What is it, dear?

MAY: Would you mind before you go, saying a prayer – a prayer about the dangers of the night, and being kept safe?

LUCY: I know. (*She kneels down beside the bed, still holding MAY's hand, and prays.*) Dear Lord, we are Thy Children, and Thou knowest what is best for us. We pray Thee now, when the night comes down over our heads and there is darkness everywhere, that Thy might may be before our eyes, and that, whether we are sleeping or waking, we may know no fear. The powers of darkness are obedient to Thy command. Our trust is in Thee, and because Thou lovest Thy children, Thou wilt give them nothing that can do them harm. So trusting we fall asleep in Thy arms, dear Lord. Amen.

MAY: What a nice prayer. I've never heard it before.

LUCY: Yes, it is a nice one. Our nurse used to say it to us when we were children. (*She tucks in the clothes at the foot of the bed.*) Now you must have a long sleep, and then you'll see how much better you'll feel in the morning.

MAY: Won't you stay a little? It isn't late.

LUCY: No, dear, you must go to sleep now. (*She bends down and kisses her.*) And no more nightmares. (*She takes the new photograph from the mantelpiece and moves to the door.*) Go to sleep and have beautiful dreams.

(*She exits, closing the door as MAY speaks.*)

MAY: Oh, please stay.

(*Meanwhile AGATHA, in her own room, has changed into an old, dirty yellow wrapper, removing the combs from her hair in preparation for the night. She listens, with her head outside her door, and, hearing LUCY approaching down the passage, hurriedly turns out the light and returns to her chair. LUCY, who has disappeared beyond the stairs, is heard outside AGATHA's door.*)

LUCY: (*Outside.*) Agatha?

(*There is no reply.*)

Agatha? Are you awake, Agatha?

(*Still receiving no reply, concluding that AGATHA is asleep, LUCY reappears at MAY's room and enters it, taking care to leave the door well ajar. AGATHA now gets out of her chair, making as little sound as possible, and lights a candle. LUCY, before undressing, sits by the dying fire to read, in solitude, her son's letter and to feast her eyes on his photograph. But her head soon begins to nod. Down in LUCY's room, MAY has got out of bed and attempted to reach the door, but her head is swimming.*)

MAY: Pip!... Where's Pip?... Pip! (*She nearly falls, but catches at the bed-post and somehow manages to get back.*)

(*AGATHA, hearing no sound from MAY's room, takes her candle and goes out of her room. Reappearing at MAY's door, she peers in. LUCY is now fast asleep. Slowly, slowly, with every precaution against noise, AGATHA pulls the door to, and shuts it fast. She reappears a moment later on the stairs, descends, and crosses to LUCY's room, where MAY is now back on the bed, sitting up with her eyes closed. As AGATHA reaches the door she opens her eyes and cries out.*)

Who's there?

(*AGATHA enters.*)

AGATHA: Good evening, Miss Beringer. I came to see if you wanted anything.

MAY: No...no... I...

(*AGATHA sits on the chair beside the bed.*)

AGATHA: Well, *I* want us to have a little talk. If you are sleepy I can wait. I am not at all sleepy myself.

(*A long silence follows. At last MAY turns round again.*)

(*Smiling.*) Why do you complain about me?

MAY: I haven't complained.

AGATHA: Yes. To Mrs Amorest. She came into my room and was very insulting. I'm sure I've been very kind to you. There are not many who would bother to be so kind.

MAY: Oh, go away. Please go away.

AGATHA: Go away? Oh, no. I'm going to be very comfortable here.

MAY: I know why you've come.

AGATHA: I came to make you more comfortable, that's
why. To smooth your pillows. (*She leans over the bed.*)
(*MAY gives a little cry and shudders to the wall.*)
MAY: Don't touch me! I'll scream. I'll rouse everybody.
Don't touch me.
(*AGATHA leans over her. Her hair has loosened and some of
it hangs untidily over her face.*)
AGATHA: Don't be so frightened! You're always frightened,
aren't you?
MAY: Leave me alone. I want to sleep, I can't stand it.
AGATHA: (*Sitting back.*) Why don't you take things more
quietly? Look, I'm sitting down. I'm kind enough, really,
but when you tremble like that it gives me pleasure...
and the more you tremble, the more I shall make you.
I lift my hand, and see!... You shake all over.
MAY: Can't you see that I'm ill? My heart's bad. It's true
what you say. I am frightened of you. I can't help it.
I always have been.
AGATHA: (*Moving her hand slowly up and down the
counterpane.*) Well, well, fancy that! I wonder why? Of
course I'm not very handsome, and sometimes I think
I'm not quite right in the head. (*She suddenly turns on her.*)
But you've no *spirit!* Why, if I were to drag you out of
bed and beat you round the room, you wouldn't object.
(*A pause.*)
MAY: What is it you want?
AGATHA: (*Shrugging her shoulders.*) Now, why don't you
give it me without all this fuss. Let's look at it. You've
got it here somewhere.
MAY: No, no, no!
AGATHA: All right, then, I can wait.
(*She sits in silence for a little. MAY begins to cry.*)
Crying? What do you do that for? I've never cried in my
life, not even when my child died.
(*MAY sits up, her grey hair hanging about her face. She keeps
her hands beneath the sheets.*)
MAY: I beg you to leave me just for tonight. You can do
what you like in the morning – I won't tell anyone, but
for tonight...

AGATHA: Yes. Give me that piece of amber, and I'll go.

MAY: No. Never. Jane gave it me.

AGATHA: Very well, then, I'll wait a little. I don't care.
I can sit up all night if need be. (*She gets up and moves over to the fire, her back to MAY.*)
(*MAY sits up, draws her knees together, slides to the side of the bed, and puts her feet to the floor. Instantly AGATHA turns.*)
Ah, So you have it in your hand. I wondered where it was.
(*MAY puts the hand that clutches the amber behind her back.*)

MAY: Ah! Let me go! Please, let me go!

AGATHA: I should think not. (*She takes a pace towards MAY.*)
You'll catch your death all naked. You get back to bed.
I'm mistress here now. You want looking after, I can see.
(*She makes another slow lurching step towards MAY, who creeps back into bed and crouches there. AGATHA comes over to the bedside chair and sits.*)
So that's what you were up to, was it? Escaping into the passage, ill as you are. I can see you're not safe to be left.
A nice report I must give the doctor tomorrow when I've let you wander all over the house.
(*MAY stares and stares. Her breathing comes in pants, her body gives little jerks.*)
So you're holding it under the bedclothes, are you? Like a schoolgirl? Give it me for a moment. I'll return it to you.

MAY: (*In a small, dry voice.*) No. I won't.

AGATHA: Oh, you won't, won't you? Perhaps I shall have to make you. In spite of my affection for you I don't think I can sit here all night. Now, come on. Give it up.
(*She leans over the bed.*)
(*MAY, with a little strangled cry, moves towards the wall. AGATHA moves her hand and touches MAY's shoulder.*)
I'm not going to hurt you, but I'm going to have that piece of amber...just because I said I would. Come now.
(*Great shivers shake MAY's body. Two tears well into her eyes and then, slowly, trickle downwards.*)
Come, give it to me.
(*She shakes MAY's shoulder, Then, suddenly, she leans right over the bed.*)

You silly fool, don't aggravate me. I *shall* hurt you if you don't take care. Give it up, now.

(*A pause.*)

Are you going to let me have it? I shan't ask you again.

(*She stretches her arm across MAY's body and reaches down below the clothes. MAY draws herself up over the pillows against the iron bars of the bed. Her body shakes. Her lips are drawn back. Between her teeth come little shuddering sobs.*)

Now then, don't be a fool any longer. You see, I mean what I say.

(*Their faces are almost touching. With a rough, strong movement, AGATHA pushes up MAY's arm. At the same moment it is as though a sudden shock galvanises MAY's body. She rises straight up against the wall, stiffly, like a rod, her eyes staring. A convulsive movement shudders through her.*)

MAY: Oh, Jane! Jane!

(*With a sigh she collapses against AGATHA's breast. AGATHA takes the amber. The body slides under the bedclothes, huddled in a heap, but the head, with staring eyes, rests on the pillow. AGATHA draws back, holding the amber in one hand, folding the wrapper over her with the other. She whispers to herself.*)

AGATHA: I didn't mean that! I didn't mean that!

(*She stands stroking the amber, thinking. Then she goes to the fire and sits crouched beside it, muttering; but now she cannot concentrate on what she has worked so hard to possess. Her eyes again and again are drawn back to the bed. Then she rises and steals from the room. LUCY by now has woken up cold, shivering, and apprehensive. Filled with foreboding, she hurries from the room and reappears on the stairs, at the foot of the which she is confronted by AGATHA.*)

LUCY: Agatha! (*She sees AGATHA's face, and her voice goes low with horror.*) Agatha!

(*AGATHA takes no notice. She stands in the gloom at the bottom of the stairs, leaning heavily on the post, breathing hard, her eyes staring in front of her. LUCY bursts into her own room and stops appalled, a moan of horror coming from her lips. She goes to the bed, but MAY is obviously dead. LUCY draws the sheet up over her face. AGATHA turns now, and comes halfway to the open door.*)

AGATHA: (*Hoarsely.*) She's dead, isn't she?

(*LUCY comes quickly out of the room, shutting the door behind her. She leans against it.*)

LUCY: Yes. Oh, poor May.

(*A pause.*)

Why didn't you call me down? I could have fetched a doctor. I could have done something.

(*AGATHA seems not to hear.*)

AGATHA: So she's dead – Miss Beringer. (*She goes on muttering.*)

(*LUCY's eyes are suddenly caught by the amber.*)

LUCY: Agatha! What's that in your hand?

(*AGATHA opens her hand and looks down dazedly, but her mind is elsewhere. Her gaze returns to LUCY.*)

AGATHA: They say if you've killed someone they stay with you for ever.

LUCY: Don't! I won't listen…it isn't true! Agatha! What have you done?

AGATHA: She'll follow me now, I know it. If I go away she'll follow me. If I die, she'll be with me just the same.

LUCY: Oh, why did I leave her? It was my fault, but I did have the door open. But I shouldn't have left her like that. (*Panic descends on her.*) Oh, what can I do? I must get away from here. I must. I don't know where to go.

(*Hardly conscious of her actions, she runs to the chair and takes up her hat and coat. AGATHA sways towards her and grasps her by the arm. Unnoticed the amber falls to the floor.*)

AGATHA: It's all right, Lucy. You stay with me. She can't come while you're here. As long as you're here, that will keep her away.

LUCY: Let me go. You're mad! You don't know what you're saying!

AGATHA: Don't leave me. I'll be all right if you're here. That's two of us against her, then.

LUCY: Stop it, will you? Poor May's dead. You have killed her. Oh, let me go.

AGATHA: Listen! What's that?

LUCY: Nothing. It isn't anything.

AGATHA: Yes, there is. I heard it. She's knocking on the wall. Listen again. Can't you hear it now?

LUCY: No! No! You're mad!

(*There is a knock at the front door. A long pause. The knock is repeated.*)

(*In a low, trembling voice.*) Oh, dear God, what is it?

(*She pulls herself away from AGATHA and runs to the front door. AGATHA lurches after her.*)

BRAND: (*Voice off. Through the letter-box.*) Anyone at home?

AGATHA: Come away from that door. Come away when I tell you.

(*She drags LUCY back to the centre of the hall, but LUCY has suddenly become a different being.*)

LUCY: Agatha, it is my boy out there.

AGATHA: What's that?

LUCY: It's Brand.

AGATHA: Don't tell those lies to me. You can't get out like that.

LUCY: Let me go, Agatha. It's Brand! My boy's outside. Will you please let me go. I'm going away!

(*AGATHA leaves go of LUCY, and moving to the front door, places herself in front of it.*)

AGATHA: Going away? Oh, no, you're not. What? Leave me in this house all alone, with that Beringer woman? You try it, that's all.

LUCY: But I am. My boy's here. (*She suddenly calls.*) Brand! Brand!

AGATHA: It's no good calling out. He can't hear. He'll knock a few times and then he'll go.

LUCY: Let me out, Agatha. I must go. Please, Agatha, please!

AGATHA: You stay here.

(*The knock is repeated.*)

LUCY: Oh, let me out. (*She tries to get to the front door again.*) Brand! Brand!

AGATHA: Just wait a little while, and he won't knock any more. He won't go on knocking much longer now. Listen, and we will hear him go away.

(*Fear suddenly drops from LUCY. She desists from struggling and, with her little figure erect, stands looking straight into AGATHA's eyes.*)

LUCY: If he does go away, Agatha, he'll find me again, but I want to go now, because it's such a long time since I have seen him.

(*The knock is repeated again.*)

Now, don't stand there any more, dear, because he's waiting for me.

(*Something lost, wandering and lonely in AGATHA's eyes touches her very heart. She bends forward and kisses her.*)

Poor Agatha... If only I could help you. Something I could do.

(*But AGATHA does not hear. LUCY waits no longer, but, fumbling wildly with the handle of the front door, calls.*)

Brand! Don't go! I'm coming! Don't go! Wait!

(*She flings the front door open and gives a moan of disappointment. There is no one there. She calls out.*)

BRAND!

(*BRAND's voice comes back to her a few yards down the street.*)

BRAND: (*Off.*) Hullo, old lady...

(*The wind howls round the house and slams the front door shut. Silence. Crushed, alone, shrunken within herself, AGATHA stands in the centre of the hall. Her breath wheezes, her old head sags forward, trembling. But before long she gathers herself together, her head goes up, the proud old gypsy look comes back into her eyes. More firmly than is her wont, she crosses to LUCY's room. She bangs imperiously with her fist upon the door, waits for a second then, bending down, puts her lips to the keyhole. Her hoarse whisper is defiant. Her voice contains no tremor.*)

AGATHA: So it's between you and me, Miss Beringer. And I'll beat you yet.

(*She turns round now and, heedless of the amber which lies glittering on the floor, makes her way slowly up the stairs as the curtain falls.*)

The End.